CONSULTATION FOR CONTEMPORARY HELPING PROFESSIONALS

THOMAS C. HARRISON

University of Nevada, Reno

Boston   New York   San Francisco
Mexico City   Montreal   Toronto   London   Madrid   Munich   Paris
Hong Kong   Singapore   Tokyo   Cape Town   Sydney

Executive Editor: *Virginia Lanigan*
Senior Marketing Manager: *Tara Whorf*
Manufacturing Buyer: *Andrew Turso*
Production Coordinator: *Pat Torelli Publishing Services*
Editorial-Production Service: *TKM Productions*
Electronic Composition: *TKM Productions*

For related titles and support materials, visit our online catalog at www.ablongman.com.

Library of Congress Cataloging-in-Publication Data

Harrison, Thomas C.
    Consultation for contemporary helping professionals / Thomas C. Harrison.
      p. cm.
    Includes bibliographical references and index.
    ISBN 0-205-33554-3
     1. Social service. 2. Human services. 3. Social service consultants. 4. Counselor and client. I. Title.
    HV40.H323 2004
    361'.06--dc22

                                    2003062761

Printed in the United States of America

10   9   8   7   6   5   4   3   2   1   07   06   05   04   03

To Elizabeth and Iain

CONTENTS

■ ■ ■ ■ ■

PART II   CONTRACTS AND CONTRACTING

CHAPTER FIVE
Formal and Psychological Contracts in Consultation   79

CHAPTER EIGHT
Ethical Decision Making in Consultation   146

PART IV   GENDER- AND RACIOETHNIC-SENSITIVE THEORIES AND APPROACHES

CHAPTER ELEVEN

Process Consultation in Organizations, Institutions, and Agencies   216

PART V   COLLABORATION AND CONSULTATION IN SPECIAL SETTINGS

CHAPTER TWELVE

School-Based Consultation and Collaboration   234

PREFACE

I am a professor, clinician, and consultant and teach in a counseling department that offers marriage and family therapy, college student development, community/mental health counseling, school counseling, and school psychology. Most of my students are required to take a course in consultation as part of their master's degree core curriculum. The goal of this course is to introduce students to the theory and practice of consultation, including learning how to actually practice consultation. In preparing to teach the consultation course, I have reviewed several books on the topic and have changed texts quite often over the semesters in an attempt to find that best "goodness of fit" for my students. Since the students still complained vociferously over the years, these efforts have largely been in vain. Many of the texts are replete with numerous empirical citations that tend to make the reading difficult. Most books cover the same issues, which include major theoretical models and approaches. Yet, no one book has really addressed to any integrated depth the various issues of diversity that are necessary for contemporary consultants. The psychological contract, a significant element in consultation, has received only paltry attention in the texts that have been reviewed. In most cases, there has been no mention of the psychological contract at all. It also seems as though many students finish reading about consultation and still do not have a grasp of how to do it. Some books have something of what students want, and other texts have other dimensions that are helpful. My goal in writing *Consultation for Contemporary Helping Professionals* is to rectify these shortcomings.

Writing a book requires the support of many individuals, and I want to express my gratitude to those whose efforts have made a difference in the writing of this book. From a professional standpoint, I express my sincere thanks to Drs. Robert O. Stripling, Larry Loesch, Joe Wittmer, Bob Myrick, and Nick Vacc. These gentlemen had a tremendous influence on how I think of consultation and consulting practice. Not only did they provide me with knowledge, but each helped me learn how to apply that knowledge effectively. Drs. Mary Maples and Marlowe Smaby are my current mentors, from whom I have learned so much. Drs. Livia D'Andrea and Paul Abney, my current colleagues, have been especially supportive of my efforts and have enhanced my understanding of the complexities of the practice. Dr. Dan Macari, a special individual, was instrumental in getting this whole process going. In addition, many graduate students helped along the way with their suggestions and criticisms of the work. Debbie Herzig was there to smile me on and keep me laughing and lighthearted. She also was able to multitask while the writing process was going on. The Family Violence Department of the National Council of Juvenile and Family Court Judges has been helpful and supportive. They are truly an "innovative culture." My dear friends and colleagues, Dr. Gary Fisher and Betty Barker, were always willing to go to great lengths to help make this text possible and meaningful. I thank them deeply. Without their individual efforts, this book would not have happened. I also extend my gratitude to Lynda Griffiths and to the reviewers of this text: Philip V. Magalong, San Francisco State University; Daniel E. Olympia, University of Utah; and Waymon Webster, Prairie View A&M University.

Finally, there is Elizabeth and Iain. Elizabeth's presence in my life is enough. Yet, her personal depth, professional acumen, and unwavering support of me concomitant with her timely proofreading only begin to reflect her contributions. For his part, my 12-year-old son, Iain, had to give up some trips to the motocross track and sacrifice some races so that Dad could write on the computer. He remains somewhat unconvinced that those days away from motocross could have been spent visualizing his races. He and Elizabeth are such blessings.

Thomas C. Harrison

CHAPTER ONE

INTRODUCTION AND OVERVIEW

CONTEXTUAL BACKGROUND OF THE BOOK

If you are reading this book, there is a good chance that you have some training in the mental health field. The aim of this book is to introduce you to the theory and practice of effective consultation in the mental health field. The book is divided into five sections: ***Contextual Dimensions, Contracts and Contracting, Ethical Dimensions, Gender- and Racioethnic-Sensitive Theories and Approaches,*** **and** ***Collaboration and Consultation in Special Settings***. The three goals of this chapter are to become acquainted with one another, to introduce you to the concept of consultation, and to orient you to the structure of the following five sections of the book.

Consultation, like counseling, is a complex interpersonal process, and it is important that you have an understanding of the principles and practices of counseling before embarking on an investigation of consultation. The reason is that professional consultation is both similar to and dramatically different from counseling. Having a rather solid grasp of counseling theory will differentiate aspects of counseling from consultation. Take a moment to imagine a counseling session and what you think a consultation would look like. If you conjured up a picture of a person or business organization working with a "trained expert" who would proceed to give advice about how to fix a problem, your image would be accurate. Caplan and Caplan (1993) state that this description or image is the most familiar form of consultation. However, this image of consultation is only one of many possible depictions of the settings in which consultation is practiced. Moreover, it is only one example of what actually occurs in consultation.

Consultation is an interpersonal process that can occur in agencies, institutions, and organizations, in which consultants work directly with some individuals (consultees) and indirectly with others (clients) to effect meaningful change in clients and client systems. Counseling is considered a direct service. Consultation is often one step removed from serving the counseling clients directly in that consultants work with the individuals who work with the clients. Schein (1969, 1987, 1999) identifies three generic types of consulting approaches: the doctor/patient model, the purchase model, and the process consultation model. When consultation clients are interested in content, the *purchase model* is the one they seek. In essence, consultation clients in this situation say to a consultant, "I have found the problem. Would you fix it?" In the *doctor/patient model,* the problem has not yet been identified by the consultation client. In this type of approach, consultation clients turn over the situation to an expert who proceeds to identify the problem and prescribe an appropriate course of action to take. The *process consultation approach* shifts the emphasis from focus on the problem or on identifying the problem to a focus on *how* the problems are solved. This approach utilizes a more collaborative or working-together perspective. All three models are effective means of helping consultation clients, and the clientele they serve become more efficient in their work.

Consultation has been found to be an effective way to help in a number of varying conditions. For instance, Bergan and Kratochwill (1990) find behavioral consultation to be an effective tool for school psychologists and school counselors. Caplan and Caplan (1993) see the practice of consultation as helping administrators deal with program and personnel issues. These same researchers find consultation to help the clinicians deliver more effective services to a variety of clients and client systems. Myrick (1977) and Wittmer and Myrick (1989) believe consultation to be an effective use of a counselor's time. Schein (1969, 1987, 1999) sees process consultation as being effective in creating change in numerous organizational cultures.

THE VOICE OF THE BOOK

The field of counseling and psychotherapy went through developmental transformations in the twentieth century, and because of its intimate relationship with counseling, consultation is the indirect beneficiary of these transformational changes. Yet, as you will note, there are really no new models of consultation. The original seminal works in mental health consultation, behavioral consultation models, and process consultation models were written within a few years of each other in the late 1960s and very early 1970s. One of the ways that diversity echoes in this book is through a selective presentation of seminal and popular models and approaches to consultation that have the greatest relevance and sensitivity to diversity in professional settings. It is my firm belief that the models and approaches of consultation themselves must possess structural flexibility in order to truly address diversity and to transform the change process into one of meaningful change. Each seminal model appearing in this book is presented in both its original form as well as its more updated form. The fundamental foundations on which these various models rest have remained the same or substantially the same in the decades following their inception. This assertion also generally holds true for the updates conducted by original authors. The implications of this essentially static state of consultation theory on diversity are monumental.

As mentioned, since the time of the original works of Caplan and Caplan's mental health consultation model (1977), Bergan's behavioral consultation (1977), Myrick's systematic consultation model (1977), and Schein's process consultation model for organizations, the helping profession field of counseling and psychotherapy has undergone profound transformations. The precursory diagnostic, objectivist, medical-model orientation operating in counseling and psychotherapy began to be challenged in the 1980s by postmodern thinkers who exclaim the virtues of the relativity of truth as a meaningful way of knowing. In direct opposition to the traditional views, this postmodern group sees truth as being subjectively constructed and socially constructed. This movement has spawned such counseling approaches and practices as narrative therapy, solution-focused therapy, strategic therapy as well as other forms of brief therapy. In general, these postmodern practitioners rail up against the objectification and functionalism of traditional theory and practice. According to some visionaries, the field of counseling and psychotherapy is transforming again through current professional interest in dialectical thought (Basseches, 1984) and dialogue (Burbules, 1993). This new movement focuses on the relationship between helper and helpee and acknowledges the existence of a power greater than each individual that is experienced when meaningful dialogue occurs between individuals. Whereas this power is *greater* than, it is not a power *apart* from the individuals. In short, the dialogic perspective transforms the polemic views of modernism and postmodernism by emphasizing the synergism that is created through the discovery of the "you within I, and the I within you." Truth is seen as existing between individuals rather than relegated to individuals. The implications for diversity are profound.

The relevance of dialogue and the reason it is mentioned here is because this book is written from this dialogic perspective. The "voice" in this book is dialogical and attempts to engage readers in such a fashion to enhance and transform their experience. The rapport that readers build with the content of this book creates a type of synergy that goes beyond what you as reader or I as author could do individually. The content of the book becomes alive and meaningful whenever you find yourself actively identifying with the words and examples contained on these pages. The inanimate words become living experiences, allowing you to resource yourself and create meaning beyond, but not apart from, the words. This is the level where information is transformed into knowledge. By using a dialogic voice, it is hoped that you can grasp the deeper relevance of consultation to your professional life through these concerted efforts. Moreover, in keeping with the tenets of traditional consultation, it is not necessary that the knowledge you gain by reading is helpful personally, because the aim of consultation is to help improve one's work—not necessarily one's personal growth.

In order for rapport to be built in such a way as to make this book meaningful, much time has been taken to formulate a working knowledge of who you (the readers) are in terms of your diverse worldviews, interests, levels of motivation, and professional orientations and abilities. As you will soon learn in your reading, the anticipation of *who* you are and *what* you are like is the first task of consultants once the process has been initiated. Effective consultants conduct rather extensive background work prior to the actual consultation itself by becoming familiar with both the persons involved and the task or problem to be solved. Since there is no opportunity to actually see who you are, many assumptions about you have been made. Primarily, an overwhelming majority of you probably are women. Many racioethnic variations exist. You are likely Hispanic American, Native American, Latino American, Euro-Caucasian (like myself), Asian American, Pacific Islanders, or African American. Some readers are disabled, many are not. Some readers are in the beginning stages of their careers, others are entering a second or third career, and still others are in other transitions. Some are married, some are gay, some feel oppressed, and some feel generally inadequate. Others might possess a more pronounced sense of efficacy. Some are spiritual, others are less so. A percentage of readers want to enter into private practice, some want to enter into agency work or school settings, and some will work in hospitals and/or institutions. There are those who are already practicing in the field. In spite of our diversity and because of it, one thing that pulls us all together is our interest in helping others.

The "voice" in this book is one of inclusion. Not only does an "inclusive" perspective relate to what models and approaches are presented but there are also direct implications for the manner in which these models are presented. Seminal models and approaches in the consulting field are included in later chapters and are discussed in detail. However, the discussion of these approaches has emphasized the *nature, scope, and operations of the consulting relationships.* If you do not have an incisive understanding of these relationships and how they change and transform in the consulting experience, your practice of consultation will be limited at best and unsuccessful at worse. As mentioned earlier, the models and approaches discussed in this book are seminal works in the professional field of consultation. Many of these have empirical support. As you might predict, the behavioral model of consultation lends itself more readily to empirical justification and validity. Yet, most, if not all, empirical studies emanate from an objectivist perspective, which is only one element of the basic tenets of a dialogical approach. Therefore, in staying congruent with both the philosophy of the dialogical approach of inclusion as well as staying congruent with the currently accepted and elevated practice of empiricism so central in the helping professions, empirical studies have been cited to punctuate certain aspects of the models and practice of consultation. However, there has been a concerted attempt to minimize the presence of this perspective as the only way of knowing or of verifying truthfulness. The importance of empirical studies in the study of consultation in the field is not to be understated, but there is an attempt to extend knowledge of how truth and practice in consultation are configured both within and beyond the traditional ways of scientific investigation and knowing. Too much empirical evidence seems to obscure the actual practice of consultation, and too little mention of empirical studies waters down the professional nature of consultation. Thus, one of my goals is to balance the book. For example, there are empirical studies examining the interpersonal skills in consultation (e.g., Horton & Brown, 1990; Martin, 1978; Merrell, 1991). Instead of listing these and discussing each one in detail or discussing them collectively as a body of research the approach in this book is to take empirical studies, blend them with practical experience, and weave them into a readable and germane discussion of the topic without an exhaustive list of citations. It is my hope that the result is a presentation of consultation that seems professional, real, and practical.

OVERVIEW OF THE CHAPTERS

Chapter Two: Counseling and Consultation

This portion of the chapter will briefly outline what you can expect from the chapters in rest of the book. Chapter Two examines the similarities and differences between counseling and consultation. The rationale for the chapter lies in the fact that most of you know something about counseling, yet probably do not know as much about consultation. In keeping with the philosophy of inclusion, I want to draw on the knowledge of professional counseling practice that you already possess and then extend it into consultation. In the process, many salient features of counseling will be identified in terms of structure and process, and these features will be compared to the same or similar salient features in consultation. Since "consultation" is a ubiquitous practice—that is, it is practiced by almost everyone, professional and nonprofessional alike—some discussion is devoted to distinguishing formal and informal consultation. There are two case studies in Chapter Two. The purpose of including these is to show you the subtle and not so subtle similarities and differences between these two practices in such a way as to be able to identify with the cases in real, practical terms. In the same practical vein, the three generic models and approaches in consultation, doctor/patient, purchase, and process, are included and discussed. The hope here is for you to quickly identify the approaches in their own right as well as to give you an initial glimpse of an orientation or approach that seems to fit your style and preferences. Eventually, as a consultant, you will want to be able move seamlessly through the different approaches as each relationship and situation requires.

Chapter Three: The Context of Consultation

Chapter Three reveals the background or context in which all consultations take place. What is different in this chapter, and may prove to be challenging for you as a reader, is the fact that all consultation is organizational in nature, but not all consultation is organizational development. If this point is understood, the chapter will have been successful in its objective. Chapter Three gives two specific examples of organizational culture. One concerns the opening of a new high school and what happens to its organization and culture as it moves from its infancy to its maturation. While particularly useful for school counselors, the process involved in opening a new high school can be generalized to how organizational culture is embedded and stabilized in agencies and institutions in general. The second example concerns itself with the levels of organizational culture and uses a mental health center to integrate the information. Again, I am using a mental health center to depict more generally what happens in organizations of all types.

Chapter Four: The Context of Intervening and Change

Once you understand the organizational nature of all consultations, it is important to glean information and knowledge about the contexts in which intervening and change take place. Since the context of consultation is the organization, it is important to have some working knowledge of how organizations change so that you can then have an incisive understanding of how individuals in a consulting relationship change in relation to their surroundings. The generic types of intervening are identified and discussed. The intervening orientation in consultation can be problem focused or solution focused, exclusive or inclusive, and aimed at first-order or second-order change at the micro-level (individual), meso-level (group), and/or macro-level (organizational). Marriage and family therapists and social workers will likely know these terms and how they operate in family therapy or in generalist social work practice; other professionals might be less familiar with these terms. An attempt has been made to discuss these various perspectives from a generalist perspective in order to help those readers who are not as familiar with these constructs understand the concepts readily. Since the types and levels of intervening and change are structural and are mediated by the roles that the consultant assumes, there are sections devoted to identifying and discussing the numerous roles that consultants assume in their work. Not only is this information important in its own right, but knowledge of various roles and the implications of each helps ensure that consultants can be more effective in their work. For example, the consulting role of "expert" may work well for some populations and in some situations. At the same time, the role of "expert" has significant implications when applied across gender, racioethnicity, and disabilities. In reality, not everyone will respond favorably to a consultant assuming the "expert" role. It is critical that consultants be aware of this fact and make every attempt to connect with those involved in the consultation in a meaningful manner, which means becoming aware of how "expert" may be viewed from different perspectives and worldviews.

Chapter Five: Formal and Psychological Contracts in Consultation

After you understand the contexts of consultation and of the intervening and change processes, it is appropriate for a discussion to ensue related to contracts. In consultation, two types of contracts exist: formal and psychological. The formal contract is what you would expect it to be. Although the psychological contract is equally significant, it is only addressed in a few places in the professional literature on consultation and in even fewer places in the counseling literature. Because of the paucity of its presence in the literature in the helping professions, much time is spent discussing what the psychological contract is, how it develops at the outset of the consulting experience, and how it changes during the consultation. When you think about it, the term *psychological contract* underscores the need for effective working relationships in consultation and punctuates the need to be sensitive to various issues related to gender, racioethnicity, and disabilities. To help ensure your sensitivity to issues of diversity as well as your advocacy of it, several dimensions of the psychological contract are discussed as they relate to special populations. The chapter's case example points out the process of developing a psychological contract and what happens when the contract indicates that it is not wise or indicated to proceed with the consultation.

Chapter Six: Gender, Disabilities, Racioethnicity, and the Psychological Contract

When the groundwork of the psychological contract has been laid, it is time for a more in-depth discussion of the nuances of the psychological contract as it relates to a variety of individuals. Chapter Six revolves around the notion that the more information consultants have about the diversity of individuals and groups in their consulting relationships, the better consultants can execute their larger charge of being change agents. As you know, counselors and psychotherapists effect change on a more individual level, whereas consultants effect change with individuals and groups in an organizational context. Consultation can change larger numbers of people because of its context as well as its structure. This chapter includes many topics related to the plight of those individuals and groups who have experienced discrimination of one sort or another. As consultants become more attentive to the deeper personal and interpersonal aspects of the consulting process, more effective and meaningful change can take place. Using the vehicle of the psychological contract, this chapter reveals the nature of social activism in consultation.

Chapter Seven: Ethical Dimensions in Consultation

Chapter Seven is the first of two chapters devoted to ethics and ethical decision making. Many of you will have had some exposure to ethics and ethical decision making in counseling, and some of the principles of counseling can be borrowed and applied to consulting. However, there are critical distinctions. To avoid repeating much of what you might already know about ethics, Chapter Seven touches on the major issues and spends more time on issues of ethics as they relate to diversity, the levels of ethical functioning, legal implications, and the application of multiple codes in consultation. A special feature of this chapter is the discussion concerning school counseling, school consulting, and the ethical implications in terms of how these services are configured. This theoretical perspective has profound implications for the ethical practice of school counseling, and hopefully it will help school counselors conceptualize their work differently while continuing to enhance their effectiveness in schools.

Chapter Eight: Ethical Decision Making in Consultation

To be aware of ethical standards and structures is not enough for consultants. The situations in which consultants readily find themselves working range from working with one person to working with hundreds or thousands (as might be the case in organizational development). My background includes a bachelor's degree in philosophy, and because ethics is grounded in philosophy, I had a particular interest in writing Chapter Eight. Writing about the grounding of ethical theory in philosophy will help you deepen your understanding of the intervening and change processes in consultation. As in some of the other chapters, case studies are used to help illuminate issues and resolutions. The first study reflects an alarming situation that occurs in the helping fields and is used to point out flaws in the consulting process while revealing the emotional anguish of a well-intentioned consultant. I believe we all can relate to the type of situation depicted in this case study. The other case study describes a typical mental health agency situation. However, the point of the second case study is to reveal the hidden consulting structure that underlies most agency work and the enormous implications these hidden structures have on practice and ethics. These two case studies are then analyzed through the perspectives and structures of two different models or approaches to ethical decision making: Kitchener's (1984) model and Shillito-Clarke's (1996) model.

Chapter Nine: Mental Health Consultation

Once you have an understanding of consultation structure and the relevant ethical issues that surround and envelop it, it is time to introduce the seminal models of consultation. The first model is the mental health consultation model of Caplan (1970) and Caplan and Caplan (1993). The first several pages of Chapter Nine address the generic structure of consultation models and discuss the implications for diversity. The essence of the mental health consultation model is presented and described in some detail. Equal attention is given to a critical analysis of the relevance of this model to diverse populations. This analysis includes discussion of the disease approach in consultation and the current status of psychodynamic theory—the perspective assumed by Caplan and Caplan—as it relates to women, racioethnicity, and disabilities. It is important to acknowledge that the mental health consultation model is practiced by a variety of professionals and professional groups in the mental health field. So, no matter what criticisms are levied against this approach, it continues to enjoy enormous popularity in such practices as school psychology, psychiatry, and in the work performed in mental health agencies, institutions, and hospitals. In order to enhance its relevance to other populations, a substantial section of the chapter is devoted to discussing the emerging issues in mental health consultation. This includes some reworking of its theoretical foundations and principles that both stabilize the original work, while making it more relevant to contemporary consulting practice.

Chapter Ten: Behavioral Person-in-Environment Approaches

Ensuring the relevancy of current models of consultation for diverse populations is carried over into Chapter Ten through the introduction of the behavioral social work perspective. This discussion precedes a formal introduction of two seminal works in behavioral consultation: Bergan's behavioral consultation model (Bergan, 1977) and Myrick's (1977) systematic consultation model. Both models work very well in schools, and the behavioral social work perspective allows for a less-biased practice in that setting. As you can imagine, behavioral consultation models focus on correct problem identification as key for successful consultation. So, there is a rather detailed discussion of the processes and procedures outlined in those two approaches. The manner and method employed in presenting both the behavioral case consultation approach (Bergan, 1977; Bergan & Kratochwill, 1990) and Myrick's (1977) systematic model are aimed at achieving two main goals: The first goal is to inform you of the process itself, and the second goal is to provide you with enough detail for you to be able to utilize their principles in your practice of consultation. In keeping with the interest in relationships, much time is spent on critically analyzing the relationships between helpers and helpees across these two models. In addition, Myrick's use of facilitative responding is detailed because of its generalizability and effective method of communicating across various diverse groups.

Chapter Eleven: Process Consultation in Organizations, Institutions, and Agencies

Even though consultation is organizational in nature, not all consultation is organizational development (OD). I have included Schein's (1969, 1987, 1999) process consultation approach to organizational development for several reasons. Primarily, I would be remiss in my duty to you if I did not discuss organizational consulting in some form. To conduct effective organizational consultation, consultants need extensive training in organizational behavior. This probably lies outside the interest and practices of common consulting in the mental health field.

As a practicing professional, you will probably be approached at some time with questions related to organizational development. Some knowledge of it is appropriate and likely necessary. However, this is not the main reason for discussing Schein's work. The main reason the process consultation approach is included is because of Schein's distinct emphasis on the relationship in the consulting process. His research on effective consulting relationships extends well beyond organizational consulting and is applicable to almost every consulting setting and situation. You will notice that the chapters on mental health consultation and behavioral consultation include essentially only the original theorists and practitioners. One purpose was to present the original models and the significant alterations that were made to those models by their authors. This allows for a critical analysis of each model's generalizability for diversity. This same focus is reflected in Chapter Eleven. There is only one "process consultation" approach, and that is the one outlined by Schein. As you read and study the chapter, you will surely see how relevant Schein's discussion of relationships and relationship building in consultation is across diverse populations. The chapter closes with a discussion of Schein's 10 principles of successful consultation. These principles are equally important and relevant to a variety of consulting situations.

Chapter Twelve: School-Based Consultation and Collaboration

Schein's 10 principles act as a point of closure for a discussion of models and approaches. Hopefully, the discussion of these principles will leave you with a simple and profound yardstick by which you can measure the progress and process of almost every consultation in which you will be involved. Chapters Twelve, Thirteen, and Fourteen reflect a movement toward more situation-specific consultation that includes schools and agencies. The main topics in Chapter Twelve are school-based consultation and the concept of collaboration. Collaboration, yet another dimension in consulting, refocuses which relationships are primary and how responsibility is apportioned. Some professionals consider collaboration to be different from consultation. Others maintain its similarity with it. Once collaboration is understood structurally, attention is turned in the chapter to how collaboration works in various settings and in school settings in particular. Because of the significant influence that school has on the socialization of its students, a social activist approach is again employed to help consultants ascertain the seriousness of their work and the ethical implications of it. The chapter closes with a discussion of the collaborative/interdependent school-based model of helping that is grounded in practical terms.

Chapter Thirteen: Agency-Based Consultation and Collaborative Cultures

Agency-based consultation is conducted everyday, and this is an important setting about which consultants need to become familiar. With the identification of coexisting disorders in the mental health field, which often includes a mental disorder as well as a substance-abuse disorder, I have used an example of consulting with substance-addicted clients. Consulting with counselors about their substance-abusing clients has its own set of unique challenges, and these are pointed out and discussed.

Agencies also hire consultants for program development and evaluation. Essentially, program consultation includes both the development of an idea and the development of the method and manner for evaluating it. Program consultation is prevalent in the mental health field, and almost every practicing professional is involved in some type of evaluation of mental health programs. This type of consulting does require some specialized knowledge, and this is discussed. A four-step model of program consultation is presented. Because of its importance and centrality to program development, several pages are devoted to a discussion of program evaluation. This includes the identification of models of evaluation and an overview of their assumptions and methods. The chapter concludes with a presentation of collaborative cultures and innovative cultures. The importance of developing and maintaining collaborative cultures is underscored in the discussion.

Chapter Fourteen: Structuring Workshops/Seminars in Consultation

Many professional consultants do not consider workshops to be consultation. The main reason for this view stems from the variety of individuals—professionals and nonprofessionals alike—who conduct workshops and seminars. If anyone can conduct a workshop, then it is not necessarily a professional endeavor. Chapter Fourteen attempts to present a valid argument for including workshops/seminars as consultation. Much discussion is focused on the theoretical grounding of workshops in terms of learning theory and theory of group and individual change. The psychological contract for workshops/seminars is examined as well as the characteristics of effective workshop consultants. The chapter concludes with a discussion of the elements of effective workshops in the hopes that you can identify potential obstacles that need to be overcome concomitant with strategies on how to structure the workshop/seminar experience so as to enhance the chances of it being meaningful for all.

I have not included a list of objectives at the outset of each chapter. Rather, it is hoped that you can determine your own goals for the reading. Each chapter does have a summary, followed by a list of questions that can help integrate the information presented in the chapter.

CHAPTER TWO

COUNSELING AND CONSULTATION

DEFINITIONS OF CONSULTATION

One of the early criticisms of consultation was the fact that there were too many definitions of the term *consultation.* In the early years of professional consultation practice for mental health professionals, the definitions that were promulgated in the professional literature either did not agree with previous definitions or were too general or so obtuse as to not be very meaningful. This held true for the early definitions advanced by those who would eventually be considered "giants in the field." For example, in the early years, Schein (1969) believed that consultation was really aimed at helping clients effectively organize, synthesize, and utilize knowledge and perceptions. Another eminent researcher/practitioner, Caplan (1970), asserted that consultation was the process of assisting helpees in dealing with problems that impeded their professional growth. Writing about school psychologists, Williams (1972) said that consultation was the process of modeling effective coping and problem-solving skills to consultees and clients. In studying the effects of consultation with teachers, Tyler and Fine (1974) asserted that consultation involved teaching new skills to teachers. A more refined definition is cited by Reschly (1976), who referred to consultation as an interpersonal process whereby helpers attempt to aid helpees in increasing awareness of their affective domain and its relationship to their professional identity, help develop helpees' awareness of how their intrapersonal feelings influence their interactions with their clients, and help develop more positive attitudes and feelings so that helpees can change and become more effective in the work setting.

At the same time that their definitions were ambiguous, these very definitions were guiding professional research and practice. For instance, Caplan's (1970) initial work on mental health consultation was considered to be the first systematic description of *mental health consultation* and continues to be widely acclaimed. Schein's (1969) initial definition may have been broad, but the ideas contained in process consultation were considered revolutionary at a time of traditional organizational development practice. *Process consultation* continues to be widely accepted. These early ideas of consultation were joined by others' attempts to define the process. The *behavioral consultation* model (Bergan, 1977) was readily accepted by school psychologists, who found the assumptions and practices of behaviorism effective with their respective populations. Another effective consultation model for schools, *systematic consultation*, was forwarded by Myrick in 1977. Yet, by 1979, there continued to be some ambiguity in the definitions appearing in the professional literature. This led Lounsbury, Roisium, Pakarney, Sills, and Meissen (1979) to conclude that consultation was a term used to describe a wide variety of activities and relationships. More recently, Hansen, Himes, and Meier (1990) concur with Lounsbury and colleagues by stating that under the rubric of "consultation," services can cover a wide variety of tasks and activities in which an expert provides specialized assistance to another person (p. 2). Another definition is forwarded by Dougherty (1990), who maintains that consultation is a type of helping relationship in which a human service professional (consultant) delivers assistance to another person (consultee) so as to solve a work-related or care-giving related problem that the consultee has with a client/system. In the final analysis, it may simply be that the word *consultation* will always elude efforts aimed to precisely define and categorize it.

In spite of the lack of consistent definitions, the practice of consultation had clearly "caught on" in the mental health field by the very early 1970s and was seen as an especially valuable tool for school psychologists. However, the dearth of consistent and precise definitions was and continues to be a nightmare from an empirical research point of view. Similar to the problems in researching the counseling process, the inconsistency of definitions makes it nearly impossible to replicate studies in consultation as well. A result is reflected in a body of research that continues to grow, yet remains somewhat fragmented (Brown, Pryzwansky, & Schulte, 2001). In many of these cases, researchers research what is available, feasible, and accessible. The lack of consistency also renders it very difficult to generalize results. Because of the consistency of inconsistent definitions, it may be that an effective way to begin to understand the principles and practices of consultation is to understand it from a broad perspective, simply because too much detail may reflect the differences in definitions and muddy the waters once again. Hopefully, a broad definition will allow at least some structural definition to remain consistent while the varied forms and processes of consultation are explored.

For instance, the example of an expert consultant coming in and rescuing the organization is rather straightforward. However, a closer examination reveals that this simple example also provides enough information to be able to make four further observations that are significant to professional consultation: First, professional consultation contains some type of financial arrangement between the parties. In the image of the consultant coming in and fixing an organization, there is a presumption that the consultant will be paid—perhaps paid quite well. Second, consultation involves some expertise as a basis for help. The consultant who comes in to fix the organization is an expert in some relevant aspects of the organization's problem. Third, professional consultation involves a focus on improving issues that are related to work and the workplace. The expert is going to fix the organizational problem(s) whether the problems are personnel related or technologically related. Finally, consultation presumes that some action will take place as a result of the process. Whether the consultant in the example is actually going to fix the problem herself or work toward having the consultee assume that role is a professional decision. In any case, some action is inferred in the depicted example.

In summary, *consultation* is an interpersonal process in which the first party (consultant) provides some type of assistance to a second party (consultee) in helping the consultee find a solution that concerns a third party (client) (Harrison, 2000). As you can tell, this definition is not meant to be either exacting or limiting. Consultation is a complex interpersonal process that can easily intimidate the inexperienced. Even the most experienced consultant will likely want to adhere to the principle of "keeping it simple" as often as possible. As the more complex nuances of consultation are discussed in later chapters, being parsimonious will prove to be a blessing for consultants-in-training from a conceptual as well as practical point of view.

FORMAL AND INFORMAL CONSULTATION

In the preceding discussion, consultation was depicted as occurring in professional situations requiring some expertise. There are less formal situations in which consultation can occur. For instance, two co-workers discussing ways to help a troubled colleague improve her morale at work could be configured as a consultation. Whether a professional interaction involving three entities can be considered a consultation is often a matter of legitimacy and functionality. For example, it may not be particularly useful to configure a conversation that takes place between two co-workers during a lunch hour about how to help a troubled colleague as a consultancy. However, labeling a conversation occurring between a counselor and his colleague about a difficult client would have a useful function. This would be especially true if the discussion related to devising an effective treatment plan or focused on the counselor's feelings about the case. It would then be a more formal, focused conversation.

In the example of the two co-workers talking over lunch, there is no overt mandate for either co-worker to help the colleague. That is not so in the case of the counselor and his colleague. There was a specific purpose that involved an obligation to the counselor's client. This ethical obligation relates to best practices for the client, which dictates that some formal action will be taken. The lunch conversation between friends could be configured as consultation because it took place at work and related to another's work performance, but there was no financial obligation involved—other than the fact that both are being paid to work. Formal consultations involve a financial arrangement in some form or another. Formal consultation also includes the notion that some type of action will be taken. In the example of the lunchroom discussion, neither employee had the mandated responsibility to act on the discussion. If either one of them had been a supervisor, then an action might have been implied by their titles and duties. One of the reasons the delineation of formal and informal consultation is necessary relates to the ethics involved in formal consultation. If there is no professional obligation involved, there is no ethic. Obligation suggests a course of action guided by ethical standards.

PROFESSIONAL CONSULTATION

Aside from the issue of formal versus informal consultations, another distinction needs to be made concerning professional versus nonprofessional consulting. There are individuals who identify themselves as "consultants" and organizations that consider themselves as "consulting firms." These individuals can be found listed in the yellow pages of phone books in large metropolitan areas. Many of these consulting firms offer professional consulting services and are staffed by bachelor-degreed or graduate-degreed professionals from the fields of social and industrial psychology, logistics, organizational development, accounting, and business. In some other consulting firms, however, the consultants have little or no formal training and often may have learned their trade on the job by selling consulting packages to businesses. An example of this occurs when a consultant makes an appointment with a local business owner for the purpose of presenting a strategy for improving sales by training the owner's sales staff. In the business world, this scenario is called an "outside sale" (as opposed to an "inside" sale, in which the customer initiates the request for service). These consulting firms, whether staffed by professionals or nonprofessionals, exist in the business world because there is a need for them and because these firms are successful business endeavors themselves and can survive in the free marketplace. Nevertheless, consultation in the mental health field is a professional endeavor because it is conducted by practitioners who have some formal and specialized training.

Generally speaking, an occupation is considered to be a "profession" when there is some specialized and formal training required, when there is an organization to which an individual can affiliate, when the organization has a formal publication, and when that occupation is regulated by some codified standards of practice that are usually administered or overseen by a state board of examiners. In the mental health field, the most obvious examples of professions are psychiatry, college counseling, social work, community counseling, counseling, psychology, marriage and family therapy, school counseling, and psychiatric nursing. Interestingly, many practitioners of these various professions utilize various forms of consultation but would rarely consider themselves to be "consultants."

With the exception of the variety of organizational consultants (OD consultants), most mental health professionals consider consultation to be an adjunct to standard professional therapy practice. This statement is especially relevant when talking about master's-level practitioners in all professions. Those professionals holding doctoral degrees may be more familiar with a consulting role simply because they may be considered "more expert" and may have been involved in situations where their expertise was enlisted. For example, psychiatrists in mental health centers are medical consultants who often carry a small caseload, but spend a majority of their time acting as psychopharmacological consultants, diagnosticians, and collaborators. Many doctoral-level psychologists and counselors may be in positions of overseeing the clinical operations of mental health centers. Some social workers and psychiatric nurses may also be familiar with the role of consultant. However, regardless of the level of education, almost all mental health practitioners consult in their daily practices in some form or another.

One way to understand consultation is to draw from counseling training experiences in order to initiate some conceptualization of consultation. This is not to say that there are categorical similarities between the two processes, because there are some marked structural and conceptual differences. However, it is assumed that you are most familiar with counseling and the counseling process and, thus, such a discussion can prove insightful to the consulting process.

THREE CONCEPTUAL IMPLICATIONS OF CONSULTATION

The "Third Party"

The fact that consultation is an interpersonal process in which the first party (consultant) provides some type of assistance to a second party (consultee) in helping the consultee find a solution that concerns a third party (client) suggests several conceptual concerns. Some of these concerns are structural, and some concerns are process oriented. The first implication is structural and reflects the fact that the "third party" entity in consultation can be a person or an inanimate object. In the example where the organization calls in an expert from the outside to help fix a management problem, the third party (client) is defined as either problematic personnel or some problematic technological concern such as designing a new financial statement going out to customers in order to increase revenue collection rates. In another case, a CEO might want to have a consultant design a new managerial flowchart for the organization. Here, the third party is an inanimate object: the flowchart. In a mental health setting, suppose two counselors consult about the best treatment venue for a client. The third party would be the client who would be benefiting indirectly from the consultation. Third parties vary in their structural composition.

Nature of Assistance

The implications of the third party logically segue into the second broad implication, which is also conceptual. This has to do with the nature of the "assistance" or interactions between the entities and the intentional interventions used by consultants. For example, imagine a situation where a mental health patient requires home visits by a nurse. After the nurse provides the outreach service to the client in the client's home, the nurse then consults with the client's physician about the treatment plan. Certainly, the physician knows her patient, but the home health-care nurse acts as a conduit of valuable information and, because of the nurse's expert training and previous home visits, the need for the physician to go for a face-to-face interview with the patient at the patient's home is precluded. This example reflects the variation in the types of assistance proffered in consultation. Sometimes the assistance comes in the form of direct advice, as it did in this brief example. Other times, however, the assistance can be simply helping someone figure out a problem at work without giving him or her advice. The assistance can also come in the form of a workshop, as depicted in the case where teachers receive an in-service training on how to address conduct disorders in the classroom. The point is that consultation involves at least two people interacting together while focusing on a third entity—be it an idea or a third person—and the types of assistance offered can vary from straightforward advice giving to exploring the consultee's experiences with a particular client.

Direct versus Indirect Service

The third broad implication relates to the structural focus of the direct and indirect interactions that occur in consultation. Counseling is considered to be a direct service to clients. It is conducted with clients present either connected by phone, Internet, or an actual face-to-face interaction. A client who comes in alone for couples counseling in order to sort out difficulties with a partner is the one receiving direct help, whereas the client's partner is being helped indirectly. A couple coming in to explore better parenting skills receive the help directly from the marriage and family therapist, whereas the couple's children receive the help indirectly as a result of their parents' changes. Although in these case examples the children and spouse receive help indirectly, the counselor's primary interest is the client or client system.

Consultants can work with both consultees and clients simultaneously. Because of the triadic structure of consultation, the consultants' interest includes both consultees and clients. For instance, imagine the work performed by school counselors, who often counsel with students who have behavioral problems. Although working directly with such a student, school counselors may simultaneously make suggestions to the student's teachers on strategies to manage classroom behavior of the student. In this case, the school counselor is acting as a consultant to the teacher who requested help for the student (client). This situation is similar to when a mental health clinician refers a client to a psychiatrist for a psychiatric work-up. The psychiatrist would be helping the client directly and the clinician indirectly. In another example, assume that a patient's insurance company is paying for the home health-care nurse and her consultation with the physician. When the nurse consults directly with the physician about the patient, the physician helps the nurse directly and helps the patient indirectly. This situation changes in another situation where the nurse refers a patient directly to a psychiatrist for a work-up. When the physician sees the patient, the patient is helped directly and the nurse is helped indirectly. In organizational consulting, there may be many who are helped directly through interactions with the consultant. At the same time, there may be numerous individuals who never see the consultant but who, nonetheless, indirectly benefit from those conversations conducted with others. In reviewing these examples, one can begin to see how the professional services of counseling and consultation are similar and different.

COUNSELING AND CONSULTATION

Time after time, during debriefing sessions following a classroom demonstration of a problem-solving model of consultation, I have heard graduate students make comments such as, "That was just like counseling!" and "I couldn't tell if you were counseling or consulting!" From the students playing the role of "consultee," comments might be heard such as, "It seemed similar to counseling, but you were more directive and asked a lot more questions," and "I was waiting for you to address my feelings, but you seemed only to acknowledge them and did not spend much time with them." These comments are powerful statements and act to help as a jumping off point for a discussion examining similarities and differences between counseling and consultation.

Some models of consultation, as well as some techniques used in other consulting models, may at first appear to have similarities with counseling and the counseling process. Other consulting models will not have the same familiarity with counseling at first glance. Although some consulting models appear similar to counseling, there are nevertheless several distinguishing structural differences between consultation and counseling and the counseling process. The following two case studies are presented to structure an ensuing discussion outlining some of the fundamental differences between these two processes.

CASE STUDY ONE
COUNSELING

A few years ago, a client called and requested counseling services. He came in somewhat distraught, stating that he felt that his performance had dropped off at work, and he was concerned about the problem so as to prevent it from getting any worse. The client believed that some of his customers were bad-mouthing him to his manager and that, in fact, the manager might have been joining in on the criticism of his work. After discussing some of the details surrounding his experience at work, attention turned to his private life. The client revealed that there had been new developments in his life: His wife had given birth to twins a few months previous. Not only did the client feel excited about being a new father but he also felt the added pressure of needing to provide more for his newly expanded family. This pressure, coupled with his concern about his performance, added fuel to his discomfort and left him feeling unworthy, inadequate, and overwhelmed.

The dialogue then focused on how the client was adjusting to his new role as father and the impact of this family change on his expectations of work performance. After two sessions, the client became more aware of the relationship between his fears about fathering and his newly heightened fears about his performance at work. The new insights he gained about the pressures of fathering and his fear of not being a good-enough father and how that related to his work concerns served as motivation for change. The fact that his boss had passed on some of the client's customers' comments to him was indeed upsetting, and the client feared that he had lost the trust of his customers when in fact it was also true that he had lost trust with himself. He still felt that he needed to act. Subsequently, the client had a conversation with his manager about his concerns and decided to share the pressures he had been feeling. The dialogue with his boss helped out a lot, and in the end she offered her unwavering support for her highly competent and respected employee.

■ ■ ■ ■ ■

CASE STUDY TWO
CONSULTING

A director of an organization phoned for help. A meeting was set up at her office to discuss her concerns and to see how a consultant might help. The director stated that the organization had a new executive director and that her department had lost two people while gaining four new ones. With the addition of four new employees, concomitant with the anticipated hiring of others planned for the near future, she had wanted to physically move her department to another location, and asked her staff to prepare for the move. The director stated that these changes had created a stressful environment for everyone, and she was concerned about morale—especially the morale of two individuals. In addition, three of her managers confided that they had heard rumors to the effect that some other staff members were thinking about looking elsewhere for employment because of the stress of the job, the change at the executive director level, and the ensuing physical splitting up of the department.

During the course of the first dialogue with the director, she mentioned that these changes had created a lot of stress for her as well and that she, too, felt overwhelmed. After agreeing on a fee for service, the director asked if the consultant could find out how staff members were doing with all of the changes and offer some advice on ways the department could handle the stress better. After some further discussion and clarification, the director and the consultant agreed on a procedure.

A confidential survey with open-ended questions was sent out to all department members, and a confidential face-to-face interview was conducted with each person, including the managers and the director. Three staff members who had recently undergone significant personal transitions asked for, and were granted, additional time with the consultant so they could discuss ways they could negotiate their personal changes and the realities of a stressful work environment. At a subsequent meeting with the director and the three department managers, the consultant provided a general overview of the attitudes of the department gleaned from the survey and interviews. After lengthy discussion, the administrative team and the consultant jointly decided to involve everyone in the intervention. The plan was to have everyone meet as a large group for the purpose of identifying and addressing the issues that were before them as well as identifying which individuals, if any, would want to initiate the move to the adjacent building. Through a series of meetings, stress was reduced and certain individuals identified themselves as willing to move. Two employees requested some more time with the consultant to discuss more "personal concerns" about the move.

These two case studies indeed have some similarities. Both were interpersonal processes aimed at helping individuals deal with work-related issues, both processes involved some clarification and discussion of the issues, both involved the concerns of a boss, and both included an employee's personal concerns: The first case involved the client becoming a new father and the second case included the personal stress reactions of several employees, including the director herself. Both cases resulted in some action being taken to resolve issues.

Nonetheless, there are clear differences in the two examples. For instance, it is also often the case where it is appropriate for the consultant to intervene directly with clients as well as consultees. This situation was reflected in Case Study Two. When the consultant was conversing directly with the director (consultee), the staff (clients) were indirectly benefiting as well. In other words, even though there was a direct discussion between the consultant and the director, the outcome of that discussion had an indirect effect on the staff. Likewise, when the consultant conducted individual sessions with three staff members, it was the consultee (and remaining staff members) who was indirectly impacted. When the consultant facilitated an organizationwide meeting that included everyone in the organization, all staff received direct service from the consultant. The only ones impacted indirectly were the department's clients and client systems. So, consulting, like counseling, has a dimension of direct service. The difference in service is found in those situations where the consultant delivers a direct service to some and a deliberate indirect service to others.

SIMILARITIES AND DIFFERENCES IN COUNSELING AND CONSULTATION

Triadic versus Dyadic Structure

In counseling, the direct interaction that occurs is only between the counselor and the client. This makes the structure of counseling a *dyadic* process, as reflected in Case Study One. From your experiences in counseling, you are aware that the counseling "client" can actually be more than one person. This is particularly true for marriage and family therapists, who can conceptualize a "client" as the entire family. Social workers might configure the "client" as both the individual client and the larger social system within which the individual client is interacting. A psychologist trained in family therapy might see an entire family for an intake and conceptualize the client as being an individual family member. Regardless of how different professionals configure their respective client systems for counseling purposes, the dyadic structure remains stable: There is one counselor, and the direct intervention is always on one client at a time; however, the client or client system is configured.

Case Study Two reflects the *triadic* nature of consulting. In Case Study Two, there is the consultant, the director who is identified as the consultee, and a client system comprised of all the department's employees. (In this case, the client system is also comprised of those who receive services from the consultee's department. These clients remain outside the actual department.) Fundamental to consultation is the fact that there is always one consultant, one consultee, and at least one other person (client) or a thing ("third entity") directly involved in the situation. This structural configuration propels consultation away from counseling.

Settings and Clientele

Case Study One was clearly a counseling session. Even though the sessions involved the exploration and resolution of work-related concerns, it was the client who initiated the request for help, and the process took place in the counselor's office. The client gained new insights and behaviors that had a positive impact on himself, and subsequently on his work environment and performance. There are obviously times in counseling when a parent calls for help with a child or when one spouse calls and requests help for the other spouse. Most often, counselors understand that, regardless of the source of the referral, the client reserves the right to refuse treatment. Consultation is different. In Case Study Two, the director called in help for her staff. The staff may or may not have had input into that request. Yet, the staff were "required" to participate by virtue of their being employed by the organization. So, one of the differences between counseling and consultation is who can initiate the call for help. In counseling, the person calling for his child or his partner may or may not be a focus of the intervention. In consultation, the person who calls (the consultee) is conceptualized as an inherent structural entity who receives direct and indirect benefits from the consultant.

Another difference between counseling and consulting is that counselors counsel with their clients in the counselors' offices, on the phone, via computer, or, as in the case of mental health outreach services, wherever the client is living at the time. That can include, among other settings, the client's home, a nursing home, or a transitional housing facility, hospice, or hospital. Clearly, the counselor's office is not the only place to meet. The propriety of locations for counseling is governed largely by the desire to eliminate distractions as well as the need to protect client confidentiality. For instance, a counselor who works in an adolescent treatment center for addictive behaviors might conduct groups or individual sessions outside because it may be a more relaxed environment for adolescents and confidentially is not an issue.

It would be somewhat unusual for a counselor to drive to the client's business address for the purpose of conducting a counseling session. This is not necessarily the case for consultants. More often than not, consultants can and do work in the consultee's environment, and Case Study Two is an example of this. All of the meetings conducted with the consultee and clients took place at the physical location of the organization. In other cases, consultations can take place in the consultee/client's idiosyncratic venue. For instance, I regularly consult with athletic teams for sports performance, and these consultancies take place in a variety of physical settings of which almost all are located in the consultee's venue. I consult with players and coaches on the athletic field, on the gym floor, at the swimming pool, or at the track during practice or during competitions. Consultations also take place in the coach's office, in the team meeting room, or in the training room. Occasionally, meetings take place in my university office. Hence, generally speaking, when a consultant works with an organization, the consultation meetings most often take place in the consultee's setting, such as in their office, staff meeting room, or actual workspace. In the case of workshops, consultations can also occur away from an office at a neutral location, such as a retreat or convention center. From these examples, one can see that consultants have a broader range of physical locations that can be considered "appropriate" for consulting, whereas counselors are more limited in where they conduct counseling sessions.

With respect to the clientele, Case Study Two depicts a consultancy that occurred with an organization. Whereas counselors counsel with individuals, couples, groups, and families, *consultants can consult with individuals, groups or families, institutions, and/or organizations.* When comparing counseling and consultation, the ability of consultants to work with a broad range of consultees and clients is a distinguishing feature of consultation. In Case Study Two, notice that the consultant worked with several staff members ("clients") in addition to working with the director (consultee). Whereas counselors counsel with one client or client system at a time, consultants can and often do work with many clients simultaneously.

Goals and Processes

The goals of counseling and consultation also differ in terms of outcomes and intraprocess stage goals. Caplan (1970), Myrick (1977), and others mentioned previously maintain that *the broad goal of consultation is to enhance the help-seeker's work performance.* Behavioral change included, the general goal of counseling can be said to enhance the client's general emotional well-being. The issue of the client's emotional adjustment being the focus of counseling and work performance being the focus in consultation is a distinguishing feature between the two processes. However, it is not that they are conceptually exclusive. In consultation, the consultee's and client's personal well-being is important, but, at best, it is of secondary importance. For instance, Caplan (1970; Caplan & Caplan, 1993) maintains that in consultation, the focus on the helpee's emotional qualities in the case are more for diagnostic purposes and serve only to help guide the professional in choosing a particular intervention style. This is the obverse of counseling, where counselors are concerned with the client's emotional well-being as a primary, if not only, aim.

In terms of the intraprocess stages of both helping relationships, evidence indicates that clients' goals in counseling differ from consultees' goals in consultation (see Egan, 1975, 2002; Schein, 1969, 1999). Egan (1975, p. 30) presents a "pre-helping" phase and a three-stage developmental model in attempting to demonstrate the process of counseling. The pre-helping phase concerns the helpers' attending behaviors of warmth and openness. The goal of the first stage is the clients' increased self-exploration and awareness. The goal of the second stage is to have clients begin having a "dynamic understanding" in which the client identifies the need for change and action, and identifies the potential resources available, which may have been previously unavailable to the client. The goal in the third stage of counseling is action. Salient throughout Egan's description is a focus on the helping relationship and on the client's self-exploration, dynamic understanding, and action.

Consultation has a different process and focus. Whereas the goal of counseling is to increase the client's (or client system's, as in the case of couples and family therapy) emotional and behavioral adjustment, the goal of consultation is to increase work performance. Thus, in a generic developmental model of consultation, the pre-helping phase is similar to counseling and is also aimed at establishing rapport. However, the first stage of consultation is directed toward problem identification and exploration—particularly in the behavioral case consultation model (discussed later in the text). The goal of the second stage is to have consultants, either with or without consultees, determine a style and type of intervention. This intervention might include suggesting personal counseling for employees, interviewing employees, conducting specific in-service training, developing goals and appropriate reinforcement schedules, altering the physical and/or social environment of the consultee or client setting, and/or a variety of other interventions. Stage three of consultation is characterized as having the same goal as the third stage of counseling: action. However, unlike counseling, where clients always initiate the action, the action in consultation can be initiated by the consultant, consultee, or both.

In addition, consultants can and often do operate from what Strong (1968) calls an "ecological" power base. This power base further distinguishes counseling and consultation because by using the ecological power base, consultants can directly suggest ways to alter the client's physical and social environment. This can be accomplished through several means, such as helping in the reorganizing of a company, creating a new management flowchart, moving or creating new office space, deconstructing and reconstructing work groups, and a host of other ways. Thus, although similar in some phases, there are distinctive structural differences in other stages or phases of each professional helping process.

Stages

In an early work, Gallessich (1982) sees consulting as occurring in steps: preliminary exploration, contracting, entry, building working relationships, data gathering, diagnosis, intervention, evaluation, and termination. Dougherty (1990) identifies the stages of consultation as entry, diagnosis, implementation, and disengagement. Hansen, Himes, and Meier (1990) distinguish the stages as pre-entry, initial contact, assessment and diagnosis, intervention, and termination. Parsons (1996) sees consultation stages as entry, identifying the problem and setting goals, intervention planning, and evaluation. Brown, Pryzwansky, and Schulte (2001) see consultation as happening in stages that include entry, initiation of a consulting relationship, assessment, problem definition and goal setting, strategy selection, implementation, evaluation, and termination. These various stages clearly reflect the expert orientation in consultation that is not as punctuated or pronounced as in a counseling venue. Moreover, these various stages suggest the preponderance of diagnosis, implementation, and evaluation in the consulting process. Although these various researchers identify different stages, it is apparent that the tasks contained within each particular stage are similar across consultation models. In comparing the two professional practices, it seems accurate to say that in counseling, the process is achieved through the reiterative dialogue that is occurring between counselor and client essentially at the time that the session is taking place. In traditional consultation models, this dialogue serves to help consultants diagnose the issue(s) and results in planned, formal intervention.

Financial Arrangements

Because of the dyadic nature of counseling, the client is responsible for payment. Thus, as in Case Study One, the client or his insurance company would be paying the counselor. His boss was not financially responsible for the sessions, even though she was going to benefit directly from her employee's successful counseling experience. Suppose that instead of seeing a counselor, the client in Case Study One had seen a therapist who was employed by a mental health agency. In this situation, the financial structure takes on an interesting and more complicated facade. Counselors who are employed by mental health agencies are paid directly by their employer (the agency) to see clients. In this sense, the counselors in agency settings can be considered "consultants" for the agency (who is configured as the "consultee"). The agency pays their clinicians to see the agency's mental health client population. At the same time, the clients being served have any number of financial arrangements available to them. For instance, the clients can pay the agency directly themselves as they leave the session (or be billed for the same). Clients may also have another agency, such as vocational rehabilitation, pay for the counseling that the client receives at the mental health center. In this situation, the mental health agency becomes the "consultant" to the vocational rehabilitation program (considered the "consultee"), and the counselor is not set apart from the agency in which she or he works. In other words, when a mental health agency is paid by a third party to counsel the third party's clients, the counselors and the mental health agency are considered to be one and the same—as a single consultant. The mental health client is the "client" in the structure.

In the case of counseling children, an early childhood program grant may pay for the counseling conducted at the mental health center. In yet another scenario, the mental health agency may have applied for and been awarded a state and/or federal grant that covers the cost of counseling services for numerous eligible clients. In the case where client services are paid for by the grant, the consultation structure remains similar to that just described. The granting agency is the "consultee" who hires a mental health agency and all of its counselors ("consultant") through awarding the agency money to provide services to eligible mental health clients. Clearly, there are more possible financial structures involved in consultation.

Even though the financial scenarios can be and often are quite complicated, there is an easy rule of thumb to follow when trying to identify the "consultee." The rule is: *The consultee is always the one who is responsible for paying your fee or bill.* In other words, the signature on the formal consultation contract identifies who is responsible for payment and thus defines who the consultee is. Designating the person/agency responsible for payment as the "consultee" is stable, meaning it does not change in structure. This structural stability is similar to counseling, where the client is always responsible for the financial arrangements in some form or another. This is important because consultants and counselors each have legal and ethical obligations to their respective clients and clientele. In the case of counseling, the ethical obligation to help is often more closely aligned with who is paying and who is benefiting. Consultation is different, as depicted in Case Study Two. The director was paying the consultant to deal directly with her employees. In that case, the consultant's responsibilities were seemingly divided between the director/consultee who was actually paying the consultant and the employees/clients who received services as well.

Obligations and Responsibilities

Counselors have a clear and direct duty and obligation to the clients whom they serve. Although there may be other personnel involved in the client's "problem," such as would be the case in family therapy approaches, counselors work exclusively with clients. When clients sign a Release of Confidential Information, counselors may discuss the client's situation with clearly identified or specified others. However, short of a release being signed by clients, counselors have an ethical mandate to restrict discussion of their work with clients. Consultants, on the other hand, have a different structure of obligation and duty.

The consultant is involved in two categorically important relationships simultaneously: One relationship is with the consultee who is paying for and may be receiving the service, and another relationship is with the client or clients who are receiving the service and yet not paying for it. Hence, *as far as structural obligation goes, consultants have a dual obligation.* Both obligations are critical to the process, and neither is more important than the other. In Case Study Two, the consultant is obligated to the consultee because she is paying for the consultancy. Yet, the consultant also saw several staff members for individual consultations and worked with the management team comprised of the director/consultee and three of her management staff—all the while interviewing every staff member. In this case study, the consultant had an obligation to everyone seen. In cases where the consultant does not see every employee, the consultant incurs some obligation to them nonetheless. Naturally, there would need to be a primary obligation if for no other reason than to help the consultant keep all of the relationships with everyone straight. Actually, the primary obligation is with the consultee because without the consultee agreeing to the consultation, it would not take place. Yet, as mentioned earlier, edifying the obligation to the consultee as being the more important obligation elevates money as the primary driver of that conceptualization. For mental health providers and consultants, this elevation has ethical overtones. Therefore, one of the balancing acts for consultants lies on a tightrope existing between the obligation to the consultee and the obligation to the clients.

Influence of Managed Care.   When managed-care organizations came into existence in the United States and established a dominating presence in the 1980s and 1990s, the relationship between clients and their insurance companies took on more of an *in loco parentis* structure (much like colleges and universities used to do). Clients became significantly less influential in their own mental health care. The insurance company became a type of caretaker for their clients and wanted to determine the best course of treatment as well as managing the cost of those treatments. This structure also realigned the financial relationships and obligations that previously existed between clients, counselors, and insurance companies. The presence of managed-care organizations has reformed the financial responsibilities of clients and has created a structure whereby counselors are seen as quasi-employees of managed-care organizations by virtue of their acting under the auspices of a preferred provider. Currently, it is a fact that in many cases, mental health professionals are either employed directly by managed-care organizations or are under contract with them (Fisher & Harrison, 2000). The client is still the client, but the counselor's responsibilities are now divided between the organization authorizing and paying for counseling on behalf of the client and the client who is actually receiving counseling services. With this has come the theoretical shift from a counseling paradigm to a consulting paradigm for many mental health professionals.

Helper Characteristics

As one would expect, since both counseling and consultation are interpersonal processes, helpers acting across both venues share some similar characteristics. Among these characteristics are the person-centered core conditions of empathy, genuineness, and positive regard (Rogers, 1951). Most consultants would agree on the importance of these characteristics, but Schein (1969, 1987, 1999) actually advances a theory of organizational consultation called *process consultation* that is based on these characteristics of a helping relationship. Brown, Pryzwansky, and Schulte (2001) believe that consultants also need to be able to take interpersonal risks. Maher (1993) takes the risk-taking characteristics and refines them by saying that organizational consultants need to possess a certain *entrepreneurship,* defined as the ability to create new professional opportunities while skillfully handling the risks that are incurred in such a creation. According to Brown and colleagues (2001), Maher also maintains that effective consultants need to possess commitment, persistence, and determination, and a desire to achieve, be open to feedback, and to be risk-seekers. It is apparent that consultants do indeed need to possess characteristics that are both similar to and different from counselors. It seems as though consultants need to demonstrate many of the same core conditions with their clientele as counselors do with theirs. At the same time, consultants need to go beyond the boundaries adhered to in counseling and match the values held in a competitive culture in which consultations take place. This posture is appropriate given that consultation is about work and takes place in the work venue.

Diversity.   The fact that consultation takes place in a work paradigm has profound implications on gender and racioethnicity. At this stage of professional development, it goes without saying that both counselors and consultants need to be culturally sensitive. However, the need for consultants to be attuned to diversity relates to their ability to effect systems change by virtue of their possessing an "ecological" power base (Strong, 1968), alluded to earlier. Changing physical and social environments is a significant responsibility that carries with it philosophical, moral, and ethical overtones (discussed in depth in later chapters). Hence, consultants need to be very attuned with the cultural Zeitgeist in a similar and different manner than counselors need to be sensitive. To be sure, each needs to be culturally sensitive. At the same time, consultants need to be very aware of how the forces present in the workplace operate to create some of the very problems that they are often asked to solve. Moreover, the implications of their solutions, whether or not they are arrived at jointly through collaboration with consultees, will impact the social, psychological, and economic climate of the organization.

Barriers to Free Expression. One of the differences in counseling and consultation lies in the type of barriers that exist in each venue that impede individual expression, equality, and growth. Although this inequity certainly is present in intimate relationships, and may be the presenting problem in counseling, the fact that consultation takes place in the work venue means that the inequities that do exist there will be punctuated. Only moral laws guide emotional oppression in the home—for example, it is not a crime to have nonviolent power struggles at home, which then can become a focus for counseling. However, there are laws that govern many interpersonal dynamics that occur in the workplace. These laws govern such things as hiring and firing, sexual harassment, oppression, equality in compensation, equality of opportunity, and a multitude of other dynamics.

Because counseling focuses on the more "private" experiences and consultation focuses on those same social dimensions from a more public and legalistic perspective, a critical component of a consultant's work is to have a working understanding of the stressors and social forces operating in the work world—especially as they relate to gender and racioethnic issues. This is not to say that counselors do not need to know about the world of work; they do. However, because counselors work with individuals, groups, and families while consultants work with the same population plus institutions and agencies, consultants are in a different position than counselors in terms of their ability to effect change on a more global scale. Changing individuals in an organization, institution, and/or agency, similar to family therapy, requires knowledge of the larger social system in which people work. Perhaps it could be generally stated that while counselors mostly deal with the psychological contracts operating in the home, consultants deal with those psychological contracts operating once the person leaves home and arrives at work. Another gross generalization can help conceptualize the similarities and differences between counseling and consultation: *Counseling deals with a person's private life, whereas consultation deals with a person's public work life.*

Approaches and Models

Just as there are approaches in counseling, there are approaches in consultation. Generally speaking, one of the ways to delineate approaches in counseling and consultation is along the traditional spectrum of the helper being "directive" versus being "nondirective." Person-centered therapy (Rogers, 1951) is considered by many as the penultimate nondirective approach. In comparison, a directive behavioral approach might anchor the other end of the spectrum. When the same delineation is used to compare consultation models, Schein's (1969, 1987, 1999) process-oriented approach to consultation lies on the more "nondirective" end of the spectrum, whereas Bergan's (1977) behavioral case consultation could be seen at the other end. Broadly speaking, Schein focuses on the relationship and Bergan focuses on the behaviors.

Another way to differentiate approaches is by the theoretical assumptions inherent in different approaches. For example, there is discussion among mental health professionals regarding "mental illness" versus "mental health" models of helping (see Fisher & Harrison, 2000). The former is considered focused on pathology, whereas the latter is considered as developmental in nature. Some consultation models, such as

Caplan and Caplan's (1993) mental health consultation model, are more illness or pathologically oriented, whereas Myrick's systematic consultation model (1977) is more developmental in its theoretical perspective.

A third manner in which approaches can be differentially conceptualized is through the theoretical tenets and practical applications. For instance, the gestalt approach (Perls, 1969) is based on experiencing, and the techniques used in gestalt therapy are vastly different from the learning theory approaches advocated by Bandura (1977) or Gerber (2001). The same holds true in comparing consultation models. Bergan's (1977) behavioral consultation model and Bergan and Kratochwill's (1990) model differ vastly from the mental health consultation model advocated by Caplan (1970) and Caplan and Caplan (1993).

Generic Models.   Schein (1969, 1987) divided the approaches in organizational consulting into the purchase model, the doctor/patient model, and the process consultation model. If one were again to arrange consulting models along a continuum, the process consultation approach would most closely approximate the "nondirective" end of the spectrum, and the doctor/patient model would anchor the "directive" approach end of the spectrum. Similar to some principles of person-centered therapy, the process consultation approach assumes that the most efficacious consultant engages in a process of "joint diagnosis" and "joint problem-solving" with consultees. In the doctor/patient approach, the assumption is that the consultant knows best and can be called into an organization to give it a look to see what problems exist (Schein, 1987, p. 7). Consultants then make recommendations and direct efforts at problem solving.

The third generic approach in consultation is the purchase model. This is best likened to a mental health counselor specializing in a focus area (e.g., eating disorders) and being paid to do work in that specialty. Another example of the purchase model in counseling is reflected in situations where a counselor refers a client to a psychiatrist for a psychopharmacological evaluation. In the purchase model of consultation, the consultant is seen as possessing a certain focused expertise, such as having expert information or an expert service, and consultees "purchase" that expertise. For example, a principal hiring a facilitator to run an in-service workshop on increasing math scores on national tests would "purchase" the expertise of the facilitator. Interestingly, as will be discussed in Chapter Fourteen, the facilitator could be more of an expert in facilitating change through workshops as opposed to an expert at the content area per se. Or, the principal could purchase a facilitator's content expertise and minimize somewhat the facilitator's expertise as a change agent. In both situations, the helper is presumed to have some expert knowledge or information either about the change process or the content.

Research

As mentioned earlier in the chapter, problematic methodologies plague the research in consultation (Brown, Pryzwansky, & Schulte, 2001; Gutkin, 1993). In actuality, the problems in research on consultation parallel many of the problems with research in counseling. That is, using control groups and manipulating variables during real-life or real-world counseling and consulting situations is difficult. The difficulty is divided between the ethics involved and the real work-world considerations. The combination of the two often precludes the use of appropriate designs and instruments that can get at the complexities of the process. Similar to the research in counseling, critical areas of research for consultation include process and outcome studies. Nonetheless, this has not deterred researchers from attempting to investigate various aspects of consultation. According to Pryzwansky (1986) and cited in Brown, Pryzwansky, and Schulte (2001), 173 data-based studies in consultation were referenced in *Psychological Abstracts* and 81 doctoral dissertations reported in *Doctoral Dissertations International* between the years 1978 to 1985. The number may not seem to be high, but it is important to note that consultation is considered an adjunct to normal mental health practice and not a stand-alone profession per se. As such, much of its content base is borrowed from the counseling literature.

The research on effective helper characteristics (e.g., Strong, 1968) is one example of counseling research being applicable to consultants. In an unpublished dissertation, Harrison (1983) measured the responses of undergraduate students who looked at videotapes of initial and action stages of various counseling and consultation models. Subjects were asked to rate the counselor and consultant characteristics on the Counselor Rating Form (CRF) (Barak & LaCrosse, 1975), which measures helper characteristics along the dimensions of perceived expertness, interpersonal attractiveness, and trustworthiness. Results indicated that the characteristics of helpers were similar, although they varied in strength according to whether the process was in the initial phases or action phases. Although interesting, the study was an analogue study, which removes it from real-world practice.

Qualitative research does not fair much better in terms of consultation. Brown, Pryzwanski, and Schulte (2001) advocate the need for more case studies. Citing Pryzwansky and Noblit (1990), Brown and colleagues believe that the hypothesis-generating value of qualitative studies of consultation can be very helpful in advancing knowledge about this helping process (p. 314). Likely, the current problems identified in the research on consultation can be addressed through a combination of quantitative and qualitative efforts. As mentioned, it may prove to be impossible to quantify specifically the intricate dynamics of consultation because problems with definitions in consultation abound. Moreover, from some gender and racioethnic perspectives, it may not appropriate to undertake such a task. Exacting precision in science, such as attempting to quantify and categorize "consultation," is seen by some professional circles as an example of a masculine male model that is not an appropriate stage upon which to embark research investigations. This male model in research reflects attempts to objectify the construct, creating a dualism with the ultimate aim being to gain intellectual control over the process (e.g., Plumwood, 1993). Although this is clearly a feminist perspective, and would seemingly unite women on the issue, it does not. There are those racioethnic women who do not subscribe to feminism as the vehicle for social justice (e.g., Fox-Genovese, 1996). Thus, the issue of what type of research is important and appropriate for consultation is debatable. Fortunately, the current movement toward using qualitative and quantitative designs in social sciences research in general should provide valid options for investigation.

SUMMARY

Problematic definitions notwithstanding, consultation is a professional practice that has some similarities and distinct structural differences with counseling. One helpful manner in which to understand the similarities is to understand the categorical importance of the helping relationship. Specifically, counselors and consultants both need to build effective rapport and trust that needs to grow and/or be enhanced throughout process. Given that structural similarity, the two processes diverge rapidly. Consultation is triadic in nature, and this requires consultants to pay attention to the relationships that are built with both consultees as well as with the client and client system. There are at least two sets of obligations in consultation that serve to separate it from counseling. Whereas counseling clients are responsible for payment in some form or through some insurance or managed care structure, clients in consultation receive the service for "free" in the sense that it is the consultee who pays for the consultant's services. Graduate students in counselor training programs are warned against advice giving. If a consultant shies away from giving advice, it might be very inappropriate and could lead to a termination of the consulting relationship. Consultants can consult almost anywhere and can consult with numerous individuals at the same time. A discussion of consultation stages often includes a diagnostic and intervention stage. The emphatic emphasis on diagnosis and intervention in consultation is not reflected in counseling. There are many models of counseling in which diagnosis is not a central component. Intervention is rather formalized in consulting, whereas formal intervening in counseling can be seen occurring throughout the process of working with a client face to face.

A very good text categorizing and summarizing various empirical studies of consultation is Brown, Pryzwansky, and Schulte's *Psychological Consultation* (2001). There is an increased effort to conduct empirical investigations and publish results in professional journals. These attempts will satisfy those who adhere to scientific and objectified approaches to knowledge. At the same time, Brown and colleagues call for more case studies as a means to understand the effective operations and processes of consultation. Qualitative approaches, which do not attempt to separate out and categorize consultation in the same manner, may be more appealing to women and some racioethnic groups. In the final analysis, a combination of methodologies may be an effective way to go about the task.

QUESTIONS

1. What is the impact of ambiguous definitions on research in consultation?

2. Why it is important to differentiate between formal and informal consultation and between professional and nonprofessional consultation?

3. The example of an expert coming in and "fixing" an organization is a common perception of consultation. How accurate is that perception?

4. What are three generic approaches to consultation?

5. If you had to determine the one salient feature distinguishing counseling from consultation, what would that one distinction be?

CHAPTER THREE

THE CONTEXT OF CONSULTATION

Counseling and consultation have been shown to operate on similar, yet different, structural and process levels. Although many dimensions were discussed in the previous chapter, the contexts in which these two helping processes occur were not central to the discussion. The contextual differences between these two processes is perhaps the hardest concept to glean (and maybe the most difficult to write about clearly or succinctly). Those professionals who were first trained in individual approaches to treatment and then became marriage and family therapists by virtue of training in family systems and systemic therapy understand the cognitive struggle being referred to here. In asking these dually trained professionals about the results of the experience, they will likely say something to the effect that once one moves from individual perspectives to a systems perspective, one cannot go back to individual therapy and see it or practice it in the same way. For these professionals, the experience is cognitively transforming. All this is to say that understanding the context of consultation is like moving from individual psychotherapy to a systems point of view. The reason for this is that the context of consultation is dramatically different from that of counseling, and this "context" is itself significantly different from the "work versus personal context" alluded to previously.

Since there are three structural entities in consultation (consultant, consultee, and client), consultation can be conceptualized as taking place in a social or group venue, as opposed to an individual venue. Moreover, since consultation is about work, the context of consultation is also "the organization" in the world of work. There are two main reasons for this: Most workers work for someone else or own companies that employ others. A notable exception might be the solo private mental health practitioner. However, even those who are in private practice belong to organizations. For instance, imagine a social worker consulting with a psychiatric nurse about a treatment plan for a single client. Even though both professionals may be in solo private practices, there is an inherent organizational context related to the discussion. The organizational context is seen by the fact that the discussion between these two professionals is guided by ethical codes. These codes are generated by the professsionals' national organizations and serve to organize the cluster of appropriate behavior expected during the discussion. In other words, the organizational influence is reflected in the fact that any solutions or calls to action occurring as a result of the consultation between professionals will be organized and structured by the ethics of their respective professions. So, professional ethics provide the organizational context in this example.

Another example of organizational context is a school counselor/consultant working with a principal on reducing the principal's stress. The impact of such an intervention with the principal clearly impacts the school as a whole, even though the intervention is with a singular consultee. In yet another instance, a psychologist consulting with a mental health therapist employed by a local mental health agency needs to understand the context in which these consultations are taking place, because the therapist needs to conform to the agency's particular ethos in order for the efficacy of help to be enhanced. Suggesting a course of action for the consultee that runs counter to the organizational culture will likely render the consultation less than effective. Typically for the school counselor, the larger context may include all the teachers, students, parents, and administrators of that school that affect any given teacher at any given time. In the case of the mental health worker, the larger context could be configured to include the administrators, the clinical staff, the system of agency policies and procedures, and the funding sources that impose certain structural guidelines for the agency to follow. If you are a graduate student reading this book, you belong to the larger contexts of the profession—students in general, students of higher education, plus a host of other nonwork-related contexts such as family and so on. The point is not so much to define "contexts" as it is to introduce the concept that *almost all consultations have some organizational context.* In many cases, the organizational context operates only as a backdrop context for the consultant. In other cases, even in the ethics example, the context is very present and visible.

THE ORGANIZATIONAL CONTEXT OF CONSULTATION

The Ethic of Context

When speaking about the context of consultation being the "organization," the organization being referred to is the same "organization" that exists in the business world. That is the realm that organizational development (OD) consultants work in. However, this is not a discussion about organizational development per se. One purpose in reviewing the issues related to organizations and organizational change for most mental health professionals is to provide a backdrop for consultants to conceptualize the context of the consultee's concerns. Nonetheless, aside from the practical value of such information, there are ethical imperatives involved.

The first ethical imperative concerns what French and Raven (1957) and Strong (1968) refer to as the *ecological power base*—the same power base discussed in Chapter Two. The ecological power base allows consultants to affect change in the social and/or physical environment of the consultee or client. Since consultants operate from this (and other) power bases, ignoring the ecological context of the problem could be argued as questionable ethics. In other words, if the true context of all consultations is the organization, then ignoring such a central concept could be questionable ethics. As for the second ethical imperative, it may seem at first incongruent and confusing to conceptualize all consultations as a type of organizational consulting. This is especially true if one adheres to the traditional notions of organizational consulting and organizational development. However, such a conceptual distinction helps clarify a perspective of change and intervening in consulting that incorporates the individual in the context of the organization. This seems to be the appropriate context in which consultation is conducted. If helping to change one individual affects others in the organizational context, then consultants need to be aware of the context in which they are intervening.

Schein (1969, 1987, 1999) believes that all organizational problems are essentially human problems. Schneider, Brief, and Guzzo (1996) state, "Organizations as we know them are the people in them; if the people do not change, there is no organizational change" (p. 7). These same authors go on to say that structural changes such as technology, communication networks, and hierarchies are effective to the degree that the changes are implemented in the psychology of the individual employee. This perspective is echoed by research into diversity and personal culture (e.g., Sue & Sue, 1999) as well as research into organizational culture (e.g., Schein, 1992), all of which strongly suggests that a consultant's intentional attempts at change need to be focused with individual differences in mind. So, theoretically and practically, the changing and intervening process effectively begins at the individual and idiosyncratic level. Conceptually, this ethic would be true for change and intervening in organizations as well. A review of the history of organizational development consulting shows that the relationship between the individual and the organization has not always been clearly delineated, even to professional consultants in the field.

For school counselors, it is rather clear that their interventions have traditionally been aimed at the individual, the individual-within-a-system, or at the micro-level. However, their current use of a consultation approach to their counseling practices in schools commands a third ethical imperative with regard to the context of their consultations. Although ethics will be discussed in depth in Chapters Six and Seven, the relevancy of this imperative necessitates attention here. School counselors do a great deal of consulting in their work, and by nature they are considered to be "inside consultants" by many theorists and practitioners alike (e.g., Harrison, 2000; Dollarhide & Saginak, 2003). The position of school counselors within an existing school is similar to what many large corporations might have in their own human resources departments. These large corporations, such as Exxon, have inside consultants who deal with a variety of organizational issues. Inside consultants such as school counselors seem to have an ethical imperative to have some knowledge of organizations and organizational life in order to appropriately contextualize their work at schools. For these reasons, some consideration of organizations and organizational culture is needed.

Organizations and the Individual

The historical overview of organizational development (OD) suggests, even as late as the mid-1990s, professional consultants continued to be influenced by individual psychology. Schein (1996) suggests that often in OD consulting, the direction of conceptualization has been from group to the individual. Hence, while acknowledging the impact of group dynamics, Schein punctuates the need to conceptualize the individual as well. Schein (1969, 1987, 1999) maintains that all problems in organizations are essentially human problems. As such, the identification of problems and potential solutions in organizations is always mediated, if not relegated, as a result of consultants working directly and indirectly with consultees and clients.

In situations where an organization requests help from an outside expert consultant, it is actually the consultee and not the "organization" per se who is requesting the service, although the "organization" obviously acts as a Greek Chorus (i.e., the group in a classical Greek drama that presents a disengaged commentary or narrative on the action). Clearly, there may be organizational problems. In actuality, it is the people in the organization who have the problem; and it may well be that only some of the people experience the problem directly. Since the problem is essentially with individuals, only those individuals can solve it. So, for Schein, it is helpful and appropriate to understand that it is the people within various organizations who actually are affected by any intervening and change process that is taking place.

No doubt there are group and organizational dynamics that occur in organizations that enable consultants to conceptualize the existence of "an organization" as such. However, if the concept of "organization" is taken myopically at face value to be the only real and breathing entity, consultants could feasibly overlook the dynamic power of the people within who actually identify and make the necessary changes. Moreover, an overly objectified conceptualization of total organizations as the primary change target may not punctuate the primary position of the human factor in organizations.

Organizations change only when the individual people within the organizations' structural confines themselves change. Nevertheless, this is not a discussion debating whether organizations have a power in and of themselves that transcends the individuals working within it. From a gestalt perspective, and from that of many systems theorists and practitioners in the field, the collective whole does transcend individuals. However, aside from the ethical considerations, the concern here is that fledgling consultants might mistake the "organization" as the large change target, and may therefore focus their conceptualizations of intervening exclusively on a larger organizational picture than might be necessary for any given consultancy. Since "organizations" are people, consultants need to have some grasp of how the people arrived in the workplace. This "arrival" reflects a history of occupational choice, career decision making, and a host of sociopolitical influences that are not left at the door of the workplace. Instead, these influences are alive and operating within and about the organization. Consultants simply cannot ignore the variety of individual perspectives on work and on opportunities in the workplace.

Career Theory and Diversity

Another concern for consultants is that they may conceptualize the organization in such a way as to diminish individual differences within the organization or agency. Some of these differences are profound and are embedded in differing worldviews regarding work and the choices available to racioethnic minorities and women. Brown (2002) maintains that "work values" are those that individuals believe should be satisfied as a result of their participation in the worker role. Typically, these work-related values include, but are not limited to, financial prosperity, altruism, achievement, responsibility, and leadership (p. 49). Certainly, consultants need to identify and listen to the important consultee values, but they need also to be aware of the pressing forces that shaped the consultees' values as well as affecting on their occupational choice. This is especially true when one considers the fact that career development theories "have all but ignored the career development of ethnic and cultural minorities" (Brooks, 1990; Brown, 2002; Cheatham, 1990; Issacson & Brown, 2000; Osipow & Littlejohn, 1995).

Brown (2000) maintains that although values may be the primary factor in choosing, deriving satisfaction from, and advancing in one's career, there are a host of other variables that actually influence occupational choice. Given this assertion, the issue for consultants is not whether these factors guiding occupational choice will influence consultees and clients, but in what ways and how are they influencing these individuals. Hotchkiss and Borow (1996) and Sinha (1990) find that *socioeconomic status* influences both the decision-making process as well as the career chosen among subjects. Leong and Serifica (1995) note the *family and/or group influence* in choosing careers among Asian Americans in their study. These same researchers, as well as others (see Melamed, 1995; Robinson & Ginter, 1999), identify a *history of discrimination* as being another variable influencing career decision making and career choice among minority groups. The issues raised by these researchers provide a structure in which to explore critical areas of the psychological contract that will be developed between consultants and consultees. It is imperative that consultants appreciate the variety of ways that individuals have "arrived" in the workplace.

These different avenues to the workplace form a basis on which the particular organizational culture develops. All too often, consultants ignore these differences because they do not see the "organization" as the backgrounded client system, are not sensitive to the issues of diversity, do not conceptualize the larger context of the consultation, are unsure of how to impact such a diverse group of individuals, do not infuse this view into the psychological contract, and/or may fall prey to the easy way out, which is to ignore things that are foreign, scary, or threatening. Contemporary consultants need to incorporate diversity as a reality, not simply as an add-on, afterthought, or something that is politically correct. Diversity *is.* It is not something out of place or in the future.

For instance, the masculine male ethic perpetuates a belief in individualism and in the organization. However, this is only one perspective, and it has been promulgated widely to the exclusion of a collectivist perspective, whose tenets may be vastly different. For example, the traditional Euro-American ethos of individualism makes it difficult to imagine an "organization" without some sort of hierarchy. Yet, the Aborigines of Australia have not had tribes, headmen, chiefs, or warriors because they do not subscribe to the concept of "tribe" as being a group that defends and uses a certain territory (Lawlor, 1993). Instead, there is a web of rights and responsibilities that has been spun out of their birthplace and reflected in an extensive kinship system that spreads human relationships across vast distances. If a mother or father was born far away from the birthplace of his or her child, that child still has responsibilities in those distant areas. Aborigines have lived this fluid, widespread kinship for perhaps 150,000 years without destruction to each other or the environment. The idea of possession does not exist in

Aboriginal culture because they do not think of owning anything. Instead, they have a concept of belonging to the land, of belonging to their kin, and of beholding (meaning that Aborigines observe their environment, spiritually as well as physically, and are responsive to their observations). They do not own; they belong.

How different this perspective is from the traditional Euro-American views of organizations, ownership, and individualism! That you may discredit the argument by saying that the chances of having an Aborigine as a consultee are negligible does not diminish the profound implications of difference. You, as a consultant, may never work with an Aborigine as a consultee or client, but the fact that this group exists should underscore the reality that individuals in organizations have differing worldviews. That is the reality, and these differing worldviews, however expressed or unexpressed in the workplace, form the basis of the organization's culture. Hence, organizational culture impacts everyone—every consultee and every client—regardless of how the actual focus on consultation is configured. Since organizations are essentially groups of individuals, the social context of every consultation needs to include some aspect of organizational life.

THE CONSULTEE'S CONTEXT: ORGANIZATIONAL CULTURE

Whenever a group or organization experiences enough situations together, a culture develops. Organizational culture is an elusive yet popular concept that is used in the research to capture the essence of organizations operating in the world of work. The term *organizational culture* has been defined in a number of different ways. Deal and Kennedy (1982) capture the essence of organizational culture by saying it is "the way we do things around here." Others offer more detailed versions. For instance, Trice and Beyer (1984) believe that organizational culture is a system of publicly and collectively accepted meanings that operate for a group at a particular time. In earlier works, Schein (1987) describes organizational culture as a pattern of basic assumptions developed as a group or organization learns to cope with its environment. More recently, Schein (1999, 2000) elaborates in saying that organizational culture is a pattern of shared basic assumptions that is learned by members of the group as they go about attempting to solve their external problems of survival in a competitive marketplace and their internal problems of integration. Theoretically and practically, these shared assumptions work well enough so that they can be taught to new group members as the correct way of perceiving, thinking, and feeling about all aspects of their daily work life.

For professional organizational development (OD) consultants, organizational culture is conceptualized as a strong operative force, yet, it is an elusive concept. For example, according to Silvester, Anderson, and Patterson (1999), quantitative research aimed at investigating organizational culture has been hindered by ambiguous theoretical models. Nonetheless, the number of qualitative-oriented research articles appearing throughout various OD journals underscores the fact that it is a meaningful way to conceptualize and understand what goes on in organizations. Since organizational development consulting requires specialized training, most mental health practitioners simply need to know something about the concept. Therefore, the following discussion of organizational culture is not meant to be in-depth nor particularly broad in scope. The lack of depth given to the discussion, however, should not be confused as indicating its lack of importance. The ethical considerations alone with regard to organizational culture and its inherent impact on the lives of individual consultees and clients make it imperative that mental health professionals be familiar with the larger social context in which their consultations are taking place.

Contents of Culture

Schein (1992, 1999), Smith and Vecchio (1997), Smircich (1983), and Weiner (1988) all essentially agree that organizational culture has three main ingredients: norms, shared values, and the premises that are taken for granted by members of the organization. According to Smith and Vecchio (1997), these three ingredients are reflected in the informal systems that emerge within organizations over time. These informal systems embrace the habits and routines that develop into the unwritten understandings of "how business gets done around here" and "what it is like out there" (p. 485).

Culture provides members with an ordered approach to routine problems that arise based on approved perspectives. The decisions that are made in solving the routine problems help to continually reaffirm the organization's culture by reinforcing the expected and acceptable behavior across the entire organization (Schwartz & Davis, 1981, p. 35). The orientation that is produced helps form the homogeneity of the organization in terms of helping with the communication and shared understandings about what is being experienced. However, according to Tushman and Romanelli (1985), culture is often tied to tradition and sometimes is less successful at changing because culture is rooted in a history that has probably been successful enough to allow the organization to survive. As such, organizational culture tends to be inertial and can diminish an organization's ability to adapt and survive under external new conditions. This is critical information for any consultant to know because in attempting to effect change in an individual consultee or client, in an agency, hospital, or institution, interventions that run counter to the larger system's culture will not likely be successful. So, when an individual consultee calls and needs some help, even though the help might be aimed at the individual level, the "individual level" really does not ever exist. There is always some relationship that exists between the individual and the larger organizational venue in which that individual works. Thus, even though the focus of the intervention might be aimed at the individual, consultants need to know about the ethos and culture in which that individual operates.

Smith and Vecchio (1997) identify six central elements of organizational culture:

1. Critical decisions of founding members
2. Guiding ideas
3. Social structure
4. Norms, values, and premises
5. Remembered history and symbolism
6. Institutional arrangements

The founding members are those individuals who start the firm or who are on board from the very beginning. These individuals play a particularly important role in the development of the organization's culture by bringing their personal goals, values, and dreams to the neophyte organization. These personal perspectives guide the early strategic decisions and define the market scope. Interactions with the competitive environment and the nature of the decisions that are made in response serve to shape the organization's experiences. When the firm is in its early years, founding individuals help create a set of values or guiding ideas that become validated by accomplishments in the marketplace. As a result, the organization takes on what Clark (1972) describes as a distinctive identity that cannot be readily abandoned. The social structure that is initiated and sustained within organizations reflects patterns of interactions that develop among individuals, between people and their jobs, and among groups. Over time, attitudes about themselves and what others are doing in the organization, and about the organization itself develop.

Selznick (1957) believes that the organization may eventually become valued for itself as members come to see it as a source of personal satisfaction. This evolves into the idea that the organization becomes an institutional fulfillment of group integrity and aspiration. As the organization survives over time, some parts of the original history become forgotten, while other more salient aspects of history become punctuated. Hence, the "history" takes on a remembered history as opposed to actual history and is remembered through sagas, stories, and myths. Clark (1972) believes that sagas provide connections between history and the organization's purposes or values, and serves to maintain the image of distinctiveness about the organization. An offshoot of sagas are the myths, folklore, and rituals that help communicate values and legitimize current organizational practices by appealing to the explanations offered by the myths of past events. Finally, institutional arrangements go beyond the remembered history to include formal management systems that exert a powerful form of control in that they fundamentally influence behavior. Formal information systems include the measurement of reward as well as the nature and type of information available for planning and training systems. Stinchcombe (1990) believes that the policies and systems that develop reflect the adaptation of the organization to its environment.

External Organizational Survival.   Schein (1999) collapses the various elements of organizational culture into (1) learned responses to external survival issues, (2) learned responses to internal integration issues, and (3) core basic assumptions (higher-order abstractions). *External survival* means simply that the organization competes in a marketplace and in a context of changing economic and social conditions. Without successful adaptation to those conditions, the organization eventually ceases to exist. The learned responses to external survival issues include:

- A shared definition of the primary task, mission, and strategy of the organization
- Shared goals
- A shared sense of the means to be used in goal accomplishment
- A shared definition of the measurement systems to assess the progress as well as the errors in the process
- A shared sense of the means to be used to correct the errors in the process

Even in working with individual consultees and clients, consultants need to have at least some familiarity with how the individual's organization copes with its survival. Is the organization cutthroat in its attempts to be competitive or effective in such endeavors? Is it top-down in its management ethos? What are the real-world pressures of organizational survival that impact individual consultees and clients? How do the individuals handle those pressures? These are important questions for all consultants in any consulting situation to consider because the issues raised in these questions are operating in almost every consultation to one degree or another.

The "error detection" device is a concept used in organizations to ensure that the organization is on target with its mission, aims, goals, and objectives. For most organizations, this error detection devise is actually the financial bottom line. However, it is the organizational culture that determines what type of information is gathered and processed in the course of detecting errors in the system. In organizations such as in-patient treatment facilities, the bottom line might be reflected in the concern with the census or number of beds still available. Those who work in in-patient treatment centers often joke that the first question their administration asks each morning is "What is the bed census?" rather than "How are the clients?" In community mental health agencies, the error detection might come in the form of the number of clients on the therapist's caseload. Too heavy a caseload might indicate that some rearrangement of cases might need to be done. Schools are no different. Some school districts have error detection systems that identify schools whose student achievement scores are in need of improvement. Sometimes these schools are labeled "at risk," and this reflects a "school in error." Error correction for these institutions can come in the form of a new principal, transferring teachers, and/or the retooling of teachers in areas of academic concern so that they can improve instruction to raise test scores. All of these varied responses to external survival issues essentially form the contact boundaries around the organization as it goes about interacting with its environment.

Internal Organizational Integration.   At the same time that the organization is interacting with the external environment, the individuals go about integrating themselves into the organization. Smith and Vecchio (1997) assert that all individuals within the context of their location in the organization will develop norms or expectations about what the organization, along with its constituent units and individual members, should do or not do in a given situation. Individuals will develop a set of assumptions that are taken for granted, and they will use this to interpret events that occur. Hence, individual employees, subgroups or units of employees, as well as the total organization itself become sensitized to the "ways things are done around here." Schein (1999) believes that the issues surrounding this internal integration include:

- Shared language and concepts
- Shared definition of group boundaries indicting who is in and who is out
- Shared criteria for acquiring power and status
- Shared rules of face and intimacy
- Shared criteria for rewards and punishments
- Shared ideology

Internal integration has something to do with formal and informal power structures within any organization. With regard to "who is in and who is out" of the power circle, there are often professional boundaries that structure this pecking order. In mental health agencies, professional credentials and/or responsibilities often depict who is in and who is out of the power circle. For instance, psychiatrists may automatically be "in" the inner circle simply by virtue of their ability to prescribe medication and hospitalize patients. Likewise, master's-level clinical therapists may be "out" of the inner circle of influence because they cannot prescribe or hospitalize patients without the approval of the psychiatrist. In addition to the structural delineations, there can be interpersonal dynamics that determine who is in power and who is not. For example, all schools have principals. However, not all principals are powerful inside their own schools. In fact, there can even be cliques and coalitions of teachers who actually hold more power in the school. These individuals determine who is in and who is out. *Thus, it is often the case where the leader of an organization owns the title but does not possess the process.* That is, the title of principal or clinical director affords the person a certain amount of power, but often another individual or group of individuals actually has the power to get things done.

Cultures also have shared understandings about how open individuals can and should be in the organization. It may be presumed that mental health professionals are supposed to be open, whereas employees in a high-tech firm may draw very different boundaries around how open they are with each other. Some organizations "require" employees to leave their personal lives outside whenever they come to work. At the same time, there may be other organizations where a discussion of personal reactions is acceptable as long as it does not interfere with the overall mission of the organization. Some organizations, such as a mental health crisis center, may set up a structure whereby volunteers can be debriefed by other staff about their reactions to particularly difficult crisis calls. In these situations, a lack of openness might be construed as a type of defensiveness that needs to be addressed. The extent to which an organizational ethos allows for openness is important information for consultants to have.

Core Basic Assumptions.   As mentioned, only over time can an environment create a culture. If something works repeatedly, it becomes part of the culture. Because of this, culture always implies history. So, a "new way of working" is not considered a part of the culture until that "new way" becomes an accepted way of working and integrated into culture over time. Specific to consultation, any intervention that implies a new way of working will only become effective over time. Thus, consultants need to measure their interventions with this in mind. All cultures have fundamental assumptions that lie deep within a given culture and serve to guide what culture is formed over time (Schein, 1992, 1999; Smircich, 1983; Weiner, 1988). Rokeach (1960), in *The Open and Closed Mind*, considers these fundamental assumptions to be "unconscious beliefs." Every culture rests on some set of tacit assumptions regarding who its members are, what kind of universe they live in, and what is ultimately important to them.

According to Rokeach (1960), one's total belief system is an organization of beliefs and expectancies that the person accepts as true of the world in which he or she lives. This includes the verbal and nonverbal, the implicit and explicit, and the conscious and unconscious. The purpose of belief systems centers on the need for a cognitive framework to interpret new experiences as well as the need to ward off threatening aspects of reality. In other words, these tacit assumptions form cognitive *paradigms* that serve to filter events seen as coming from the outside. These paradigms serve to organize information into the basic ways that individuals and cultures perceive, value, and act in the world. Rokeach believes that all individuals and cultures believe, value, choose, and know based on these belief systems. In organizational cultures, the paradigms that are formed through systematic ways of perceiving, valuing, and doing result in an accumulated experience that depicts what works and what does not work for the organization and for the individuals. Argyris (1970) refers to these basic assumptions as "theories-in-use." These theories are not often confronted or debated and, as a result, they are very hard to change. According to Schein (1992, 1999) the theories-in-use or higher-order abstractions relate to the following:

- Nature of reality and truth
- Nature of time and space
- Nature of human nature
- Nature of human activity
- Nature of human relations

When taken as a composite whole, these higher-order abstractions guide the culture from all aspects. Another way to conceptualize what these core assumptions are and do is to reflect on a counseling theory such as Rogers's person-centered counseling. The underlying assumptions of Rogers's theory (1951) reflect a deep belief in the goodness of human nature and human activity. Individuals are viewed as teleological in that they are seen as inherently goal oriented. The goal is aimed at self-actualization. The nature of the relationship between counselor and client is characterized as reflecting respect for the client's reality, offering no judgments, accepting clients as they are, and demonstrating warmth, empathy, and positive regard. In this manner, Rogers believes that the relationship that develops between counselors and clients is a powerful medium for growth. At the same time, Rogers's belief in humans to be self-determining mandates that he reflect back to clients what they are saying and seem to be feeling so that clients can make sense of it. Eventually, in terms of space and time, the client's problems, which are originally defined as "there and then" move toward the "here and now." As a result, clients begin to talk in terms of "I" instead of using the euphemistic or distant "you."

In today's public schools, the nature of reality and truth is measured by the institutional arrangements depicting an emphasis on test scores and on learning math and science. That is their "reality." Time is measured by the school year and by grade-level criterion referencing. Time is also measured in the "now" because science and math need to be learned for the immediate future. Time is precious for school districts. So, students must attend school for a certain number of days. Space is allotted for schools in neighborhoods, and classrooms are arranged in a certain spatial fashion so as to enhance the learning experience. In schools, there are "public" or shared spaces, such as hallways, cafeterias, media centers, and libraries. In other places, space is measured by learning stations in classrooms. There is a belief that competition begets competition and humans learn best when they compete for grades. Thus, there are assumptions about the power of statistical averages as being reality and truth. Elementary students are generally segregated from middle school students who are segregated from high school students. Learning is assumed to be most successful when students feel safe. Therefore, drug-free and violent-free schools are valued. In terms of relationships, there is an assumption of equal opportunity, so there are laws protecting the rights to learn for all students. On a fundamental level, schools operate on the assumption that humans are malleable and can learn. As you can see, "culture as a set of basic assumptions defines for us what to pay attention to, what things mean, how to react emotionally to what is going on, and what actions to take in various kinds of situations" (Schein, 1992, p. 22).

EXAMPLES OF ORGANIZATIONAL CULTURE

Embedding and Stabilizing Culture

According to Smith and Vecchio (1997) and Schein (1999), culture is embedded in organizations in several ways. Culture develops over the life cycle of the organization and is revealed through artifacts, espoused values, and core basic assumptions. The culture gradually embeds itself into the deepest structures of individual consultees and clients as well as into the organization as a whole. Schein believes that culture is embedded through:

- The leader's attention to the measurement, rewards, and controls that are implemented
- The leader's reactions to critical incidents
- The leader's role modeling and coaching
- Establishing systems for recruitment, promotion, retirement, and ex-communication
- The formal and informal socialization that takes place
- Recurring systems and procedures
- The organization's design, structure, and physical space
- Stories and myths about key people and events
- Formal statements, charters, creeds, and ethical codes

The opening of a new public high school is a good example of how culture is embedded in an organization as it moves from its infancy to maturity. A second example of an established mental health center will depict the levels of culture.

Organizational Life Cycles: The New High School

The opening of a new public high school would be considered its *birth or founding phase* of organizational culture. The actual opening, of course, is the result of a series of events that occur upstream of the official opening. All new schools are founded within an existing organizational culture made up of the accepted social and educational norms operating in the community in which the school will be located. This local culture is embraced on a national scale by the cultural norms toward education held by citizens of the United States.

These two prevailing organizational cultures guide all aspects of the development of the school. The local venue will dictate physical locality, size, and the type of school (elementary, middle, or high school) that is proposed to voters. The national culture will be reflected more in the influence over such elements as the curriculum, the issues surrounding equality of education, student and parental privacy, academic achievement and its measurement, students with disabilities and special needs, and the like. The system used to measure and evaluate the school operates on both local and national levels as well. Locally, a superintendent may impose an evaluative measure designed to identify schools that do not meet local standards. On a national level, governments legislate certain national standards set through the Department of Education. A local community may reflect a high overall socioeconomic level that enables such programs as art, music, dance, and theatre to be added to conventional, federally controlled curriculums. It could also be the case that the community decides to build the school simply out of a desire for more space for these programs. Another school might be proposed to handle a problem of overcrowding based on newly created federal guidelines for student-to-teacher ratios. There are myriad agendas for opening a new school.

In terms of culture, principals often bring staff with them from their previous schools. Some people apply for staff positions and are hired from the outside. Those teachers who transfer with the new principal bring with them an established culture that interacts with the loosely developing culture of new hires. A value of diversity is immediately reflected by the composition of the faculty. The principal and perhaps a few "founding members" become the dominant influence, and the new culture that develops builds through the success of whatever initial strategy was agreed on and laid in place. This "strategy" includes such things as the success the school has had in meeting the challenges imposed from the external environment, the success it has had in the integration of its members to each other, and the extent to which artifacts such as the mission statements, goal attainment charts, and the like have become a congruent system. Often, a new high school will not incorporate juniors and seniors its first year. Thus, the high school will not usually field an athletic team nor compete at the varsity level for the first year or two of its existence. The assumption operating here concerns the merits of equal opportunity in a competitive and free marketplace.

The following paragraphs describe the school's first year. Basically, the first year went relatively well. The first problem to surface was that the school's construction project manager nor anyone on the construction crew checked the specifications for handicapped access. The result was that the wheelchair ramps were 6 inches too narrow. No wheelchair, except for the ones handicapped athletes use, could make it up the ramps. Since the principal had hired three teachers with disabilities, this could have been a horrendous situation. Fortunately, this error was caught in the inspection and was rectified before it became an issue and an embarrassment for everyone. There were some other minor, but nonetheless dramatic, problems. For example, there was a flood in the school cafeteria during the first week of school that closed the cafeteria down for three days and forced the students to eat off campus. There was an incident in which three students received minor injuries in an auto accident in the school parking lot while attempting to go to a fast-food restaurant during a 25-minute lunch break. In this case, one of the student's parents was a member of the school board, so the problem of insurance was quickly and decisively taken care of and no blame was levied against the school or its principal.

Nonetheless, according to some, this incident contradicted the school policy of being a *closed campus.* Ordinarily, this would not have been a problem except that the issue of whether to open or close the campus had been hotly contested among the community and school officials for months prior to the school's opening. The vociferous group that lost the debate wasted no time in deflecting the car accident to poor supervision on the school parking lot.

As for the flooding, it turned out that the janitor had forgotten to shut off a water valve timer on Friday afternoon. This led to the sink becoming flooded almost as soon as school closed for the weekend. By Monday morning, things were not good. The janitor came in to open the school that morning only to find all of the garbage floating on the flooded cafeteria floor. The architectural design of the cafeteria included a sunken floor, which required that a drain be installed in the middle of the cafeteria floor. No one noticed that the drain had never been installed as per the blueprint plans until it became obvious due to the flooding. This comic relief enjoyed by the students was upstaged in the school's saga only by the fact that lawsuits were immediately filed against the contractor and the county building department as a result. In the meantime, the financially strapped school district had to repair the floor immediately at the cost of $300,000. The local newspaper took the new school's name, Riverfront High School, and dubbed it "Sinkhole High" to reflect how much money it cost to build and maintain the school during its first year.

Nevertheless, in spite of it, or perhaps because of it, the freshman and sophomore men's and women's debate teams took first place in the district, and placed third and second, respectively, in the state championships. The new computers finally arrived during the December holidays—four months late. Nine teachers left at the end of the year. Fortunately, none of those who left was a minority, so the percentage of minority teachers (13 percent) remained constant. Four teachers had babies. Six teachers were in the throes of divorce. The school's favorite male and female teachers got engaged during one of the school assemblies. The principal was chastised by a good-natured group of teachers for not allowing the orchestra to play "Here Comes the Bride" during its recital that day. Every time the principal had the opportunity to speak to the student body that first year, she made vague and not-so-vague references to her "mistake." She also vowed if anyone else wanted to become engaged during an assembly, she would personally love to lead the orchestra. However, in the same breath, she said that it might not be legal to do so. Nonetheless, her attempts to win over the student body were reasonably successful, and she enjoyed good rapport with almost everyone.

Not surprisingly, the students at the new school soon had achievement scores above the national norm in science, social studies, and humanities. The school's new sobriquet was now "Brainy High," thanks to the local media's attention to the high achievement scores. At the year-end assembly, the science, social studies, and humanities teachers were given a resounding salute. One of the students sitting in the audience yelled that they forgot to congratulate the students. The entire student body clapped and cheered along with the embarrassed principal and excited teachers. In the school yearbook there was a section titled "Hey, what about us?" This title page was followed by numerous pictures of the principal, teachers, and students in various friendly poses.

In the *adolescent phase,* continued success of the organization (the school) is built on the established culture and becomes a source of strength and identity (Schein, 1992). In this phase, the school's culture acts as the glue holding the various components and elements together. The events of the first year serve as threads weaving a tapestry of culture. During this phase, there is strong pressure to conform to the new culture, and most individuals will become highly committed to what is working. In the first year of the new high school, nine teachers transferred. Only two teachers requested transfers in the second year. The faculty was beginning to gel together and stabilize. Naturally, subgroups among teachers will form by virtue of the differences in history. The teachers who previously worked for the principal are more "in" than the other teachers. These "insiders" carry more influence on the formation of the new culture. In this example, the math and science teachers would appear to be the "insiders." Those teachers whose student scores were not among the nation's best would probably fall into another group, and be more on the outside of the power circle. Over time, the events occurring in the school are represented in the myths, folklore, and sagas for the school.

During this adolescent phase, the foundations of school spirit are formed in an attempt to develop its "distinctive identity" (Selznick, 1957). The car washes of the previous year, designed to gather funds, were distributed to the school's athletic teams, now competing with other schools in the district. Regarding the school's status as an athletic powerhouse, it may have only two or three years to establish itself among the district's athletic elite before it becomes labeled as "no threat." So, if the athletic teams are to be competitive, the pressure to win becomes acute in this phase of the school's development.

The manner in which the principal models acceptable and valued behaviors is also embedded into the culture during this phase and becomes a standard. In this example, when the principal took full responsibility for the flood in order to help keep the janitor from being fired, she taught the rest of the school that she would stand behind her staff under almost any conditions. For some reason that hardly any educator can explain, the new school's parent-teacher organization (PTO) became the paragon example of activist thinking for the district. It seems that a group of PTO members got together and located a grass/sod company that was willing to donate enough grass to sod two entire practice fields for women's soccer and softball. Other schools in the district managed some success with other joint ventures, but none as noteworthy as Riverfront High's efforts. The achievement scores in math and science led the district in the third year. Softball and baseball teams won the district playoffs, but both lost in the state playoffs. The basketball teams were decent, but the football team still struggled. It was hard to keep a football coach (there were three different coaches during the first five years).

Nonetheless, the crowd loved the cool and eccentric marching band, and this sustained the hungry crowd during the cold, snowy football games.

In the *midlife phase,* differentiation and diversification emerge, allowing for the formation of subcultures, which gravitate around the core culture (Schein, 1992). In this phase, there can be a lack of integration and conflict that is of a deeper nature than that experienced during the adolescent phase. In the example, the chaos that occurs during the school's adolescent phase is centered more around the structural conflicts and the formation of the opening of and development of any new school or organization. The chaos that follows in the midlife phase is tied more to the developing culture.

The formal and informal socialization creates subcultures that become the basis for evolving in new directions. In this example, as long as the achievement scores remain high, the science and math teachers will probably be on the inside of the power circle. If the football team begins winning, that will be reflected in a new-found respect for the school. In some instances, new subgroups that emerge can be more powerful than the principal. These influential subgroups become elements of the school's culture, and perhaps become part of the myth and saga of the school. At the same time, the competition between the teachers whose students score high in science and math may become the object of jealousy by other teachers. The principal's attitude and behavior toward teachers on the inside and those on the outside influence the level and type of culture embedded at this phase of the school life cycle. The manner in which these problems are addressed become integral in the functioning of the school and guides the culture in its problem-solving evolution.

During the *maturity/decline phase,* the school becomes more stabilized and established in the larger organizational culture of which it is a part. In other words, its "place" in the organization of the larger district's schools is reserved. Initially, the school established its relationship with the external environment and began addressing those demands to varying degrees. In the maturity/decline phase, the school has a history that comes to define "how things are done around here." As long as the school can meet the demands valued by the larger school system, it will survive. It can even excel. However, if the internal integration of staff members has not been deep or effective, or if there is a dramatic change in the immediate surroundings, the school culture can change. For example, a new cluster of apartments may be built close to the school that attracts a more transient population. As the student population changes, the culture would eventually change over time. In another instance, a school's achievement scores may fall to the point that the school district identifies the school as being an "at-risk" school. Teachers may transfer out to other schools, pressures to raise academic standards may become intensified, and a new principal may be installed. The school's culture becomes reworked to incorporate the new demands made from the external environment in order to address the new issues.

The *strength and stability* of organizations, and the school in this example, will depend on many things (Clark, 1972; Schein, 1999; Smith & Vecchio, 1997). Among them are the *stability of the environment* and the *stability of the group.* If the new high school was built in a community that was growing with new homes, the community might be considered less stable than an older neighborhood. However, the size and type of homes being built (e.g., single-family dwellings) might reflect an environment that is more stable economically. The stability of the group relates directly to the turnover rates of the school's teaching and administrative staff. The rather minimal turnover rate after the first year of the school in this example would act to stabilize the group of teachers.

Generally speaking, *the longer the staff has worked together,* the more stable the organizational culture will be. Two other factors affecting the stability of the organization's culture relate to *the length of time the principal or leader has been a leader* and the *intensity of that person's convictions.* In general, a principal's reputation often precedes him or her to a new school, and with that comes perceptions regarding her or his abilities. The stories, myths, and sagas surrounding the newly appointed principal will serve as a harbinger and set up expectations. Some principals are recognized for their management style, others are known for their abilities to raise test scores, and still others may be known for their abilities to garner school spirit. Some exceptional ones may be known for possessing all three traits. In any case, the convictions advanced by the principal or leader tends to help stabilize the culture. The incidents of the first year together at Riverfront High School, together with how the principal handled the various incidents, became well known throughout the district. She was perceived as a principal who was progressive, very sensitive to diversity issues, creative, direct, and fair.

Another factor affecting the stability of the culture relates to the *number of problems the group has attempted to solve* and *the intensity of emotions* that were called on in the problem-solving process. The more that the intense emotions are discharged in a helpful and solution-focused manner, the more the culture will stabilize and strengthen. If, during the process of problem solving, the learning that takes place has been oriented toward positive reinforcement, then the culture is strengthened in one direction. However, if the learning that takes place comes through the venue of reducing pain, instead of promoting positive reinforcement, the culture will be strengthened in a different direction. What is remembered about these experiences becomes a part of the remembered history and symbolism (Smith & Vecchio, 1997) of organizations. The fact that the Riverfront High principal stood up for her custodian was seen throughout the district as a win for the underclass.

Consultants must be able to relate to how these various elements of culture are reflected in the types of problems that are identified as needing to be solved. The organization has its own life, and the individuals within it subscribe to various aspects of the organizational culture to varying degrees and in a number of ways. Even though a consultant may work with a single consultee and single client within an organization, both consultee and client are significantly impacted by the organization's "goings on." In many cases, consultants will not be addressing the entire organization. For example, most mental health consultants will be working with only a few of those who work in the organization. Nevertheless, everyone is being impacted to some degree by the manner in which the organization is going about doing its business. Some information about an individual consultee's organizational culture is necessary to help ensure the efficacy of the consulting help.

Levels of Culture: The Mental Health Center

According to researchers such as Schein (1999), Smith and Vecchio (1997), and others, there are three levels of culture. The *artifacts* are the most observable elements of culture; the other two are harder to measure. *Espoused values* underlie the artifacts that we see, such as dress style, organization of documents, and office location, and these values rest on *core basic assumptions*. So, the *contents* of culture include learned responses to external survival issues, internal integration issues, and core basic assumptions, whereas the *levels* of culture include artifacts, espoused values, and core assumptions. Whenever dissonance exists between any one of these three elements, problems can occur. Conversely, the more congruent these three elements are with one another, the less problematic life should be in that particular organization. Familiarity with these structural levels of culture helps consultants in the overall understanding of the context in which consultation will occur. As mentioned previously, not all consultants will be organizational development specialists, but all consultants will need to know something about organizational culture. Obviously, an incisive understanding of organizational culture is mandated for any large-scale organizational development project. However, for most mental health professionals, familiarity with a consultee's organizational culture will help in the formulating of issues to be addressed and have direct implications for any informal and formal interventions.

Imagine that a newly graduated mental health therapist has just been hired as a clinician at a mental health center. Assume that the center has been in existence for several years and is funded by grants through the federal government. The newly hired professional is walking into a culture of practicing mental health professionals. The larger culture of the general mental health field serves as a context for this agency's existence. Funding is directed at helping a particular population, and the money that is attached is to be used for that larger, federal agenda. Sometimes the funding includes provisions for a wide variety of mental health services needed for a given population.

In terms of *core assumptions,* several possible scenarios exist. Usually, the financial grants that are awarded are competitive, so the basic culture of the mental health center likely assumes that *time is scarce* and *space is open* by virtue of competitive grants *yet limited* due to the paltry number of awards. The culture of this hypothetical mental health center might also be founded on the "medical model," since a psychiatrist will probably act as the medical director. The medical model is based on assumptions that form a paradigm. In this paradigm, science holds that truth is truth only if it is demonstrable, controllable, and measurable. Moreover, as will be shown in Chapters Four and Five, the medical model assumes that (1) humans are perfectible, (2) science alone can discover the technology to handle medical problems, and (3) for any problems that arise along the way, a technology can be developed to take care of it.

At this core cultural assumptive level, science is seen as greater than the forces of nature. As such, an *artifact* of this paradigm might reflect the fact that most clinicians in the center dress conservatively, as opposed to a relaxed, "sandals-type" look. Another artifact of this mental health center culture would be the amount of time allotted to each client. If the psychiatrist is acting as a medical consultant, the vast majority of his work centers on chemotherapeutic follow-up. Those sessions usually last about

20 minutes for each client, and are scheduled roughly for every three months. The clinicians might see clients for an hour—or more likely a culturally enforced "50-minute" hour so that the clinician has time to write notes. (Most mental health professionals practicing in agencies, institutions, and hospitals will attest to the need to write notes as soon as possible after sessions in an attempt to avoid paperwork that can quickly reach overwhelming proportions.)

The culture will also include the instrumentation of medical charts, psychometrics and normal curves, as well as treatment plans. The accepted instrumentation for understanding and conceptualizing clients is the *Diagnostic and Statistical Manual-IV-TR (DSM-IV-R)* (American Psychiatric Association, 2000). The various ethical codes that apply to the respective professionals working at the mental health center serve to guide the agency's culture along a certain ethical and moral pathway. It will also be likely that the culture of this center will also include conflict over which paradigm is "right." In other words, there will likely be differing philosophies among the staff regarding the propriety of the "medical model" or such things as whether mental health is a privilege or a right. If everyone has to pay for services, the prevailing culture is likely based on the assumption that mental health is not a right and that individuals are responsible for all their actions. The amount of money devoted through the various federal grants and through the local fiscal department of the mental health center will reflect the relative standing of the philosophic assumption that mental health is a social right.

The *espoused values* will reflect the methods the center uses to arrive at solutions. In other words, in discussing differences among staff members, *the way the differences are discussed or how the meeting goes* will reflect the organization's values. The artifact of these espoused values will be seen in the number and type of staff meetings that are held. In addition, the process of meetings and the amount of time devoted to the discussing of philosophical issues also mirrors the organization's values. On a more micro-level, the structure of the discussion involving individual staff members is indicative of the espoused values. For instance, the structure of the interactions in the staff meetings will show, among other things, such things as who speaks to whom and how often, who interrupts whom, and the circumstances in which this talking occurs.

In addition to these core basic assumptions, the mental health center's espoused values will reflect a number of other artifacts. There is a formal and an informal pecking order that will have been established among professionals. This hierarchy will be reflected in the ways that clients are conceptualized. For example, a linguistic artifact will be seen in whether the term *clients* or *patients* is used. Another artifact reflecting a certain cultural espoused value is the expectation for clinicians regarding the number of clients each should carry on their caseloads. Some agencies expect clinicians to handle enormous caseloads (although they are nowhere near the 300 to 800 individuals to whom school counselors typically may be responsible). The center may also have a value expressed through the artifact of "on-call." In other words, there may be a formal expectation of taking an on-call night, and an informal expectation that new hires take the holiday on-call until someone else is hired behind them.

Certain salient clients and a certain client population may become identified as part of the center's ongoing saga and history. The artifacts of this situation will be the group of clients or patients who are remembered as opposed to those who are not remembered in the stories. The *content* of the client's story becomes an artifact reflecting the cultural values. For instance, if the clinicians remember a particular client, the espoused values might be reflected along the following dimensions: How much help did the client need? What kind of help was needed? Who provided the help? Under what circumstances was the help provided? Underneath the words of the story are values that help make up the prevailing paradigm that operates in the center's culture.

An artifact of the values placed on the executive of this hypothetical mental health center will be the amount and type of paperwork involved. The history of mental health executive directors in general will likely reveal some who were clinically oriented and some who were more financially oriented. For instance, an executive director who is oriented toward the financial bottom-line might institute a management information system (MIS) to track how clinicians spend their time. This can promote a perception that clinicians are not to be trusted, or that where one spends one's time (in or out of session) becomes more important than the quality of care given. Another executive director might institute regular case conferences, mandating attendance for all clinicians, as a means of enhancing the level of care given to clients while paying less attention to the amount of time each client is seen. This would likely create a different perception among clinicians.

Another value will be exemplified in the number of clients who are designated as needing partial hospitalization. This group will populate the center's day treatment facilities. The number of clients, how close the day treatment facility is placed to the center and clinicians, the activities undertaken at day treatment, and the number and type of professionals who are staffing the day treatment are all artifacts that are based on some espoused values and tacit core assumptions.

In this mental health center example, the newly hired clinician will also notice that certain professional units within the center may have more prestige than others. For example, therapists in the Child, Youth, and Family unit may have the nicest offices and the most number of therapists. Concomitantly, those working in addictions might be set off to the end of the building in older offices. On the surface, it may seem as though the center does not value the addictions counselors as much as the marriage and family therapists simply due to the artifacts. However, in this particular example, the newly hired clinician may come to find out that the addictions counselors voted to have their offices in the more "private" and remote areas of the center due to their espoused value of helping to provide anonymity for those in recovery. In this case, the artifact of "location" matched the value of wanting to be anonymous. Moreover, the artifact of location was based on the tacit assumptions that human beings are good and are capable of self-direction because they were voting for office space. For a smooth organizational flow to occur, there needs to be a relatively close match between artifacts, values, and core tacit and unconscious assumptions. The more smoothly the center runs, the more likely there is a congruence between all three levels of culture.

CULTURE AND CONSULTATION

The purpose of presenting information about organizational culture is to help in the conceptualization of the context within which all consultees and clients experience their work lives. A consultant who comes in to consult on cases with the mental health clinicians at the center might want to know the context and culture in which these consultations will take place for a number of reasons. For instance, in intervening with a group of clinicians at the center, a private practitioner/consultant might need to know how overwhelming caseloads typically are in community mental health agencies so that there is little, if any, suggestions that connote or denote "more" work. Information about the hierarchical structure of the center can help identify potential barriers a clinician might have when attempting to "go to the top" with information about inefficiencies in the center. A consultant who is aware of the political structure along with who is "in" and who is "out" of the power loop can direct interventions toward consultees that are more congruent with the political culture in which the clinicians must interact. For instance, a school counselor might work with a single teacher about an issue involving a single student. However, both teacher and student belong to the larger organizational context. Any intervention that pulls the teacher too far away from her culture or the student too far away from his culture may not really be helping at the level the situation may require.

If the consultant believes the resistance felt in the intervening process is due to simple resistance to change and does not correctly associate the resistance as anchored to an organization's cultural norm, the consultation may fail to come to completion. In such cases, consultees and clients can find numerous ways to be "unavailable" for consultation. Clearly, there are times when the organization's culture is more in the background and times when the culture is seen as foreground. However, *organizational culture is always present.* Even though a particular situation does not appear to call for some awareness of the consultee's culture, consultants need to be able to differentiate such issues. For example, if an organization's cultural value centers on "we do not discuss our business outside the company" and it calls in a consultant, the consultant can expect a certain amount of resistance to the consulting process based more on the collective value of privacy rather than simply resistance to the consulting process.

It is also true that information about the culture in which the consultee is operating will be reflected in the conversation between the consultant and the consultee. The actual content of what the consultee presents will reveal a level of organizational culture in which the consultee works. For instance, a consultee may be discussing poor management practices and offer solutions about how things ought to be prior to discussing the issue with organizational insiders. In another situation, there may be several individuals who are in agreement about what a particular problem is. Yet, these several individuals may make up only a small percentage of those affected by the situation. The key for consultants is to listen and observe. Listen to the consultee's story and note artifacts. This will reveal the personal and organizational cultural context in which any formal intervention will take place.

In another instance, a school counselor who is asked by the assistant principal to consult with a teacher about a particular student might benefit from knowing if the teacher is on the "ins" or "outs" with the administrator. It may also be important to determine the relative level of coercion involved between the administrator and the teacher. If the teacher is on the outs, or has no power, then the question needs to become one involving the power and control needs of the administrator making the request in order to more accurately identify a solution that will work for the teacher. It is not that the school counselor will directly or even actually address whatever issues are raised as a result of this understanding of culture; rather, it is simply that the intervention with the teacher will be more effective if it is placed in context of the teacher's organizational culture. This is critically true if one believes what Schein (2000) purports: "Key interventions happen early on in the consulting process." Engaging the consultee's cultural context early on in the process helps ensure that those "key interventions" are effective.

THE CULTURE OF CONTEXT

Fundamentally, *consultation* is a term, a concept, a cognitive form, or a cognitive paradigm. The term allows us to talk about consultation as if it occurs "out there." Ultimately, *consultation* describes a certain cluster of culturally and professionally acceptable behaviors that occur in a specific context. As such, the fundamental operations of consultation do not occur "out there"; rather, they are occurring as we speak. This dialogic perspective of consultation requires attention to the issues of diversity that occurs on the individual as well as professional organizational levels.

In attempting to understand the consulting situation, consultants are listening for key elements in the consultee's organizational context as well as listening for key elements in the individual consultee's personal culture. Norton (1978), in discussing a perspective to understand a client's cultural life in social work practice, suggests the need for a *dual perspective*. This perspective advocates the conscious and systematic way of perceiving, understanding, and simultaneously comparing the values, attitudes, and behaviors of a given minority person's immediate family, community, or cultural system with those of the larger system. In earlier research, Chestang (1972) suggests that a dual perspective for social workers needs to include the idea that everyone is a part of two systems: a dominant or sustaining system, and a nurturing system. The *dominant system* is the accepted source of economic, social, and political power. The *nurturing system* is comprised of the person's immediate social environment of the family and system. These various systems will also be significantly influenced by gender (Gilligan, 1982). Gilligan points out that male and female constructions of and beliefs about the nature of reality are very different. In oversimplistic terms, men are "linear" thinkers and females are "relational" thinkers. Gilligan asserts that the male model of thinking tends to focus on results and the achievement of a specified goal. On the other hand, women tend to think about possibilities and relationships among possibilities before acting. This also comprises an organization's culture. The understanding of differences in how individuals perceive and act in their culture is basic to effective and ethical consultation practice.

The value system that individuals have and express within these two domains (i.e., dominant and nurturing systems) contains all values held by individuals. As was reflected in the section on organizational culture, individual value systems typically include several grounding perspectives of the world. According to Brown (2002) and other researchers, among these perspectives are views of human nature as being good, bad, or neutral. Another perspective includes views regarding the person-environment relationship. In simplistic terms, the person-environment relationship can be categorized as nature dominating humans, people dominating nature, or humans and nature living harmoniously. Time and activity are important components in one's value system. The orientation to time is characterized along dimensions of past, present, past-future, and circular. Orientations to time involve perspectives on digital or chromatic time (see Fisher & Harrison, 2000). The notion of activity relates to one's "being" and one's "doing." In the perspective of "being," spontaneous behaviors are important. In the perspective of "being-in-becoming," self-control is revered. In addition, values are guided by perspectives on social relationships: individual versus collective. Carter (1991) asserts that there is a considerable amount of diverse and overlapping values within and across systems of people from the same cultural groups. This is an important issue for consultants when acknowledging that one's value system also includes the work values (Brown, 2002) that consultees will be expressing to consultants.

In consultation, an understanding of the concept of "culture" is critical in every way that one can imagine. The consultee's individual culture will be reflected in his or her subscription to and participation in the person's organizational culture at work. Because the contextual background of almost every consultation includes both the individual as well as the organizational culture, consultants need to listen to important elements of the consultee's story in order to help the person formulate a clear picture what is going on in the consultation. Because Schein believes that many key interventions occur early on in the consulting process, consultants need to pay particular attention to the personal and work values as well as the espoused values of the organization during the initial proceedings of consultation. This will most often happen in the formulation of the psychological contract, discussed in a later chapter.

Clearly, the consultee's personal values will be inherent in any conversation with consultants. However, the espoused values held by the larger organizational cultural in which consultees work may be harder to discern and may not be a focus of interest of consultees in the consultation. Nevertheless, it is critical that consultants endeavor to glean a glimpse of the organizational culture to clearly see issues and concerns. In all cases, obtaining sufficient information about the consultee's culture needs to be a central aim in the earlier interactions with consultees and clients. Rather than invoking new and sophisticated skills in organizational culture assessments, consultants need to appreciate cultural similarities and differences on an individual level, exercise the same appreciation on a professional level, and listen and discern important words, phrases, beliefs, stories, and other elements of conversations with consultees and clients. These skills are basic to effective helpers—not simply those relegated to professional consultants.

SUMMARY

The context of consultation is the organization. This is not the same as being an organizational consultant. The consultee's and the client's affiliations with their respective organizations provides a backdrop in which consultants can examine consultee and client concerns. These concerns will be identified and framed in accordance with the organizational culture in which they exist. Problems in one organization might not be seen as problems in another organization, and it is important that consultants understand the idiosyncratic nature of problem definition and resolution.

All organizations have a culture that is made up of artifacts, values, and core basic assumptions. According to some researchers, there are six elements of culture: critical ideas of founding members; guiding ideas; social structure; norms, values, and premises; remembered history and symbolism; and institutional arrangement. This culture develops over time and includes the external survival issues facing the organization as well as helping with the internal integration of its members. There are processes through which organizations embed and stabilize this culture. Consultants need to have knowledge of organizational culture and these processes in order to understand more fully the experiences of their consultees and clients, who are members of organizations. Such an understanding helps consultants conceptualize a context in which they will be operating. Even in one-on-one consultations, the consultees and clients are engaged in systems.

QUESTIONS

1. What is the difference between the context of consulting being the organization and OD consulting?

2. Why is it important to have knowledge of the consultee's and client's organizational culture?

3. What are the ingredients of culture?

4. What are the processes by which this culture is embedded and stabilized?

5. What is the relationship between organization culture and personal culture?

6. How does knowing the stage of development that an organization is in help consultants?

7. What are the core basic assumptions operating in your work or school life?

8. What is one meaningful piece of information or concept you will remember about this chapter?

CHAPTER FOUR

THE CONTEXT OF INTERVENING AND CHANGE

When mental health professionals conceptualize "consultation," they are conceptualizing "intervening and change" in the same breath because, as Schein (1987) states, "Rarely is the goal of a helping process to maintain the status quo" (p. 92). The context of change and intervention in consultation includes both an individual and an organizational dimension. It is important to understand that consultants do indeed intervene to help create change. Yet, they are always intervening in consultee and client systems that themselves are in an inherent and constant state of flux themselves.

Consultants' interventions with consultees and clients can range from two seconds, to 20 minutes, to years. Schein (1999) believes everything a consultant says and does is an intervention; thus, a two-second sentence uttered by a consultant is an intervention. In fact, it could possibly be *the* intervention that helps the consultee and client change. An example of a consultation lasting 20 minutes typically occurs when a school counselor consults in the hallway or in an office with a teacher who is having difficulty with a particular student. Consultants may also be hired to intervene over longer periods of time. For instance, internal consultants and school counselors may be hired to intervene on an ongoing basis. Having a consultee or a client work with a consultant to simply reframe an issue or redefine a situation may be all that is required for a significant change to take place at the individual and/or organizational level. On the other hand, complex organizational change might also require consultants to spend a great deal of time assessing the organization's culture and intervening with various consultee and client systems at a variety of levels.

As mentioned in the previous chapter, when consultants work with schools, agencies, institutions, and organizations, it is important that consultants understand the stage of change of the organization. The same is true for consultants working with groups and individuals in those settings. By considering whether the organization is in the founding adolescent, midlife, or maturity/decline stage, consultants can better conceptualize intervening and change with consultees and clients in their appropriate cultural context. For instance, imagine that a vice-principal of a school opened only three years complains to a school counselor about the low morale at the school. The vice-principal says that there seems to be an increase in interpersonal conflicts occurring among the teaching staff. As seen in Chapter 3, a school opened for only three years may be experiencing its "adolescent" life in which these interpersonal conflicts, as unpleasant as they are, should be somewhat expected. Hence, although while the result could be a lowering of morale, conceptualizing "low morale" as the problem without placing it in the context in which it occurs could lead to an intervening process that may be misguided. If conflict is expected at this stage of the consultee/vice-principal's organizational life, then the issue becomes the amount of conflict present that exceeds the "expected amount." If the vice-principal wants something to be done, the school counselor/consultant could intervene with an educational workshop. The purpose might be to help teachers generally understand what is to be expected at this stage of the school's development. The workshop might also include some skills to help reduce stress.

Consultants intervene at the micro (individual), meso (intermediate/group), and/or macro (organization/agency/institutional) level. In all likelihood, most mental health professionals will be working with individuals and groups of individuals who are members of a larger organizational context. Working with the organization itself as an OD consultant will fall outside most generic training in consultation for mental health professionals. However, school counseling is an exception. The work of school counselors is clearly organizational development. For consultants to help create change at the individual and group levels, there is little need to conduct a cultural assessment of the organization. This is due to the fact that a cultural assessment is a complex task undertaken by OD consultants when intervening on the macro-level of organizations.

Clearly, it stands to reason that the stresses experienced by an individual can be understood or explained by knowing something of the context in which the stress occurs. Without this information, a rather predictable and familiar situation can occur where a consultant works with a consultee or client only to send her or him back into a system where the intervention does not fit. The classic example is a school counselor who works with a given student in such a fashion as to inadequately conceptualize the context of the problem as including the school's culture. Without paying some attention to the context of the change needed, the student comes back into the classroom having changed, but having changed in a way that made no difference to the situation. Had the school counselor/consultant attended to those larger, more amorphous contextual elements, the intervention would have a better "fit" in the situation.

THEORIES OF SYSTEMS AND CHANGE

Professional consultants' perspectives of organizations and organizational change have largely been influenced by the general systems theory (GST) of von Bertalanffy (1950), Lewin's (1951) field theory, and, more recently, organizational chaos theory as described by Massarik (1990). The general systems theory of von Bertalanffy (1950) is a fundamental tenet in marriage and family therapy approaches as well as a widely held view maintained in the fields of medicine, psychiatry, psychology, sociology, biology, history, education, philosophy, biology, and organizational development. Davidson (1983) summarized the definition of GST as being any entity maintained by the mutual interaction of its parts, from atom to cosmos, and including such mundane examples as telephone, postal, and rapid transit systems. A von Bertalanffian system can be physical like a television set, biological like a cocker spaniel, psychological like a personality, sociological like a labor union, or symbolic like a set of laws. . . . A system can be composed of smaller systems and can also be a part of a larger system, just as a state or province is composed of smaller jurisdictions and also is part of a nation. Consequently, the same organized entity can be regarded as either a system or a subsystem, depending on the observer's focus of interest. (p. 26)

Although maintaining aspects of linear causality (see below), Lewin's (1948, 1951) views of systems were similar to those purported by von Bertalanffy except that Lewin restricted his views more toward organizations themselves. Lewin (1948) believes that organizational problems must be solved in such a manner as to incorporate all individuals in the organization. The reason is simple: Individuals act and are acted on by forces within the organization, and learning and change can only result by involving the learner. According to Leonard and Freidman (2000), Lewin contends that the best way to understand an organization is to try to change it, study the effects of the action taken, plan the next step, provide training if needed, and then take action again (p. 16). Since Lewin's works were first published, researchers have reexamined many of Lewin's original concepts and begun to question their relevancy for today's institutions, agencies, and organizations (e.g., Feigenbaum, 1981; Gleick, 1987; Mandelbrot, 1983; Massarik, 1980, 1990; Massarik, Tannenbaum, Kahane, & Weschler, 1961). In essence, these researchers point to the fact that fairly well established approaches to understanding organizational change fail because there is an increase in rapid and discontinuous change occurring in organizations today. Both Senge (1999) and Leonard and Freidman (2000) believe that traditional approaches have relied on Lewin's (1951) field theory and on the general systems theory of von Bertalanffy (1950) that cannot explain such events as transformational or discontinuous change. For these researchers, adding notions of chaos theory concepts to general systems theory would provide models for understanding systems and organizational behavior in dynamic flux, in disequilibrium, or on the edge of disorganization and chaos (Silvester, Anderson, & Patterson, 1999).

Linear and Circular Causality

A profound impact of systems theory is reflected in the area of diagnosing and intervening in systems. Systems theorists do not adhere to linear causality; rather, they believe in circular causality. The metaphor for *linear causality* is a pool table in which the cue ball sets all other balls rolling in a sequential chain reaction. The problem systems theorists have with linear causality is they maintain that it is possible to hit the cue ball and miss some of the other balls. Such is not the case in circular causality. *Circular causality* is the idea that change in one individual member of a system affects all other members of the system as well as affects the system as a whole. Circular causality sees actions as components of a causal chain in which each action influences and is influenced by other actions (Gladding, 1998).

Clearly, there are numerous direct implications for consultants in terms of how they will direct and manage the change efforts based on the principles of circular causality and general systems theory. The conceptualization of circular causality is reflected in Dougherty's (1990) notions of "synergy." In organizations, a type of synergy results when individuals are put together in a certain environment for a certain purpose. The result is something greater than any individual entity. The interactions among these components result in a product that transcends any given component. If the people were reorganized, if the environment were altered, if the purpose was reconfigured, the result would be another product that would also transcend any individual entity. Since, according to systems theory, every entity affects every other entity, a consultant who helps an individual consultee or client change is, in effect, changing the entire organization. This is not to suggest that every consultant who works with an organization must work with every component of that organization. This is to suggest that consultants must at least be aware of how their interventions will potentially affect other individuals and organizational entities.

Another impact of circular causality on intervening is seen in the linear attempt to understand root causes. Consultants should not become beguiled by what Schein (2000) refers to as "root cause analysis." Root cause analysis occurs when consultants attempt to define a consultee's or client's problem in terms of a single cause. The idea is that if the single discrete cause can be identified, the solution becomes more evident. Attempting this course of analysis is not often very appropriate. For instance, almost all school counselors with whom I am familiar will attest to the fact that it is impossible to conduct an accurate root cause analysis in a school system. Society attempts to conduct a root cause analysis for problems in schools by identifying teachers as the problem, while the teachers' associations vociferously exclaim that parents need to do a better job so teachers can teach. It is important to distinguish a root cause analysis that leads nowhere from one that is appropriate. For instance, there is a good, if not mandated, justification for conducting a root cause analysis on a technical problem occurring in a computer. The viruses cause damage, and a root cause analysis leading to knowledge of the virus life cycle is critical to its purging from the computer. In early 2003, the *Columbia* space shuttle broke up upon reentering the earth's atmosphere. A concerted effort was undertaken to find all of the missing pieces of the shuttle in order to determine the root cause of the catastrophe. This is an example where a root cause analysis is appropriate.

CONCEPTUALIZING ORGANIZATIONAL CHANGE

Approaches to Change in Schools, Agencies, and Organizations

A review of the current literature will reflect two essential prevailing thoughts used to conceptualize organizational change (Dunphy & Stace, 1988). Effective change in organizations proceeds linearly in small, incremental adjustments. This is known as *incremental change*. Change in this conceptual paradigm is synonymous with natural growth. However, many researchers now agree that it is common for organizations to go through an abrupt, *transformational change* over a short period of time. Both terms, *incremental change* and *transformative change,* have a host of synonyms that appear in the professional literature. For instance, Levy (1986) refers to these two changes as "first-order" and "second-order" change. Tushman, Newman, and Romanelli (1986) use "convergence" and "frame-breaking" change to describe the same phenomena. Pettigrew (1985) refers to "evolutions" (or lower-order change) as opposed to "revolutions" (or higher-order changes). Miller (1982) and an earlier researcher, Greiner (1972), use "evolutionary" and "revolutionary." Miller and Friesen (1984) use "incremental, piecemeal" and "multifaceted, concerted change" to describe the two ways that agencies, schools, and organizations change.

Incremental Change

Dunphy and Stace (1988) cite research arguing the pros and cons of managerial approaches to change. Beer (1980) and Quinn (1977, 1980) believe that effective management moves organizations in small, logical steps. This is achieved by assuring that the organization collects and analyzes appropriate information from the outside over a long period of time. As this information is collected, shared, and then assimilated and integrated by employees, relevant subsystems can be adjusted incrementally and progressively as opposed to discontinuously. Reliance on incrementalism as a means of managing schools, agencies, and organizations is based on three assumptions.

The first assumption is that principals, administrators, and senior business managers have the *capacity to anticipate* fully the external survival issues or environmental forces that impact their school or organization. Dunphy and Stace (1988) believe that in stable times this assumption is a reasonable one. The second assumption is that schools, mental health agencies, and organizations are *run by intelligent, proactive individuals.* According to these same researchers, the societal selection process specifically for business managers reflects them to be of average intelligence who have limited experience outside of their own industry. These same managers are seen as being ill equipped to judge accurately all of the complex information generated from the environment.

Specific to schools, principals are assigned to schools by superintendents who themselves are political appointments. Principals often become principals by rising through the ranks of education first as teachers, then as assistant principals. Although there are many, many competent and caring principals operating in the public school systems of the United States, there are those principals who rise to their positions because they are good at playing the politics needed for appointments. Some principals can be good at politics and less than adequate managers. Other principals are good at managing teachers, students, and parents. Yet, these individuals might be stifled by an inability to become politically powerful. Moreover, new principals do not have as much power as those who have been in their positions longer and have been exposed to the district principal culture and to the "way things are done at this level."

Mental health agencies have a similar situation. Administrators of mental health agencies may or may not have risen through the ranks of the mental health system. There may even be administrators who are not licensed or trained specifically in mental health. Instead, they may be hired by their respective board of directors for any number of differing agendas. Some are hired because of their relevant backgrounds. Some are hired because of their reputations or because of their acquaintances. Administrators for mental health agencies may also be hired because of their abilities to manage a not-for-profit agency effectively. Some are hired because of their abilities to garner grants and funding for services.

The third assumption regarding incremental change assumes that *large-scale school or organizational change can be accomplished through small, planned, and logical steps.* Johnson and Scholes (1984) believe the forces that impinge on the school or organization cannot be controlled by principals and managers. In fact, these researchers believe that there are both determinate forces that can be controlled and indeterminate forces that lie outside of the direct control of principals and managers. Contextually, incrementalism reveres evolutionary as opposed to revolutionary change. Incrementalism is based on order rather than disorder. Those subscribing to this incrementalism and the small-steps approach value consensus and collaboration versus conflict and power. Moreover, incrementalism uses expert authority and persuasiveness of data rather than relying on the dictates of an emotional or charismatic leader, executive director, or principal.

Transformative Change

According to researchers, incrementalism is particularly well-suited to social, political, and economic environments that are stable and can promote normal growth. However, Bell (1976), Ferguson (1980), and Ginsberg and Vojta (1981) point to the fact that these stable conditions have disappeared, resulting in an external environment that is so complex and turbulent that it is sometimes impossible to predict future situations accurately. This is in spite of any exceptional skills held by principals or managers.

There are numerous examples of transformative change in organizations. For example, a principal might be transferred immediately if a problem arises that needs such drastic action. A CEO might suddenly quit over a difference with a board of directors regarding the direction that the organization is taking. Rumors of massive layoffs, fueled by other rumors of a hostile takeover, can dramatically change the way an organization functions. The sudden onset of new technology can require organizations to drastically alter their operations. A board of directors of a mental health agency might abruptly fire an executive director. News of accounting fraud can cause stocks to plummet overnight. Organizations can secretly arrange for bankruptcy, and then publicly declare bankruptcy and seemingly reorganize themselves overnight. In the nonprofit world, funding sources might suddenly dry up with the change of governmental administrations. With contemporary technology, almost all points in the world are either connected directly or are a click of a computer mouse away. Economic, social, and political changes in another country can impact organizations positively and/or negatively almost immediately.

Dunphy and Stace (1988) point to the fact that administrators, principals, and managers have little, if any, control over the fluctuations that occur in the financial and political realms that directly affect their schools and organizations. Perhaps, as a result, the strategies for change that are adopted in these situations often reflect a top-down coercion method. This top-down approach to solving problems is either achieved by outsiders or from newly appointed leaders in the business world and achieved by transferring in a new principal or through charismatic leadership of a single principal in the schools (Dunphy & Stace, 1988).

Those administrators, principals, and managers adhering to the transformative approach to change embrace Drucker's (1969) notions of society living in an "age of discontinuity." The large-scale efforts at organizational and economic restructuring that occurred in the United States during the 1970s and 1980s is seen as antithetical to the incrementalist approach to managing change. The discontinuities that arise are often beyond the capacities of principals, managers, and executive directors. A result is that principals, administrators, and managers often need to respond and react as opposed to act. Those directors, principals, and managers who trap themselves into an incrementalist approach mind-set can find great difficulty in managing change if the environmental conditions change abruptly (Dunphy & Stace, 1988). Massarik (1990), in identifying three types of chaos that occur in organizations, says,

> We may think of a very large corporate entity in an uncertain economic and market environment and one individual person, such as a lone OD consultant, standing at its doorstep, trying to understand what's going on. Or then again there may be a group of effective line managers and OD generalists enmeshed in the web of a major merger whose organizational and practical implications remain largely uncertain. In each instance, what seems to be "out there" contains some determinate (i.e., specifiable) elements with which the observer(s) (e.g., the lone OD consultant or the manager-OD group) presumably have had some generic if not necessarily particular acquaintance. Beyond that, lots and lots of stuff is unknown and, significantly, in major flux. . . . In spite of the hypothetical wealth of data, as may be gathered by interviews, observations, reviews of published material, examination of artifacts and symbols (such as buildings or spaces), significant and massive changes may again rapidly burst upon the scene— removal of a CEO, the launching of a hostile takeover bid, the sale of established divisions, "downsizing" resulting in separations of large numbers of employees, or the introduction of a revolutionary new technology—any one or several of these, occurring simultaneously, may cause regression to chaos. (pp. 3–5)

These crises often precipitate transformative change in schools, mental health agencies, and organizations. For example, to address school overcrowding, some districts adopt a year-round school system. Often, schools only have one year to plan this transformative change process, which involves shifting numerous layers within the school system. Mental health agencies live and die by government administrations. Mostly, there are federal and/or state funds granted that keep mainstream mental health agencies afloat. However, in mental health agencies it is not uncommon to hear rumors to the effect that certain programs will close due to a lack of funding. Sometimes they close; sometimes they do not. Sometimes they are restructured and incorporated into other facets of the agency where money is available. The point is that there are circumstances lying outside the immediate control of the school, agency, or organization that almost mandate a type of rapid, transformational change.

Dunphy and Stace (1988) identify four types of situations or scenarios in which an approach to incremental change is not indicated. First, there is what is referred to as *environmental creep*. This occurs when the external environment itself may be changing incrementally and in ways that are imperceptible to administrators and managers. The degree of change over time may be so large that a major readjustment is required in the organization. Second, *organizational creep* is similar to environmental creep except that it is the organization itself that gets out of alignment with the environment. Public schools experience both types of creep. Second, society's values toward education shift on some levels and remain stable on other levels. Sometimes values shift as new information is relayed to the administration that another country's students score better on certain tests. Over time, adjustments are required in the curriculums of public schools in an attempt to regain the lost competitive edge. Charter schools rose up almost overnight in the U.S. education culture. Many school districts instituted charter schools in an attempt to address rising dropout rates and in an attempt to individualize educational experiences for students. Public debate continues on how to fund these schools appropriately and how to ensure quality management. Charter schools are the artifact of a culture that values educational change over a period of time.

The establishment of charter schools is an attempt at *diversification*, a third scenario that requires a large-scale transformational change process. In the business world, this process is seen as resulting from mergers, acquisitions, and shutdowns. Because these types of business dealings are sometimes hostile, or at least secret until the last minute, there is a clash of cultures that demand an immediate change process, in which an incrementalist approach will not suffice. A school may be adjusting appropriately within the larger system of schools in the United States, yet, at the same time, the larger school structure is changing. A superintendent might be hired who immediately infuses a "site-based" management approach in the school district. Some principals can adjust quickly and some cannot. In either case, the reorganization of how local schools are managed creates a shift in the local educational industry. In the medical and clinical mental health field, the evolution of managed-care systems called for rapid adjustments of a transformational nature. Scandals involving accounting practices of major corporations have created environmental conditions in the business world where board of directors' meetings are now characterized as financial inquisitions.

The fourth scenario proposed by Dunphy and Stace (1988) relates to technological breakthroughs that require a large-scale change. An example of this occurring in the education field was the rise of computer-assisted technologies to aid in education. First, there were issues related to the acquisition of hardware. Then, the acquisition of software became the focus. After that, Internet access became important, along with new artifacts detailing policies and procedures for using the Internet on school grounds. All schools scrambled to obtain computers. Schools that could afford computers and the software faired better than their poorer counterparts. Inequities existed that created problems for school districts. Yet, social pressure continues: Even if a school cannot afford it, there is constant pressure to have Internet access. The survival of a school's students in a world marketplace will ultimately depend partly on the accumulation of computers and appropriate software. Computer issues catapulted schools into a type of transformative change.

The two approaches to change, incrementalism and transformation, are based on conditions in the environment. Incrementalism rose in a time where the economy of the United States was unidirectional and stable. Schools, agencies, and corporations were experienced as operating primarily within the bounds of national economies. Now that the economy is global, there are good arguments for transformative change. The radical times characterized by widespread economic restructuring, recessions, and discontinuous change conditions almost require radical remedies (Dunphy & Stace, 1988). These same researchers exclaim that the fundamental difference between these two approaches to change is not the simple difference between slow and rapid change, nor is it a simple difference between normal and exceptional change. The difference is whether the school, agency, or organization is effecting change on a continuous or discontinuous basis (p. 91). As an inside consultant, school counselors can use this conceptualization to help them diagnose issues in the workplace and determine levels of intervention based on the manner in which the school experiences the change process.

Levels of Intervening

During the formulation of the psychological contract, the consultant and the consultee will not only explore the culture of intervention but there will also likely be some discussion concerning the level of anticipated intervention that the situation might require. In that initial discussion, some notion of where to begin will need to be identified and agreed upon. Given that the theoretical context of consultation is the organization, consultants' interventions will always occur in "organizations" to some degree.

Social workers are familiar with the terms *macro, meso,* and *micro* in delineating the levels at which their interventions will be aimed. Consultants who are trained to work with organizations at the macro-level focus on organizational culture as a means of understanding the macro, meso, and micro levels of the workplace. Interestingly, as will be discussed, even at the large-scale organizational level of change, consultants can invoke a clinical approach to change. Consultants also work at the meso-level, which includes groups of individuals. At this level, consultees can be from the same or different "organizations." An example is a workshop where participants are comprised of clinicians employed at a variety of local mental health agencies and organizations. An example of intervening at the meso-level in business occurs when OD consultants are helping develop effective management teams in large organizations. At the micro-level, consultants work with individual consultees and clients. An example is when a school counselor is consulting with parents about their child's behavioral problems at school.

The concept of micro-, meso-, and macro-levels of change can be described from a gestalt perspective. Imagine an OD consultant working to effect a large-scale organizational change. That conceptualization occurs at the macro-level. At this macro-level, the "organization" is the target of change, thus it moves toward the consultant's conceptual foreground. The meso- and micro-levels remain in the conceptual background. At the meso-level of conceptualizing interventions, the "organization" becomes somewhat backgrounded while the particular group or groups inside the organization move into the foreground and become targets of change. When intervening with individual consultees and clients, the micro-level is in the immediate conceptual foreground. The organization per se is almost completely backgrounded, whereas the meso or group level to which the individual belongs is more conceptually immediate, yet not structurally in the foreground.

Traditionally, OD consultants claim the larger organization, the macro-level, as their domain. Those mental health professionals who are not formally trained in organizational development and industrial psychology will likely be working at the meso- and micro-levels with groups of individuals and individual consultees and clients. School counselors, by virtue of their being inside consultants, are inherently structured to work at the macro-, meso-, and micro-levels. For these professionals, the macro-level of intervening is considered to be the systems support services that many comprehensive career guidance programs incorporate (Gysbers & Henderson, 1988). This would include their work with administrators and principals in their respective schools. School counselors' meso-levels are conceptualized as including groups of teachers, groups of parents, and the various counseling groups they run. This would be seen as falling into the responsive services of Gysbers and Henderson's model. At the micro-level, school counselors work in responsive services with individuals such as students, parents, and teachers. For other mental health consultants, they might work with individual clinicians, their clients, or administrators. Organizational development consultants might work with individual employees or individual managers.

CONCEPTUALIZING CONTEXTS OF INTERVENING

Not only will consultants intervene at various levels of "organizational life," they will also intervene by assuming a variety of roles. Professional researchers in the field have identified the numerous roles that consultants assume in their efforts to effect change. Organizational culture and the culture of these roles and subsequent interventions both include artifacts, espoused values, and core basic assumptions. Knowledge of these roles and their cultural assumptions is important to help ensure a "goodness of fit" with the cultural assumptions held by the school, agency, or organization. Another context relates to the levels of intervening. As already mentioned, consultants can intervene in three levels: micro, meso, and macro. At each of these three contextual levels, research suggests that consultants can help create change at two levels. These two levels are referred to as "first-order" and "second-order" change.

Problem- and Solution-Oriented Intervening

Consultants intervene from basic orientations that depict either a problem-oriented or solution-focused approach. *Problem-focused* approaches are represented by deficit-oriented or disease models of consultation. Examples of this are Caplan and Caplan's (1993) mental health consultation model and behavioral consultation (Bergan, 1977; Bergan & Kratochwill, 1990). The problem-focused, medical model paradigm values hierarchies. It is a paradigm where prediction is the valued goal, and prediction is made possible through controlling the environment. Technology and know-how are highly valued. This paradigm is more outcome oriented than process oriented. Competence, perfection, and content expertise are revered. The kind of expertise utilized in the problem-oriented approaches is mirrored in the doctor/patient and purchase models of consultation (see Chapter 2).

The *solution-oriented* approaches are more developmental in nature and are also known as *process approaches*. Schein's (1969, 1987, 1999) process consultation model fits the "focusing on a solution" paradigm. In this paradigm, collaboration is valued. Normalizing experiences and co-equal relationships between consultant and consultees and clients are valued as a way of connecting. Expertise is also valued. However, consultant expertise is more process oriented, structurally engaging, and mutual as opposed to being only a content expert. Solution-focused approaches theoretically assume that individuals experience problems not because they are lazy; rather, they experience problems because they have been trying hard to solve the problem, and their efforts have been in vain (de Shazer, 1985). The core basic assumption in solution-focused approaches is the idea that consultees and clients already possess what they need to know to solve their issues. The roles and interventions emanating from this paradigm assume that students, teachers, administrators, counselors, and clients are inherently good and capable.

The two paradigms through which consultants conceptualize issues and solutions are vastly different from each other. The problem-focused paradigm may seem less viable to those mental health professionals who have been trained in a developmental-, strengths-, or solution-focused approach. Nonetheless, it is important to remember that school districts, mental health agencies, institutions, and organizations often operate from a problem-focused paradigm. Knowledge of the cultural paradigm that prevails in the consultee's organization is important. As such, it is a significant perspective to explore during the formulation of the psychological contract with consultees and clients. Essentially, the solution-oriented roles examine "what is and what can be," whereas the problem-oriented approaches examine "what is wrong, why, and what can be."

Inclusion and Exclusion Intervening

In arriving at solutions, consultants, consultees, and clients will interact each other, and the nature of that engagement can be conceptualized as falling along a continuum of inclusion–exclusion. The paradigm of inclusion is a postmodern concept and suggests that reality, meaning, and truth are best arrived at through a joint process of connection. Individuals can never really know truth and reality without some association with another person. The nature of this association is inclusion and embracing as opposed to excluding and rejecting. Intuition is included in this paradigm. In contrast, the paradigm of exclusion holds that truth is best arrived at through objectification. Gaining distance in situations and relationships allows for a better understanding because truth stands by itself apart from one's experience of it. This paradigm essentially separates the knower from the thing known. Both paradigms will be reflected in the types of roles that consultants assume, in the model used, and subsequently in the types of verbal and nonverbal interactions that occur between consultants and their consultees and clients. For instance, the fact-finder who is focusing on information about a problem assumes that the process of gathering information in an objective manner is the most efficacious way to arrive at a solution. In the process, the consultant assuming the role of fact-finder gains "distance" from the consultee in an effort to be more objective. It is important to note that the exclusion domain does not suggest that consultants physically exclude consultees and clients professionally, personally, or otherwise.

Inclusion and exclusion are fundamental orientations, and inside of each orientation is a myriad of combinations and permutations of inclusion–exclusion that lie along the continuum. In fact, even though consultees and clients may operate from a deficit or problem-oriented conceptual orientation, it does not mean that consultants have to operate from the same orientation in order to be helpful. Helping problem-oriented consultees and clients conceptualize their own issues based on the idea that they already possess the solution does not in any way impede or infringe on the consultee's conceptual paradigms. However, this point might be moot because pragmatically the issue of a problem-oriented consultee or client not wanting to proceed in a consulting process that is emphasizing and exploring solutions would probably be handled during the formulation of the psychological contract.

THE CULTURE OF INTERVENING

Hopefully, it can be seen by now that all mental health professionals who are in the role of consulting share a common "organization." Since consultation is synonymous with intervention and change, it is important to understand the culture of intervening. The idea of there being a culture of intervention suggests that every intervention itself has artifacts, espoused or underlying values, and core basic assumptions upon which it rests. For example, a consultant might decide to survey employees of a mental health agency to determine if there are morale problems. The survey is an artifact based on the value that rigorous scientific methodology is the best means to knowledge. Science itself is built on a set of core assumptions about the nature of truth and reality. In another situation, a consultant might invoke a group approach to solving problems. The group convened to solve the problem is the artifact. This approach is based on a set of values indicating the benefits of social interactions and the notion that truth is best arrived at conjointly. Again, these values are based on a set of core assumptions related to the social nature of human beings. Hence, the interventions used in consultation are considered artifacts of deeper beliefs regarding the nature of knowledge and how best to arrive at it.

The content areas of the culture of intervention also reflect the varied roles that consultants assume. As you would expect, the structural assumptions or higher-order abstractions contained in each role relate to the nature of reality and truth, the nature of human nature, the nature of human activity, the nature of human relations, and the nature of time and space. As such, intervening opens the possibility of having the culture of the organization clash with the culture of intervention from time to time in the same manner as the medical model clashes with a mental health perspective. Whether these differences can be worked through successfully depends partly on the psychological contract that is developed between consultant and consultee and through the appropriate use of consultant roles.

Consultant Roles: Artifacts, Values, and Core Assumptions

All cultures operate on core assumptions about who we are, the kind of world we live in, and what is ultimately important to us (Rokeach, 1960). Consultants assume various roles based on these assumptions. These roles include being an expert, advocate, fact-finder, trainer/educator, collaborator, information specialist, sanitation engineer, and process consultant. These roles themselves are also founded on a set of core assumptions. One of the ways to conceptualize the roles consultants take is to arrange the roles along a continuum ranging from directive to nondirective, as Lippitt and Lippitt (1986) and Dougherty (1990) suggest. The doctor/patient model of consultation reflects a more directive role. Schein's (1969, 1999) process consultation model lies closer to the nondirective pole of the continuum. Brown, Pryzwansky, and Schulte (2001) conceptualize consultants' roles as delineated by the amount the consultant's values are infused into the process of consulting. Applying this conceptualization to the doctor/patient model of consultation, the more directive consultants are, the more they infuse their own values into the consulting process.

Brown and colleagues (2001), Gallessich (1982), and Lippitt and Lippitt (1986) are often cited for their identification and discussions of the various roles that consultants assume. In many of the consulting models, these roles are not identified specifically. For example, there is little discussion of these roles per se in mental health consultation (Caplan & Caplan, 1993). Neither is there much discussion of these roles in behavioral consultation models per se (Bergan, 1977; Bergan & Kratochwill, 1990). The same is true for the systematic consultation model (Myrick, 1977) as well as for the atheoretical consultation model (Vacc & Loesch, 2000). Schein (1969, 1987, 1999) only implies these roles.

Regardless of the extent to which roles are overtly discussed or only implied in the various models, different consulting situations call for different roles. A mental health professional might intervene by mediating differences between a supervisor and an employee. School counselors might advocate for a student in the face of a possible suspension. These roles reflect certain types of processes that occur in consultation. For instance, if you were to witness a doctor/patient consulting approach, you would likely hear a systematic approach utilizing specific types of verbal exchanges between consultant and consultee. You might hear consultants asking consultees lots of questions. The idea would be to gather as much information as possible in order to make a correct diagnosis. You might also hear the consultant giving advice and prescriptions. This approach assumes that if enough information is gleaned by consultants, they could prescribe correct courses of action for consultees. In the doctor/patient approach, consultants hold the power to effect change. This lies in opposition to consultants who share the power of diagnosis and prescription, such as is the case in process consultation. If the situation calls for advice, and the consultant does not assume the appropriate role of expert, the consultee might not deem the consultant as understanding the situation and may be more hesitant to proceed.

The role of *expert* lies on a continuum. Consultants assume the expert role in almost every consultation. It is really a matter of degrees. Technical problems require technical expertise. Process problems require a process expert. Sometimes situations call for a combination of the two. In general, the role of expert, at its core, assumes that there is a relational power differential existing between consultants and consultees. Consultants have more power by virtue of their being "experts." The reason for this is because in traditional Euro-American culture, experts become experts by having more education, more experience, more intelligence, and/or more of some other construct. In closed systems, *more* on the part of one implies *less* on the part of the other. Thus, when consultants engage in the expert role, they set up a relationship with consultees based on a power differential. Consultees and clients hold power in terms of the nature, type, and amount of information they are willing to share. At the same time, when that information is shared, they loan the power over to the consultant.

Another role is that of *advocate*. The role of advocate assumes that on some level the environment is a hostile one. Although a noble undertaking, the role of advocate fundamentally presumes that the consultee and/or client are unable to help themselves sufficiently. The role of advocate allows consultants to promote their values and orientations to consultees and clients. This role is seen as a high-risk role because of the possibility of misuse by consultants. The reasons cited for positing the advocacy role as "high risk" include the potential misuse of power, politics, and influence to help induce change which, at the same time, can alienate peers (Conoley & Conoley, 1982). School counselors are acutely aware of their roles as student advocates in the school. Sometimes school counselors are faced with severe opposition to their advocacy of particular students—especially in those situations where the student being advocated for has had numerous problems with other school officials.

The *trainer/educator* is another role played by consultants. School counselors who are asked to facilitate in-services assume this trainer/educator role. Workshop facilitators, such as those described in Chapter Fourteen, utilize this role as well. Since this trainer/educator role may be more closely aligned with the purchase model of consultation, this role is more usually directive. In short, the trainer/educator may impart information and skill building to consultees and clients

Consultants also assume the role of *fact-finder*. In this very common role, consultants utilize various diagnostic interventions such as interviews and questionnaires in order to generate data. Reality, and therefore solutions, can be identified, observed, measured, and predicted if enough information is known. The data are then provided to the consultee in the form of feedback. Similar to the role of expert, the fact-finding role assumes that reality is better understood from an objective standpoint.

Collaborator is another role. School counselors collaborate, or share responsibility for the educational well-being of students, with a variety of school teachers, parents, and administrators. Mental health professionals regularly collaborate in the substance-abuse field. In collaborative roles, the expertise for handling a particular case is shared among professionals. For instance, a mental health counselor working with a client with an eating disorder might see the client for counseling and refer the client to a physician for follow-up and hospitalization. The client is receiving help from both professionals, and each professional is responsible for his or her part in the diagnosis and treatment.

At its core, the role of collaborator assumes the inherent goodness of being social. People can be trusted. Moreover, collaborating roles assume that "two heads are better than one."

Yet another important role is the role of *process consultant.* At its core, this role assumes the importance of the "here and now" as opposed to the "when and where" dimension of time. This is in direct opposition to the role of fact-finder. Another way of understanding this is to imagine a consultant interacting in a nondirective manner with consultees and clients while using reflection as a mainstay of the approach. For the consultant in this example, time is in the present, moment-by-moment interactions occurring between consultant and consultee. The connection in the relationship is significant, and one might hear the dialogue between consultant and consultee characterized by the consultant reflecting back to consultees what they say or think, much in the same fashion as Rogers (1951) would do in person-centered therapy. In contrast, imagine another consultant, assuming the role of fact-finder, interviewing a consultee in a series of questions. For this fact-finding consultant, time is in the past and is reflected in questions such as, "When did this problem start?" and "How did this happen (back then)"? Reflection might be used to punctuate points to the consultee rather than as a methodology aimed at direct problem resolution.

In addition to these roles, consultants can also assume the roles of *information specialist, joint problem solver, identifier of alternatives, process expert,* and/or *sanitation engineer.* This latter role occurs when the consultee hands a messy problem off to the consultant and says, "Here's the mess. You fix it." The consultant then proceeds to clean up the mess. The information specialist is more of a resource consultant for consultees and clients.

There are several significant points to remember about the culture of consultants' roles. Primarily and simplistically, *consultants assume many roles, whereas counselors assume only the role of counselor.* It is important that consultants do assume various roles, because the situations in which consultants find themselves are quite varied. No single role is sufficient for most consultations. For instance, even though a technical consultant will likely expect to be diagnosing technical problems in computers, the consultant will need to assume a fact-finding role in order to proceed. School counselors assume numerous roles throughout the day. One minute they are counseling with a student, and the next minute they are attempting to advocate for another student in an IEP (individualized educational plan) meeting. That afternoon, they may be conducting a training session on new federal guidelines for special education students. Each role assumed in consultation has its own culture or philosophical context. Certain roles belie certain core basic assumptions and may not match well with a particular organizational culture. For instance, a mental health center may have a culture that assumes all therapists are coequals. A consultant who comes in and proceeds to utilize a fact-finding or expert role may not fit well with the ethos of the agency's culture. Consultants need to be able to assume a variety of roles in order to be helpful in any given situation.

Intervening at the Meso-Level

Site-based management teams are becoming increasingly popular among schools and school districts. With ever-increasing numbers, business organizations are utilizing special-purpose teams, improvement teams, and task teams to carry out essential or core functions of the organization (Mohrman & Quam, 2000). According to these same researchers, OD consultants are being called on to help organizations transition to team-based approaches, or they are being asked to help or actually design the process. This type of consultation differs from traditional "team building," where consultants help team members with their internal integration processes and connections to the larger organizational scheme. Team-based designs are business performance strategies. As the strategies and activities of the organization change, designs change. Hence, team-based groups are dynamic and operate in a dynamic environment. Consultants who are involved in these types of OD consultations will be continually redesigning their strategies to help at this meso-level.

Peck's Community Making: Benchmark of Healthy Group Development. Organizational development consulting occurs at the macro-level of agencies, schools, and institutions. With the exception of school counselors, most mental health professionals will be consulting at the meso- and micro-levels. Generally speaking, mental health professionals who consult with groups will either be working with intact groups from the same school, agency, or organization, or will be working with a heterogeneous group comprised of individuals from various organizational contexts, as would be the case with workshops. In working with intact groups, it is important that consultants have knowledge of group stages and dynamics in order to more adequately anticipate or recognize situations that are to be expected. However, because consultation takes place in a work venue, the traditional research into counseling group stages and dynamics may not always be the appropriate conceptualization (e.g., Corey & Corey, 2002; Posthuma, 1999).

A model of group development that may be applicable to consultation at the meso-level of organizations is Peck's (1987) work on community making. English (1992) built on Peck's model and extended it into a model for promoting pluralism in the twenty-first century. Hence, not only do these two models act to organize conceptualizations of the meso-level of intervening, but these community making models are particularly appropriate for diverse populations. Peck (1987) and English (1992) both write about the stages of group development, referred to as "community making." Peck's and English's work is significant to consultation because each describes phases and stages involved whenever a group gets together that are distinctly different from processes of counseling groups. Moreover, both researchers point out reasons why a group is or is not moving through the phases successfully. English and Peck both see the need for community making to reach out to diverse cultures. Without such extension, community making would not be community making, and the researchers are acutely aware of this. The community-making model provides consultants with a conceptual yardstick by which they can identify and evaluate the stage of group development. Knowing the context or stage helps consultants understand the context of what they are experiencing as well as determine critical levels of intervening.

According to both Peck and English, *pseudo-community* is the first stage of group development. In this stage, the group has a goal of avoiding conflict. Facades are characteristic of this phase, and the interactions are punctuated by group members' attempts to deny anything that is offensive or irritable or that would create disagreement among group members. Denial and ignoring potential conflict is the rule in this stage of development. For example, a mental health center clinical director might be holding a staff meeting for therapists. Since a characteristic of pseudo-community is to avoid disagreements, one might see a conversation centering on platitudes, with some individuals being overly agreeable. Everyone would seem to be getting along. Interestingly, in moving forward with the agenda of the staff meeting, this mental health group might seem quite cohesive and experiencing a real sense of community. However, both Peck (1987) and English (1992) maintain their belief that in this stage of group development, individuals will often avoid too much detail and speak in generalities so as to remain somewhat anonymous. Individuals will not be as free in using the word *I*. Thus, a consultant who is listening to and observing such artifacts would correctly surmise that the group is in its initial forming stages. It is important to know that some groups can remain in pseudo-community for a long time, and this might well be the case for many groups in the workplace. Therefore, the length of time that a group has been together is not always indicative of where they "should be." In this example, the group could have been together a period of time in which the culture espoused the values of pseudo-community as a means of getting things done.

Chaos is the second stage of group development for both Peck and English. For those mental health professionals working with counseling groups, this stage would be associated with the storming or transitional stage of counseling groups. Chaos results from a natural progression of interactions between group members in which individuals begin struggling for power, control, and influence while assessing whether the group can meet individual goals (Schein, 1999). When individual differences occur, there are attempts to minimize the potential chaos by normalizing experiences. For example, in the example of the clinic staff meeting, one might hear a therapist complain about the amount of difficult cases on her caseload only to be met by a host of friendly, yet beguiling, comments to the effect that everyone has tough cases. The result is to play down the complaint by normalizing it. In diminishing the complaint of this one therapist by telling her that her complaint is normal, the group "avoids" overt conflict. However, at a deeper level, the group is actually ignoring individual differences. At the same time, the meeting would likely continue with the group members assuming that the complaining therapist's concerns are appropriately quelled. Yet, an experienced consultant would note that there does not seem to be any rhythm to the meeting. It is as if the group is going nowhere. Nor is there much fun.

In listening to conversations and discussions taking place during the chaos phase, one would likely hear comments such as, "We don't have the time," "We don't have the money," and "We just don't have the person-power to get it done." All of these comments are seen by Peck and English as *appeals to principles and dogmatism*. In other words, groups can invoke structural and hackneyed phrases such as those described to keep the status quo. These appeals are often borne out of fear and feelings of being threatened. Therefore, appeals to policies, laws, and the like serve to keep group members' anxieties and fears in check and, at the same time, keep the group from moving ahead.

The third stage of Peck's and English's work is *emptiness*, which would roughly correlate with the norming stage of counseling groups. English (1992) asserts that this stage reflects a state of deep questioning and doubt. However, in Peck's (1987) community-making model, emptiness denotes a quietness of the mind as individuals let go of expectations, prejudices, ideologies, theologies, as well as the need to fix, solve, or control. This third stage of community making is potentially transformational in changing the group. It is critical for another reason, as well, and this reason has direct implications for consultants. In the third stage, one option the group is faced with is to empty and reorganize itself in a different paradigm. The other option in this third stage is to reorganize back into the "old" organization or organizational culture. In other words, if there is not enough questioning occurring in the third stage, groups will inevitably return to pseudo-community. Eventually, the group will become chaotic and have another opportunity to question deeply. If not, it will once again return to pseudo-community. It is very important to note that although it may appear as though a group vacillating between pseudo-community and chaos is undesirable, that is not always the case. There are significant exceptions where a type of pseudo-community is appropriate. For instance, intimate relationships may not be the rule of the particular school's organizational culture. Athletic teams may also be a significant exception. Athletes can function well and play cohesively without having much personally in common or knowing intimate details about a teammate's private life. There are numerous other exceptions where pseudo-community works well.

Nonetheless, the result of the oscillation between stages one and two is to create a system that loops back to the "old" organization and the old ways of doing things. This can be frustrating for some group members. Interestingly, in the example of the mental health center, the very individuals who helped create the loop back to the "old" organizations of time, thoughts, ideas, and behaviors by denying and normalizing also have the very training it takes to move the group through a process of deepened questioning. The same can be said for school counselors who sit in various meetings throughout the week. School counselors and other mental health professionals do not need specialized training in consultation nor sophisticated tools to intervene in these types of meetings. They can simply use the knowledge and skills already available to them.

For instance, when individuals are speaking in the euphemistic "you" or third person and are in stage one, mental health consultants can invite the expression of "I-statements." This will encourage individual differences, which will lead to chaos. In the second stage, chaos, consultants simply want to encourage the helpful expression of feelings and ideas (English, 1992; Peck, 1987). A simple intervention aimed to encourage others eventually begins to put a rhythm to a group that is going nowhere nor having much fun at it. A school counselor, sitting in an IEP meeting and noticing that a teacher has not been given the opportunity to share his or her ideas can be invited to speak. Other group members may be encouraged to provide more detail, thus diminishing the "distance" in the conversation while promoting expression. At all times, consultants need to be careful to ensure that the intervening process aligns with the established organizational culture at whatever level or however present the organization is in the consultation.

According to English (1992), if individual group members question deeply enough, the group can move into the fourth stage, *community,* where there is a set of new values and assumptions about the group's experience. In this stage, the group transforms itself into a dynamic entity both separate from each group member as well as connected to each member. The researchers describe the characteristics of community as being

- A group of leaders
- A place of reality
- A place where there is fighting with grace
- A place of reflection
- A place of vulnerability
- A safe place
- A place of spirituality
- A place run by consensus

A group of leaders means that all individuals are in charge of themselves in terms of being responsible for their own feelings of both adequacy and inadequacy. In situations where everyone is a leader, each person diminishes his or her ego investment in the outcome of a particular group task. This does not mean that the outcome is eliminated, nor that the group does not value the outcome. In reality, it is quite the opposite. The theory is that an ego-less group functions more efficiently. There are several real-world situations in which this philosophy is seen in action. For instance, a successful athletic team clearly depicts this ego-less situation. Even though there may be huge egos involved, part of the team's task is to transform those individual egos into a collective team ego. As you can imagine, this task is very difficult to achieve. Yet, when it is achieved, performance and cohesion increase.

The notion of *reality* is aligned with the concept of a group of leaders. It helps to create a group of leaders by encouraging everyone in the group to share their ideas, opinions, and thoughts about a given current situation. The theory behind this is that the more input that everyone one has into a work situation, the more real it becomes. In terms of problem identification, the problem becomes more clearly defined when others have the opportunity to share their ideas about it. If only a few individuals share their perceptions, the problem may be only partially defined. The more input individuals have in defining the problem, the more accurately the problem becomes defined. This segues into more efficient solutions.

Fighting with grace means simply that fighting among group members is inevitable; it is the manner in which individuals argue or differ that either makes or breaks the group. Fighting with grace means that differences are appreciated, not obliterated. Fighting with grace is fighting with an inclusion-oriented perspective. That means that when differences are discussed, not only are individual group members graceful in their exchanges but they also allow others to experience their own grace. There are no put-downs, no sarcasm, and no attempts to power-play others or otherwise coerce them into a position of submission or giving in. Instead, the ego-less group welcomes the diversity of individuals and viewpoints as a means of helping them transform their work group.

A place of reflection means that there is time made for individuals and groups of individuals to reflect on the processes in which they are involved. This reflection can be as short as a five-minute debriefing of the process after a staff meeting, or more formalized, such as an agency or staff retreat. On a more abstract level, a place of reflection would mean having an atmosphere or ambiance of openness about the processes that occur in the everyday workings of the institution or agency. Reflection would include the ability of individuals as well as the group(s) as a whole to comment on the process to one another and among themselves. Being able to sit alone outside during lunch without folks thinking something is wrong or taking time out for watering plants is a behavior that mirrors reflection in the workplace. A private conversation about one's concerns at work with another staff member(s) is another example of being able to reflect. A place of reflection also would be characterized by the presence or potential for deepened levels of interpersonal vulnerability. These levels would be flexible enough to reflect a dynamic relationship or organizational system and, at the same time, would be appropriate to the workplace.

It is interesting to note that *a place of vulnerability* can exist in almost every work environment. The vulnerability referred to here concerns the psychic space that is made available in the organization for individuals to reflect on themselves in relation to other individuals, the group, and the organization as a whole. This reflection allows individuals an "error-detection" mechanism in which they can examine the congruence they experience between themselves and their own values and those of the group and/or organization. Being vulnerable may or may not mean that individuals should discuss their deeper experiences, their inner-most feelings, and/or their fears in the workplace. Certainly, individuals can be vulnerable in this way in some organizations. However, the permission to feel vulnerable in the workplace is regulated more by an organization's culture. Some organizational cultures allow or promote this, whereas other cultures seem to prohibit this vulnerability. A place of vulnerability essentially means that if one chooses to be vulnerable at whatever level he or she does, the choice is respected by other group members. This creates a type of *safe place,* which is another element of community.

When referring to community as being *a place of spirituality*, Peck means that the individual's personal spirituality, the manner in which one connects herself or himself to a larger entity and sense of ongoingness, is acknowledged and appreciated. It may not ever be the focus of conversation in the workplace, and it does not have to be. A place in which the deeper aspects of the organization's mission can be entertained and acknowledged overtly and covertly is a place of spirituality. An example of this would be reflected in a situation where a group of teachers, counselors, and administrators discuss the deeper levels of their educational aims with one another. In this discussion, compassion would be present as well as passion. The ultimate meaning of education and its relevance to students would also be included in the dialogue. Again, other group members would be accepting of each individual's views and worldviews. If there were differences, these would be included in the discussion as necessary for a group to transform itself.

Decision by consensus means that when it comes to group decisions, there is no vote. Everyone has the opportunity and is encouraged to speak. Having done so, consensus means that everyone has an understanding of the issue, and the "feel" of the group points it into a direction for action. Consensus does not mean that everyone agrees on the action. Rather, it means that everyone has had the opportunity for input and has been appreciated and respected by other group members. Individuals shed their egos that, if left unchecked, would result in power-plays over others. Individuals let go of the outcome in order to become immersed in the process. Decision by consensus differs from other forms of group decision making. Schein (1969, 1999) identifies other forms of group decision making, including decision by majority, decision by minority, decision by authority, decision by unanimity, and decision by lack of group response. With the possible exceptions of unanimity and lack of group response, the other three forms of decision making promote adversarial relationships. In other words, there are winners and losers whenever decisions are arrived at by majority, minority, or autocratic responses. Deciding on a course of action through the lack of group response occurs when a group member makes a suggestion that is met with a loud silence. The silence makes the decision because the person who offered up the idea often will withdraw it as a result of the group's silent response. Making decisions by unanimity is not the same as consensus. In a unanimous decision-making style, there is a vote, and everyone votes in the same direction. Moreover, this style takes a great deal of time and persuasion and is often not an efficient way to conduct business whenever decisions need to be made quickly. On the other hand, consensus gets at the same sense of unanimity. Yet, the unanimity is centered on the process of deciding, rather than the actual decision itself, in a style of consensus decision making.

Consultants can use Peck's and English's group models as a benchmark to understand what is happening in groups in the workplace. As with other benchmarks, an understanding of the context in which a consultant is seeing individual behavior in a group setting helps as an "error-detection" mechanism. This means that consultants can predict certain types of behaviors that will surface in a given group stage. When observing a work group, consultants can use their understanding of the components of community to determine how close or how far off the group is from that benchmark. It is not that Peck's or English's model is appropriate for all work-group situations. However, these models have tremendous application for diversity. If you review the tenets of their respective works, it is difficult to find that the elements of community are anything less than revolutionary and profoundly inclusive of diverse others.

Intervening at the Micro-Level

Given that the smallest structural unit in consultation is a single triadic system, the most simplistic consultation occurs in situations where there is one consultee and one client rather than a client system. An example of this simplistic unit occurs when a school counselor works with a student (client) whose been referred by a teacher (consultee). Here, although the actual situation might be quite complex, the consultant is working with the individual student and the individual teacher in various ways to effect change. Another example occurs when a mental health professional is seeking consultation from another professional regarding a problem the former is having with an individual client. Again, even though there might be complex issues at stake, the consultant's field of vision in these two common examples is focused on the consultee and a single client. There is little doubt that the interventions invoked by the consultant in these simplistic situations will, in fact, actually affect the larger system of teachers and students in that particular school or affect the group of all mental health clients seeking services in a mental health center. For instance, other classmates and teachers might benefit from a consultant's successful intervention with a single student who acts out in the classroom. A mental health professional's new understanding gleaned from the consultation with another professional over a particular client's issue may well generalize to other similar client issues, and hopefully will. However, these examples depict consulting situations that have a primary aim to improve the performance of an individual, and hopefully others, rather than focusing on improving the organization as a whole.

Caplan (1970), Caplan and Caplan (1993), Bergan (1977), Bergan and Kratochwill (1990), and Myrick (1977) all describe the intervening process at the micro-level. These approaches will be examined in detail in their respective chapters. It is germane here to note how Caplan and Caplan (1993) differentiate approaches to consultation at the micro-level. Caplan and Caplan's views of *consultee-centered case consultation* and *client-centered case consultation* describe consulting perspectives involving individual consultees and clients. In the client-centered case consultation, the model most often used is the doctor-patient model briefly alluded to in Chapter Two, where the expert consultant is called in to diagnostically assess a client and make recommendations for remediation and treatment. According to Caplan and Caplan, the "primary goal of this type of consultation is to develop a plan that will help the client" (p. 86). In consultee-centered case consultation, the consultant's primary focus is on clarifying and providing remedies for the shortcomings of the consultee's professional functioning. Bergan (1977) and Bergan and Kratochwill (1990) offer a behavioral case consultation model. It is important to note that the main focus of behavioral case consultation is on teaching the consultee about behavioral principles that will help in the disposition of the consultee's case. In behavioral case consultation, the consultant's job is to manage the case manager. Myrick's model, systematic consultation, is an individual model in that consultants focus on sequential steps to help individual consultees and clients. Even though the single triad is the most simple form of consultation, what happens within these types of consultancies can range from the simple to the complex and profound.

FIRST- AND SECOND-ORDER CHANGE

As mentioned earlier, consultants can intervene at the micro-, meso-, and/or macro-levels. In each of the levels, consultants can intervene to help create *first-order* or *second-order change*. Both levels can produce meaningful change in consultees, clients, and client systems. However, as you would imagine, these two levels relate to different depths of intervening. One might conceptualize the first level as a more superficial intervention, and the second level can be conceptualized as the more structural level of intervention. Fiol and Lyles (1985) view change as organizational learning and use "constant learning" and "periodic learning" to describe incremental and transformative change respectively. Continuous or incremental change is a type of *constant learning,* whereas discontinuous or transformative change reflects *periodic learning.* You have heard of organizations "reorganizing." Organizations undergoing periodic learning can often regain "fit" through a series of large-scale shifts and recalibrations in such things as strategy, structure, process, or a combination of these three. These readjustments occur at two levels, according to Levy (1986). The first level, considered first-order change, occurs when the changes that occur do not alter the basic structural core of the organization. The second level, referred to as second-order change, happens in situations where the changes actually alter the organization's structural core. Levy argues that second-order change involves a change at the level of cultural basic core assumptions or the system's basic governing rules. At this level, multidimensional, multicomponent, and multilevel changes that are made actually shift the system irreversibly to a new and revolutionary paradigm.

Levy's first- and second-order change concepts for organizations are similar to the notions of change used by therapists in a variety of settings. For instance, in working with couples in conflict, a marriage and family therapist can focus on first-order change. According to Carter and McGoldrick (2000) this type of first-order intervention occurs when there are changes in the family that do not rearrange the basic rules of operations for that particular family. Helping the couple work on interpersonal skills to handle the conflict is an example of a first-order level intervention. Second-order change in families occurs when the family members change the rules of operation for how they solve their problems. Working on the power structure differentials in a relationship can clear up many conflicts. In learning more effective ways of communicating with each other, a marriage and family therapist might discover that a basic component of a couple's psychological contract includes a "no-talk rule" about emotions. Encouraging each partner to talk about his or her emotional experience violates the structural "rule" and gets at the basic core structure of the psychological contract. By talking about something the couple agreed to not talk about, they effectively change the rules and structure of their relationship. Perhaps the new rule is that unpleasant feelings can now be talked about and worked through.

In a mental health center, treating patients with chemotherapy is an example of first-order change. Having a client see the psychiatrist for medical and chemotherapy concerns while continuing to see the client in group or individual therapy is an example of intervening at both levels of change. In OD consulting, changing the location of staff offices is an example of first-order change, whereas changing how the people who occupy those offices communicate with one another would be second-order change.

Levy (1986) believes that oftentimes, OD consultants make the mistake of not intervening deeply enough at the second-order change level. Whenever school counselors intervene at the system level of the school, such as would be the case when designing and initiating a new program to address drug use by students, they are intervening with second-order change. Working with a student to change the words used during a conflict at recess to avoid a future fight is an example of a first-order change. Moving the student to another homeroom with a different recess period to avoid the conflict would also be an example of first-order change. In this case, the student's interpersonal interactions are not altered per se. The change is a change in physical location only. If another situation occurs with another student, the problem may remain. Examining the playground conditions that promote a conflict in terms of the why, when, and where the fighting takes place, and intervening in those structural areas is an example of a second-order change. A mental health agency program director who is suggesting that two staff members change offices in order to give each more space as a method of solving a personality conflict is an example of first-order change because changing the physical locale only changes the physical conditions that lead up to a problem. The problem of two staffers not liking each other remains and would likely spark if the two were to be in contact again.

SUMMARY

The emphasis on individual psychology, present to varying degrees in traditional organizational developmental consulting, is familiar ground to mental health professionals. The mental health profession itself is founded on fundamental knowledge of individual human behavior. At the same instance, this knowledge base is useful to mental health professionals in another way. Conducting consultations with an organization at any level can be complex and intimidating. This is especially true if the school's, organization's, or agency's problems are deep-seated and long standing. Thinking about how to change or how to intervene can feel overwhelming to consultants. Remembering that mental health professionals are experts at change in interpersonal relationships, it is often useful and appropriate to conceptualize change as occurring in a conversation with a consultee or client, much in the way that Schein might. Collapsing change into such a small step as a conversation with one individual can help enhance the consultants' feelings of self-efficacy (Bandura, 1977).

However, perhaps the most significant implications relate to how consultants go about conceptualizing intervening with consultees and clients when delivering direct and indirect service. Change occurring in consultees also affects clients. Concomitantly, changes in clients also affect the consultee. With this knowledge, consultants can then be better prepared to understand and predict the short- and longer-term effects of their intervening efforts. As mentioned in Chapter One, consultants have differential obligations to consultees and clients/client systems, and it is clear that general systems theory plays an important and influencing role in how consultants go about discharging their duties and obligations. Although a consultant's primary responsibilities are to the consultee, one can see that the principles of general systems theory helps to texture and broaden the issue of consultant responsibility.

Intervening has its own culture and is reflected in the various roles that consultants assume during their work with consultees and clients. As consultants glean a better understanding of the culture of intervention, including the assumptions assumed in the various roles, they can be more effective in their work. Interventions need to have a reasonable "goodness of fit" for them to be effective. This means that interventions invoked through various roles undertaken by consultants need to fit with the organization culture inherent in almost every consultee and client. A consultant assuming an expert role in a situation where the culture presumes the expertise of everyone might run into resistances. Finding facts to determine causes and solutions will work in some consultations and will be ill-advised in other situations. In many cases, this fit can be initially assessed during the formulation of the formal and psychological contract, which will be discussed in the next chapters.

QUESTIONS

1. What are the assumptions inherent in incremental change in organizations?

2. Why is it important to have an understanding of how organizations change?

3. What is meant by a culture of intervention?

4. What are some of the roles that consultants assume?

5. What are the fundamental assumptions surrounding the expert role? A process consultant role?

6. Is it possible for a work group to be a community? Why or why not? What, if any, are the disadvantages?

7. How does the notion of community and community-making relate to diversity?

CHAPTER FIVE

FORMAL AND PSYCHOLOGICAL CONTRACTS IN CONSULTATION

In consultation, there are two types of contracts: formal and psychological. Both types of contracts have elements to them that are important for consultants to know. The formal, written contract is explicit, whereas the psychological contract is implied. Both help to establish the parameters of the consulting process in that both types of contracts have implications for intervening with consultees and clients. From my experience, mental health professionals who are learning about consultation will need to know something about formal contracting, but will need to know more about the psychological contract.

Ironically, many formal contracts used in the field of mental health consulting are written in an ambiguous manner, and this seems to work for many practitioners who may consult with individuals, groups, and local agencies and institutions. If a consultant were working full time and had several clients, a standard formal contract might be more useful and more prevalent. However, for most mental health practitioners, consultation is a part-time professional endeavor. Thus, the need for a lengthy discussion on formal contracting is beyond the scope of this chapter. Nevertheless, the structural elements of a standard formal written contract used in consultation will be outlined, and examples will be provided to help clarify significant points. The psychological contract is a different story and will be addressed in this chapter as well as Chapter Six.

FORMAL CONTRACTS

As you would expect, most consultations require some type of written contract for services. These formal contracts can vary in length and in detail. For example, when working with local school systems, the written contract may be about one page in length and contain standard language. In these situations, the contract will probably indicate only the dates of service, the fee for services, a short description of what is expected (for example, a workshop), some legal information about how the contract can be disclaimed by either parties, and a place for signatures. If the consultation is for a state agency, the contract will be roughly the same as those often used by school districts, but may be more comprehensive. It still will likely contain standard legal information and disclaimers. Consulting in a local mental health agency will likely require a contract similar to other governmental agencies since these agencies usually have some form of federal funding. Again, these contracts are binding and yet are somewhat simplified in their language and length. There are formal consulting situations where no money is exchanged. In these situations, a contract may or may not be executed. This often occurs when consultants are doing the work pro bono. The general rule is: If money is exchanged, there will likely be a formal contract. If the consultation is being done pro bono, there will probably be no written formal contract. In any and all cases of consultation, some type of agreement is involved that implies a mutual consent to participate in the consulting process.

I was recently involved in a consulting relationship with a particular sports team. All of the consulting that I do with sports teams has been conducted without a formal written contract. Instead, I have relied on developing strong and effective psychological contracts. There has never been a problem until recently. I assumed that since my working relationships with other coaches and teams was working well without formal contracts, the same structure would suffice with this particular team. I failed to assess the coach's needs and ways of doing business correctly. At the end of the season, I asked for the sum of money we had agreed on only to find out that the coach did not have the same understanding. As a result, I felt my ethical obligation was to conform to the coach's understanding, which left me with a significant loss of income. In this case, the failure to adequately assess the coach's expectations resulted in a situation where my main aim shifted to wanting to preserve the relationship with the consultee (coach) and clients (players) at all costs. Even though my mistake cost me money, it did not cost me future consultations with this team. I was asked back to do more work. Obviously, a written contract was drawn up for the ensuing work with the team.

Informed Consent in Counseling and Consultation

As you would expect, all consultations require that attention be paid related to informed consent. Informed consent in consultation is both similar to and different from the idea of informed consent in counseling. In general, informed consent in counseling requires counselors to outline with their clients the problems to be solved and the manner in which the counseling process will aim to achieve the solutions. Everstine, Everstine, Geymann, True, Frey, Johnson, and Seiden (1980) assert that there are three elements of informed consent for counselors that make it legal. The first requirement is that the client is *competent* and can engage in rational thought processes to a degree that he or she can make competent decisions about his or her life. Minors cannot give informed consent; rather, consent must be sought from their parents or legal guardians. The second requirement relates to the notion of *informed*. This element requires that information must be given in a manner that is understandable. The American Counseling Association (1995) is very specific about the information that should be disclosed to clients in order for them to give adequate consent to treatment. Finally, the consent needs to be given *voluntarily*. A fourth issue comes from the American Psychological Association (2003), which requires that the consent be appropriately *documented*. In the practice of counseling, the manifestation of that documentation is a type of "Consent to Treatment Form."

There are important ethical and legal implications of informed consent in counseling, and the same holds true for consultation. Some of these ethical and legal issues are the same for both practices, and other issues clearly distinguish components of the two processes. For instance, in the practice of consulting, the consulting contract is the legal "consent to treatment." Interestingly, and a marked difference from that of counseling, the clients who receive direct and indirect service in consultation do not sign the contract. In this sense, they do not ever consent formally. Only the consultee, the one responsible for payment, signs off on the contract.

Objectives of the Formal Contract

One main benefit of contracting is that it can help establish goals, objectives, and the processes by which the goals will be reached. Hansen, Himes, and Meier (1990) assert that contracts also help set limits and aid in making clear "what will and will not be done" (p. 78). Dougherty (1990) claims that the contract is an explicit exchange of expectations that are expressed orally, in writing, or in a combination of the two. The contract reflects and clarifies the shared understanding between the consultant and consultee. Contracts outline what each person expects from the consulting experience and the approximate (or explicit) time involved and for what price. The use of formal contracts essentially explicates to some degree the ground rules under which the consultant, consultee, and consultee system will operate (Weisbord, 1985, p. 306). Mann (1972, p. 218) believes that the consultation contract is an agreement that clarifies as much as possible the expectations of and the obligations incurred by each party. Included would be information about the frequency of meetings and the scheduling of appointments. Further, the agreement should address how the client/client system will be accessed. Wherever appropriate, the contract should outline the data to be collected, the provisions for review and modification of the program, and the amount and manner of payment for services rendered.

As will be discussed later, awareness of the dimensions and obligations outlined in the contract is the responsibility of both consultees and consultants, and the more descriptive and informative the contract is, the more clear and objective the responsibilities become. There are situations in which the contract does not go far enough or goes too far. In the former case, where it does not go far enough, the contract may fail to provide a certain latitude to make adjustments to the agreed upon plans when something new develops during the consultation. An example might be if the consultants find an unexpected situation arising from their interventions in another arena of the consultancy. For instance, a consultant might begin to intervene with the employees of an organization only to find that one or more of the managers or supervisors suddenly quits to take another job elsewhere. The consultant may need to address the loss with the remaining employee clients before the agreed upon consulting goals can be addressed. There may also be situations in which consultants find more resistance to their interventions than had been originally planned. This may require more time than was originally specified in the contract, and adjustments to the contract will need to be made. Sometimes this will come in the form of an amendment, and in other cases, there will be no rewriting of the original contract. In cases where the consultation is a workshop, consultants will rarely need to readjust the contract because of the nature of the intervention. Workshops are almost always time limited and contain specified content.

Components of the Formal Contract

Although the notion of informed consent is specified in the ethics of practice for counselors, one can readily see from the preceeding discussion how informed consent is approached in consultation through the formal contract. Both Fisher (1986) and Mc-Gonagle (1981) describe the elements of a standard formal contract in consultation. These researchers see the standard contract as determining informed consent in consultation. Fisher advocates that formal contracts need to have six elements. McGonagle makes minor alterations to Fisher's notions and extends the contract to include six other components. McGonagle's aim is to increase the consultant's insulation from litigation. Gallessich (1982) has some components of contracts that neither Fisher nor McGonagle identifies. Many of these elements are described next. In general and regardless of the intent of the contract, the order of components contained in the formal contract usually varies, based on consultee preference.

Problem Identification.   Both Fisher (1986) and McGonagle (1981) believe that the identification of the problem needs to be addressed in the beginning paragraphs of the formal contract. More specifically, McGonagle believes that the first paragraph should describe the start and end dates of the consultation, whereas Fisher advocates that the first paragraph ought to describe the problem to be addressed. Obviously, describing the problem requires some diagnostic language. Diagnostic language that only a professional would understand is not recommended. It is usually best if the language is worded in such a way as to be clear, concise, and understandable. The use of pedantic language might create more distance in the consulting relationship, and this would be a critical error in situations where the consultee is already feeling threatened and vulnerable by the consultation. Language that is difficult for consultees to understand might also increase resistance to the consulting process by making the diagnosis somewhat "mysterious." In situations where the consultee has issues related to dependency, the use of obtuse or pedantic language might increase his or her dependencies to an undesired or ineffective level. On the other hand, using language that everyone can understand helps "reduce" the problem into more manageable terms. In the process of doing so, the contract may actually help provide encouragement that the problem can actually be solved.

Description of Activities and the Consultant's Role.   The second element or paragraph of the formal contract, according to Fisher, should include a general description of the approach that will be used. The approach should be mutually agreed upon by the consultant and consultee. Similar to Fisher, McGonagle believes the second paragraph should include a detailed description of the consulting activities mutually agreed upon by both. The description of services essentially acts as an important element in that it helps the consultee to give informed consent. For both Fisher and McGonagle, this description also needs to be as clear and concise as possible. An example in the mental health field might be a situation where a social worker is hired to consult with the clinical staff of a community mental health center about cases. The description of services might include statements detailing the consultant's activities and purposes of the consultation. For instance, there should be language describing whether the consultant will attend clinical staff meetings or whether meetings will take place outside of the regularly scheduled case consultations. In addition, this section might indicate the process used, such as meeting with individual therapists or with a group of therapists. The purpose should also be outlined. For example, the purpose of the consultation might be "to help clinical staff members identify problematic clients and to increase the clinical staff's abilities to conceptualize issues and help clients."

The Number of Meetings.   This section of the formal contract should simply identify the length of the contracted service and the number of times the consultant will directly intervene in the process. Sometimes, the length of time is less important than the actual number of times the consultant will meet. Other times, the length of time is specified but the number of meetings taking place during that period is less specific. For example, a contract might specify that the consultant will meet periodically for three months. Another contract might state that the consultant will meet for a total of eight times during the course of three months. The important issue is that there needs to be a mutually understood time period identified.

Remuneration for Services.   The amount of expenditure needs to be identified and agreed upon, and this depends on the problem identified, the consultants' activities, and the number of meetings determined. Some consultants have a standard hourly rate for services. This is similar to counselors, who usually charge a standard hourly fee. Other consultants assess the actual consultation and determine a flat fee for services. Sometimes, consultants charge by the day rather than by the hour or by the job. Consultants who are hired to conduct a workshop might charge a flat fee. An OD consultant working with an organization might charge an hourly fee, a fee for the total amount of work anticipated, or be on a retainer. In many school situations, grant-funded agencies, and institutions, there will often be specific funds set aside for consulting services. The fee is not negotiable; it is set by the funding agency with whom the consultant will likely have no contact. In other situations, the fee for service can be mutually agreed upon through discussion between consultant and consultee. Beginning consultants need to be aware of the hazards of giving their services away for free. This can set up expectations for future consultees who may have gotten the consultant's name from a former consultee who received service pro bono. It is also difficult to provide free service and then ask for payment on subsequent consultancies.

Gallesich (1982) agrees with both Fisher and McGonagle in that the consultee's financial responsibilities need to be identified in the formal contract. However, Gallessich also thinks that contracts should specify to whom the consultant is responsible as well as clarifying the clients to be served in the consultation. It may be that the consultant has access to only certain individuals or groups while other groups may lie outside of the consulting venue. Sometimes, it is the case that the consultees initially desire to be ruled out as "clients" or participants other than acting as contact persons. Later, it may be that the consultee needs to be involved. It is a good idea to get this clarified if language to that effect is going to be included in a formal contract.

Settings of the Consultation.   McGonagle and Gallessich both believe that formal contracts need to identify the actual settings in which the consulting process will occur.

There may be legal implications affecting the physical location of the consultation. For instance, if the meetings take place in locations away from the central offices, consultants may find that their consultees and clients are not covered by insurance. Convenience and purpose may also play a role in determining the location of the consulting process. A school often can use the cafeteria or library to conduct meetings with administrators and teachers. Although not always the best ambience for some types of consultations, these school rooms are readily available and provide convenience to the participants. There may also be situations where consultees agree to provide a physical location for the consultant. For instance, a social worker might be hired to consult with the clinical staff of a mental health agency. The director may offer a temporary room in which individual meetings can take place.

Access to equipment such as a copier, overhead projector, and fax, along with the need for any secretarial services, ought to be identified in the setting component of the formal contract. As much as possible, an estimation of the amount of this type of help needs to be specified, and if there is to be a charge incurred, that figure needs to become a part of the discussion. Often, the consultant will receive some secretarial services or other needs gratis. In those situations, it is helpful for consultants to be reasonable and respectful in their requests. For instance, when consulting with athletic teams, I do not often require the use of copiers. The question becomes, "Who will copy the material?" This may seem trivial, but to secretaries who already feel oppressed by the amount of work, making copies can be seen as inconvenient and can initiate some resistance on their part. Imagine if that secretary was one of the clients in the consultation! Usually, I provide my own copies, often at my own expense.

Reports, Work Products, and Strategies.   This part of the formal contract will almost always depend on how precisely the problem has been identified. In the case of the social worker consulting with the clinical staff, the problem may be construed as ongoing and noncrisis. In this example, the problem is not precisely identified. Yet, the intervention is quite specific. In general, the more precisely the problem is identified, the more precisely the interventions ought to be outlined. Contracts can be quite explicit, or they can be rather broad. The social worker's contract might be somewhat specific. A consultant brought in to help with a problem related to morale in an inpatient treatment center may draw up a broader contract. This would be due to the unknowns, complexities, and nuances involved in such a situation.

If the consultant is to provide reports or other documentation, this needs to be identified in the formal contract as well. McGonagle (1981) believes that the issue of the confidentiality of the reports and of the consultation itself needs to be included in this section of the formal contract. There was a situation in which I failed to specify this element in a consultation only to find that the consultee became upset when a mid-consultation evaluation report was not provided. I then provided the report without charging the consultee. Some detail about what the report(s) should contain and who will be privy to it is also specified in this section of the contract. There was another situation where I failed to specify who would have access to a report submitted after several days of consulting. I assumed it would be between me and the consultee. Soon after, I came to find out that the CEO of the organization as well as the clients with whom I had worked were also given copies of the report. Had I taken the time to determine those who would have access to the report instead of simply assuming access, the report would have been written differently than it was. Conversely, can you imagine how the consultee would have felt in a situation where the report had identified some weaknesses in the consultee and he or she had been required (unbeknownst to the consultant) to provide a report to his or her supervisor or boss? From my experiences, it is critical to know who will be reading the report.

Evaluation of Consulting Services.   It is important for the formal contract to include some language describing how the consultation (and subsequently, the consultant) will be evaluated. There are a myriad of ways to evaluate consulting services. Some consultees want an ongoing evaluation, whereas others may require only a formal evaluation at the end of the contract. Some evaluations are standard forms, such as might be the case for school districts, and other evaluations are generated by either the consultant or consultee. As a general rule, the elements of the evaluation need to relate to the problem identified. This is a good reason why the problem needs to be stated in clear and concise terms. In this way, the evaluation will be relevant to the work performed.

Other Elements.   McGonagle believes that sections in the formal contract should deal with assignment of the contract, arbitration of disputes, integration, and closing the contract. *Assignability* has to do with the ability of the consultant to assign all or part of the work to another party (another consultant, for example). *Arbitration* deals with the mechanism that will be used to settle any contract disputes. *Integration* deals with any changes that need to be made to the contract. In general, both parties would need to agree on changes to the original contract. Finally, the *Closing* section simply closes the contract by providing a place for signatures approving the contract. These other elements are often too detailed for most contracts involving mental health consultants.

PSYCHOLOGICAL CONTRACTS

Social Psychological Contracts

Psychological contracts are not relegated to professional consultation; rather, they exist between humans and those who believe in God or a Higher Power. These contracts exist everywhere in the world, in every religion. Psychological contracts exist between people and between countries. They exist between governments and those they govern. They exist between employers and employees. They exist between nuclear and extended family members. A psychological contract even exists between you, the reader, and me, the purchase model consultant.

Schein (1987, p. 126) describes a psychological contract in consulting as one that involves an understanding of implicit or explicit expectations on the part of the consultant and the consultee. This will include the gains expected and the obligations that the consultee will accept. The contract will also include an understanding of what each will give to the relationship. In everyday situations, psychological contracts can be conceptualized in a similar fashion. For example, some traditional religions in the United States promote a type of psychological contract in which one's behavior is eventually rewarded in Heaven. This understanding acts in one way as a powerful guide for moral behavior. Yet, there are those religions that maintain that one's "reward" is here—not after death, for there is "nothingness" after death. This contract, although different from the former, still acts to mitigate moral behavior. If one were to switch religions, one would, in effect, be switching components of psychological contracts. During the years of the Cold War, the United States and Russia engaged in a psychological contract that drew stringent and threatening boundaries around the two nations. It was explicitly and implicitly understood that a transgression by either side would result in Armageddon.

In business, employers and their employees have formal and psychological contracts that involve quality-of-life issues. These include such issues as having ongoing trainings and other efforts to improve morale at work, employee profit sharing, free and convenient parking, providing windows for offices, and a host of other concerns. The presence and amount of employee benefits packages also reflect psychological contracts or an implied understanding of the value of any given employee to the company organization. There is also an implied understanding that operates between managers/ supervisors and their supervisees. A given supervisory style impacts supervisees on both a behavioral and a psychological level. Employees who can effectively manage the psychological contract with their supervisors are more likely to stay.

Social psychological contracts exert a tremendous and profound direct force on the contract members as well as on those with whom the members involved themselves. There is clear and unabashed evidence that the psychological contract operating on a diurnal basis in people's lives is changing dramatically. For example, a major corporation in northwestern United States, the Boeing Company—a world leader in aircraft manufacturing—announced in March 2001 that it would be moving its corporate headquarters from Seattle, Washington, where it had been housed for 85 years. The reason given for the move was the need to have Boeing headquarters closer to the center of its operations. The state's own delegation to Washington, including one senior U.S. Congressman well known for his staunch support of Boeing, was notified only a few minutes before the public announcement. This episode illustrates the presence of a psychological contract as well as the abrupt violation of it. It appears to have been the understanding (a psychological contract) that if anything of such magnitude should ever occur, the senators and congressmen and congresswomen would be made aware of it long before a public declaration. Boeing also appears to have violated the psychological contract it had with the surrounding community as well. Economically, this move would help Boeing. Yet, it was an economical and psychological blow to the region.

Diversity and the Changing Psychological Contract

As will be examined in Chapter Six, psychological contracts are rooted in fundamental worldviews. Worldviews act both as the seeds from which psychological contracts germinate and as structures that define the breadth and scope of those involved. Worldviews can and do change for individuals. As they change, so do the ensuing psychological contracts. Examples of changing contracts in areas of diversity can be seen throughout American history.

For instance, a significant shift in a psychological contract occurred between Native Americans, whites, and alcohol. According to Fisher and Harrison (2000) and Attneave (1982), trappers and other frontiersmen introduced alcohol to Native Americans as a social beverage in the late 1700s. Eventually, many natives drank as a means to increase social relations with whites and hoped that drinking would increase favorable trade relations. This newly formulated psychological contract violated an older one held by many woodland and plains tribes. It was understood in the old contract that alcohol was to be used exclusively for certain ceremonial purposes (Fisher & Harrison, 2000; Westermeyer & Baker, 1986). As a result of a newly renegotiated contract, Native Americans began to differ among themselves over views of alcohol because some members of the same tribe would drink socially and others would drink only during ceremonies to help them communicate with the powers. Each style of behavior had a concomitant psychological contract that was both superficial and profound: On one level, the some tribal members drank based on the core assumption that they and the tribe needed the economic benefits that drinking with whites could provide. On another level, this shifted their psychological contract from ethereal faith to a more mundane faith in the absolute benefits of trade and commerce.

This newly renegotiated psychological contract had broad-ranging effects and involved many parties. For instance, there were renegotiated understandings regarding the role that alcohol would play in tribes themselves. It would redefine the role alcohol would play in relations with whites. It would spiritually reconfigure the ceremonial rituals of some tribal members (some of whom might have eventually converted to Christianity as a result of protracted association with whites). American Indians have continued to renegotiate contracts with alcohol in order to keep it a part of their modern culture. One aspect of the current psychological contract that Native Americans have with alcohol is that alcohol is now seen by some researchers as a grieving response to the loss of the Native American homeland and heritage (Fisher & Harrison, 2000; Young, 1991).

Social psychological contracts have been the subject of intense renegotiation when one examines the professional literature on gender and racioethnic issues (see Plumwood, 1993; Gilligan, 1982). The contracts between males and females and between the majority population and different races and ethnicities are undergoing profound changes. The psychological contracts within each group are also being renegotiated. For example, women differ among themselves on such issues as abortion and the death penalty; men have differences on what it means to be a man; African Americans differ among themselves on such issues as victimology and separatism; and Native Americans differ on the value of living on reservations. Each position on the issue generates a psychological contract with those advocating for it.

In discussing social psychological contracts, it is important to be aware of their existence in everyday life because they clearly function in significant ways. As far as consulting is concerned, psychological contracts are a significant component of all consultations and critical and defining components in many consulting experiences. For that reason, it is important to have an incisive understanding of what psychological contracts are in consultation and how they function in this professional practice. The psychological contracts that are formed and exist between minorities and the larger social systems are significantly different from those formed with a majority population. The situation is not rectified in the workplace to any significant degree in that women, racio-ethnic minorities, and people with disabilities continue to experience inequalities (e.g., Brief, 1998; Schuman, Steeh, & Bobo, 1985). Because of this, consultants will need to work hard during the formulation of the psychological contract to understand the impact of those various psychological contracts on consultees and clients who experience these inequities.

Psychological Contracts in Counseling and Consultation

As stated, most professional consultations will have some type of formal contract either in written or in oral form. Regardless of the presence of a formal contract, consultations always have an informal contract known as a psychological contract (Schein, 1969, 1987, 1999). The psychological contract is both a type of implied contract and a process in which consultants are assessing a myriad of variables present in the consultee and the consultee's organization or system. The psychological contract is first formulated while the consultant is determining the "lay of the land." On a more global level, the psychological contract is essentially a name given for an often silent and ongoing interpersonal process with consultees and clients during a time when consultants are forming effective working relationships. Even though the psychological contract does not occur in written form, both consultants as well as consultees and clients essentially agree to be able to work together through this mechanism.

The structure and function of the psychological contract is likely familiar to most mental health professionals. For example, the psychological contract in counseling is implied in the nature of the business of professional counselors, psychologists, social workers, psychiatric nurses, and marriage and family therapists. Most clients going in for counseling have some idea that the process will likely include a discussion of painful experiences. Once there, clients and counselors engage in a process that establishes the "timing and nature" of the discussion. The framing of this psychological contract is more or less tied to the strength of the counselor/client relationship and to the stage of the counseling process. In other words, a counselor and a client might "agree" that they will not immediately begin their counseling relationship with a thorough and incisive discussion of the client's painful feelings about a lost relationship. This discussion would wait until the counselor and/or client determines that the timing is right for such an undertaking. This timing is partially mitigated by an assessment of the counseling stage they are in and through an informal assessment of the "client's readiness." Yet, this "agreement" is an unspoken one. And since counselors almost always eventually confront the clients' painful feelings when appropriate, the "agreement" needs to be renegotiated in an ongoing fashion. Sometimes the renegotiation of a psychological contract in counseling takes the form of immediacy and confrontation. For example, when a counselor comments to a client that the client seems reluctant to discuss a painful feeling, there is the introduction of a new element to the original contract: The new element suggests that the counselor believes it is time for this discussion to occur, and this changes certain aspects of the original psychological contract.

THE TWO PSYCHOLOGICAL CONTRACTS IN CONSULTATION

There are two significant types of psychological contracts in consultation. One contract exists between consultants and consultees, and the other exists between consultees (organizations) and their client/client systems (employees) (Astrachan & Astrachan, 2000). In many situations, consultants will need to have an understanding of both contracts. Regarding the contract between consultants and consultees, it has already been stated that parts of the psychological contract will be manifested in a formal written contract. Nevertheless, there are critical components and underlying assumptions that affect consultants and are related to the psychological contract with consultees that are reflected in sections of a formal contract. Hence, they are not recorded.

The earlier discussion about social psychological contracts in U.S. culture clearly suggests that any psychological contracts that are developed during the process of consultation will have numerous levels of equal complexities. Many mental health professionals endeavor to comprehend such complexities of psychological contracts every day in their work with clients. So, it will come as no surprise to know that as complex as the psychological contracts are in consultation, consultants will not likely have to remember what they are or how they are formed effectively. The interpersonal complexities involved in a psychological contract are mirrored in the research on it. There is a dearth of research about the psychological contract in the professional literature—although it is doubtful that any consultant would negate its presence or its impact in the consulting process. Empirically measuring psychological contracts and their impact on the consulting process present some difficult methodological problems. For instance, deciding on a unified definition of "psychological contract" is almost impossible. Attempting to measure the ostensible effects of such a covert and unspoken contract appears equally difficult. The very act of talking with the consultee about what is contained in a psychological contract begs the question because the discussion can no longer be about an "unspoken contract." Thus, any conclusions drawn from an assessment of the psychological contract are subject to serious flaws in interpretation and experimenter (or consultant) bias. It seems understandable why there is a dearth of empirical research on the topic. Although no research to date has documented the effectiveness of consultants' abilities to understand the psychological contract, it also seems plausible to acknowledge that the better consultants are in understanding the psychological contracts involved in their work, the more successful the consultation is likely to be.

Bifocal Conceptualization

There are numerous instances where consultants are not dealing directly with the clinical aspects of consultees or clients, and yet a psychological contract still exists between consultant and consultee. The consultant is attempting to glean an in-depth understanding of the consultee's world so that an accurate assessment of both the consultee and the client system can be undertaken. In the formulation of the psychological contract, the consultant listens to the consultee's explanation of the events while attempting to understand the consultee's worldview, her or his views of the current situation, as well as the views that might be held by the larger client system. By "splitting" vision and focusing on these three aspects, consultants can then formulate a more incisive understanding of the situation.

One might think of this "splitting of vision" as wearing a pair of bifocal glasses. The "close-up lens" magnifies the elements of the psychological contract that reflects the developing consultant/consultee relationship. The "distance lens" magnifies the psychological contract that exists between the consultee and the client/client system. Using the "close-up lens" allows consultants to assess what the consultee wants and what avenues will ultimately be available to the consultant in the process. That lens also allows the consultant and consultee to determine the "goodness of fit" for the consultation. Using the "distance lens" allows consultants to conceptualize the broader range of issues that the consultant is presenting. For instance, in first talking with a principal (consultee) about presenting a workshop for motivating students, a consultant might sense that it is the teachers who are having difficulty with motivation and resent the principal's strict, micro-management style of leadership. Without some conceptualization of the context for the request, the consultant might have gone on to design a workshop only to find the participants resisting. Worse, the teachers might resent the experience.

Although relevant in this example with the principal, an incisive understanding of all of a consultee's unconscious motivations is not necessary nor appropriate for any given consultation. The awareness of this unspoken contract of understanding does seem to increase knowledge of how the consultant/consultee relationship will likely proceed. Another benefit is that it allows for a more accurate prediction of barriers that might impede the process. Using another example, if the psychological contract between a director and staff of a mental health agency reflects micro-management and a rigid top-down style, a consultant could anticipate resistance from the client or client system within that agency. The resistances may not occur across the board because there may well be staff members who respond positively to that style. However, there will clearly be some staff members who take overt or covert umbrage with that particular style. As a result, a consultant might be caught in between needing to satiate both groups who appear to oppose each other. Knowledge of this potentiality can aid consultants in formulating diagnostic interventions with an intention of diminishing the distance and resistance inherent in the system. As you would expect, which focus is germane to which consulting situation is quite varied.

Consultants can conceptualize both psychological contracts similar to the way that Bateson (1951) conceptualized communication. Bateson proposed using the idea of "report" and "command" levels to examine the communication patterns of family members. For him, the "report" level is simply the superficial behavior level indicating the content level of what has been said. "Please clean up your room" would be the report level. Bateson maintains that this same statement carries an implied understanding about "what will happen if you don't." This is the "command" level—the level that structures the rule for the exchange. Although not every communication carries with it the punitive nuance as this example depicts, Bateson believes that every communication categorically has these two levels.

Psychological contracts operate in a similar fashion. They carry with them both overt and covert levels of communication. A teacher who requests aid from a school counselor/consultant to help with a problem student or parent is also implying information about what is going to happen if help does not come. The unspoken consequence reflects some psychological contract that exists. For instance, suppose a teacher insists on help from a school counselor. The teacher explains to the school counselor that there are many students who seem to resent almost anything the teacher suggests in the way of help. In describing the situation, the teacher uses guilt to elicit help from the school counselor by implying that the school counselor should help. Requesting help through guilt may be isomorphic for what happens in the teacher's classroom and may be a significant contributing factor escalating the problem. An effective consultant usually can and does sense this. This understanding then becomes part of the intervention for the school counselor, who might work with the reasons the teacher uses guilt to motivate and how that might be occurring in the classroom to the detriment of everyone, including the teacher.

When an administrator of a local community mental health agency calls and requests a consultant to come in and provide ongoing case consultation, the prospective consultant should immediately become curious as to other dimensions of the request. The request looks quite legitimate through the "close-up lens," but it may be that the real issue is that the agency is coming up on a grant compliance review and is delinquent in having this type of consultation occur. This more subtle level has significant implications for the consulting process, and it underscores the importance of consultants conceptualizing consultations through two lenses.

Contextual Dimensions of the Psychological Contract

Transmitting Core Basic Assumptions and Values among Cultures.   The role that values play during the formulation of the psychological contract is important to consider. As Rokeach (1960) stated, the fundamental context for any and all interactions between people ultimately includes the individuals' core basic assumptions, including their views about the universe, the world, and their positions in it. Ultimately, the various individuals' core basic assumptions and worldviews help shape the organizational culture that develops.

LeVine (1967) and Ogbu (1978) discuss a process by which various cultures transmit core assumptions related to getting ahead in the workplace across generations. The transmission process, known as *folk theory,* underscores the significant effects of core basic assumptions and how they guide minority (and majority) views of and subsequent behavior aimed at getting ahead. Although work is valued in the culture of the United States, there are differing values placed on the importance of work. Some view work as a positive experience and an opportunity for expression. Others see it as a means to an end. Still other workers do not see the relevance of work. This is especially true if they do not believe that they can get ahead. It is important to see the diversity within diverse populations because the implications for consulting are significant. For instance, Hong, Morris, Chui, and Benet-Martinez (2000) and Rosenberger (1992) state that cultural responses are often context dependent. Moreover, there is a growing recognition that individuals' concepts about themselves are inextricably woven with their social situations and relational domains.

Gushue and Constantine (2003, p. 11) and Markus and Kitayama (1991) maintain that in certain cultures, being able to adapt and adjust oneself to meet the various role demands and expectations across differing contexts is a sign of interpersonal strength. For instance, Gomez, Fassinger, Prosser, Cooke, Mejia, and Luna (2001) note that many of the Latinas they interviewed reported cultural differences in their behaviors at home and at work. One of the conclusions drawn by Gushue and Constantine is that one should not assume that African American women, for example, who present for counseling or consultation are necessarily endorsing a cultural perspective commonly attributed to their group (i.e., collectivism). These same researchers state that some of the beliefs, attitudes, and values that may motivate African American women may be specific to their presence and survival at particular settings. The results of these studies underscore the necessity of consultants paying particular attention to the cultural values of their consultees and clients during the formulation of the psychological contract.

Structural Dimensions

Goodness of Fit.   A psychological contract between consultants and consultees can be conceptualized as not only having two focal points but two dimensions as well. One dimension of the psychological contract relates to an initial and reciprocal assessment of the personal characteristics of consultants and consultees with an aim toward finding a "good match." This "goodness of fit" will likely determine if the consultant and consultee can agree on the services that are wanted and determine the ability of the consultant to deliver appropriate services. The second dimension relates to the need for an ongoing and negotiated understanding between the consultant and consultee as to how the consultation is progressing. Thus, the psychological contract commences in the initial conversations with the consultee prior to an agreement for services as well as occurring throughout the consultation. In essence, after the dimensions of the psychological contract are documented orally or in writing in a formal contract, whatever is left is grist for the mill. Key is an understanding of whether consultees' desires and wants actually match what consultees are able and willing to do.

Components of the Psychological Contract

Schein (1999) suggests that the formulation of the psychological contract with consultees be started as early as possible in the consulting process. From earlier discussion, one can clearly see the need for this assessment to be initiated early in the process.

Aside from the overall assessment of the "goodness of fit," the psychological contract between consultant and consultee will include a conceptualization of the working relationship between them. This notion is similar to the fit between a counselor and client. Research appearing in professional publications underscores the need for good rapport to exist between consultant and consultee (see Bergan, 1977; Bergan & Kratochwill, 1990; Myrick, 1977). In general, consultants want to assess the consultee and client/client system along the following two broad dimensions:

1. The nature of the relationship between the consultant and the consultee
2. The nature of the relationship between the consultee and the client/client system

There are five components of the nature of the relationship, and there are two components that help consultants conceptualize the relationship between the consultee and the client/client system. Primarily, consultants are interested in the *consultee's openness*. This will include an assessment of the degree of openness to the consultation itself, an assessment of the degree of openness to the consultant, and an assessment of the degree of openness to the process that will develop. In a consulting with a single consultee and a single client in a school or community mental health agency, the degree of consultee openness will be relevant to the intervention.

The second component in the psychological contract relates to the *consultee's issues of power and control*. This dimension, of course, will have far-reaching effects in terms of conceptualizing the consulting problem. One element of this dimension concerns the relationship of power and control as they relate directly to the consultee's relationship with the consultant. Another element of this dimension will be reflected in the *consultee's descriptions of the interactions with the client/client system*. During this discussion, consultants need to be listening to consultees for clues reflecting to the extent to which the consultee is attempting to "overcontrol" or "undercontrol" the client/client system. The issues of power and control may not be an appropriate or relevant change target for any given consultation, but these issues clearly impact the process and the consultant's conceptualizations of the problem.

The third component of the psychological contract relates to an assessment of the *consultee's unconscious and/or hidden agenda(s)*. Consultees can have agendas that may be somewhat obscure, ill defined, or even hidden from themselves and the consultant, and these need to be identified and addressed in some manner during the formulation of the psychological contract. More often than not, the forces that are operating in and around organizations are complex and difficult to ascertain. Consultees may be attempting to solve one problem, but their lack of awareness of the impact of other variables can create situations where the solutions they seek actually exacerbate other problems. In other situations, consultees may be attempting to "go through the motions" when it comes to getting consulting help—even though it may appear to the consultant that there is a serious effort being made on the part of the consultee.

An assessment of the *consultee's independence and dependency issues* is the fourth component in the psychological contract. This relates to the client's openness and his or her issues of power and control. Rather than significantly affecting their relationship with the client/client system, consultees' issues along this dimension will likely be most apparent in the relationship with the consultant. A consultee may portend to be staunchly independent only to suddenly switch gears and appear to be obsequious during a particularly difficult decision-making time during the consulting process.

The fifth component relates to the *consultee's strengths and flexibility*. It is a good idea to draw on the strengths of consultees and client/client systems. Assuming this position greatly enhances the rapport with consultees and client/client systems and it allows for more "solution-focused approaches" to be considered.

In addition to an assessment of the relationship between consultant and consultee, the second mainstream assessment centers on the consultant's conceptualizations of his or her ability to actually access the client/client system. This accessibility relates to the client system and its *physical, emotional, and structural availability*. Remember, the first contact is often conducted with the consultee. As such, the client/client system is usually one step away from the consultant. This implies that any access to the client/ client system will be initiated and mitigated through the consultee. It is difficult to ask for consultation in many cases because it suggests a weakness to some (Caplan & Caplan, 1993). Consultees may be conflicted so that on the one hand, they need and want help, and on the other hand, they are simultaneously concerned and fearful of the process. Given that potentiality, consultees may often covertly resist the consultant's attempts to access the client/client system. As in the case of counseling, consultants who spend time developing rapport and trust can help consultees loosen their grip on their employee/clients where and when it is appropriate. Ensuring that, in fact, the particular client/group needing attention is actually available physically is a first step to gaining access, and this should be addressed at the outset of the psychological contract. Extreme loyalty to the consultee can also present a situation where clients and client systems may resist the consultant's attempts to help them change. This type of "access" is more subtle than that related to the client's physical availability, but no less significant and impactful on the consulting process.

■ ■ ■ ■ ■

CASE STUDY ONE
THE PSYCHOLOGICAL CONTRACT

There are occasions when the initial discussions aimed at establishing a formal written contract are interrupted by what is uncovered during the formulation of the psychological contract with the consultee. For instance, I was asked to consult with a governmental agency. During the initial face-to-face discussions, it was determined that the consultee had identified the problem as being one of low morale among his staff members. As a result, he wanted a one-day workshop aimed at elevating employee morale. During the course of this initial discussion, the consultee also revealed that he was going through a bitter divorce and that his morale was clearly being affected. Given what the consultee had revealed, I was hesitant to conduct a workshop aimed exclusively at the employees. So, I suggested that perhaps it might be a good idea to talk again with the consultee to better clarify the "real" issues. At that point, the consultee became somewhat defensive and reiterated his desire for a one-day workshop aimed at the employees. Again, I suggested that both the consultee and I rethink the situation so that both of us would be in agreement. If the consultee desired another meeting, he could phone and set one up. Moreover, if the consultee wanted to interview another consultant, I could provide the names of several good consultants. As a gesture of good will and to help enhance the credibility of consultation in general, I stated that if the consultee did not wish to pursue work with me, there would be no charge for the initial consultation meeting. If the consultee wanted to proceed, the initial meeting would be billed. The consultee never called back.

In this case study, the consultant conceptualized the issues differently than did the consultee. The suggestion that the consultee may have, in fact, been a part of the issue that needed solving clearly was not what the consultee wanted to hear. As a result, the psychological contract that was being formed between the consultant and the consultee implied that the consultant needed to perform what the consultee wanted—regardless of how the consultant conceptualized the issue. The consultant determined the consultee's unconscious or hidden agenda as being "I am always in charge. I have already diagnosed my own problems and the problems with my staff, and I want you (consultant) to agree with my assessment and do exactly what I am asking." Clearly, consultees have every right to make such a statement. It is up to consultants to assess the psychological contract being formed with consultees and to determine if the work can be performed under those psychological conditions. The problem in this case with the psychological contract being formulated was that the consultant assessed the consultee as being rigidly fixed on his own hypothesis while seeming to be quite resistant to entertaining any other interpretations for the situation. Even if the workshop approach had been agreed upon, it was this issue of the consultee's rigidity that indicated that trouble might lie ahead if the consultation had been pursued.

One may ask at this point, "Why couldn't the consultant simply do what the consultee asked?" Some consultants could and would have executed the workshop. However, in this case, the consultant's values came into conflict with the consultee's values. The consultant, as does Schein (1999), valued the belief that it is often very difficult for supervisors to accurately diagnose their own problems. Therefore, upon entry into the initial discussion with the consultee, the consultant already had some concerns about the accuracy of the diagnosis and wanted to pursue a discussion with the consultee. In the process, the consultant recognized that the consultee's deeper wish was to have his ideas not questioned. The consultant then determined that if there was a morale problem, the consultee's rigidity may have had a significant impact in helping to create the problem. As such, the consultant had questions about the efficacy of performing a workshop in which this issue would likely not be addressed. For the consultant, it was a question of efficacy: "Would a workshop actually work?" When the consultee maintained his rigidity, the consultant was not in a psychological position to follow through with the consultation. Interestingly, the consultant heard many months later that a workshop had been conducted and was seen by most employees as "helpful." So, while the consultant did not feel comfortable with the consultee's diagnosing, the consultee's perceptions were accurate so that a workshop did help diminish the morale problem. This situation underscores the influence of consultants' values and the role they play in the psychological contract.

SUMMARY

Psychological contracts operate in all aspects of people's lives and therefore operate in the consulting process. The contracts that are formed in consultation are significant ones. The notion of a formal written or oral contract has legal and ethical implications. As mentioned, the formal contracts that mental health professionals will likely come into contact with will be standard ones. Far more important is the ground upon which the psychological contract is formulated in the process. In some cases, the information gleaned during the forming of this contract will not be directly relevant to the consultant's work. However, there is the presence of psychological contracts in all consultations and they do influence the process to greater or lesser degrees.

The two significant dimensions that should concern consultants are those contracts that involve the consultant/consultee relationship and the one operating between consultees and the client/client system. In many ways, many of the psychological contracts that have been developed between consultees (employers) and clients (employees) have been undergoing fundamental changes over the past several decades. Such phenomena as corporate takeovers, massive layoffs, right-sizing, and relocating corporate offices have impacted the covert understandings that have been guiding interactions in the workplace. Even though many mental health professionals may not undertake organizational development on a large scale, these changes do affect individuals and their orientations at work. Since most formal consultations take place in an organizational venue of some type and at some level, it is important for consultants to have at least a cursory understanding of some of the larger contextual issues surrounding the workplace. In only a few cases will these psychological contracts be insignificant factors in the consulting process.

The psychological contracts operating between different genders and racioethnic groups will almost always be significant factors in any interactions that occur during the consulting process. Consultants need to be aware of the dimensions of those unspoken contracts in order to be able to mitigate unintentional gender and racial biases. Research strongly suggests that minority values at home may actually shift at the workplace. Therefore, consultants should not assume that the homework they have done on diversity and diverse value systems necessarily rolls over categorically to the workplace. Adaptability to situational cultures is seen as a strength in some cultures.

In the formulation of psychological contracts, the values held by consultants, consultees, and clients all play a significant role. In fact, Gallessich (1982) warns consultants against proceeding with a formal contract in consultations where there is "significant incompatibility" on fundamental difference of values between consultant and consultee. These values are driven by basic core assumptions and are reflected in the ensuing behaviors of all consulting participants. This was exemplified in the case study discussed. Because consultants always work with consultee and client value systems on some level, it is imperative to have an understanding of the roles that different values play in the process. In the case example, the consultee and I (consultant) conceptualized the issue and subsequent solutions differently. Each conceptualization was borne out of each individual's respective core basic assumptions. I assessed the consultee as not doing enough "work on himself." For his part, the consultee held the basic orientation that home and work need to be separated. For him, there was no room for personal problems to be discussed at work. This was one of the consutlees's core beliefs that had been embedded in the organization's culture. For the consultant valuing personal growth in the workplace, this was a conflict that eventually led to not pursuing the consultation.

QUESTIONS

1. What is the major difference between a formal contract and a psychological contract?

2. What are social psychological contracts?

3. Why is the psychological contract so critical to the consulting process?

4. What are the two psychological contracts operating in consultation?

5. What are the major components of the psychological contract?

CHAPTER SIX

GENDER, DISABILITIES, RACIOETHNICITY, AND THE PSYCHOLOGICAL CONTRACT

Diversity and the psychological contract are discussed together in this chapter based on the idea that one aspect of the consulting process is, indeed, a social change process that takes place in a work venue. This is a social activist perspective, and an important concept to entertain because of the ethical implications of diversity and social change relevant to the consulting process. It is not ethical for consultants to reinforce values that promote gender and racioethnic oppression. To avert potential improprieties in ethical decision making, consultants need to enhance their understanding of both gender and racioethnic perspectives as well as the economic and social pressures operating in the workplace around racioethnicity and gender.

To date, there has been a paucity of empirical research conducted on diversity and consultation (Brown, Pryzwansky, & Schulte, 2001). Yet, when one sees the significance of the psychological contract, one also sees the need for consultants to have an incisive understanding of and appreciation for the diversity of individuals and the values to which they adhere. This is because the psychological contract is so crucial to the process of determining the nature, type, scope, breadth, and downstream implications of the interventions that ensue. Because the psychological contract is essentially formulated through an interpersonal process, effective consultants need also to be acutely aware of their own worldviews in order for the process of formulating the psychological contract to be more fully genuine and effective.

Effective consultants need to challenge themselves by entertaining paradigms of diversity that stretch their cognitive and affective domains. Without sensitivity to diversity, the psychological contract may contain dimensions of bias and prejudice that may be unconscious to the consultant and perhaps to the consultee as well. A result can be a reinforcement of the status quo, which is not the goal. Torres-Rivera, Smaby, and Maddux (1998) maintain that more needs to be known by mental health professionals about the socioeconomic status, education, language, employment, and health characteristics of Latino clients in order to work more effectively with this group. It seems logical to assume the same would be true for the need to have a broader understanding of the similar influences that would affect gender and racioethnic groups.

Formal consultation is aimed at increasing the work effectiveness of consultees and clients. Because of that fact, the financial bottom line is involved at some level and to some degree in every consultation. This impact on the bottom line occurs without respect to gender and racioethnicity. As has been pointed out, not every formal consultation will be aimed at directly affecting the bottom line as a forefront issue. In fact, this may not even be addressed directly or indirectly at all. Nonetheless, effective consultation requires consultants to be aware of issues that can affect the overall consulting process and subsequent bottom line. The issue of gender is one such concern because if any one worker is not living up to her or his potential, it stands to reason that the bottom line is already being affected.

A simple consultation with a teacher regarding a problem student may not appear to have direct implications to the bottom-line notion until one considers the further reaches of the consultation. As the teacher becomes more effective at handling the student, that student's learning should increase. As that occurs, that individual student's test scores should theoretically increase and will impact the overall test score average for the school, which ultimately impacts teachers' salaries for performance. The student's newly developed participation can help the entire learning environment in the classroom. In a mental health agency, the same scenario can be seen to occur. The better the counselor becomes at diagnosing or at handling cases as a result of consultation, the more efficient counseling becomes, and the number of individuals receiving effective help can increase. This is reflected in the more efficient use of resources.

Although these examples may seem far-fetched in terms of configuring the impact of consultation on the financial bottom line, it is hard to argue against these notions. As such, any overt and covert issues that serve to hinder the bottom line are seen as inefficient and affect the bottom line adversely. Some of the issues relate to biases and prejudices regarding gender, racioethnicity, and disabilities. When these structural oppressive barriers exist, bottom lines are always affected to some degree.

GENDER AND DISABILITY ISSUES IN CONSULTATION

The issue of gender in consultation is a significant one. This is especially true given the latest statistics published by the United States Department of Labor through the Bureau of Labor Statistics (U.S. Department of Labor, 2000).

- The number of women workers between 1990 and 2000 has increased 25 percent.
- The number of women working in elementary and secondary schools has increased 61 percent.
- The number of women working in social services has increased 81 percent.
- The number of women working in individual and family services has increased 78 percent.
- The total number of women working in managerial services has increased 32 percent.

Barriers in the Workplace

Glass Ceilings.   The increase of women over age 16 in the workplace has been a trend since the 1970s and is seen as the main cause behind the overall rise in the employment rates (Bureau of Labor Statistics, 2000). This sounds like very good news for women of all racioethnic minorities. However, a review of the professional literature on women in the workplace indicates that serious issues remain. A so-called glass ceiling continues to exist in the corporate world in spite of all of the changes that occurred in the last decades of the twentieth century. For example, according to Gilbert, Stead, and Ivancevich (1999):

- Only 14 percent of sales managers are women.
- The number of women serving on corporate boards is slightly under 7 percent of the total membership of the Top 1,000 organizations.
- Ninety-five percent of senior-level managers in the largest U.S. organizations are men.
- It will take 475 years for parity to be achieved between men and women in top-level managerial and administrative positions.
- Less than 3 percent of federal government contracts go to women.

According to Baxter and Wright (2000), the *glass ceiling* is one of the more compelling metaphors that reflect the inequalities that women face in the workplace. Essentially, the metaphor suggests that although women may actually make it through the front door of managerial hierarchies, they will eventually hit an invisible barrier that serves to block their advancement to upper-management. It is important to understand that the metaphor applies to women as a group who face almost insurmountable barriers to achieving upper-management status *because they are women* (Morrison, White, & Van Velsor, 1987, p. 13). The issue of the glass ceiling has always been a critical one, but never as important as it might be now because of the increase in women working outside the home environment.

The reasons for the paucity of female managers in business settings vary. Some research, however, suggests that the problems may start in the graduate training programs for business. For instance, Stevens and Brenner (1990) suggest that business schools may not be effectively training women to become managers because many training methods may be based on fundamental biases toward women. These same authors go on to state that, as a result, many women may be "grateful for mere acceptance [in a job] and do not expect to surpass males in either authority or position" (p. 885). Ohlott, Ruderman, and McCauley (1994) suggest that one reason so few women have been promoted to senior-level management positions is because they experience fewer developmental job opportunities during their careers than do men.

The importance of having "challenging experiences" for women to advance upward is underscored in the research of McCauley (1986), McCauley, Ohlott, and Ruderman (1989), and McCauley, Ruderman, Ohlott, and Morrow (1994). The challenging experiences for women include, among other things, situations where women can have an opportunity to turn around a business that is in trouble and the opportunity to start a business from scratch. Van Velsor and Hughes (1990) find that certain types of job assignments and challenging experiences are less available for women in the workplace and make it more difficult for women to get the training needed to advance. The women in their survey reported that the nature and scope of their job assignments were more limited than that of their male counterparts, and the experiences seen as "stepping-stones" for advancement were also more available for men (Morrison, White, & Van Velsor, 1987; Van Velsor & Hughes, 1990).

More controversial findings are stated in the research of Maupin (1993). Citing earlier works of Brenner, Tomkiewicz, and Schein (1989) and of Hennig and Jardim (1977), Maupin describes *person-centered* explanations and *situation-centered* explanations for the lack of women in senior-level management positions. Briefly, the person-centered explanations suggest that it is the female socialization practices that encourage the development of personality traits and behavior patterns that are contrary to the demands of the managerial role. The situation-centered explanations emphasize the nature of the work environment faced by women. That is, rather than it being a problem with socialization, it is a problem of organizations.

There may be discriminatory personnel practices regarding gender and the perceived "gender appropriateness" of a given occupational position. Maupin gathered written comments from 188 male accountants and 184 female accountants. Results indicate that men perceive the scarcity of women in senior-level partnership positions as a result of person-centered variables and less a function of organizational or situation-centered variables. On the contrary, the most common response of the women interviewed reflected a belief that their lack of mobility was due to the situation-centered variables. Specifically, the women claimed that, at least in the field of accounting, the senior-level positions were seen as masculine and therefore inappropriate for women. This was coupled by the perception that sexual harassment also exists concomitant with a belief held by women that women are exhausted from having to be a mother, a housewife, and a professional accountant (Maupin, 1993). Although the sample in the Maupin study included accountants, it may be important to consider the themes of her findings as they might relate to other occupations.

Given the increase of women in the work force and the information regarding the status of female managers, it would seem that there needs to be a concomitant decrease in the structural and interpersonal barriers that continue to inhibit the free expression and acknowledgment of abilities of all women in the workplace. In spite of the obvious benefits to having every worker perform up to her or his potential, a review of the professional literature suggests that women of all racioethnicities continue to face serious barriers in the workplace. Since many consultees will be women, consultants need to be able to discern such contextual issues during the formulation of the psychological contract. This helps consultants understand the interaction effect occurring between consultees/clients and their environments. Interventions can be more appropriately planned.

Potential Gender Bias in Consultation. Research also demonstrates that the attitudes of male co-workers is one of the greatest barriers facing women managers who strive to develop organizational careers with possibilities for advancement (Burke,

1994; Burke & McKeen, 1992; Morrison, 1992; O'Leary & Ickovics, 1992). Moreover, Burke (1994) maintains that "men are not likely to be supportive of initiatives to develop women's careers and may actively endorse views of backlash" (p. 1128). Even hiring practices can affect women negatively. For example, Heilman, Kaplow, Amato, and Stathatos (1993) state that women who perceive themselves as being hired based on their gender rather than on their qualifications would tend to report negative self-perceptions of competence. Gilbert and Stead (1999) reveal similar results in reporting that women hired under affirmative action mandates suffered increased levels of job stress, experienced less job satisfaction, and selected less-demanding work assignments. Aside from the impact of hiring practices, gender also appears to function in organizations as a powerful independent bias. Jobs are grouped into separate promotion ladders and clustered into positions on the ladder that afford little chance for promotion (Hood & Koberg, 1994).

Finally, Ragins and Sundstrom (1989) state that women in powerful positions face two forms of gender-role conflicts. One conflict relates to the incompatibility of gender and power, and the other conflict relates to conflicting expectations regarding work role and gender role. These same authors also maintain that male subordinates, peers, and supervisors may also experience gender-role conflict as a consequence of having women in positions adjacent to theirs. Consultants need to listen closely to female consultees and clients who are in positions of power to help determine attitudes related to these potential conflicts.

Feminism and Technology

There is little question that the United States is a country that is technologically advanced. Many assume this is a good position in which to be. What often goes unnoticed is an examination of the significant core basic assumptions lying beneath a value of technology. Habermas (1970) claims that the philosophical roots of technology reflect that (mother) nature is seen as capricious, wild, unpredictable, and hostile. Examples that tend to support this view include the devastation caused by earthquakes, monsoon rains, hurricanes, tornados, and the like. According to Habermas, it is logical that humans would want to tame nature. Therefore, for Habermas, the fundamental drive of technology is a drive toward domination of a hostile nature. This is especially true since nature is seen as such an enemy. In other words, technology is an attempt to free people from the arbitrary forces of nature, and the history of technology is a history of persistent attempts to address this threat as well as to lighten the burden of work and improve yield.

At first glance, this philosophical argument seems to have some merit—if not viewed as harmlessly entertaining. However, in the Western tradition, earth and nature have been proclaimed as feminine, and the implications are far from innocuous. Many primitive cultures as well as many contemporary cultures in the West relegate male characteristics to the sun and feminine characteristics to the moon. Moreover, in traditional Western culture, the heavens are seen as masculine (Heavenly Father) and the earth is affixed with feminine characteristics such as "earth mother" or "mother earth." If one were to reflect on this association more closely, it would be clear that an association with earth (as in earth mother) in a technological culture is not such a noble thing. In fact, being associated with something that needs to be dominated, such as a hostile earth, is not desirable. This is exactly what many feminists state. This perspective is reinforced by Plumwood (1997), who states that feminine "closeness with nature" has hardly been a compliment. She maintains that the Age of Enlightenment is a rationalist perspective and, because of that, is a masculine perspective—since masculinity and rationality are closely associated in the traditional Western culture. Plumwood argues that nature, since it is seen as hostile, is posited as the excluded and devalued contrast to reason, and the implications of such devaluing are devastating for women. Through a philosophical association with earth, women become the "excluded" environment against which "male achievement" takes place. According to Plumwood:

> Both rationality and nature have a confusing array of meanings; in most of these meanings reason contrasts systematically with nature in one of its many senses. Nature, as the excluded and devalued contrast of reason, includes the emotions, the body, the passions, animality, the primitive or uncivilized, the non-human world, matter, physicality and sense experience, as well as the sphere of irrationality, of faith and of madness. In other words, nature includes everything that reason excludes. (1993, pp.19–20)

Implications of Feminism and Technology.   Agreement or disagreement with the preceding philosophy is not the issue. The issue is that there are far more female teachers and school counselors than there are male counterparts. Subsequently, consultants of either gender who work in the schools will likely have numerous more female consultees than male consultees. Whether or not any given female teacher is aware of or cares about the "dangerous" association with earth, male consultants working with female consultees (and females in general) need to be very mindful of the further reaches of this association with technology and its covert and overt impact on females in traditional Western culture. One could surmise that this association is a fundamental reason why there is a "glass ceiling." However, that aside, the more important issue relates to the interactions that may occur between male consultants and female consultees and between female consultants and their male consultees. The basis of these interactions is founded on deep social core assumptions. Moreover, these assumptions clearly impact the foundations of the psychological contract. The important issue is for consultants, both female and male, to be sensitive to the overt and covert processes that impede the freedom of all women (and men) in the workplace.

Persons with Disabilities

Whereas there may be a dangerous association between women and technology, this is not the case for the 54 million persons with disabilities who live in the United States. In fact, regarding persons with disabilities, technology is considered "the great equalizer" that provides better opportunities to communicate, learn, participate, and achieve greater overall levels of independence. Of great significance is the idea that new technologies enable people with disabilities to perform at competitive levels with others in the workplace (National Organization on Disability, 2003). According to the State of the Union 2002 for Americans with Disabilities (National Organization on Disability, 2002), computer and Internet technology offers real hope for persons with disabilities. People who are deaf are using "instant messaging" to have real-time conversations. People who are blind use voice-synthesis technology to write and read documents and website information. Finally, people with disabilities who have difficulties getting to an office can use technology to work from home.

The term *disability* runs a wide gamut that can include mental and physical conditions; visible and nonvisible conditions; conditions that people are born with or develop during their lifetimes as a result of illness, age, accident, or attack; and conditions that have varying degrees of severity. All of these conditions meet one common criteria: They all in some way limit people's abilities to participate fully in one or more major life activities (National Organization on Disability, 2002). According to the State of the Union 2002 for Americans with Disabilities (National Organization on Disability, 2002), a clear majority of people with disabilities (63 percent) say that although life has improved since 1990, only 33 percent say that they are very satisfied with their life in general. This is alarming, given the fact that the minority group defined as people with disabilities is the only minority group existing where anyone can become a member.

The limitations for people with disabilities are not only relegated to those described in the preceding paragraph, but are placed on people with disabilities by a social/cultural structure in the United States that reinforces the notion that persons with disabilities cannot perform as well as persons without disabilities. Short of this, persons with disabilities face some other type of discrimination. For instance, 36 percent of persons with disabilities say that they have encountered some form of discrimination in the workplace due to their disabilities. The most often cited discrimination is reflected in not being offered the job for which they are qualified. Other discriminatory practices are mirrored in being denied workplace accommodations, being given less responsibility than co-workers, being paid less than other workers with similar skills, being refused a job promotion, and being refused a job interview. Perhaps, as a result, unemployment is one of the most profound issues facing the disability community. According to the National Organization on Disability (NOD) (2003), only 32 percent of persons with disabilities aged 18 to 64 are working (compared to the general population of 81 percent). Yet, two-thirds of those not working would like to do so. Even though the percentage of all people with disabilities who are working remained relatively stable from 1986 to 2000, there has been a significant increase in the percentage of people with disabilities who are able to and are working. Of those who are working, 20 percent say their jobs involve only a small amount or none of their full capabilities and talents.

Aside from moral and ethical concerns, consultants need to know something about persons with disabilities because, as mentioned, many times the disability is invisible. For instance, a learning disability is invisible to many except teachers. The same holds true for attention disorder hyperactivity disorder (ADHD). Given the number and types of successful programs in public schools to help those with these types of learning differences move through the educational system and on to productive work lives, it may well be that numbers of those with these types of disabilities are underinflated. This can and often does go unnoticed by employers. The main reason for this is likely due to the fact that a person who is learning disabled will not reveal his or her condition out of fear of discrimination. However, it may be that a large number of adults with learning disabilities are not aware of their condition (Vogel, 1998). According to the same researcher, there are "significant" numbers of adults in the United States who have learning disabilities. As such, consultees can have problems with their employees as a result and not even be aware of the origin of the problems. Thus, whenever problems that consultees discuss with consultants suggest the possibility of a learning disability, consultants should pursue such avenues of exploration.

Women, Persons with Disabilities, and the Psychological Contract

Consultants need to be aware of how they might unintentionally maintain or reinforce the status quo and subsequent plight of women and persons with disabilities by failing to understand their experiences in the workplace—regardless of whether the female and/or person with disabilities is a consultant, consultee, or client. Without paying attention to the experiences of these groups, a consultant may interact with a consultee in ways that may inadvertently (or deliberately) undermine the hopefulness of women and persons with disabilities in the workplace. With regard to women, for example, Ely (1995) states that there may be pressures on women to conform to stereotypic behaviors in organizations where there are few women employees. In addition, Ely asserts that in organizations where there are few women, those women who are present often display more "masculine traits," such as aggressiveness. (One of the issues here, of course, is whether males have a corner on such attributes as aggressiveness or whether women can be aggressive and still "considered" feminine.) Pressures to conform to stereotypic behaviors may or may not be appropriate for any given female in any given consulting situation. Nonetheless, it is at this level that consultants need to be open to a larger worldview in formulating a psychological contract with female consultees and clients.

If the consultant assesses subtle gender or disability bias early on in the formulation of the psychological contract with consultees, then subsequent interventions may "work" on one level but actually reinforce discrimination of women and persons with disabilities on another level. For example, suppose a male clinical director of a local mental health center requests a consultant to consult with staff members, many of whom are female. The consultee wants help in improving the efficiency of weekly staff meetings. In the initial conversations between consultant and consultee, the consultee mentions that "the meetings could be over and done with quickly except for the fact that most of my staff like to spend more time gossiping." As a result, the consultee believes that the staff meetings go on longer than they should. For this consultee, this situation is inefficient and precludes other agenda items from being discussed. Now, if the consultant were a female, how do you think she would react to the consultee's statements regarding "gossiping"? If the consultant were a male, how would he react to the consultee's conceptualization? In both cases, if the gender bias of "gossiping" were not addressed at some level during the formulation of the psychological contract, both consultant and consultee might aim to make the meetings "more efficient" by eliminating "gossiping." The result of such action could actually increase resistance to altering the structure of the meetings because of the premise that the problem was with the women. In fact, the problem may have been in the conceptualization: The conversations between staff members was being conceptualized as "gossiping" rather than as an informal exchange of work-related information and ideas.

Another example can be seen in the ways that traditional collectivist cultures view "gossip." Generally speaking, traditional Euro-American culture admonishes gossiping and views it as being deleterious to group and organizational functioning. However, according to McGoldrick (1998), gossiping serves an important function in many cultures. Cimmarusti (1996) agrees and states that in traditional Filipino culture, gossip is an intricate means of criticizing another without causing open conflict. Thus, assessing the consultee to be gossiping and judging the consultee to be rigidly adhering to that form of social control without understanding its contextual function would be poor practice for consultants. A consultant who was aware of the consultee's bias could address the issue during the initial phases of the psychological contract to ensure that the consultee was flexible and willing to entertain the possibility that the issue may not be one of "gossiping" at all. The consultant might address the issue directly by asking, "How do you know that the staff members are gossiping?" The consultant could also ask for a clarification about the meaning of "gossiping" while assessing the consultee's openness and flexibility.

In responding to the consultee, the consultant might say, "It has been my experience that this type of social interaction (gossiping) might actually be helping the staff members communicate about important things and feel more connected to one another. It might also be the case that some of your employees have undeclared learning disabilities that might necessitate the need for this type of interpersonal exchange." At that point, the assessment of potential gender and disability bias goes deeper. How would the situation have changed if the so-called gossiping were actually a learning method for one or more of the clinicians who had difficulties in reading emails and appreciated the auditory method of exchanging information?

Another example occurred during a consultation I conducted with a group of women professionals. A retreat or workshop format was used for this consultation, and during one part of the retreat, I was attempting to address the group as a whole. At that time, there were several female staff members involved in a discussion. I asked the individuals to be quiet, which caused unpleasant feelings among those who were talking. Before lunch, a few of the staff members came over to me and shared their anger and resentment at being told to "be quiet" when they were actually debriefing the exercise that had been just concluded. Rather than dealing directly with their concerns, I suggested that after lunch I would address the issue to the entire group. After lunch, I apologized to the whole group for my timing error and specifically apologized to "those who were having intense discussions about the day's work" when I interrupted them with my need to address the entire group. I assured the group that I would listen more closely to when they were ready for me to address them. It seemed as though the gesture was greatly appreciated by all. Later, one individual came up to me and shared that all her life she had had difficulty sitting still, holding attention for long periods of time, and reading. She told me she had an appointment with her doctor to see if she had ADHD. In leaving, she mentioned that she was "a bit embarrassed, but did not want me to think poorly of her."

RACIOETHNIC ISSUES IN CONSULTATION

Classification of Diversity in Organizations

According to Cox (1993) and Larkey (1996), the term *racioethnicity* is used in theory to denote the socially constructed combination of racial and cultural characteristics expressed in values, norms, and communicative behavior. It covers a range of identities across categories of race, national/cultural origins, and domestic as well as foreign ethnic identifications. Organizations might be classified along a continuum indicating their level of integration of diverse populations. There is what is referred to as the *monolithic organization.* This organization is seen as being nearly homogenous, with a limited number of minority employees. Even though affirmative action plans may be in place, these monolithic organizations reflect a subtle resistance to it. In this type of organization, members exhibit prejudice and discrimination in the form of pressure on minorities to conform or assimilate to the mainstream culture.

Another type of organization is the *plural organization.* In this organization, minority members are present in moderate numbers. Yet, they will hold down the lower-level jobs. Although accommodations may be in place to improve the hiring rates of minorities, once hired they are expected to conform to the majority population cultural mores and values (Nkomo, 1992). As in the monolithic organization, prejudice and discrimination still exist, but may be less intense. This type of organization can be seen as giving lip service to valuing diversity, fairness, and equality.

Consultants will often be working in these types of organizations where consultees and clients do not see themselves as discriminatory or prejudicial. This is a difficult situation with which to work. The reason for this is due to the fact that in the early stages of developing cultural acceptance, individuals tend to interpret differences negatively, minimize them in order to maintain their own worldview, or utilize other strategies to deal with differences other than true acceptance (Bennett, 1986). At the same time, minority members in these organizations acknowledge that they are in subtle ways at a disadvantage and know they are being left out of opportunities because of their differences.

The third type of organization is the *multicultural organization.* Here, minorities "are represented at all levels of the organization, and the expression of cultural ways of thinking and working are encouraged rather than suppressed" (Larkey, 1996, p. 466). Prejudice and discrimination are almost nonexistent. What replaces it is an environment in which employees encourage pluralism in ideas, communication, management styles, and ways of working.

Cox (1993) suggests that organizations may progress through these types as stages on a continuum. The important point for consultants is to recognize the type of organization to which consultees and clients belong. The issues of prejudice and discrimination that exist in monolithic and plural organizations may not be the focus of the consultation. Yet, these issues should be addressed on some levels, either indirectly or directly. When prejudice and discrimination are not the central focus, consultants need to be careful to align their diversity work as closely as possible with the prevailing organizational culture. In this fashion, consultee and client resistances may be lowered to appropriate levels for change to take place.

Typology of Racioethnic Minorities

As a consultant, you will be confronted with a variety of racioethnic consultees and clients. Ogbu (1978, 1988) and others (e.g., Attneave, 1982) have described minorities in terms of different types. Ogbu identifies and classifies three types of minorities in the United States and elsewhere. "*Autonomous minorities* are minorities in the numerical sense who may possess a distinct ethnic, religious, linguistic, or cultural identity" (Ogbu, 1988, p. 140). In general, autonomous minorities are not usually socially, economically, or politically subordinated. Ogbu states that Jews and Mormons are examples of autonomous minorities. *Immigrant minorities* are those who voluntarily move to the United States in order to improve their economic stature, social conditions, or political status (p. 140). Examples of immigrant minorities are the Chinese Americans in Stockton, California; the Punjabi Indians in Yuba City, California; and the Hispanic population in San Francisco. Ogbu asserts that these groups of minorities maintain their expectations of getting ahead and these expectations help them to negotiate the social, political, and economic barriers that they face once they arrive in the United States. The third minorities type is known as the caste-like or *involuntary* minorities. Ogbu states that this group is comprised of people who were originally brought in to the United States involuntarily through slavery, conquest, or colonization (p. 140). Currently, the American Indians, African Americans, Mexican Americans, and Native Hawaiians are "relegated to menial positions and denied true assimilation into the mainstream of American society" (p. 140), which maintains the caste-like system. Similar to the plight of women's deleterious association with nature, the caste-like system of minority populations is reinforced by core basic assumptions as well.

The New Managerial Class

As the philosophical assumptions of technology have had considerable implications for women, these same fundamental principles also have noteworthy implications for African Americans, Hispanic/Latino Americans, Native Americans, and Asian Americans. A subtle form of discrimination and prejudice likely operates in many organizations as a core basic assumption. Darity (1983) writes a compelling account of how technology and a technological mind-set are creating a *new class* of people in the workplace. This new class of workers is known as the "managerial class," and they are seen as operating with the "Law of the Progressive Elimination of an Undesirable Population." Essentially, this class is the technological intelligentsia who have steered the western economy from the pursuit of profit to a pursuit of scientific and technological know-how. In the business marketplace, managers now have the technological knowledge of the forces of production and administration, and the result is a battle over possession and ownership. There are significant implications for consultants. For instance, Darity (1983) maintains that the United States is witnessing a shift in power from owners to managers. Owners may *own* the businesses, but it is the managers who actually *possess* the businesses. The difference between ownership and possession needs to be understood during the formulation of the psychological contract.

In the larger social scheme, the new managerial class believes that society needs to be organized by people with technological expertise, intelligence, and wherewithal.

Moreover, the new managerial class locates itself in institutionally prestigious think tanks, universities, and the lower reaches of educational systems (e.g., classroom teachers and school counselors). *The aim of this new class is to provide new technology on how to manage large groups of people through such symbols as welfare, governmental regulatory agencies, guidance and counseling practices, social agencies, and the like.* Since the largest users of social services are women and minorities, Darity claims that the new class is learning how to manage these populations, which, in the end, leads to their progressive demise as productive members of society. Due to the 1990–2000 census statistics that reflect an increase of women into social and family services work venues, the implications are enormous.

Darity (1983) cites other examples that suggest that this notion of the progressive elimination of a surplus population should not be taken lightly. For instance, the old means of controlling the surplus population—such as spatial isolation of minorities in the nation's inner cities, utilizing a volunteer army that attracts minorities, and passing laws that seem to be related to an increase in the percentage of minorities in prison—have been supplanted in the last decades of the twentieth century. Currently, there is debate on the humanity of executions, euthanasia, genetic engineering, abortion, and policies for unwed mothers (the majority of whom are racioethnic minorities). All of these have significant and direct implications for racioethnic minorities. For example, building more prisons will enable the nation to house more African Americans. Genetic engineering is feared to become a gift for the elite and healthy and a bane for those identified as "undesirable." Executions target African Americans, since they are the group that makes up the overwhelming majority of death-row inmates. Other examples exist. For instance, policies for family violence are formulated by members of the new class, and most state laws currently advocate laws that can lead to the splitting up of families with domestic violence (Websdale, Sheeran, & Johnson, 1997). Many traditional African American families want to keep their families intact—given the high number of minorities in prison already. Thus, there is philosophical debate among the nation's leaders in the family violence movement as to how best to handle these cultural differences.

Should judges be trained to treat all families equal? Or, is it better not to telescope laws that address the cultural differences of families experiencing violence? In Los Angeles, there is an African American battered women's shelter where the women who come in are asked to think about the situation for a month before any restraining orders or charges are pressed. Action in whatever direction can take place after this "thinking period." Conversely, in a traditional Euro-Caucasian battered women's shelter, a restraining order and other legal action are almost an immediate undertaking. The shelter for African American women is based on the idea that since many young African American males are in jail, why would they want to continue to disintegrate families that are already disintegrating? This is an interesting and challenging notion.

Other minority populations are affected as well. For instance, one way in which Native Americans are "managed" by this new class is seen in the research of Tinker and Bush (1991), who maintain that Native Americans are seriously undercounted in unemployment figures reported for any particular locale in the United States. These undercounts "mask the reality of Native Americans' unemployment rates that are apparently, in some cases, almost twenty-times higher than what is reported by government agencies" (p. 119). The undercounts essentially serve to keep funding for federal programs that attempt to alleviate these problems at a less than adequate level. Although not necessarily "intentional," the management of Native American unemployment numbers is inconsistent and deleterious to this population. The notion of a managerial class, whose sole aim is to be the only class, and therefore have an aim to eliminate other classes, is rather alarmist. Yet, one would find it hard to fully refute the existence of this new managerial class. For example, Schuman, Steeh, and Bobo (1985) maintain that white opposition to governmental policies aimed at increasing opportunities for African Americans and other groups remains intense. This is especially true in areas of busing, open-housing laws, and various affirmative action efforts in education and employment.

Consultants need to be aware of the proclivity to "manage" consultees and clients in ways that lead to their progressive elimination. Similar to the nuances of technology and the feminine association with nature, the philosophical (and unconscious) assumptions on which this "new class" rests may well serve to diminish the hopefulness of African Americans and other racioethnic groups. It is not that anyone will get fired immediately. The significant and deleterious implications occur downstream, many years later.

Modern Racism and Gender Oppression

Sexism continues to be rampant in the world of work, and according to Swim, Aikin, Hall, and Hunter (1995), sexism and racism have a long history of association. Female abolitionists in the 1830s became incited by their inability to work as equals with male abolitionists, and began speaking out vehemently against the subjugation of African Americans and women in general. One hundred twenty years later, Hacker (1951) and others have noted differences between the status of women and African Americans and have argued that sufficient parallels exist to generalize findings of sexism to racism against African Americans. Swim and colleagues maintain that "national surveys on women's equality support the possibility of structural similarities between modern racism and modern sexism" (pp. 199–200). These same authors cite Sears's (1988) study that describes similarities between modern racism and modern sexism. Sears asserts the underlying beliefs of modern racism and sexism revolve around

- The denial of continuing discrimination
- Antagonism toward African American demands
- Resentment about special favors for African Americans

According to Sears, these same beliefs can be applied to women—and to persons with disabilities as well. Sears (1988) maintains that people may resent women, persons with disabilities, and African Americans because these groups have made demands for equality, demanded more political and economic parity, and have argued for the passage of antidiscrimination laws (p. 200). Similarities are also noted by Brief (1998), who cites the work of McConahay (1986) on racism. According to McConahay, the principal beliefs of a modern racism are as follows:

- Discrimination is a thing of the past because blacks now have the freedom to compete in the marketplace and to enjoy those things they can afford.
- Blacks are pushing too hard, too fast, and into places they are not wanted.
- These tactics and demands are unfair.
- Therefore, recent gains are undeserved. The prestige-granting institutions of society are giving blacks more attention and the concomitant status than they deserve.
- The first four beliefs do not constitute racism because they are empirical facts.
- Racism is bad.

According to Brief (1998), modern racists think racism is socially undesirable, yet they feel negatively toward African Americans, particularly because they believe that the gains made by African Americans were not earned. Although there has been some research that opposes the views of McConahay's work (e.g., Montieth, 1993; Montieth, Devine, & Zuwerink, 1993), Brief (1998) maintains that McConahay's views are largely accurate. When this research is coupled with that of Cox (1993), Larkey (1996), and Nkomo (1992), it is clear that consultants will be faced numerous times with overt and covert prejudice and discrimination in their work with consultees and clients.

Folk Theory about Getting Ahead

Shenhav (1992) found that during the years from 1982 to 1986, only 3 to 4 percent of managers in the United States were African Americans. Brief (1998) found that there were 52,000 allegations of discrimination in the workplace in the year 1992–1993 alone. According to the United States Census Bureau (U.S. Bureau of the Census, 2000), the real income of Caucasian families increased by 9 percent, whereas the real income of African American families did not change. The bureau also reported that in 1993, African Americans earned less than their Caucasian counterparts in all jobs at all levels. Similar to women and persons with disabilities, studies indicate that African Americans (and other minority groups) "do not proportionally occupy certain types of positions at work, particularly those above the bottom of organizational hierarchies (Brief, 1998, pp. 136–137).

LeVine (1967) promulgates the notion of "folk theory " to explain ways that many minorities think about getting ahead, and current researchers have used LeVine's ideas to help explain the plight of minorities in the workplace (see Ogbu, 1988; Reed & Noumair, 2000; Weis, 1985). Clearly, consultants who are working with racioethnic minorities need to be aware of differing approaches to work and getting ahead. Known as the "people's status mobility system," this theory holds that minorities tend to share a theory of getting ahead that is based on their past and present experiences. The theory becomes punctuated for any given minority group as long as the folk beliefs are confirmed by the actual experiences of the members. In the United States, the folk theory of success for minorities differs from the theory of success for the majority population, and Ogbu (1978, 1989) provides three reasons for the differences that lead to disadvantages for minorities. Primarily, there are *job ceilings* and other barriers limiting minority access to jobs, wages, and other societal benefits. Second, minorities are often subtly required to provide *additional qualifications for employment* aside from the traditional educational credentials. Finally, many minority members who face a persistent job ceiling tend to develop

> an *institutionalized discrimination perspective* or a belief that they cannot advance into the mainstream like the majority population (whites) by merely adopting rules of behavior for achievement and the cultural practices that work for white people. As a result, the minorities spend a good deal of time and effort attacking such rules of behavior for achievement or such criteria of selection for jobs and other societal positions defined by white Americans. (pp. 109–110)

Job Ceilings.   The notion of the existence of "glass ceilings" for women, persons with disabilities, and racioethnic minorities has enjoyed broad popular and professional recognition (see Gysbers, Heppner, & Johnston, 1998; Morrison, White, & Van Velsor, 1987). In reviewing the climate of organizations, these researchers state that women continue to face hostile environments in workplaces that often devalue them. Moreover, women continue to work in environments where informal networks exclude them and all but preclude effective mentoring of women. Racioethnic groups have not fared well in the workplace either. Instead of the "glass ceiling," minorities face "job ceilings." Brown, Minor, and Jepsen (1991) report that 75 percent of Hispanic/Latinos and 71 percent of Asian Pacific Islanders wished they had received more career planning assistance. In another study, Brown (1995) indicates that although African Americans represent approximately 12 percent of the general United States population, their average family income is 58 percent of that of Caucasians. Brown (1995) also states that African American teenagers have an unemployment rate that is double that of Caucasian teens.

The Women's Bureau of the U.S. Department of Labor (1997) cites some alarming statistics concerning the plight of African American women in the workforce. They are seen as having made great progress in terms of improving their economic status between 1986 and 1996. Unemployment for African American women went down over 4 percent (4.2 percent), teen unemployment dropped almost 9 percent (8.9 percent), and total employment rose by over one and one-half million persons (5.4 million to 7.1 million). Also, there was a significant increase in the total number of African American women employed in the higher-paying managerial/professional occupations. More African American women are owning their own businesses than ever before. Nonetheless, of those African American women who were working full time in 1996, they made only 88 percent of what their African American male counterparts earned in similar employment (U.S. Department of Labor, 1997). In addition, African American women made only 85 percent of what Euro-Caucasian women in similar employment situations made and only 62 percent of what Euro-Caucasian males made in similar situations. Hispanic women continue to have a lower participation rate in the workforce than either Euro-Caucasian or African American women.

One of the offshoots of folk theory for minorities is that, in their efforts to pass through the job ceiling, some minorities may include alternative strategies that are not necessarily approved by the majority population of the particular organization in which they are working. Moreover, some of these strategies may, in fact, serve to hinder the chances of these minority groups from achieving success in school and mainstream employment simply because of the resistance of dominant groups. Consultees in monolithic and plural organizations may complain about some employees not "following the rules" or about the behavior of a minority individual. It would be important for consultants to determine the extent to which employees are attempting to utilize a strategy to circumvent the job ceiling, which may be backfiring on them. In this situation, the psychological contract could include some attention to working with these clients in order to help them strategize more "acceptable" means of moving up. However, these acceptable means need to work for the minorities involved. In order to enhance the probability that the strategies will work, it is helpful for consultants to have more contextual knowledge of the group with whom they are working. McWhorter (2000) offers some interesting insight into black American culture that can prove invaluable in consulting.

Theory of Self-Sabotage in Black America

McWhorter's (2000) work on racioethnic minorities helps provide some realistic hopefulness for change. Consultants can use this information to discern consultees' and clients' values during the formulation of the psychological contract. McWhorter extends the notion of folk theory and calls for a reworking of the current folk theories utilized by minorities. He does not believe in the idea that white racism is the true obstacle to black success and achievement; rather, he maintains that this notion is "all but obsolete." In its place, McWhorter advances three ideological manifestations that currently plague Black America: victimology, separatism, and anti-intellectualism. He also issues the warning that Black America is on a "tragic detour." To McWhorter, nothing short of profound adjustments in black identity will be needed. Consultants need to be able to discern the diversity within diverse populations so as to avoid stereotyping. Whereas some minorities will subscribe to more traditional folk theories about getting ahead, others may embrace opposing views and perspectives.

Cult of Victimology.   According to McWhorter (2000), a cult of victimology has become a keystone of cultural blackness to treat victimhood not as a problem to be solved but as an identity to be nurtured. Victimology is the result of calling attention to victimhood in Black America where the view is "less toward solutions and more toward fostering and nurturing an unfocused brand of resentment and sense of alienation from the mainstream" (p. 2). One of myths about victimology is that it is an inner-city affair—typified by students dropping out of high school under the assumption that they will not be accepted in the white world. Victimology is "just as prevalent among educated [black] people with ample opportunities" (p. 31). It is not a conscious process, nor one that is the result of white political chicanery. Victimology infects the subconscious and all but makes it impossible to be open to all sides of the issue. As a result, victimology has become a cultural keystone, likened to religion or bigotry, and is passed on from one generation to another in the same way as folk theory is sustained.

According to McWhorter (2000), victimology is an expression of insecurity at its core. He maintains that this inner-doubt and insecurity manifests itself by calling attention to the faults of others through blaming. Contrary to myth, victimology is rather prevalent among black leaders, and increasingly the leaders are coming from the educated black population. Not surprisingly, McWhorter does not advocate affirmative action. He believes that many black students go to selective universities already wary that white students suspect them of being admitted under the affirmative action guidelines and are thus not really qualified. He suggests that by doing away with affirmative action, it will eliminate a subtle but deleterious dynamic that leaves black students feeling inferior from the outset. Because affirmative action is a federal issue in the workplace, every consultation will relate to views on this hotly debated issue. Some consultees and clients will subscribe to the tenets of affirmative action, while others will not. It is important to have some understanding of where consultees and clients are on the issue. Rather than outright asking consultees and clients, consultants should attend to those remarks made by consultees and clients as they relate to the issue.

The Cult of Separatism.   Another dimension plaguing Black America is separatism —a natural outgrowth of victimology. According to McWhorter (2000), separatism fosters and encourages black Americans to conceive of themselves as an unofficial sovereign entity. As such, many rules governing other Americans' lives are suspended out of the belief that black victimhood renders them morally exempt from those laws. Separatism may at first appear to be simply a matter of self-protection, but McWhorter claims that in practice, separatism actually narrows horizons and holds black people back from being the best that they can be (p. 51).

According to McWhorter (2000), separatism is expressed in three ways. First is the idea that mainstream culture is a "white" culture according to many, if not most, black Americans. This serves to alienate many black Americans from the total culture and narrows the horizons of American culture. Moreover, separatism also closes off black people to foreign cultures as well. The second issue in separatism relates to black history. Much academic work on black history downplays rational arguments and factual evidence and serves as an idealized and preconceived version of the "truth" of black history. For instance, McWhorter claims that "Afrocentric history" is "primarily focused upon a fragile assemblage of misreadings of classical texts which constructs a scenario under which Ancient Egypt was a 'black civilization'" (p. 54). Black scholarship is often devoted to chronicling black victimhood, past and present. One result of such inadequate or inaccurate inquiry is to leave black Americans in conflict with mainstream academia, which serves to continue alienating black Americans through a separatist conception in academia. Through "black" academia, folk wisdom often prevails over scholarly arguments to the contrary. Ideally, McWhorter would like to see an increase in Afrocentric academia in which people simply apply tools of conventional academia to illuminating black concerns rather than the present state in which sociopolitical content carries more weight than empirical rigor.

The third expression of separatism comes through the conviction that because black people have been treated so poorly, they cannot be held responsible for their moral or destructive actions. Irresponsibility is supplanted by the "understanding" that these actions are the response to frustration and pain. According to McWhorter, "Victimology channels through Separatism to create the sentiment that black people are still so mired in oppression that to express any real criticism of them is to kick them while they are down" (2000, p. 62). McWhorter claims that the harm that separatism wreaks is serious. For one, separatism reinforces the "dumb black myth." Separatism also sabotages black people in that it can have a harmful effect on hiring and employment. Perhaps the most alarming and harmful effects of separatism are that it sabotages black Americans through the excusing of immoral behavior. A result of this is the promulgation of a folk theory that encourages black Americans, generation after generation, to settle for less.

The Cult of Anti-Intellectualism. The effects of victimology and separatism are reflected in a strong tendency toward what McWhorter (2000) refers to as *anti-intellectualism* at all levels of the black community. The origins of this anti-intellectualism are rooted in the notion that school is a "white" endeavor as well as in the fact that generation after generation of black Americans lived and died in a culture where books and learning were actively withheld or lent only begrudgingly (p. 138). Because of this, black American culture emerged in contexts that could not emphasize ways of thinking that would necessarily lead to scholarly success. This, concomitant with the difficulties facing blacks in public schools, has had a tendency through the generations to downplay the need for education.

Fordham and Ogbu (1986) demonstrate that the factors that create and perpetuate black anti-intellectualism are rather typical of dispossessed groups in terms of their first lagging behind in scholastic aptitude, but then quickly catching up through schooling and upward mobility. McWhorter (2000) suggests that black American students "are hindered because new ways of thinking entail an openness—a sense of integral commitment and belonging, to the realm of school that black students tend to teach one another out of" (p. 143). It is not just the children in the ghettos who tend to reject school, but blacks of all classes. In other words, McWhorter claims that if one were to abolish the inner-cities tomorrow, black school performance would continue to be the weakest in the United States. In fact, he points out that folk theory for blacks includes the phrase that "books are not us" (p. 161). This phrase keeps blacks from getting as far ahead as whites and other minorities. The process is rather subconscious and, as a result, most black students are inhibited from performing well in school because of the cultural heritage that schooling is only to get a piece of paper.

McWhorter (2000) states that once a race has been disparaged and disenfranchised for hundreds of years and then is abruptly given freedom, victimology and separatism develop naturally. Victimology leads to anti-intellectualism, because victimology perpetuates the idea that mediocre scholarly achievement for blacks is inevitable. Moreover, separatism casts scholarly achievement as "what white people do," and the result is a sanctioning of mediocre black scholastic achievement. In the final analysis, McWhorter believes that the most important thing is to realize the grip of victimology, separatism, and anti-intellectualism on black Americans. McWhorter writes:

> Whites cannot solve the problem in any other way but allowing black people the dignity of true competition. . . . When whites try to bridge the separation between the races by adopting aspects of black culture, they are accused of co-optation; when they try to intro-

duce their culture to blacks, they are accused of cultural imperialism. Whites have tried to bring blacks into the academia arena with permanently lowered admission standards, only to see black scholarly performance freeze at a substandard level, while black college students occupy administrators' offices crying "facism" at the very schools that admitted them with scores that would have barred any white student from admission. (p. 258)

The implications for Euro-Caucasian consultants is significant. McWhorter (2000) claims that whites do nothing less than encourage victimology, separatism, and anti-intellectualism. These are seen as "understandable" responses to the horrors of the past. Whites also unwittingly have encouraged these responses by way of a "well-intentioned" managerial class (Darity, 1983) that has created social policies like open-ended welfare and permanent affirmative action. These were created to help blacks and other minorities overcome disadvantages, yet they only serve to boil the waters on which these responses rest. Interracial relations in America have congealed into a "coded kind of dance" that subconsciously encourages black people to preserve and reinforce their status as "other."

DIVERSITY AND THE
PSYCHOLOGICAL CONTRACT

There should be little question about the significance of diversity and its relationship to the psychological contract. Remember, this is not simply a discussion about diversity among people; this also refers to a diversity of ideas that diverse individuals have. Notwithstanding the moral implications, the imperatives for a consultant relate to what she or he believes the larger aim to be in the consulting process. This requires consultants to develop a larger, more diverse picture and subsequent understanding of the factors that influence the context of the consulting process. Without an accurate assessment of both the overt and covert factors in consultation during the formulation of the psychological contract, the interventions that ensue will likely be less effective because they will fail to address the larger, more subtle issues related to the consultation. Does this mean that the total consulting process will have been wasted? No. It is simply an issue of the level of effectiveness. On some level, the consultation may be effective at identifying and resolving issues. However, remember that solutions to problems always create other problems. The key is to have the new problems be less serious. It may take some time for the new problems to surface. So, it is up to the consultant to visualize the breadth, depth, and long-range impact of any and all interventions during the process.

The point is simple: Consultants can have an enormous influence on individuals, and it is very important for consultants to recognize their power in order to diminish the chances of their reinforcing the status quo inappropriately. Are consultants change agents? Most assuredly, they are. The issue relates to what changes, with whom, for what purposes, and how the change process takes place. Is it necessary for a consultant to help an organization change into one that reflects the greater social diversity? In other words, is it appropriate for consultants to help monolithic and plural organizations to change? That is a moral and legal issue. Many organizations are currently attempting to enhance underrepresented individuals through proactive efforts to manage their diversity (Gilbert, Stead, & Ivancevich, 1999). Does this mean that all organizations should have a similar aim to eliminate racism and gender bias in the workplace? Current writings on modern racial oppression would certainly underscore this need. But, is that the consultant's job? The psychological contract will help clarify exactly what the boundaries of the consultation will be. However, the boundaries of the consultation need to be negotiated in terms of the larger values being purported by both consultants and their consultees and clients.

Assessing the Relationship and Degree of Openness

Consultees of any background and belief will need to be open to the process of consultation itself. Simply requesting consulting service indicates a degree of openness on the part of the consultee, but the extent to which the consultee is open and remains open throughout the process is a key ingredient to assess in the psychological contract. It is often the case that consultees are open to the prospect of requesting help, but then find themselves hesitant or ambivalent once the process has actually begun. It is up to the consultant to prepare consultees for this natural occurrence during the process. One thing that is almost certain is the fact that no matter what intervention is determined and acted on, it will create new problems that will require some flexibility and openness on the part of the consultee in order for the consultation to be successful.

Consultee openness must always start with the consultant's openness. That is, consultants are not really in a position to assess the openness of consultees unless consultants have some idea of what "openness" actually looks and feels like across gender and racioethnicity. There are some cultural mores that take precedence over who is "open" and under what conditions the openness will occur. For example, traditional Native American and other traditional racioethnic families, such as African Americans and Pacific Islanders, often place credence on the notion that the group takes precedence over the individual (Attneave, 1982; Fisher & Harrison, 2000). A crucial question becomes: How *possible* is it for this (Native American) consultee to be "open" to the traditional Euro-Caucasian view that the individual is more important than the group? The reversal of roles would lend the same situation in the other direction: A traditional Native American consultant would need to assess how open her or his Euro-Caucasian consultee is to an orientation of "group."

Regardless of who is in the consultant or consultee role, consultants who ponder this question when working with consultees who embrace such an ideology will automatically position themselves into a posture of "openness" themselves by virtue of reflecting on this issue. Then, consultants can more accurately assess the consultee's "openness" to ideas about intervention. Being open in consultation is not the same as agreeing with what is being said; rather, it means that there is a sense that the consultant and consultee can *work together*. This means that the relationship needs to be able to bend without breaking. Caplan and Caplan (1993) use the term *entre nous* ("between the two of us") to describe the attitudes and structural relationship between consultant and consultee in their "work together."

The most important issue here is for Euro-Caucasian consultants not to assume that they know much about the African American experience, or any other minority experience per se, in the workplace. In this manner, consultants will assume a position of curiosity that, while reflecting a more honest situation, can also enhance the consulting process greatly. Working together naturally implies an element of "ongoingness" to the process of mutual exchange and growth. That is, consultants need to be open to what consultees are thinking, the ways that consultees think, and the means through which the consultees' thinking is imparted to the consultant throughout the process of forming the psychological contract as well as throughout the consulting process itself.

For instance, Taoism, which stresses harmony, is quite prevalent among the traditional Asian population (Burns & D'Avanzo, 1993). It may well be the case that a traditional Asian American consultant will conceptualize a consultee's consulting concerns as one indicating disharmony rather than seeing morale problems or problems of output or production. The terms *harmony* and *disharmony* may be used to conceptualize the issue by either party in the consultation, but both consultant and consultee need to agree on the meaning of these terms and how they will be translated across cultural boundaries during the consulting process. This will require a mutual openness because harmony and disharmony are valid ways to conceptualize problems, and openness to these terms and the concomitant nuances of such terms will only enhance the relationship between consultants and consultees. In this manner, neither consultant nor consultee has to be in an adversarial position with each other, which would be defined by contrary terms to the same problem. It is likely the case that one Euro-Caucasian consultant might utilize a group intervention approach to restore *efficiency* to clients, whereas another interpretation is that the consultant restored *harmony* to the group of clients. It is more than semantics. It is a way of being, and effective consultants are able to be open to such reconceptualizations. There are clear benefits to be obtained—the least of which is that it diminishes ethnocentrism.

Assessing Power and Control Issues

Ragins and Sundstrom (1989) researched gender and power in organizations and found a consistent difference favoring men in accessibility to, and utility of, resources for power. Their research suggests that males and females differ in the development of power in organizations, with women facing more of an "obstacle course." It is critically important for consultants to analyze the more subtle obstacles to advancement for women because, if assessed incorrectly, these obstacles will clearly surface during the intervention phases. A result can be an ineffective intervention process and the subsequent failure of the consultation. For example, a consultant who is unaware of such barriers in the workplace might mistakenly suggest a course of action that might work for a "good old boy" and be occupational suicide for a woman or a racioethnic minority.

Critical to the discussion of power and control is the notion of hierarchies. The very constructs of "supervisor," "manager," "boss," "CEO," and "principal" (to name a few) imply a structure of hierarchy and power differentials. Part of the psychological contract is aimed at assessing how individuals and groups manage the power differentials. The reason is because it is very likely that consultants will also face the same issues with their consultees. Hierarchies in and of themselves are not inherently bad or inappropriate. However, it is important to understand some of the implications of hierarchies as they relate to women and racioethnic minorities. For instance, a group of women who are working together at eliminating family violence might have problems with a hierarchical structure in an organization. This might be due to the experience of being subjugated in a family where they did not hold a position of power. Any hierarchy at all might be problematic for this group of women.

On a philosophical level, the very notion of hierarchy implies a dualism or a separation between individuals and/or groups. According to many feminist theorists, it is the very notion of hierarchies that help create situations where women and racioethnic minorities are "backgrounded" in work and nonwork settings (Plumwood, 1993). For Plumwood, *hierarchical structures promote males and "background" or diminish the important contributions of women and racioethnic minorities.* According to Plumwood, what is needed is a "gender-neutral" position that is nonhierarchical in nature. Although consultants will undoubtedly have consultations that involve hierarchical relationships and structures, there are larger issues at stake. The larger issues to be assessed relate to the rigidity of the hierarchy, the access to the upper echelons of the hierarchy, and the subtle ways that the hierarchy is maintained that may contribute to the problem needing a solution.

Consultees' Vulnerability and Fears

At the time that consultees request help from consultants, it can be accurately assumed that consultees are feeling some sense of the need for help and a concomitant willingness to lend some power over to a consultant. This, of course, would depend on the nature of the request. For instance, a consultee may feel little vulnerability when requesting a consultant to put on a workshop. However, a consultee who requests help in solving a complicated morale problem will likely leave the consultee feeling much more vulnerable. In the case of a workshop request, an assessment of the consultee's power and control issues might not be categorically indicated. The request could simply be coming through the venue of a purchase consultation where the consultee does not possess the related expertise and desires an expert to come in and deliver a product. The latter case in which morale is a problem would suggest the need for consultants to have a more incisive understanding of how the consultee is processing such issues as independence and dependence because of the direct effect on the more lengthy consulting process. Consultees who have a high need to be in control of situations may initially challenge the consultant for power by withholding some important information, thereby making it difficult for the consultant to accurately conceptualize the issues needing to be addressed. Direct challenges to the consultee's legitimate power to intervene will likely be met with resistance. This is due to the fact that one of hardest things for powerful people to do is to give up that power. On the other hand, an individual consultee and clients of minority status may already be in positions of little power due to an organizational structure and/or due to prejudice and discrimination. In a situation such as this, the fear of losing power and/or control takes on a very different context.

A consultant needs to respect the consultee's power as well as see through the guise of power to recognize the consultee's underlying fear of losing control. In this manner, an effective consultant will be both acknowledging the overt need for power while understanding the inherent fears that drive such a posture. The consultant can then become strategic in his or her interactions so as to help the consultee retain power and save face, and, at the same time, help the consultee to loosen up dogmatic control which, itself, may be contributing significantly to the problem. In the process, there will almost always be surprises in consulting processes. Schein (1999) maintains that errors are inevitable and can be a source of information about the consultation. The aim here is to minimize the number of times the consultant gets surprised. If consultants assess consultees to be less into power than they actually are, consultants may find problems later on in the process when attempting to intervene directly. For example, a consultant who is expecting to have access to a group of (employee) clients for the purpose of talking openly and confidentially about problems in an organization may be surprised when that group is suddenly "unavailable" or when the supervisor suddenly switches positions and arbitrarily decides to sit in on the discussions. Although this may be construed as sabotage, it may also be a case in which the consultant did not accurately anticipate this potential consultee shift while formulating the psychological contract.

One manner that can prove useful in helping manage a traditional Asian American consultee's fears and vulnerabilities is through an appreciation of the concept of "saving face." For instance, Fisher and Harrison (2000) and others have asserted that shame and saving face are important variables in traditional Asian American families. Clearly, there is a strong possibility that these values will be present during the formulation of the psychological contract. Therefore, effective consultants need to ensure that their conceptualizations and assessments of the problems to be addressed in consulting have allowances for all to save face. It may well be that there has already been a loss of face, which led to a consultant being sought out. A good rule to follow is for consultants to guide their work with all groups with a sense of wanting everyone to be able to save face. If consultants can exude this attitude and concomitant behaviors, it may help traditional Asian Americans become more amenable to consultation.

Assessing Hidden Agendas

For most mental health professionals, the issue of assessing a client's hidden agenda is a rather standard procedure. The same is true in consultation. The difference between hidden agendas in counseling and those in consultation lies mostly in how the consultant will go about assessing the agenda. Clients rather expect that counselors will assess the underlying or hidden motives that operate in clients' lives. However, consultees often are not interested in giving permission for consultants to assess the same unconscious drives and motivations. This is especially true with racioethnic consultees who may not experience a level of trust with the consultant.

For example, an African American consultee was referred to me for help in solving his "anger problem" at work. It just so happened that the consultee was the CEO of this particular organization, and the referral came through the guise of a mandate from the organization's board of directors. Clearly, one of the consultee's overt agendas was to obey the mandate of his board. On a more hidden level was the need for the consultee to be "exonerated" from this accusation related to his anger management so that he could continue to point his finger back at those who were pointing fingers at him. The consultee did not believe that he had an "anger problem." He felt that "they" had a problem.

As long as I had an understanding of this context and hidden agenda, the consultation was able to proceed. Without an understanding of the consultee's hidden motives, he might well have resisted my misguided attempts to intervene. The consultee, however, was not in a position to initiate the consultation with this hidden agenda or he would have risked appearing irresponsible and immature. His fears of being vulnerable and appearing incompetent outweighed his need to be open.

The issue of hidden agendas has particular dramatic implications when working with diverse populations. For instance, an Hispanic consultee, seeing morale problems in her organization, may be very aware of Hispanic poverty in the United States and the discrimination of Hispanics in the workplace. As a result, she may proclaim a need for everyone to be treated equally. On another level, this same consultee may understandably desire more Hispanics to be promoted to more positions of power in her organization. She may consciously or unconsciously use means to accomplish her goals in such a way as to appear to discriminate among her other employees. By ferreting out the hidden agenda, the consultant can address the real issue, which is a morale problem related to her desire to help Hispanics in her organization advance. Through the consultant's understanding of the consultee's hidden agenda, the morale problem is correctly conceptualized in context. The consultant can then explore the possibility of rectifying the morale problem by working with the consultee on ways to increase both morale and Hispanic upward mobility. The two are not mutually exclusive.

In this circumstance, the consultant was able to identify the consultee's hidden agenda first by simply revering the consultee's Hispanic roots. A nonjudgmental understanding and acceptance of the plight of the majority of Hispanics in the United States allowed for the consultant to anticipate that there would naturally be an interest in having the consultee's own people be able to better themselves. The issue was really concerning how she was going to go about helping her people. Would it be at her Hispanic employees' expense? The consultee's own expense? The expense of other employees? The desire to help some without hurting others is a noble one. However, the process by which she went about attempting to achieve her goals may have been problematic and may have required the assistance of a sensitive consultant.

Assessing Independence/Dependence Issues

As mentioned in the preceding paragraphs, consultees are often not interested in an assessment of their own issues related to independence and dependence any more than they are interested in consultants overtly addressing consultees' unconscious motivations and hidden agendas. Yet, similar to hidden agendas, consultants need to assess consultees along this continuum of independence/dependence because it will greatly affect the consulting process in terms of interpersonal dynamics, interventions, and responsibilities. A consultee may at first appear to be one way and then abruptly change.

For instance, a consultant might initially assess a particular consultee as standoffish or very independent only to find himself or herself in a situation where the consultee suddenly turns to the consultant and says, "So, what should I do?" This change may be reflected in asking for more time than was initially agreed on for the consulting services. Rather than being a problem that can be rectified by altering the formal contract, this sudden switch from independence to dependence can mean that more time will be required to conduct the consultation than the consultant can give. If this inclination is not sensed or assessed during the formulation of the psychological contract, the consultee may need more than the consultant can actually give at the time. A result can be a negative experience for all.

Theories of Attachment.   In general, the issues related to independence and dependency are usually derived from various theories of attachment (see Bowlby, 1969; Hawkins, 1986). Theories of attachment allow one to draw implications about the formation and separation processes that occur in consulting relationships. For example, in family systems theory, there are patterns of interactions that are highlighted by enmeshment and disengagement. *Enmeshed relationships* is a term used to describe traditional Euro-Caucasian families characterized by diffuse boundaries to the point that individuals lose their sense of individualism while concomitantly becoming overly dependent on another. In *disengaged relationships,* individuals have rigid boundaries that almost preclude their ability to attach to another in meaningful ways. Consultees who have difficulty attaching to others may have difficulty in attaching to consultants, thus making an assessment of the problem situation difficult. This results from the consultee not being forthcoming with information due to an underlying and generalized mistrust of others. Moving slowly and nonjudgmentally in acknowledging the consultee's experiences can prove effective when consultees seem distant and/or disengaged in the process. The consultant would be moving slowly, assessing the ability of the consultee to join in the consulting relationship and the extent to which the consultee's mistrust of others contributes to the need for consulting services.

It is critical to note that issues and concepts related to independence and dependence vary across gender and racioethnicity. For instance, it is not appropriate to use the term *enmeshed* carelessly to describe racioethnic families in which such close relationships are valued. It is important to have an awareness and understanding of various cultural views of independence during the initial formulation of the psychological contract and to assess as much as possible how consultees will handle these issues throughout the process of the consultation. This will help diminish inappropriate conceptualizations on the part of the consultant. For example, a traditional Hispanic individual who values close family relations, and who mirrors that value in the workplace by having many close relationships, could be misconstrued as unhealthily "enmeshed" by an uninformed consultant. In a traditional Native American culture, an individual cannot be conceived as extricated from the larger whole of humanity and nature.

A traditional Asian American might present a rather "passive" approach to the state of consulting affairs. This is not because he or she is dependent in the Euro-Caucasian sense of the term. It may be the result of traditional Asian culture, which sees being too independent, disengaged, or assertive as actually disrupting harmony and perfection. In a situation involving traditional Asian Americans, the fact that many may bow during greetings and good-byes may appear to be obsequious in the eyes of Anglos when, in actuality, the bows are indications of status and power—a polar opposite of dependency! For instance, I worked with an Asian American female in a consultation. As we finished up the day's work, I shook her hand and then bowed my head as a gesture of thanks and honor. Much to my surprise, she immediately and instinctively bowed her head twice in return. At that moment, something deep was exchanged and we experienced heightened rapport.

Assessing Strengths and Flexibility

In assessing a consultee's strengths, the consultant needs to understand how the term *strength* is interpreted by various and diverse groups. A Euro-Caucasian consultant might assess a consultee's strength to be openness, sensitivity to employees' or clients' needs, and approachable. At the same time, the consultee might not consider herself or himself in the same way. For instance, a Native American female consultee might consider herself to be very strong in terms of her being able to hold a family together. This would be due to the fact that many such families are held together without the help of a live-in male counterpart (Shinagawa & Jang, 1998). Her strength might be reflected in having a sense of purpose, a strong will to achieve in what she believes to be important, and a resolved sense of purpose in her relationship with her people and nature. These are indeed different concepts of "strength."

Fisher and Harrison (2000) state that many traditional Native Americans do not believe that nature can be controlled, so many of these individuals may see consultants' plans of action as attempts to control something that cannot be controlled. Moreover, the traditional Native American notions of group taking precedence over individuals can run counter to consultants' proposals to deal with individual clients. Consultants need to address such issues with consultees (traditional Native Americans, in this case) by first having some working knowledge of the prevailing mores and beliefs held by persons of that traditional culture. Then, an accurate assessment of the consultees' flexibility can be undertaken. In this fashion, consultants can test out their hunches about how to proceed through an informed discussion about differences in approaches. These various approaches might include a combination of individual and group interventions or only the latter.

The purpose of assessing the consultee's flexibility during the formulation of the psychological contract is to help determine how willing the consultee will be to accept shifts in the consulting process that will inevitably occur. One of the opposites of flexibility is rigidity, and there is a large body of professional literature describing the downfalls of individuals and systems characterized by ultra-rigidity (see Fisher & Harrison, 2000; Jenkins, Fisher, & Harrison, 1993). So, consultants would clearly want to assess the extent to which consultees are overly rigid because that may, in fact, be the problem needing to be addressed—in spite of the consultee's conceptualizations to the contrary. Remember, when some consultees feel threatened, they may appear rigid. That does not mean that they are rigid. Bateson (1951) says that the thing named is not necessarily the name of the thing.

If consultants are not careful, they can assess a consultee as being too flexible (or too rigid) when in fact the consultant is simply behaving according to his or her own cultural norms. An example might be reflected where a traditional Native American or Alaskan Native consultee is assessed by an uninformed consultant as needing to be more assertive in requiring employees to be on time for meetings with the consultant. Since traditional Native culture views time in terms of it being chromatic (as opposed to digital time), it is not appropriate for the consultant to suggest that the consultee change her or his views on time so as to require clients to be "on time." In all likelihood, the employees are already "on time" when they come in 10 minutes after the official start of a meeting.

Race Relations and the Psychological Contract

The formulation of the psychological contract is a good place to improve race relations while helping consultees and clients work more efficiently. In the past, white males in the United States have benefited from racism (Bowser & Hunt, 1996, p. 174). In today's workplace, this population of white males is having to deal with the negative impacts of racism and sexism. Nonetheless, in most cases, below-average white and average white males continue to retain significant advantages over women and racioethnic minorities of the same ability in the workplace. This is important information to have when entering into consultation because racioethnic minority workers and women view white men's position in the workplace from a dramatically different perspective (Bowser & Hunt, 1996). For instance, some stereotypes used to describe white male co-workers by their minority counterparts are *arrogant, crazy, ignorant, insensitive, out of control, spoiled,* and *selfish.* The more positive stereotypes include *privileged, shrewd, in control, dominant, smart,* and *powerful.*

These same researchers assert that many white males, themselves, feel discriminated against in the workplace. In addition, these white males are afraid of unintentionally offending minorities or women. Bowser and Hunt (1996) believe that this fear can be rather unhealthy in that it can inhibit open, healthy communication among people. Moreover, this fear can lead to more misunderstandings and lower the efficiency of the particular workplace.

In assessing the psychological contract when working with the diversity of consultees, it is important to determine each other's sensitivity to status. That is, Euro-Caucasian consultants who work with racioethnic and female consultees need to be sensitive to the issues of hierarchy and status. Using the moniker *doctor* or the label *expert* might not be indicated in situations where the minority consultee does not hold similar status. Consultants need to work their way into a position of equality in terms of status when working with consultees and clients. Moreover, since the psychological contract is usually formulated between the consultant and a single consultee, there is opportunity for the interactions to be one on one. This can provide the venue for more in-depth exploration of differences and similarities between consultants and consultees. For instance, Euro-Caucasian consultants working with African American consultees might need to explore how racioethnicity will impact the process. Here, compassion needs to be the guiding light for consultants during these discussions. Consultants can come from a position of curiosity about the implications of such a racioethnic consulting arrangement. This can be extremely valuable and educational for both consultant and consultee. The Caucasian consultant might say to a Latino consultee, "I'm not sure how well my Anglo values will match up with your values on this particular issue. What do you think?"

Assessing the Psychological Contract between Consultees and Their Clients

A critical component to be assessed involves the psychological contract that exists between the consultee and client/client system. This is important because, to some degree, the contract between consultees and clients will be reflected in the ways in which consultees will approach and conduct themselves with consultants. Because of the nature of psychological contracts, an analysis and understanding of the psychological contract that exists between consultees and client/client systems will also help consultants identify boundaries and barriers to the consulting process. Many times, the boundaries and barriers will not be identified in overt discussion with consultees. Nevertheless, their influence cannot be understated.

As mentioned previously, it is important to understand how available the client and client system will actually be to the consultant in terms of willingness for consultation. The psychological contract that exists between the consultee and the client/client system can usually be seen through an analysis of the existing organizational culture. At this point, a good rule to follow in assessing the contract that exists between consultees and their client/client systems is to conceptualize the contract as emanating from the interaction of the other assessment components. In other words, by assessing the consultee relationship and degree of consultee openness, issues related to their power and control, hidden agendas, independence/dependence issues, and strengths and flexibilities, consultants can get a "good feel" for what they can expect to see and experience once they actually enter into the client/client system.

SUMMARY

Aside from the information about the formulation of the psychological contract, the intent of this chapter was aimed to broaden the consultant's conceptualizations of the issues that influence most formal consultations. Even though many consultations will be a clinical model in which there is a simple structure of consultee and singular client, numerous other consultations will involve the larger organizational system to varying degrees. The information presented in this chapter is meant to aid in the conceptualization process because all interventions will ensue from these conceptualizations.

Although the actual formal consultation contract may not specify issues related to disabilities, racioethnicity, and gender, it does not mean that these issues should be overlooked. They clearly and inexorably impact the psychological contract. If consultants are not able to establish good, meaningful rapport with consultees (and clients), the process will be severely affected. Because psychological contracts exist everywhere and among all peoples, consultants need to have a more incisive understanding of the larger issues at work. As consultants understand racioethnic and gender issues in consultation, the process will become more broad-based, deep, and effective. The actual intervention should parallel what has been specified in the formal contract, but the foundations on which those interventions are conceptualized and understood by consultants are contained in the psychological contract

The information presented in this chapter was also aimed at creating a general profile of the current state of affairs as they relate to gender, disabilities, and racioethnic aspects and perspectives in the workplace. These values will vary across all organizations and across most consultations. It is far better for consultants to be overprepared than underprepared for a consultation. If the organization's espoused values include nonhierarchies and equal advancement for all workers, the consultant needs to discern this as best he or she can early on in the process. Conflicting values can surface during the intervention phase and interrupt or significantly alter the course of the consultation. On another level, there are ethical considerations involved when discussing gender, disabilities, and racioethnic issues in consultation.

QUESTIONS

1. What experiences do you have with disabilities and racioethnicity issues? How do you see these experiences translating into consultation?

2. What kinds of experiences have you had with glass or job ceilings? Explain how you felt as a result.

3. From your experience of discrimination and/or prejudice, what qualities in a consultant would you like to see?

4. To what extent can you relate to McWhorter's notions of self-sabotage in Black America?

5. What would be your major concern in working with a consultee who is culturally different?

CHAPTER SEVEN

ETHICAL DIMENSIONS IN CONSULTATION

It may be surprising to learn that the practice of professional consultation is generally conceptualized by professionals in the field as a subset of general counseling, psychotherapy, and social work practices. The reasons for this conceptual subordination of consultation are complex. It is hard to conceive of any practicing mental health professional who would not engage in the process of professional consultation at some point of time. Because every professional consults at one time or another in the course of carrying out professional duties, it is imperative to be informed of the expectations of professional conduct. Newman (1993) states that consultants will often base their primary sources of information about how to proceed through established ethical standards as well as through their own personal and professional values. Newman emphasizes the need for consultants to have a clear understanding of both ethical standards and personal and professional values prior to problems occurring (p. 152).

PROFESSIONAL CONSULTATION VERSUS PROFESSIONAL CONSULTING

When it comes to a discussion of consultation and ethics, it is critical to understand the difference between professional consultants and professional consultation. As discussed in Chapter Two, there is a critical distinction between formal and informal consultation, and the same concern prevails with professional consultants and professional consultation. The term *professional consultant* may or may not indicate that the person is a professional per se. The term likely describes a person who consults for a living. For instance, both palm readers and consulting psychologists would consider themselves professional consultants. Aside from their orientations and interests, a significant difference between these two groups of professional consultants is that the latter is legally regulated and bound to a code of ethical behavior, whereas the former is not. *Professional consultation,* however, describes an interactional process that occurs when the consultant is a member of a profession. For mental health professionals, the distinction is crucial when discussing consultation because it means the difference between being legally regulated and not being legally regulated, or perhaps not being regulated at all.

The term *professional* has many meanings to many people. The Department of Labor may use the term to describe someone performing a type of work, whereas a given professional organization may use the term to describe someone performing something entirely different or at a different level. In addition, drawing a distinction between the terms is not a significant issue in many cases. For mental health professionals, the term *professional* has a specific and decisive meaning. It is generally recognized that a "profession" usually requires some specialized training or education. Also, a profession has an organization to which practitioners can belong, such as the American Counseling Association, the National Association of Social Workers, the American School Counselors Association, and/or the American Psychological Association. Professions are regulated by their respective state board of examiners and are created for the purpose of protecting the public. The regulating board of the profession requires professional members to hold national certification and/or state licensure. Along with that is some requirement for the continuing education of its practitioners. In addition, a profession usually promulgates its research findings in a professional journal. Finally, a profession has an ethical code of conduct to which its members must adhere or risk legal action or professional censure and/or sanctions.

The Regulation of Professional Consultation

The codes for conduct for the various mental health professions are conceptualized and documented by their respective professional organizations—the American Counseling Association, the National Association of Social Workers, the American School Counselors Association, and the American Psychological Association. The regulation of professional behavior for consultants is overseen by both the professional mental health organization to which that particular consultant belongs as well as the respective state board of examiners. In the situations where state law actually binds the profession to the organization's code of ethics, the consultant is legally bound to adhere to the professional code. For instance, the State of Nevada Revised Statutes (NRS) actually states that marriage and family therapists will adhere to the code of ethics for the American Association of Marriage and Family Therapy (Nevada Revised Statutes: Chapter 641A, 2003). So, when consulting with families, the practitioner would be in violation of the law if she or he behaved unethically.

State Examining Boards. Unlike state examining boards specific to psychologists, social workers, counselors, and marriage and family therapists, there is no examining board that is exclusively concerned with consulting practices. There are reasons for this, the first of which is fundamental. As pointed out previously, generic consultation (not professional or formal consultation per se) is practiced all over the world in an immeasurable number of ways and in an equally innumerable number of settings by almost everyone at one time or another. Because of the prevalence of consulting practices throughout the world, it is prohibitive to attempt to regulate the generic practice of consultation. Even on a more mundane level, it would be difficult. Aside from the differences between informal and formal consultation and professional and nonprofessional consultation, there is a vast difference between how consultation may be practiced in the business world and how it may be practiced in professional settings. Again, it would be impracticable and impossible to attempt to regulate consultation even on this level because of a lack of consistency in the definition of it.

Even among regulated mental health professions, consultation is operationalized differently across their respective ethical codes of ethics. This adds to the difficulty in finding consistency in actual process and practice. The term *consultation* does appear in various mental health codes. Yet, not every mental health profession agrees unequivocally on which specific aspects of "consultation" to codify. Nevertheless, the various mental health professions seem to agree on how the practice of consultation should be conceptualized in relation to the practices of counseling, psychotherapy, and social work. It is not conceptualized as a stand-alone professionally regulated practice.

Regulating a "Backgrounded" Profession.   The practice of consultation is conceptualized in such a manner so as to be *backgrounded* into professions already regulated. *Backgrounded* means that the specific codes for consultation appear only in a few sections and/or standards of that respective profession's comprehensive code of ethics. For example, only five sections of the Code of Ethics and Standards of Practice for the American Counseling Association (ACA) contains ethical guidelines related to the practice of consultation (ACA, 1995). The National Association of Social Workers (NASW) recognizes the practice of "consultation" by including the term in the list of acceptable activities in their Preamble to the Code of Ethics (NASW, 1996). The social work code also contains guidelines related to consultation in four of its sections. The American Psychological Association (APA) lists the term *consultation* in its General Standards and the section on Privacy and Confidentiality (APA, 2003). In the expanded document, the APA discusses consultation in several sections and cites the activity again in the principles section (e.g., Principle B, Fidelity and Responsibility). The American Association of Marriage and Family Therapy cites consultation in seven sections of its ethical codes. Because of this background effect, the voice of consultation has had a difficult time finding an audience of its own, which is similar to the findings of researchers who cite similar effects in the backgrounding of gender and racioethnicity minorities (see Plumwood, 1993). Consultation shares the stage as a minor actor in the conventional helping processes and is thus regulated by standards of conduct applicable to that more comprehensive professional practice.

ETHICS AND CONSULTATION

Research on Consultation Ethics

Although the term *consultation* appears only in relevant sections of various professional codes of ethics for mental health professionals, it should not be construed or mistaken to be an insignificant professional interest or concern. To the contrary, recently published textbooks on consultation have devoted entire chapters or at least several sections of a chapter on ethics. For example, Brown, Pryzwansky, and Schulte (2001), Parsons (1996), and Dougherty (1990) all devote chapters to ethics in consultation, and Hansen,

Himes, and Meier (1990) provide several sections on ethics in their book. Yet, two well-written and popular texts on ethical issues in marriage and family therapy do not include the term *consultation* in their indexes (see Gladding, Remley, & Huber, 2001; Sturkie & Bergen, 2001). Reasons for this seeming conflict over the significance of consultation as a mental health practice are numerous. Nonetheless, Brown, Pryzwansky, and Schulte (2001) report that since 1981, there has been an increased emphasis on ethics in consultation. However, in spite of this and the works of Hughes (1986), Pryzwansky (1993), and Newman (1993), a review of the professional literature reflects a general lack of information that can be used to guide ethical decision making in consultation (Newman, 1993).

Due to the potential complexities experienced in consultation, concomitant with the lack of professional research on ethics in consultation, an examination of the structure of a practicing consultant's decision making may reveal a process-toward-solution that at times seems to conform to conventional professional ethics and at other times seems to defy the same ethos. This incongruence should be seen as logical extension, given the decisive structural differences between the two processes. The foundations on which the generic decisions that consultants will be making, although structurally different from those of counseling, will not appear entirely foreign to practicing mental professionals. Certainly, consultants' decisions will need to be firmly grounded in ethics. The level of interpretation of the ethic will also be a factor in how a particular decision is made in consultation. Decisions will also be strongly influenced by the existence of multiple codes to which consultants must adhere. As such, there will also be legal considerations. In all of that lies the consultants' visions and values that serve to mediate interpretations of any of the above. These values will be based on deeper philosophical core assumptions or worldviews. When consultants intervene in the process, all of the factors come together to revolutionize the process and maintain its momentum.

Limits of Professional Codes

The code of ethics sets the structural standard for decision making in any consultation. However, the "subordinate" status ascribed to professional consultation via the various codes of ethics does not allow the unique practice to escape from the confounding variables that plague mental health codes in general. As good as any code might be, it still represents an ideal state that frames the boundaries of acceptable professional behavior. There are limitations to the already existing professional codes, and researchers have identified several, but not all, of these limitations (see Bersoff, 1995; Corey, Corey, & Callanan, 1993; Herlihy & Corey, 1996). The ambiguities that exist in the current codes for counseling, psychotherapy, and social work are likely amplified when applied to the triadic practice of consultation.

Lack of Specificity.   Since a code of ethics is an ideal, there may be a deliberate lack of specificity in any given paragraph. The purpose is not to confuse but rather to provide the broadest possible venue framing the correct interpretation of professional behavior. A downside of this will be an occasional inability to enforce the code adequately. Some of this inability may be the result of a lack of a deeper understanding of the process of consultation by state examining board members. Part of this may be the result of a situation where a particular code is in conflict with a law. In these types of situations, the dilemma that is produced by consultants' need to adhere to multiple codes, and perhaps legal expectations, requires that some level of professional development be executed appropriately. Consultants can find themselves caught between the laws governing the profession and the "laws" governing the work world. To aid in the development of a more sophisticated level of professional decision making in general, state examining boards attempt to guarantee the public a certain level of professional competency in its constituents through the requirement of continuing education for license renewals. However, many practicing professionals need and desire other continuing education requirements that seem to fit better with their practices and thus would not see the benefit of becoming more educated in the practice of consultation. This idea may be the reason why there is a paucity of formal workshops on consultation offered as continuing education at professional conferences. All of this tends to lead to a general and superficial understanding of consultation and the consulting process by many in the mental health field.

Problems of Adherence.   Another limitation of ethical codes is reflected in situations where the consulting issue cannot be resolved by adherence to a single ethical code. This can occur when the client is being treated for dual disorders. For example, in some states, a client with a primary Axis I diagnosis of Substance Abuse disorder (APA, 2000) may be treated only by a licensed drug and alcohol counselor. To complicate matters, it may be that the client's therapist is dually licensed as a substance-abuse counselor and psychotherapist. The issue of which code is appropriate for which counselor/client interaction is a confusing one indeed. In matters of confidentially regarding alcohol and drug-abuse patient records, the 42 Code of Federal Regulations, Part 2 (42 CFR) can supercede less restrictive state laws governing other types of counseling. Hence, there are three domains of ethics to which the counselor in this example must adhere. This scenario is only compounded further in situations where consultation is conceptualized as the foreground practice and counseling is conceptualized as the background practice. The direct result would be a conflict within a single professional code of ethics.

Difficulties Enforcing Codes.   Corey, Corey, and Callanan (1998) and Goodyear and Sinnett (1984) cite research indicating instances where there are difficulties in enforcing ethical codes. A related limitation is reflected where a court may decide that the ethical provisions are not applicable or too broad or too narrow to be of use in a given legal case. A result can be inconsistent findings and court rulings. Sometimes particular community standards may be more salient than a specific code in deciding the disposition of a case involving consultation. For example, assume that a mental health professional is being sued for damages by another professional's client for alleged improper advice given to the mental health professional during a consultation. Assume also that the client is a high-profile person in the community and politically well connected. This and other facts "persuade" a judge to hear the case that might not have been heard in another jurisdiction.

Another type of community standard conflict can be seen within the mental health community itself. There can be conflicts that emerge within a mental health agency's philosophy and the actual mental health practice of its employees. For example, imagine that the administration of a mental health clinic determines that it wants to change the ways it delivers services to clients. The new way is based on brief therapy, which would limit the number of sessions offered to clients. The purpose may be to help diminish a long waiting list that leaves the agency potentially liable for behaviors of those on the waiting list. In the process of solving a waiting list problem, a new problem might arise related to the need to terminate certain clients who have had their limit of sessions. Other clients may be referred to sources designed to handle more long-term cases. In the process of transitioning, there may be some specific cases that are prematurely terminated in order to reach a macro-goal of serving more clients. At this point, the system is in conflict. Part of the conflict relates to the ethics of terminating clients who may feel as though they are not ready. This may be in spite of the therapist thinking that the client is ready. If the mental health director enlisted the services of a consultant, the consultant may find herself or himself caught between the desires of consultees wanting to diminish the waiting list, the frustrated therapists, and the scared clients.

Consultant Characteristics.   Another limitation inherent in codes of ethics concerns the idiosyncrasies and characteristics of individual professionals who interpret them. Not every professional agrees with every other professional about every detail of every code. The differences in opinions can range from the dramatic to the miniscule. Nevertheless, the fact remains that there are different interpretations of the codes. Varying interpretations can be associated with differences in professional experience, differences in the personalities of practitioners, different contexts of interpretation, consultants' differing values and biases, and different levels of ethical functioning subscribed to by the consultant.

Ethical Codes and Diversity.   Critical outcry has come from professional researchers examining feminism and ethics. Thus, a serious limitation to ethical codes relates to the cultural context. Corey, Corey, and Callanan (1998) believe that all codes of ethical conduct need to be understood within a cultural framework, and this includes the context of gender, racioethnicity, and the culture of the professional as well as the culture of the profession itself. This is crucial because a practitioner's personal values may conflict with a specific standard contained within a given code. In addition and on a deeper level, the committees who comprise the various recommending units about ethical revisions may or may not be progressive or function effectively as a working unit. Inevitable conflicts arise during the course of developing new codes. The gender and racioethnic makeup of the recommending units may not be representative of the population to which the profession serves. Moreover, Goodyear and Sinnett (1984) assert that many times these committees can be negatively impacted by the fact that the members are voluntary. A covert but significant result can be a lack of a more full integration of minority issues into the foundations of ethical codes. Given the context of potential underrepresentation of gender, disabilities, and racioethnicity in codifying the practice, consultees and client/client systems may be the recipients of less than what is ideally considered "best practice."

For example, both the American Counseling Association (ACA, 1995) and the American Psychological Association (2003) have sections in their respective ethical codes that address discrimination. As pointed out in the last chapter, conflicts can arise easily in consulting situations where consultees may be overtly or covertly behaving in a prejudicial fashion toward minority employees. In these situations, the consultee may be requesting consulting services on a completely different matter, and the issue of prejudice may appear to be "ancillary" to the identified problem. Furthermore, what if the consultee is relatively unaware of the prejudice? What ethical standard addresses such a situation? At what point does the ethical standard for the consultant kick into play? Obviously, consultants are prohibited from behaving with prejudice or discrimination. However, does that mandate that the consultant's consultees must behave with the same value or be confronted? Do ethical standards require the consultation to stop because of a value conflict? If not, at what point does the consultant's ethical code come into conflict with the consultee's need for help? Certainly, the psychological contract can help in surfacing differences in values between consultants and consultees. So, there may be some practical wiggle-room. Yet, having the ability to maneuver through value differences does not eliminate the need for adherence to ethical codes.

In another circumstance, it may be that the consultant, in attempting to right the wrongs placed on minorities, behaves in such a fashion as to discriminate against a majority population. This is partly reflected in the debate over affirmative action or in Title IX in athletics. In both cases, the majority populations are up in arms about the issue of reverse discrimination. If a consultant is working toward equality for all and sees that as best being achieved through deconstructing affirmative action or Title IX in athletics, is that a violation of the sections of ethical codes that prohibit discrimination? Or are those respective ethical codes written with the mindset of helping primarily minorities?

Another situation can exist related to people with disabilities. Federal legislation requires equal access for all through the Americans with Disabilities Act. Yet, imagine a mental health therapist in private practice renting an office space in which there is no access for people with disabilities. Assume that this therapist contracts with the local department of rehabilitation services to act as a consultant for the department's clients. What duty does the therapist/consultant have to address the issue with the building's owner—especially if the owner is a nonprofessional? Confronting the building owner may prove contentious and can possibly result in the therapist/consultant being asked to leave. If there is no handicap access and the therapist/consultant finds out that a referral from the rehabilitation agency has a physical disability, what happens then? How does the duty and obligation shift in this situation? Refusing to see the client because the client cannot access the building conflicts with the code of ethics, likely violates the ADA law, and probably deviates from the consulting contract existing between the agency and the therapist. Should the therapist/consultant make other arrangements to see the client? For example, can the therapist/consultant and client meet in some public place where access is not a problem? What are the ethical implications of such a move?

In still another extension, how competent does a consultant have to be in order to serve a client with disabilities? Is one course in disabilities or diversity enough to deem the professional as competent? What does therapist/consultant "competence" mean in this situation? Does the consultant need to have had a certain amount of experience in working with minorities and disabilities? If so, how does one go about ethically getting that experience? On a philosophical level, the larger question that looms is: When is a consultant competent?

The Contemporary "Male" Ethic. There is concern about the philosophical relevancy of the ethical structure for racioethnic minorities, persons with disabilities, and women. Several researchers on feminist theory consider the manner in which ethics are constructed and interpreted as being essentially male (e.g., Lloyd, 1984; Parsons, 2002). Specifically, Parsons (2002) asserts that the "modern self" is a man. Therefore, the subject of ethics is modeled after a masculine model—specifically, man's self-understanding and self-determinations (p. 43). Other researchers on feminism assert that man's imagination is oppositional and dualistic (e.g., Cocks, 1989). The result is a masculine discourse of ethics built on the construct of powerful ones ruling over the powerless, subjugated others (Parsons, 2002, p. 48). Since women, persons with disabilities, and racioethnic minorities are seen as the "less powerful" ones, their voices are left out of the very structure of the masculine ethic.

Professional research into this concern has provided some guidelines for a new ethic to emerge (e.g., Benhabib, 1992; Habermas, 1970). In her book, *Situating the Self: Gender, Community, and Postmodernism in Contemporary Ethics,* Benhabib (1992) calls for a challenge to unexamined normative dualisms. For Benhabib, examples of norms needing to be scrutinized are between justice and the good life, norms and values themselves, and interests and needs. The examination should be driven by concern for the context of gender and subtext (p. 113). What can result from such an examination is a reconfiguration of the moral self in which the self is located within communities of discourse where there is an emphasis on what Benhabib refers to as "enlarged thinking" (p. 4). This concept is closely associated with the levels of ethical functioning.

LEVELS OF ETHICAL FUNCTIONING

In general, the law reflects the *minimum standard* of society's acceptance. On the other hand, ethics reflect the *ideal standard* of behavior set forth by professionals. According to Heron, Martz, and Margolis (1996), ethics focus on how the world should or ought to be. Professional ethics are systems of normative behavior that are restricted to work-related decisions. Ethical issues differ from moral or religious issues in that ethics may involve legalities or sanctions. According to Varney (1985), consultants frequently need to operate at a high level of moral reasoning.

Mandatory Ethical Functioning

There are two levels of ethical functioning that parallel the differences between laws and ethics: mandatory and aspirational. In the first level, *mandatory ethical decision making,* counselors and consultants act in compliance with the minimal standard of the ethic (Corey, Corey, & Callanan, 1993). Mental health professionals utilizing this level of ethical decision making can be seen as categorically following *what should, ought to, and/or must be done.* The American Counseling Association (ACA, 1995) has promulgated a document titled "Standards of Practice" that outlines mandatory behaviors for counselors. Yet, no mention is specifically made regarding consultation. According to Corey, Corey, and Callanan (1993), the standards of practice briefly describe the minimal standards of acceptable counselor behavior. The mandatory level of ethical behavior is a minimum standard; it functions in a manner similar to the way that a law functions. That is, both laws and mandatory ethics specify the *minimum* acceptable standards of behavior that can be evaluated by general members of society. The ACA Standards (ACA, 1995) outlines minimal acceptable counselor behaviors covering the following:

- Counseling Relationship (Section A)
- Confidentiality (Section B)
- Professional Responsibility (Section C)
- Relationship with Other Professionals (Section D)
- Evaluation, Assessment, and Interpretation (Section E)
- Teaching, Training, and Supervision (Section F)
- Research and Publication (Section G)
- Resolving Ethical Issues (Section H)

These eight sections contain 51 standards of behavior. Although the standards cover a broad range of behaviors, each standard of practice (SP) itself is rather specific. For example, SP-14 states that counselors must obtain prior consent from clients in order to record electronically or observe sessions (ACA, 1995). SP-15 specifies that counselors must obtain client consent to disclose or transfer records to third parties, unless certain exceptions exist. SP-20, which relates to advertising, states that counselors must accurately represent their credentials and services when advertising. SP-32 directs counselors to use assessment instruments only for the purpose for which they were intended. With regard to research, SP-47 implores counselors not to distort or misrepresent data, nor fabricate or intentionally bias research results. The American Psychological Association Ethical Principles and Code of Conduct (APA, 2003) outlines 10 ethical standards that include:

- Resolving Ethical Issues
- Competence
- Human Relations
- Privacy and Confidentiality
- Advertising and Other Public Statements
- Record Keeping and Fees
- Education and Training
- Research and Publication
- Assessment
- Therapy

In these standards, the term *consultation* is either implied or overtly mentioned. For instance, Section 1.03 refers to "Conflicts Between Ethics and Organization Demands,"

Section 3.05 relates to "Multiple Relationships," and Section 3.11 concerns "Psychological Services Delivered to or Through Organizations." From a mandated ethical perspective, whenever the demands of an organization with which psychologists are in conflict, psychologists need to clarify the nature of the conflict, make known their commitment to the Code of Conduct, and attempt to resolve the issue through strict adherence to the code (APA, Section 1.03, 2003). Section 3.11 (APA, 2003) states that consultants need to inform, whenever appropriate, those directly affected by the services about (1) the nature and objectives of the intended intervention; (2) which individuals are the clients; (3) the relationship with each person in the organization; (4) the probable use of services and the information that will be obtained, including who will have access to the information; and (5) the limits of confidentiality. In the ACA and APA codes of ethics, these sections outline the minimum level of ethical functioning.

According to Corey, Corey, and Callanan (1993) mental health professionals who function at the mandatory level are reasonably insulated from potential legal action and/or professional censure. Brown, Pryzwansky, and Schulte (2001) also imply that the closer one subscribes to the letter of the code related to consultation, the more legally insulated a consultant becomes. This insulation is not impermeable, however. The fact that professional consultation is folded into broader mental health practices, concomitant with the inherent complexities of any consultation, produces a potentially volatile scenario. In a review of the sections of the codes directly related to consultation, it is clear that there are fewer discrete ethical mandates for consultants; thus, consultants must exercise judgments that many times are based on a few words or a limited number of paragraphs in codes. This segues into the need for a higher level of judgment and ethical functioning.

Aspirational Ethical Functioning

The *aspirational level of ethical functioning* requires professionals to extend their vision and reflect on issues from a perspective that lies beyond what is simply mandated. At this level, practitioners comply with the law and the professional codes, and, yet, go beyond the mandate to reflect on the effects the intervention has on client welfare (Corey, Corey, & Hallinan, 1993). This aspirational level of ethics is where consultants will exercise many of their ethical judgments because of the very fact that there is a minimum amount of mandated ethical standards for consultants. It is important to keep in mind that most unethical behavior is subtle and is likely inadvertent on the part of counselors (Gladding, Remley, & Huber, 2001; Sturkie & Bergen, 2001). Even though there is little professional literature describing consultants' inadvertent behaviors, it is likely that the same holds true for consultants' other behaviors. In all probability, a consultant's unethical behavior would be inadvertent, but no less serious or consequential. What makes this issue significant is the potential deleterious consequences that can follow unintentional consultant misconduct. Because of consultants' abilities to effect change on a large scale, errors can be geometric in their impact on consultees and client/client systems. In order to reflect on a certain course of appropriate action, consultants need to be able to determine probable outcomes for any given intervention. The more aware consultants are of the context of the consultation in all of its various cultural forms, the more efficacious and ethical their decision making will become.

Although there are clear exceptions, the structural placement of professional consultation as a subset of the regulated practices of the various mental health professions is likely appropriate for many, if not the majority, of practicing counselors and psychotherapists in terms of time on task. That this structural conceptualization also acts to "background" consultation as a professional, stand-alone consulting practice may not be a relevant concern to that population of practitioners. For this population, the backgrounding of consultation and subsequent foregrounding of counseling and psychotherapy accurately reflects their diurnal practices. Nonetheless, the ethical implications of such a gestalt figure/ground perspective are significant—if not categorical—in some professional settings and practices. This is especially true in situations where multiple codes may apply.

LEGAL CONSIDERATIONS

School Counseling or Consulting?
Application of Multiple Codes

It is often the case that consultants are engaged in numerous relationships while providing a variety of services during the course of a single consultation. In the course of consulting, many different ethical codes may seem to apply. It is of paramount importance that consultants be cognizant of which helping paradigm is the predominant one through which they are providing services. Without an incisive understanding of which helping process is prevailing, consultants can make inadvertent mistakes that can prove legally costly or harmful to consultees and clients. The following discussion illustrates this point decisively.

The professional practice of school counseling is a lucid example where multiple codes may apply in a given situation. Simply in terms of time spent on task, the structure of school counseling is triadic rather than dyadic—as the name "school counseling" would imply. School counselors are paid by the district or specific school administration (consultees) to deliver services to students (clients) (Harrison, 2000). In daily practice, school counselors work with students, teachers, parents, and school administrators. Many of the relationships are dyadic, such as when a school counselor works with an individual student, teacher, parent, or administrator. However, these dyadic relationships are, in fact, subsumed into the triadic practice of consultation. The reasons for this assertion are simple.

Recall three of the structural components required for formal consultation: (1) the helping relationship is configured as triadic, (2) the goal of consultation is to improve work performance, and (3) the relationship between consultant and consultee involves financial remuneration. School counselors are not paid directly by their clients. Instead, they are paid by a third-party "consultee," which can be configured as being a school district or the principal of the school. Since school counselors work and help students, teachers, and sometimes parents "perform" better and are paid by a third party, it is reasonable to conceptualize the process as *triadic,* and therefore *consultation.* This conceptualization is also punctuated by the fact that many times school counselors have to consult with teachers and administrators about how to help specific students who are exhibiting problematic behaviors. The interactions with teachers and administrators clearly are not *counseling.* To configure these conversations as "professional conversations" does not adequately describe the professional nature of such conversations. The interactions depict a consulting arrangement whereby teachers, administrators, and student(s) are being helped to perform better in their respective "work environments."

Putting this example under closer scrutiny, it would be quite possible for the school counselor to be counseling with the student and consulting with the teachers and administrators (and parents). So, one method of conceptualizing all of the various activities in which school counselors engage would be through a consulting paradigm. By referring to school counselors conceptually as "school consultants," one can better understand the actualities of their work.

One of the major rationales for positing school counseling as school consulting is so that the actual duties that are performed are conceptualized under one organizational schema. Rather than simply organizing the activities for the sake of organizing the activities, placing the activities under one organizational conceptualization, such as consulting, allows for a clearer understanding of the obligations and responsibilities that school counselors have to those they serve. The example under discussion clearly outlines the complexities of the aspirational ethical decision making and the advantage of organizing the activities under a consulting paradigm. Although it would be possible to sift through these complexities, it might be more parsimonious to collapse both activities under "consultation." Then, "counseling the student" would be subsumed under "consulting activities." Without such a conceptualization, it could feasibly be the case that school counselors must subscribe to one set of ethics when counseling students and another set of ethics when consulting with teachers, parents, and administrators. This would be in spite of the fact that all of these activities may be concurrent and focused on helping the student perform better.

In addition to the advantages of organizing the activities under one rubric, there is another compelling rationale. When a school counselor is counseling a student, the global aim of that counseling is to improve the student's performance in the classroom (through a variety of methods, including helping the student to raise his or her self-esteem). In doing so, the school counselor clearly needs to have an understanding of the school system itself and of the specific teacher(s) involved. Any suggestions made to students about how to improve their behavior needs to be germane to the context in which the behavior change will take place. This simply helps to ensure the efficacy of interventions.

In perceiving the larger system in which the student is operating, the school counselor's aim is somewhat different than it would be if he or she were simply counseling a client outside of the school setting. Outside of the school setting, the counselor's aim may or may not include interventions related to the environment. It is not that the counselor would diminish the importance of the context in which the client is involved. It is that outside of the school setting counselors may or may not conceptualize the larger implications of any given intervention in the same manner as they would when they are paid to see their student clients in the school setting. Hence, it would almost be inappropriate—and perhaps unethical—for a school counselor to intervene with students in a way that would not aid the students in adapting to their school experience. Moreover, the school is paying the school counselor. Therefore, the school has some investment in what the school counselor does. Likewise, the counselor has some ethical obligation to honor that investment. This "investment in the outcome" is clearly different from any "investment" that is taken on in a counseling situation.

There is a third rationale for considering school counselors as being school consultants. Expanding the school counseling example further, it would also be possible for the counselor to be working with a student individually, working with the student's parents or guardians by phone or in person, working with the student's teacher(s), and intervening with the school administration all at the same time. The ethical implications are profound. For instance, is the counselor counseling with the student's parents? Does the counselor then have a dual relationship operating in terms of who is the client? Is the primary client the student or the parent(s)? Since the school is paying the school counselor to provide some services to the student's parents, how obligated is the counselor to the parent or the school? In the final analysis, the question becomes: To whom is the school counselor ultimately responsible: the student client, the parents, the teachers, or the school itself? Conceptualizing school counseling as school consulting reflects a more accurate picture of what actually happens in the life of school counselors. Therefore, it is much more than an academic or arcane discussion.

Tort Law and "The Ordinary Reasonable Consultant/Person"

The legal answers to the school counseling quandaries raised in the preceding example lie in a hypothetical construct known as *the ordinary reasonable person*. In essence, the construct of the ordinary reasonable person allows one to evaluate the ethical dilemma from the standpoint of what would be the most reasonable course of action to most reasonable nonprofessional people. The construct of the ordinary reasonable person is derived from tort law, which is the branch of law that often applies to professional mental health practices. In general, tort law seeks to protect the interests that all Americans have by virtue of being members of U.S. society. Through living in this society, people have certain rights and obligations or duties. On a broad theoretical scale, everyone living in the United States has a *right* to be free from unreasonable harm and a *duty or obligation* not to subject others to an unreasonable risk of harm. Examples of rights and duties are identified in people's everyday lives. For instance, all people have an interest in being free from harmful and/or offensive touching (Tort of Battery). In addition, people also have an interest in being free from the *threat* of harmful and/or offensive touching (Tort of Assault). The threat to an individual's reputation is covered under the Tort of Defamation. If an individual were to subject another to an *unreasonable risk* of harm, the person could be considered negligent in his or her duty. The school counselor example clearly relates to the notion of duty to others (i.e., student, parents, teachers, administrators). It also segues into the possibility of these others becoming negligent in their duty. The centrality of "duty and obligation" in the ethics of consultation cannot be punctuated enough because of the triadic structure of the practice concomitant with the multiple relationships inherent in the structure.

Naturally, the Law of Torts has some profound assumptions on which it is built. According to tort law, the "ordinary reasonable person" is one who is

- Always reasonable
- Always prudent
- Always careful
- Always informed
- Always up to the standard

Because professional mental health practices, including consulting, are covered under tort law, ethical decision making in consultation needs to be made in the context of the "ordinary reasonable person." In other words, for every ethical dilemma in consultation, the best answer on how to proceed emanates from what the ordinary reasonable person would do. This is the global construct and guiding light for the ethical practice of consulting (and counseling as well).

CONSULTANT VISION AND VALUES

The consultant's vision and values will also be of significance when it comes to ethical decision making. An earlier study by Warwick and Kelman (1973) suggests that by leaving the issue of which values are important in consultation up to the consultees, consultants may be seriously abandoning their moral and ethical responsibility. An examination into more recent research indicates that consultants' values are of crucial importance in the process, and it is important that consultants have an incisive understanding of their values (Brown, Pryzwansky, & Schulte, 2001; Caplan & Caplan, 1993; Conoley et al., 1991; Dougherty, 1990). Richardson and Molinaro (1996) warn that if consultants are not aware of their own Eurocentric value system, they may inadvertently impose their own values on consultees and clients inappropriately. This can occur regardless of the consultee's or the client's cultural background. In other words, consultants need to be aware of imposing their own values on consultees and clients of *any* culture (Carter, 1991). The implication of such issues on the psychological contract have already been identified and discussed, and the ethic of such issue is addressed in appropriate sections of various codes of ethics. For instance, all professional codes prohibit discrimination and sexual or other harassing behaviors.

Researchers have addressed the issue of consultant values (see Snow & Gersick, 1986; Warwick & Kelman, 1973). According to Newman (1993), many ethical issues that present themselves in consultation are related to values and value conflicts. The potential impact of these values on the process and outcome of consultation can be significant. Because value conflicts are inevitable in consultation, it is important to understand *how* these conflicts will influence the process—not *whether* they will affect it

(Newman, 1993). In an earlier study, Lippitt (1983) outlines three challenges for consultants with regard to their values and the roles they play in consultation: (1) consultants must clarify their values about people-helping decisions and actions, (2) consultants need to also develop knowledge and skills in using their values as part of the intervention decisions and behaviors, and (3) consultants need to learn ways to collect data gleaned through their interactions with consultees and clients in a manner that can be used to check and revise their values. Newman maintains that it is categorically important for consultants to identify their personal and professional values and to utilize them in conjunction with established ethical standards of practice. Moreover, to ignore or deny the significance of consultant values in consultation is "naïve at best, and from an ethical perspective, dangerous" (p. 151).

There is a significant dimension that needs to be addressed when consultant values are discussed. That dimension relates to how the consulting professionals' values are reflected in their relationships with consultees and clients. The issue of consultant values is central when any consideration regarding gender, persons with disabilities, and racioethnic minorities is concerned. It is the consultant's ethical responsibility to embrace diversity in all of its various forms, including diverse ideologies, ideas, and perspectives.

Snow and Gersick (1986) identify two schools of thought regarding how consultants' values need to be used in consultation. One school of thought is called the *value-independent* belief. This school of thought emphasizes the importance of maximizing the full range of choices available to consultees and clients. This way of thinking also acknowledges that consultants' values and biases can influence consultees' decision making. This is not seen as appropriate. The value-independent school of thinking advocates that consultants should not disclose their values or preferences to consultees for fear of restricting consultees' choices. This perspective punctuates the importance of consultants presenting a full range of choices to consultees from an objective standpoint.

The other school is called the *value-guided* belief. Consultants adhering to this school of thought share the view that it is appropriate for consultants to adopt a certain value orientation and to work from that orientation. This school assumes that consultants will limit the attractiveness of any given course of action that is presented to consultees whenever that course of action is not congruent with the consultant's value system. By infusing their values into the consulting process, consultants from this school of thought are seen as promoting what they consider to be the "overriding social good." Examples of promoting the compelling and overriding social good can be seen where consultants promote democracy, unity, nondiscrimination, equality, and fairness. According to Newman (1993), both positions have their advantages.

Consultees understandably have a vested interest in particular consultation outcomes. As such, they will likely recognize and reinforce the ideas that are relevant to that outcome while concomitantly ignoring information which is not congruent with their values (Warwick & Kelman, 1973). Along with this notion are several questions that need to be considered by consultants, although definitive answers to the questions are not necessary. These questions are meant to aim the consultant into the direction of a solid and informed understanding of their values and value systems. Newman (1993) outlines these questions:

- What actually constitutes "imposing" one's values on consultees and clients?
- Is there ever a time when such an imposition is acceptable?
- If consultants allow consultees to unilaterally determine the intervention goals, how much responsibility for the impact of the intervention falls onto the consultant?

Implications of "Power and Control"

Newman (1993) maintains that the concept of power often is seen in a negative light in the helping professions, and consultation is no exception. Merrell (1991) believes this negative view of power in consultation is unfortunate because one of the fundamental determinants of consultants' efficacy is their ability to influence and effect goal attainment. There are several questions related to power and control that need to be addressed when attempting to discern ethical behavior in consultation.

The issue of power and control is an important consideration in the ethics of consulting because consultants will be in positions where a significant amount of power will be "on loan" to them from their consultees and clients. Clearly, the means by which this power is "loaned" and the amount of power loaned varies across consultations and is determined by the formal and psychological contracts. The fundamental aspects of "power and control" relate to how power and control are derived and what it means in any given context. Newman's (1993) interest lies in the point at which this exertion of power by a consultant occurs to negate the consultee and client's freedom of choice. Moreover, does power always imply a differential between individuals? In other words, can two people hold equal power at the same time in the same way? If not, which power is more powerful, and how is that power determined and perpetuated? Regarding organizations, Newman (1993) believes that the consultant's responsible use of power may have a positive impact on how power is subsequently used by those people in power in organizations. In short, Newman sees the appropriate use of a consultant's power as a modeling effect for change in consultation.

What is the relationship between having personal power and having power over someone? In order to have power over someone, does the other person have to agree to being overpowered? If so, under what conditions is that true and under what cases is it not true? Finally, are people inherently powerful? If so, how is that translated into a work setting? There are really no right or wrong answers to these questions. However, the ways in which consultants answer the questions for themselves will partially determine which courses of action are considered "reasonable" in the consulting process. The implications for how consultants answer these questions will also be reflected in the types of consulting models they utilize and in the subsequent interventions that are employed. A consultant who believes that everyone is powerful might not be as likely to employ a "doctor/patient" model of consultation, since that model theoretically ascribes more power to the consultant's abilities to diagnose and prescribe treatment than to the consultee's abilities to do the same. A process consultation approach would seem to fit more with a philosophy where everyone has some power. Yet, would it be ethical for a consultant who believes in the equal distribution of power to employ a doctor/patient model? How "reasonable" would that be? The National Association of

Social Workers (NASW, 1996) implores its members to make their decisions and actions consistent with both the spirit of the code as well as the letter of the code. Although it would be doubtful that the consultant in the earlier examples is acting inappropriately with regard to a specific ethical code, there is some hint of being inconsistent with the true spirit of the consultant's beliefs and values.

Implications of "Expertness"

Similar to the ethical consideration of power and control in consultation is the issue of consultant "expertness." Tokunaga (1984) suggests that consultants should be very careful of presenting themselves as an "experts" because this might covertly influence the consultees' decision making and restrict them to alternatives more congruent with the consultants' values. In the process, consultees may violate their own value standards due to their perception that the consultant knows best.

Who is an expert and how does one become an expert? Who is more of an expert? Is it the one who knows a great deal or the one who knows that he or she doesn't know? The question, "At what point does one actually become an expert?" is intriguing because it is similar to the situation with an oak tree acorn: When does the oak tree acorn become an oak tree? Was it always an oak tree, just in a different form? Or does the acorn become an oak tree when it grows out of the ground? Or when it gets leaves? Or when it reaches maturity? Again, this question is important because it has implications for how consultants might proceed during consulting. If the consultant subscribes to the belief that an expert is one who knows more than he or she doesn't know, that belief might preclude the consultant's abilities to utilize a process consultation approach. It is not that a consultant could not employ such a model. It is to suggest that a potential conflict might surface when determining a course of action or intervention because of the incongruence of values and action.

Implications of "Autonomy and Manipulation"

Almost every beginning graduate student in the mental health profession is confronted with the question about whether human beings are autonomous and whether individuals can be manipulated. The issues surrounding autonomy and manipulation relate directly to notions of power, control, and expertness. The implications are as profound for consultation as they are for counseling.

In terms of autonomy, it is critical to understand that the construct of "autonomy" is itself a Euro-Caucasian value. Since the Age of Enlightenment, the culture of the United States has revered its ability to separate, differentiate, and objectify. The traditional African American syllogism of "We are, therefore I am" stands in diametric opposition to the Cartesian syllogism of "I think, therefore I am." The collectivistic tribal value is also reflected in Native American traditional values as well. According to McGoldrick (1998) and Walsh (1998), highly resilient people reach out to the collective other for supportiveness, such as friends, kin, extended family, and social and religious support systems. This was not always the case, though. Garmezy (1991), Rutter (1987), and Wolin and Wolin (1993) reported that, traditionally, resilience has been viewed from the perspective of the individual and individual traits. This view paralleled the view of the "rugged individualist" in which it was presumed that the individual picked herself or himself up without the help of others. These same researchers maintain that the philosophy of the individual has left the U.S. culture out of touch with the communal and the interpersonal aspects of life, which has led to fragmentation and alienation. It is not sound ethical practice to categorically subscribe to an ethos that maintains a cultural viewpoint that is not appropriate to other cultures. Hence, although a view of individualism might be appropriate for Euro-Caucasian consultees, it may clearly be in conflict with the variety of other cultures that consultees will represent. Moreover, the conflict may not always surface during the initial phases of formulation the psychological contract.

It is not critically important for consultants to have definitive answers to the queries raised in this chapter, because it is assumed that viewpoints can change across time. What is crucial is that consultants have an incisive understanding of the *implications* of these questions on their practices. It is essential for helping professionals from all disciplines to act with *informed judgments*. The term *informed* has many meanings. However, it clearly implies that consultants should be open to being informed by their consultees and clients of both the issues that need to be addressed in consultation as well as being informed of how the consultees and clients are experiencing the issues of concern. A proper conceptualization of consultee's and client's concerns needs to have gender and racioethnicity incorporated into it. Without such a paradigm, consultants are likely not behaving in an informed fashion.

SUMMARY

The ethics involved in consultation are complex and have received only moderate consideration in the professional literature. Because consultation is seen by mental health professionals as being a subset of counseling, the ethics of both helping processes will parallel each other in places and will be different in other areas. The result is that there may not be a great deal of guidance for how consultants should act. Fortunately, many models of consultation outline consultant behaviors that are presumed to be organized around ethical conduct in consultation. Examples are the mental health consultation model of Caplan and Caplan (1993), the behavioral model of Bergan (1977) and Bergan and Kratochwill (1990), Myrick's (1977) school consultant model, and Schein's (1969, 1987, 1999) process consultation approach. All of these will be discussed in later chapters.

In making ethical decisions in consultation, there are several considerations. Since all professionals likely consult at one time or another, being aware of the specific codes that relate to consultation is imperative for all mental health professionals. It is also essential that mental health professionals are aware of which paradigm, counseling or consulting, they are conceptualizing as the primary helping paradigm. The discussion of school counseling illustrates this point emphatically. The issues of confidentiality, dual relationships, informed consent, use of data, individual versus system interventions, consultee and client "right to choose," conflicts of interest, and technology all contribute to the complicated ethics involved in professional consultation. Because of that fact, an attempt has been made to present an overview of the more generic and relevant aspects of ethics in consultation.

There are two levels of ethical functioning: mandated levels and aspirational levels. Several variations of these concepts and terms exist, and these will be discussed in the next chapter. In general, it will be the aspirational level of ethics in which consultants will find themselves when making many decisions during the course of any consultancy. In dealing in the aspirational level of ethics, consultants come face to face with their values, and how their values might impact the consultation. The values referred to and discussed—such as expertness, autonomy and manipulation, and power and control—do not reflect an exhaustive list. They seem to be values that are of particular importance to consultants. In reviewing the professional literature, it seems that consultants must at least entertain these types of questions in order to behave in an informed and ethical manner.

QUESTIONS

1. What is meant by saying that consultation is a "backgrounded" profession?

2. What are the ethical implications that result from such a positioning?

3. What are the levels of ethical functioning? From which level will consultants likely make judgments? Why?

4. What are the reasons for asserting that school counseling is actually school consulting?

5. What are the major ethical implications inherent in the reworking of school counseling into school consulting?

6. Since consultants have expert power, how much of an expert do consultants need to be?

7. Can consultees and clients ever be manipulated? Support your answer.

CHAPTER EIGHT

ETHICAL DECISION MAKING IN CONSULTATION

In the last chapter, various broad dimensions of ethics in consultation were outlined. In this chapter, there is a shift of focus to a more specific analysis of ethics as it relates to the types of decisions that consultants frequently have to make during the course of consultancies. This chapter is not aimed toward providing in-depth skills in ethical decision making in consultation; rather, it will provide a scope of understanding of how consultants might proceed in their practical decision making. According to Cottone and Claus (2000), many practice-relevant models of ethical decision making can be used as guides for consulting decision making. Currently, the criteria for what makes one model better than another are yet to be determined (p. 281). A second purpose is to demonstrate the ethical complexities that occur at the meso- and micro-levels of consultations.

Because the establishment of ethical guidelines for the mental health fields in general is relatively new (Neukrug, Lovell, & Parker, 1996, p. 98), any ethical issue relating to consultation is almost "newer" than that. In other words, although the term *consultation* has been included in the codes, it has developed meanings over time and newer sections relating to consultation have been either added to or changed in established codes. The sections of the established codes for various mental health professionals that apply to consultation are focused on several general areas. As mentioned, these areas include such ethical standards as (1) informed consent, (2) confidentiality, (3) dual relationships, (4) sensitivity to gender and racioethnicity, (5) consultee/client welfare, (6) beneficence, (7) consultant "competency," and (8) intervening. As you can gather from the list of ethical constructs, some paragraphs of a given professional code relating to consultation appear to parallel counseling and therapy codes, and some paragraphs will reflect the structural differences between the two processes. These standards do not change structurally in consultation. As seen previously, the psychological contract usually addresses such dimensions as informed consent, consultee/client welfare, consultant competency, intervening, and diversity. The structural issues of dual relationships and confidentiality become more complex because of the nature of consulting. Yet, these more complex dimensions are still subsumed into the notion of consultee/client welfare. One of the distinctive differences with consulting ethics is the fact that the scope of intervention is larger than the dyadic counseling relationship. However, Dinger (1997) and Cottone and Claus (2000) concur that there is surprisingly little research on ethical decision making or models of decision making in counseling. By default, one can surmise that research in consultation ethics is even further behind.

In spite of a host of ethical decision-making models, problems remain. Primarily, ethical decision-making models for consultation do not appear in the professional literature. Thus, one must borrow from the counseling field in order to help extrapolate guidelines for decision making by consultants. In a comprehensive review of the literature on ethical decision making in counseling, Cottone and Claus (2000) conclude that there are many practical models that can be chosen as guides. Moreover, these practice-relevant models can be applied in specific settings, within specialties, with specific types of clients, and/or according to published standards of practice (p. 281). However, these researchers state that the criteria for what makes a "better" model are not clearly identified in the field. Empirical comparisons do not exist in the professional literature. In spite of these shortcomings, and perhaps because of them, models of ethical decision making used in counseling can still be applied to decision making in consultation.

CORE COMPETENCIES FOR ETHICAL CONSULTANTS

Because consultation ethics and decision making are in their infancy, one manner in which to establish a paradigm of understanding ethical decision making for consultants is to identify some core competencies that consultants need to possess. This can help establish conceptual parameters that would be available to consultants in choosing ethical courses of action. Clearly, as with counseling, consultants need to be aware of their various ethical standards and codes of conduct that apply to consultation. According to Gladding, Remley, and Huber (2001), ethical codes are adopted by professional associations for the purpose of helping its members identify the norms of behavior that are acceptable to the profession while helping members in their decision making. Once consultants understand the codes and the standards, they need to have some understanding of ethical decision-making models.

Not every consultancy will require complex decision making; however, every consultant has to make decisions in every consultancy. To varying degrees, these decisions will impact the lives and perhaps livelihoods of consultees and clients. The purpose here is to help mental health professionals develop a deepened understanding of their impact on the lives of others through the study of ethics. With regard to consultation and probably with most other professional endeavors, it is almost always better to be over-prepared than underprepared. Stevens (1999) and Van Hoose (1980) both agree that therapists must have a clear process for understanding ethical decision making in order to behave ethically. There is little reason to doubt that the same is true for consultants.

As discussed in the previous chapter, ethical decisions are driven by the system of values that are operating during the process. It is critical that mental health consultants explore their attitudes, values, and understandings of the primary conceptual paradigm of the helping service that they are providing—counseling or consultation—in order to be ethically effective. Illback, Maher, and Kopplin (1992, p. 119) outline the knowledge, skills, and attitudes necessary to ensure consultant competency. This list reflects basic core attitudes that consultants need to have in order to be able to discharge their professional duties in an effective and ethical fashion. According to Illback, Maher, and Kopplin, consultants need:

- To be able to tolerate ambiguity and inadequate data in making decisions about certain courses of action and intervention
- To be able to make a personal commitment to the precepts of the mental health profession that include the public interest, social responsibility, and service to the community
- To believe that institutions, organizations, and other social systems can change through collaborative planning and systematic intervention
- To recognize and advocate for the psychological and civil rights of individuals in society and to seek empowerment for them, especially the vulnerable
- To be able to consider the diverse and often contradictory demands of multiple client systems without behaving in a judgmental or arbitrary fashion
- To be sensitive to and appreciate cultural diversity and be willing to communicate this sensitivity to others
- To be able to maintain equanimity and personal integrity in high-stress and conflicting situations
- To engage in sophisticated reasoning about complex ethical dilemmas while using specific ethical principles in seeking effective resolutions
- To be able to respect and communicate the fundamental worth and dignity of learners, clients, and consultees
- To be able to demonstrate enthusiasm for learning, capacity for psychological growth, intellectual curiosity, openness to experience, and appreciation of empiricism

In discussing ethical and legal issues in school psychology consultation, Heron, Martz, and Margolis (1996) point out other considerations for consultants. For example, these researchers caution consultants against attempts at "being all things to all people." Although it is not stated in their research, it would seem obvious that a state of affairs where consultants are attempting to be everything to everybody suggests ethical issues of competency and scope of practice. In terms of decision making, it would seem equally obvious that this situation would also lead to faulty decision making or at least to decisions that were not conceptualized adequately. Heron, Martz, and Margolis also caution consultants to stay current with research in the field and to periodically review their respective professional codes of conduct. Garfat and Ricks (1995) believe that ethical decision making is mainly a self-driven practice and advocate that consultants need to possess attributes such as self-awareness, an ability for critical thinking, a willingness to take personal responsibility, an openness to alternative choices, and the ability to monitor and implement feedback.

As you would expect, several critical dimensions in models need to be considered as influencing the decision-making process. First is the consultant's knowledge of the ethical standards, because all models will require knowledge in this area. Second, an implied dimension that influences a consultant's decisions is the level of his or her ethical functioning (mandatory or aspirational) or orientation to that standard. Another dimension is the consultant's level of understanding of the decision-making model and processes through which ethical decisions can be analyzed. A fourth dimension relates to the level of the consultant's understanding of the context of the problem. All things being equal in the consultation and given the consultant's knowledge of the ethical codes, it is reasonable to assume that the more incisive the consultant's awareness is of the nuances of the problem needing solving, the more ethical and more effective the solution would potentially be.

GROUNDING ETHICAL DECISION MAKING

Researchers in the mental health field have attempted to ground ethics on a theory or philosophy. The theories or philosophies on which various ethical approaches are based include *moral theory* (e.g., Hare, 1991, 1981; Rest, 1984, 1983; Stadler, 1986), *probability theory* (e.g., Gutheil, Bursztajn, Brodsky, & Alexander, 1991), *feminist theory* (e.g., Hill, Glaser, & Harden, 1995), *hermeneutic perspectives* (e.g., Betan, 1997), and *social constructivism* (e.g., Cottone, 2001).

Grounding in Moral Theory

Moral theory is a fundamental ground for ethics. Hare (1991) identifies absolute thinking and utilitarian thinking as being involved in ethical decision making regarding psychiatric patients. Briefly, *absolute thinking* reflects the legal notions of tort law, focusing specifically on rights and duties. *Utilitarian thinking* emanates from the notions contained in the concept of "the greatest good for the greatest number of people." In order to deal with these two types of thinking, Hare devised a two-tier level of moral reasoning that became the basis for Kitchener's (1984, 1986) model of ethical decision making. Cottone and Claus (2000) cite the work of Rest (1983) as another example of moral philosophy guiding ethical decision making. In Rest's research, four processes are identified as major determinants of moral behavior:

1. Interpreting situations in terms of potential effects on the welfare of others
2. Formulating a moral course of action and identifying the moral ideal in a specific situation
3. Selecting an outcome from competing values in deciding whether to try to fulfill the moral ideal
4. Executing and implementing one's intention

Stadler (1986) embraces moral principles as the basis for action in a 10-step model of ethical decision making. Stadler believes that moral beliefs influence actions taken in response to ethical decisions, and holds that helpers are moral agents with special responsibilities to clients. In this model, the test of ethical decisions rests on the *universality, publicity,* and *justice* of the proposed course of action. Tymchuk (1986) held the construct of justice as being the goal of ethical decision making and bases a 7-step model upon notions of utilitarianism. Forrester-Miller and Davis (1996) uphold the constructs of *autonomy, beneficence, nonmaleficence, fidelity,* and *justice* as standards of ethical decision making. Forrester-Miller and Davis's model uses Stadler's (1986) three questions to determine the courses of action. With respect to consultants, the three questions are:

1. Is the action fair?
2. Would the consultant recommend it to a peer?
3. Would the consultant want the behavior to be made public?

Corey, Corey, and Callanan (1993) also concur with Forrester-Miller and Davis in believing that autonomy, beneficence, nonmalficence, and justice are significant ingredients that go into ethical decision making.

Causing and Allowing.   Interestingly, as profound as these moral considerations are, all are founded on more fundamental philosophical issues related to cause and effect and the natural course of nature. In conceptualizing "courses of action" in decision making, consultants can borrow from the works of Bennett (1993) and Donagan (1977) on ethical theory. Bennett provides a profound and critical discourse on the morality of "making" something happen versus "allowing" it to happen. The distinction is clearly related to the consultant's decision making. Sometimes consultants "make" something happen, as in the case of the doctor/patient model, whereby a consultant diagnoses the problem and prescribes an intervention or treatment. Another example of "making" something happen is reflected in the purchase model of consultation in which a consultant provides a needed service that directly impacts the consultee and/or client system.

   "Allowing" something to happen emanates from an entirely different perspective. Bennett (1993) uses the example of a tree in a forest to depict the point. Imagine a tree falling as a consequence of your behavior. In other words, whether or not it fell depended on how you acted. According to Bennett, you could either *make* the tree fall, fell the tree yourself, or cause it to fall. You could also *allow* it to fall, not prevent it from falling, or not save it from falling. Bennett maintains that the difference between these two paradigms is profound and significant. To illustrate the point about the crucial distinction, Bennett offers the following example:

- She fells the tree, she causes it to fall or she makes it fall.
- She lets the tree fall, she permits or allows it to be the case that the tree falls.
- It falls because of something she does.
- It falls because of something she does not do.
- It falls because she intervenes in the course of nature.
- It falls because she allows nature to take its course. (p. 75)

   The ethical distinction between "allowing" something to happen and "making" something happen is decisive for consultants, consultees, and/or their client and client systems. According to Bennett (1993), the important question for moral theory asks, "If someone's behavior has a bad state of affairs as a consequence, is the morality of the conduct affected by whether the person *made* the consequence obtainable or only *allowed* it to be so?" (p. 76).

Other Grounding Theories for Ethical Decision Making

Gutheil and colleagues (1991) advance a theoretical orientation to ethical decision making from a scientific paradigm. Formally known as *probability theory*, these researchers propose a "decision analysis" as a formal decision-making tool. Based on the uncertainty principle in science, Gutheil and colleagues believe that decisions can be broken down into components. These components can then be organized, and projected courses of action can be sequenced in terms of what might follow. Clearly, this approach draws heavily on conventional scientific approaches. For example, the researchers suggest that decision analysis involves such things as acknowledging the decision, listing the pros and cons, developing a decision tree, estimating probabilities and values, and calculating the expected value of any given behavior.

In contrast, Hill, Glaser, and Harden (1995) offer a model of ethical decision making reflecting feminism and *feminist perspectives*. In this model, both the emotional responses, concomitant with the social context in which the helping process takes place, are valued. Congruent with traditional notions in feminist theory, Hill and associates believe that clients need to be engaged as fully as possible in the decision-making process. This is seen as enhancing feelings of empowerment. As a result, this joint engagement helps ensure that the diagnosis and subsequent interventions will be more effective. The process of decision making in this feminist perspective model includes a rational-emotive component aimed at valuing emotional and intuitive dimensions of decision making. The impact of consultants' personal values, the universality of the proposed solution, and the "intuitive feel" of the proposed solution are considered to be of significance in this model.

The probability approach of Gutheil and colleagues (1991) is not only in opposition to feminist approaches but it is also in opposition to other approaches. For example, two other grounding perspectives that are reported in the professional literature include *hermeneutic perspectives* and *social constructivist perspectives*. Betan (1997) advances a hermeneutic approach that sees knowledge as being situated in the context of human relationships in which the interpreter participates in the narration of meaning. In this approach, the helpers' psychological needs and the context of the helping relationship "are fundamental considerations in the interpretation and application of ethical principles" (p. 356). Because of this, Betan believes that linear, logical-reductionist approaches may lead to a false dichotomy between reason and intuition, or between the universal and the subjective. A more "radical" approach is offered by Cottone (2001) and Cottone and Claus (2000), who ground ethical decision making into a social constructivist paradigm. According to Cottone and Claus, decision making is not a psychological process at all; rather, decision making is a social process that always involves interactions with other individuals (p. 277). These researchers believe that ethical decisions are not internally compelled, as some research has suggested. Instead, ethical decisions are socially compelled and, as such, always take place through the interactive processes that include negotiating, consensualizing, and arbitrating (p. 277).

CASE STUDY ONE

THE MORAL DILEMMA

The Situation.   A clinician approached a fellow therapist at a party and asked for some time alone to talk about a dilemma. The clinician and therapist were cohorts who practiced out of the same office building. Although their respective schedules kept them from spending much time together, both considered themselves to be friends. They had the kind of friendship that develops over the years of working together and that comes to include a certain level of trust on both a personal and a professional level. The two professionals lunched together about a half a dozen times throughout the year, and they did celebrate one or two holidays a year with each other's families.

In the ensuing conversation, the clinician revealed that he had fallen in love with his client's soon-to-be ex-boyfriend. The clinician acknowledged his ethical transgression, then he posed the question to his fellow therapist, "What should I do about the situation?" The therapist knew that she was now involved, unwittingly, in a formal consultation with serious ramifications for all parties. She asked the clinician how serious the relationship was between him and his client's soon-to-be ex-boyfriend. The clinician responded that nothing had happened as of yet, but said that they were both attracted to each other and were pursuing the relationship. The consulting therapist asked for clarification of the status of the relationship between the client and his boyfriend, and was assured by the clinician that the "relationship was over." Needing to clarify the structural concerns, the consulting therapist asked how often the clinician had met with the two of them together and asked the clinician who he was identifying as "the client." The clinician stated that the "client" did not include the boyfriend, and that he had only had two sessions with both of them in the room. The aim and focus of those two sessions was to "finish up the business of breaking up." It was during those two sessions that the clinician and the ex-boyfriend became enamored with one another.

The clinician said that the client was moving to another state the following week. At this point, immediate action was called for. Assured that there was no possibility of reconciliation between the clinician's client and his boyfriend, and assured that the relationship between the clinician and the ex-boyfriend was going to be pursued, the therapist turned discussion toward an ethical strategy to help with the unethical situation. The therapist queried the clinician about important issues related to the client. Primarily, the therapist wanted to know how stable the client was and the extent to which he had social supports. The clinician remained steadfast in his assessment that the client was in "reasonably" good mental health considering that he was going through many profound changes. For instance, the client was breaking off his relationship with his boyfriend of five years, was leaving a job to take on another, was moving to another city where he would need to establish a new social circle, and was selling his house. Moreover, there would be a temporary drop in income, new adjustments made for a new job, and the client would need to find new housing. All of these changes were considered by the consulting therapist to be major life transitions in the life of the clinician's client, which increased the client's risk factors for future mental or physical illness.

After gathering enough of the facts about the case, the consulting therapist asked the clinician what he was planning on doing. He replied, "That's why I am asking you! I have no idea what to do, given the new relationship is going to continue." The consulting therapist organized a strategy with the clinician. Primarily, the consulting therapist asserted that the clinician would need to disclose this unethical behavior to the client as soon as possible. The issue of when to disclose was mitigated by the fact that the client was experiencing many stressful events simultaneously, and this information would also be seen as a major stressful event. At the same time, the consulting therapist and the clinician agreed that there was not enough time for the clinician and the client to meet before the client left the city. Both professionals agreed that one meeting in which the clinician revealed the situation would not be enough to process the client's reactions. Thus, it was agreed that the best course of action was to wait until the client moved and became somewhat stabilized in his new environment.

The consulting therapist knew that the client was already experiencing a host of stresses, and if the client found out about the relationship before the clinician disclosed the information, the situation would turn from very bad to worse. The consulting therapist suggested that the clinician wait for two or three weeks and then arrange to fly down to see the client. The purpose would be to disclose the unethical relationship. During the meeting in which the unethical behavior would be addressed with the client, the clinician would be prepared with a list of potential mental health professionals in the client's new hometown who could potentially help the client debrief the situation. In the meantime, the clinician was directed to report himself to the state board of examiners as soon as was possible. Short of the clinician reporting himself, the consulting therapist was mandated to report her cohort and friend to the board. The clinician agreed that this was a reasonable plan of action.

In the ensuing few weeks, the clinician and the client's ex-boyfriend continued pursuing their relationship. However, a short time after the consultation and before the plan could be executed, the clinician's new boyfriend was killed in a tragic accident as the clinician looked on. So, just after the consultation and before anything was disclosed to the former client, the relationship between the clinician and the client's ex-boyfriend came to a sudden and tragic halt. The former client became aware of the relationship between his ex-boyfriend and his former therapist during the course of settling the deceased boyfriend's estate. After the funeral, both the clinician and the consulting therapist were named as co-defendants in a lawsuit. Even though the consulting therapist had never seen the clinician's client in a professional setting, the complaint against the clinician and the consulting therapist centered on a breach of contract by both parties.

Debriefing the Case.   Clearly, there were ethical issues at stake, but the morality of the case was front and center. Yet, although these were moral issues, professional ethics and the legalities of the situation superceded the deeper and more fundamental issues involved. The clinician was in violation of professional ethics and subsequently of the law. Although it is never a good idea to carry on a relationship with a former client, some professional codes of ethics state that a sexual relationship is permissible as long as the clinician waits for a period of time. In this situation, the clinician was involved before the two-year window. The consulting therapist's values came into play in the consultation that reflected a philosophy that one can never control when and where one falls in love. Hence, falling love in the workplace was seen by the consulting therapist as unethical and, yet, philosophically "permissible." This value allowed for immediate, nonjudgmental acceptance of the clinician's behavior. Nonetheless, this philosophy did not obviate any ethical responsibility. Regardless of how the consulting therapist felt about the situation in philosophical terms, an ethical action was mandated. The issue related to what type of action was mandated.

(continued)

CASE STUDY ONE   (CONTINUED)

As Hill, Glaser, and Harden's (1995) feminist model suggests, the consulting therapist's intuitive feel for the case as well as the need to enhance the empowerment of her clinician friend were two aspects of the situation that were important to the consulting therapist. The suggestion that the clinician report himself to the state examining board was aimed at two things: solving the awkwardness of a situation in which the consulting therapist would be turning in a friend, co-worker, and consultee; and helping empower the clinician to take responsibility for his actions on a deep and meaningful level. Clearly, there would be sanctions as a result of turning himself in to the board. However, the consulting therapist believed that by having her colleague turn himself in, he would be moving his relationship out of a shame paradigm into one in which he could be proud of his choice of love while "paying the price" for it by assuming his responsibility in the act of falling in love. The need of the consulting therapist to avoid the awkwardness of reporting the clinician and the suggestion that the latter report himself reflects notions of Betan's (1997) hermeneutic model, which emphasizes the relevance of interpretation. In that model, the consulting therapist's psychological needs and the context of the relationship with the clinician are fundamental to the ethical decision-making process. In this manner, the consulting therapist was exercising valid ethical decision making. This is also supported in the more radical model proposed by Cottone (2001) and Cottone and Claus (2000). These authors believe that decisions are always made in the context of interacting with others. In interacting with the clinician, the consulting therapist was well aware of the impact the discussion was having on her relationship with the clinician. At the same time, the consulting therapist was very cognizant of the clinician's unethical behavior and did not attempt to exonerate her cohort.

Disposition of the Case.   The case did go forward to a judge who heard the case and attempted to settle it. There were two main overriding elements in the case. One related to the unethical and inexcusable behavior on the part of the clinician—in spite of the philosophy that love finds its own lovers. The second overriding feature of the case was the tragic death of the clinician's new boyfriend. Clearly, the actions were unethical. Yet, the tragic death had a significant emotional effect on all parties, including the plaintiff (the former client), the clinician and the consulting therapist, the lawyers, the state board of examiners, and the judge. All parties agreed that the behavior was unethical, and all parties agreed that what had resulted was tragic. Everyone involved in the case was profoundly impacted. The clinician was reprimanded, and the consulting therapist was essentially excused from the case on professional grounds. An interesting feature of the settlement process was ironic: While the judge was lecturing the consulting therapist about her responsibility to report the case to the board, the judge was smoking a cigarette in his office. Public offices have a no-smoking rule, and the judge was obviously violating the law while lecturing the consulting therapist on the prospect of her unethical conduct. The depth of the irony is seen in the fact that while chastising the consulting therapist for not turning in a fellow professional, none of the lawyers in the settlement room reported the judge on his illegal behavior! This echoes Schein's (2000) sentiment that "organizations are neither fair nor rational." This presumably includes the judicial system.

Corruptions in Ethical Decision Making

Point of No Return. Gabbard (2000) researched clinical consultation from a psychodynamic paradigm and has identified several "corruptions" that can take place in the consulting process that are interesting and particularly relevant to the case example at hand. Primarily, Gabbard states that "consultation is not a panacea" for problems (p. 213), and in earlier research, asserts that there are points of "no return on the slippery slope" (Gabbard & Lester, 1995). This occurs when whatever ethical decisions are decided upon become ineffective because the ethical situation has progressed too far. In the earlier case example, it was clear that the clinician was at a point of no return before seeking consultation. That is, even if the consulting therapist had suggested that the relationship needed to stop, the clinician was not going to do so. The consulting therapist knew this was the case through the discussion with the clinician. Gabbard (2000) states that this type of "as-if consultation is of no value whatsoever" (p. 213).

Curbside Consultation. Another type of corruption in consultation is a situation in which the consulting decisions take place "on the fly." Gabbard (2000) offers the example of a colleague seeking consultation while getting a cup of coffee or when a consultee pulls the consultant aside at a social function with the idea that the consultant will affirm and validate what the consultee is already doing. Gabbard thinks that in these situations, the client's history will often be given in a brief form followed by a "carefully edited" description of the problem. Although the "coffee machine" is not an ideal place in which to consult, school counselors know full well how effective these types of consultations can be. Time is at a premium for school counselors, and many consultations do take place in such unusual locations. Rather than these being categorical criticisms of the decision-making process, these types of school consultations can be seen as accommodating to the very real limitations school district employees face everyday. Not every teacher has the time to walk down to the counselor's office without an appointment and expect to receive immediate attention. At the same time, counselors who may be on hall or playground duty can find opportunities to interact with teachers for the benefit of students. Thus, a categorical mandate admonishing "curbside consultation" is not appropriate in all situations. Clearly, the issue here relates to the intentions of consultees, some of whom may be attempting to play down certain ethical considerations.

In many cases, the manner in which the consultee relates information positions the consultant into a decision frame that almost obligates the consultant to affirm and validate the course of action already set upon by the consultee. The case example also reflects elements of this type of corruption. After all, the consultation was requested at a party, and only a brief history of the situation was described. Perhaps the most interesting and relevant aspect of this type of corruption in consultation relates to the fact that during the settlement hearing with the judge, the clinician could not recall being instructed by the consulting therapist to turn himself into the state board of examiners. Gabbard (2000) says that "even when consultees desire help, they may unconsciously 'not hear' the consultant's words if they contradict the consultee's wishes" (p. 214). This was clearly the case in the example.

Consultant Shopping. On closer reflection, the case study suggests that the clinician may have been shopping around for validation and to limit legal liability. As it turned out, the clinician had actually already obtained consultation from "other friends" prior to requesting help from his cohort therapist. This information was not shared with the consulting therapist at the time of the consultation. So, the consulting therapist believed that she was the only one providing expert advice to a cohort and believed that the clinician was going to follow the suggestions that she had made. On a deeper and legalistic level, Gabbard (2000, p. 215) states that the duty of the consultant is only to the consultee, not to the patient. So, unlike a supervisor or a supervisory relationship, the consultant has no liability for what happens to the patient. In this case, the judge decided differently in that the case was heard. Although no liability was assessed against the consultant, she was verbally reprimanded.

Furthermore, the case is complicated by the fact that the consulting therapist was bound by confidentiality, so to report the clinician may have placed the consulting therapist in a vulnerable position had she chosen to report the unethical behavior. This does not mean that the consulting therapist would have been found guilty of breaking confidentiality by reporting the clinician to the board. Even though the code of ethics requires reporting, the consulting therapist would still have been somewhat at risk had she broken confidence with her colleague. The categorical exception to confidentiality is sexual abuse (child abuse and elder abuse), and this case could have been construed as a form of sexual abuse from the perspective of the former client. Although this would have been a legal question, the fact remains that sexual relations between the ex-boyfriend and the clinician is not considered to be dangerous in the same way that assault is. Hence, the legal entanglements in the case example served to constrain both the clinician and the consulting therapist concomitantly in terms of decisions that were actually available to make. To the credit of the clinician, he sought consultation from another professional. He did not have to seek consultation at all. The vulnerability of feeling ashamed and embarrassed by the situation was great. Nonetheless, he did reach out for help to someone with whom he had respect and he risked reprisals as a result. The example just discussed was clearly consultation. The decisions about how to proceed were framed using a consulting paradigm. There are other situations where the paradigm itself is in question.

CASE STUDY TWO:
THE COMMUNITY AGENCY COUNSELOR

A marriage and family therapist was working in a rural mental health center that was providing counseling to individuals, couples, and families. The therapist was assigned to a division in the center that was funded by a grant awarded by that particular county's court. The general purpose of the five-year grant was to provide funds for 10 sessions of marital counseling services for couples referred by the courts who had a history of family violence and who were going through the divorce process. The hope was that family counseling would decrease the stresses associated with divorcing, and thus diminish opportunities for family violence and the need to return to court.

In this particular couple's case, the therapist had been working with a couple for nine sessions. After the ninth session, the wife had solidified her plans to relocate in another state. The tenth and last session was scheduled for the day before she was moving. During the course of a brief interaction with the therapist in the waiting room immediately prior to the last session, the female client whispered that she had just told her soon-to-be ex-husband that she was pregnant. The female client then turned and moved closer to the therapist and disclosed that she was deliberately lying to her estranged husband and had no intention of telling him the truth until he had "paid" for the pain he had caused her. After disclosing this secret to the therapist, the female client abruptly left the center prior to her husband's arrival for the session. On her way out, she ran into her husband, who was arriving for the session. Yet, she kept walking, passing by without comment. The confused husband wanted to speak with the therapist.

The situation was compounded critically by the fact that both the female client and the therapist were aware that the soon-to-be ex-husband had a history of suicide in his family and at least one attempt himself. The therapist feared that the female client's lie about being pregnant might push the male client to the brink of another suicide attempt. Not knowing exactly what had transpired, the soon-to-be ex-husband heeded the urgings of the therapist to call his wife on her cell phone and request that she come back so that they could fulfill their contract with the agency and court. The female client agreed to come back in for the session. While waiting for the female client to return to the session, the therapist made some attempts to help the husband see the possibility that he was being manipulated by a false-truth without breaking confidentiality. The husband was visibly distraught about the news of the pregnancy, but said that he was not suicidal.

Soon, the wife knocked on the counseling door at which point she was invited in to sit down. The session immediately intensified and escalated, and the unanticipated speed of emotional reactivity set the therapist back in shock. Almost as soon as the session began, the female client turned around, yelled at her husband, and ran out of the office without disclosing anything about the lie. Her husband reacted as fast as his wife had. He stood up and immediately ran after her through the waiting room, out the door and into the street. The therapist was in hot pursuit. When the female client had reached the car door, she opened it and stood there without getting in. Her husband reached into his pocket and dangled the car keys in a taunting fashion in front of her, daring her to try to drive off without the keys. At that, she slammed the door and ran down the block, leaving her husband standing on the side of the road yelling at her. The therapist knew that the situation was a volatile one because both clients had a history of physical violence with one another. After a few minutes, the therapist had calmed down the husband.

In the meantime, the female client returned and the situation escalated once again—this time in the agency's parking lot. Other clinicians and employees of the center saw what was happening and contacted law enforcement. Now, the husband threw the keys at his wife who then used them to open the door. As she was getting inside, she spit on him and revealed the truth about her not being pregnant and taunting him as naïve and weak. He punched his fist through the windshield. She started to get out of the car. As she was getting up out of the car seat, she shoved the car door against him, pushing him back. He grabbed the door. Then, realizing what was happening, each backed down from the other and stepped away. The incident lasted less than two or three seconds and never escalated

(continued)

CASE STUDY TWO   (CONTINUED)

past that. The wife got back in the car and closed the door while leaving the window open. Both clients were angry and hurt. Yet, to the therapist, there was no threat of harm.

At that point, the police arrived to find the two clients quieted down, still physically apart and not talking to each other. One of the officers requested a moment with the therapist. The officer asked the therapist for information about the clients, but was told that the information was confidential and could not be discussed at present. The well-trained officer did not press the issue but did ask if the therapist had witnessed any violence.

The Therapist's Contextual Conceptualizations.   At this point, the distraught but poised therapist thought about several issues. She was aware that if she had admitted seeing the brief physical exchange, one or both of her clients might be arrested. She feared more for the husband's lethality. Although he stated earlier that he was not suicidal, the situation was perceived as possibly escalating his risks. Moreover, all this was happening the afternoon before the female client was moving away with no plans for the couple to ever see each other again!

There were clear values involved in this example. The therapist believed that it did not seem moral or fair that her male client might go off to jail. After all, the whole incident started with a lie meant to inflict hurt and humiliate him. At the same time, a desperate attempt by the female client to inflict emotional pain was seen by the therapist as another sad state of affairs. The therapist assessed the consequences of playing down the physical exchange in which both clients had demonstrated a degree of good self-regulation in deescalating the potential violence. If she did not provide full disclosure to the officer in an attempt to care for the mental health of her clients, the therapist knew she was colluding with her clients against law enforcement. She knew this was not good. By not involving law enforcement, she also knew that she was exposing each client to the other for one more night. That was risky, too. At the same time, the therapist was aware that her male client had a place to go for the night, away from the female client. She had been perspicacious enough to clarify that when the officers were arriving on the scene. The therapist also knew that the female client had already made plans to stay at her parents' house for her last night in town. Those plans would not change unless the female client was arrested and in jail. The therapist concluded that each of her clients was safe at this point—safe from suicide and safe from each other. The two clients spoke to the officers and briefly explained their situation and the fact that they would be physically separated that night and the next day. The officers left the scene with assurances from the clients that they would not have any further contact with each other that night. The male client did in fact find a place to stay for the night, and the female client followed through on her plans to leave without further contact. The divorce was handled by lawyers through the mail.

This case illustrates how quickly a consultation (or a counseling session) can intensify and how fast the helper must respond. To act in an informed manner with sound clinical judgments, helpers must be acutely aware of how they are globally conceptualizing the helping process from the outset, for one is not able to conveniently switch paradigms (i.e., from consulting to counseling) simply to fit the situation. There needs to be a prevailing helping paradigm in order for consultants to organize their thoughts, conceptualizations, and potential courses of action into a unified and consistent whole.

SHILLITO-CLARKE'S MODEL OF ETHICAL DECISION MAKING

In her discussion of ethical issues in counseling psychology, Shillito-Clarke (1996) analyzes the ethical problem-solving model of Bond (1993). Bond's model as well as Shillito-Clarke's analysis of it is written in the context of counseling psychology. Again, consultation is in a "backgrounded" position. Hence, the ensuing discussion will be drawn from a counseling foundation and applied to consultation. This application of ethical considerations from counseling to consultation can also help demonstrate how mental health professionals go about determining the best course of action based on ethical principles that bridge counseling and consultation.

Step One: Clarify

This step is likely the most important one. Clarifying the situation and problem to be solved is crucial. Sometimes clarifying the situation might involve writing down the situation and the issues that are at stake. According to Shillito-Clarke (1996), this process of clarifying encompasses a *determination of the elements* involved in the problem. In terms of the triadic structure of consultation, it is important to imagine how the consultee and clients might *describe* the problem. Once the consultant has gone through this process, it is advisable to *gather evidence* for and against a given course of action.

A. Determine the Elements.   Determination of the significant elements in the case is a structural question rather than a process one. From a counseling perspective, referring to the previous case study, the structure includes the therapist and both the female and the male clients as the basic dyad. The officers and perhaps the colleague who phoned law enforcement would be included in a collateral fashion. However, from a consulting perspective, the structure changes the situation dramatically. Employing a consulting paradigm reflects the centrality of the mental health agency (financial grantee) and the law enforcement agency (financial grantor) in the picture. Given this consulting conceptualization, the ethical issues gravitate around the following:

- Whether the therapist's conceptualization of her role as a "consultant" and all of its implications is a more appropriate role than a counselor role
- The agency's policies and procedures regarding responsibilities and obligations
- The expectations of the granting agency
- Professional competence
- Informed consent

- The therapist's relationship with each individual family member as well as with the couple as a whole
- The issue of the female client's lie about being pregnant and all of its implications on the mental health of her partner
- The male client's history with suicide
- Confidentiality
- The couple's history of mutual violence
- The timing of the issue
- The conflict(s) between law and ethics
- The issue of beneficence
- The context of intervening

B. Descriptions of the Problem.   Imagining how each party would describe the problem is an important step in the process (Bond, 1993; Shillito-Clarke, 1996). The consulting paradigm once again shifts the number of individuals involved. The viewpoints that need to be imagined would include those of the therapist, her immediate clinical supervisor at the mental health clinic, the appropriate mental health agency officials (including the executive director), the grantor (the appropriate law enforcement agency administrator), the officers who were on the scene, the clients, and the colleague who called law enforcement. *It is advisable to imagine different viewpoints from the same person.*

C. Identify the Stakes.   What was at stake? Clearly, there was a great deal at stake in this case in terms of client welfare and ethical decision making. How the therapist represented her mental health agency in the crisis was also of central focus. There were two consultees in this case: There was the mental health agency that paid the therapist directly, and there was the court that funded her position and paid the center to hire the therapist. On a global scale, because the officers are related to the courts, they were also consultees. At this level of conceptualization, the relationship between the agency and the courts was also at stake.

The primary clients in this consultation were the divorcing husband and wife. There was a lot at stake for them in terms of their mental health. The therapist believed that her actions would directly impact their mental stability. Concomitantly, the situation demanded that the mental health issue be balanced against each client's emotional welfare and physical safety. For the husband, this emotional health included being free from the threat of suicide. It included for the female the safety in being free from threat of physical harm as well as being free from the harm itself. There were legal issues at stake in terms of confidentiality and the therapist's full or semi-full disclosure of the events to the law enforcement officer. There was also the potential for the therapist to perjure herself in an attempt to protect the mental health of her clients. The question of her freedom from prosecution was a serious consideration.

Step Two: Consult

Shillito-Clarke (1996) suggests that consultants review their respective codes of ethics. She also advocates the adherence to "that code that gives you the tightest, most specific information" (p. 578). According to this model of ethical decision making, it is a good idea to consult with legal counsel prior to determining a course of action. (Many insurance companies for mental health professionals advocate that their insurance holders consult with them prior to determining a course of action when legal issues are at stake.) It is also wise to consult with colleagues and supervisors. In these situations, it is important to maintain proper boundaries of confidentiality and take notes. However, in the example, there was no time to consult with anyone or anything other than dealing with the very real crisis at hand. This situation required the consultant/therapist to have already been well versed in her ethical obligations.

Step Three: Consider Courses of Action

What choices are available? As with the foregoing components, the identification of choices available to consultants is bound to the ethical standards, by the level and type of consultants' ethical functioning, and by the imposing contextual conditions present in the situation. Some choices will be ruled out simply through mandatory adherence to the code of ethical standards. On one level in the example, the therapist was mandated by law. Perhaps she was ethically bound to report fully what she saw happen with the car door. Other choices will rule themselves out because of their conflictual effect(s) on other proposed solutions. So, some potential solutions will cancel out other options. The impact of the choices on the larger consulting system, including the consultee and client/client system, will determine the viability of some choices. Gender and the culture of the organization, institution, agency, group, and/or individual will also influence the choices that are available to consultants. Clearly, the severity of the situation in this example was a significant factor in the therapist's decision making.

The Decision Tree. The decision tree for the therapist in the example included a number of equal-appearing and conflicting choices. The choices available to her were conceptualized mainly by evaluating the severity of the situation, the history with suicide, confidentiality, and beneficence. There was the threat of violence to both the clients. This threat also included the potential threat of violence to the husband—due to his risk of suicide. The balance of this potential for harm was weighed against the breach of confidentiality and full disclosure to law enforcement, which might have been potentially harmful to both clients. There was also the threat to the therapist's safety because of her physical proximity to the action. Finally, the notion of "beneficence" was predominant in this example. Everything that was under consideration needed to be evaluated in terms of what was the "greatest good" for the greatest number of individuals. As it turned out, "beneficence" was the prevailing paradigm guiding the therapist's decision making as to what to do.

Step Four: Choose

Select the best course of action and sleep on it (Shillito-Clarke, 1996). It is good for consultants to have some time away in order to help ensure that they are thinking of everything they can. If not, it is possible that some small detail will be overlooked in the process. It is also possible that this omission can have significant deleterious effects. Sometimes situations that are not bound by a short time line may take a few days to consider the full implications. Sometimes, there is no time to sleep on it. There is only time to act, as in this case. Sometimes the decisions are made in the moment and intuitively, and consultants deal with their choices later.

Step Five: Check the Outcome

Reflect the results of the decision. Bond (1993) and Shillito-Clark (1996) both maintain the importance of reflection in terms of what consultants learn about themselves and about the situation as a result of any given course of action. In this case, the therapist was reflecting on her actions by sharing it in detail with her colleagues in a staff meeting.

KITCHENER'S MODEL OF ETHICAL DECISION MAKING

According to Gladding, Remley, and Huber (2001), who conducted an extensive review of Kitchener's (1984) work, Kitchener identified four predominant psychological processes on which applied ethics is based for psychotherapy. The application of this ethical decision-making process will be reconceptualized and reoriented to consultation.

Process 1: Interpreting a Situation as Requiring an Ethical Decision

Given that every decision should be ethical, the "interpretation" referred to here is fundamental. This includes such fundamental understanding of gender, disabilities, and racioethnic differences because the entire paradigm of diversity, cross-cultural, and/or cross-gender consultation is guided by an ethical structure. That is, the term *minorities* is mentioned in the established codes of ethics and, as such, any interaction involving those identified as minority is ethically structured.

In the original counseling paradigm, this process of interpreting a situation underscores the categorical necessity of *perceiving the effect of one's actions* on the welfare of others (Gladding, Remley, & Huber, 2001). The numbers of significant "others" in consultation can be enormous. According to the authors, there are many persons who have difficulty interpreting the nuances of situations, and one result of failing to intervene may be due to a misunderstanding of what is happening. It is partly for this reason that time was spent in the last chapter discussing the more profound and core assumptions related to autonomy, freedom, and manipulation. Ethical sensitivity and empathy are categorical requirements, and if consultants are not aware of where they are in the interactions, problems can develop quickly (as was the reflected in the latter case example).

Regarding Case Study Two, Gladding, Remley, and Huber (2001) provide a good guideline related to this notion of the reliability of empathy and feelings in ethical decision making. These researchers describe a case of a therapist who breaks confidentiality to prevent perceived "serious" harm to a client and ends up feeling bad. For instance, the therapist in the example feared that she would be feeling worse if something bad did happen as a result of her attempts to maintain confidentiality. Yet, she remained steadfast in her nondisclosure. In another situation, a therapist might break confidence in order to avoid a potential worse feeling in the future. Gladding, Remley, and Huber warn consultants that an "ethical action does not always feel good, nor does it always lead to choices that are 'good' in an absolute sense" (p. 10).

In the case example, the therapist knew that she was playing a line of confidentiality and she felt that pressure. On the one hand, there was the line between breaking confidence of her female client and disclosing to the husband that the story of his wife being pregnant was a lie. She wanted to tell him. On the other hand, she chose to maintain confidence while asking him questions that would hopefully bring him to the realization that his wife might be lying. For instance, the therapist asked the husband how sure he was that his wife was pregnant. Did he see the doctor's report? Did his wife visually share the results of the home pregnancy test with him? These questions were couched in the frame of standard procedures that any husband would want to know. This is how the therapist believed she was protecting her female client's confidentiality while, at the same time, helping the husband discover the truth by indirectly prodding him into his own realization. The therapist disclosed in a subsequent staff meeting that she knew it was "almost a no-win situation." She also knew that she "had to act quickly."

Process 2: Formulating an Ethical Course of Action

After a situation has been accurately assessed for its "ethical presence," one must conceptualize an ethically justifiable course of action (Gladding, Remley, & Huber, 2001). Kitchener (1984) delineates between two levels of ethical justification. Citing the work of Hare (1981), Kitchener maintains that there is the *intuitive level* and the *critical-evaluative level* of moral reasoning.

Intuitive Level.   With regard to the intuitive level, Kitchener (1986) believes that people develop ethical beliefs and assumptions about what is right and what is wrong and what one should and should not do over the course of normal life experiences. During the course of acquiring and shaping these ethical values, people are also seen as developing reasoning related to these values. Kitchener maintains that the intuitive level allows for decisions to be based on the professional's immediate affective response to situations.

According to Hare (1981) and Kitchener (1984), immediate moral feelings are critical to everyday ethical decisions. Everyone in the United States (and in many areas abroad) had emotional and intuitive reactions to September 11, 2001; similar reactions occurred on April 19, 1995, when the Murrah Federal Building in Oklahoma City was bombed. The guilty party, Timothy McVeigh, received a stay just prior to his execution after the federal government released documents related to the case that had not previously been presented to the court. Everyone familiar with the case "knew" what was right and what was wrong. The stay was perceived by the American public as "wrong" based on intuitive levels of understanding. Although knowing that hiding information is inappropriate and unethical, people (judges, too) also "knew" that the bombing incident was worse than the lack of disclosure by the government, and the stay was quickly overturned. The point is simply that there were intuitive reactions to the bombing and to the federal government, and these "intuitive feelings" were the foundational basis in decrying the stay of execution. The same emotional or gut feelings can help guide ethical decision making.

Mental health professionals who deal with suicidal clients often do not have the time to do anything other than act. In those cases, there is little or no time for reflection—only time to intuit the situation and act according to ethics and one's gut feeling. Hare (1981) and Kitchener (1986) both believe that *in new or unfamiliar situations, professionals will likely err if they do not adhere to their intuitive level of reasoning.* These two authors are joined in their beliefs by several other researchers, such as Van Hoose and Kottler (1977) and Corey, Corey, and Callanan (1979). In this chapter's Case Study Two, the therapist intuited that the most efficacious "action" was to help with the original plan to get her female client out of town and develop a new plan to keep her male (and perhaps her female) client out of jail. Both plans needed to be incorporated into a new plan guided by her ethical reasoning and decision making. Reverting back to the description of *mandated ethics* discussed in Chapter Seven, the therapist could not have responded effectively to the situation simply by adhering to the mandated charge for her behavior. Clearly, the mandated level was necessary for ethical information, but it was not sufficient enough on which to base a decision. However, it is also critical to note that even though the therapist believed that her intuition was on target, that does not mean that it, in fact, she behaved ethically. Nor does it ensure that she did the right thing. Nevertheless, it is likely that the case discussion brought up emotions for you, as readers, too. It is likely that you were making intuitive understandings and assessments as to what the therapist should have done. Your intuitive understanding is the intuitive level of ethical decision making.

Critical-Evaluative Level.   Because mandated and intuitive levels of ethical decision making are not always sufficient, there needs to be another level of ethical reasoning to augment the efficacy of decisions. As mentioned earlier, this second level is referred to as the *critical-evaluative level* (Beauchamp & Childress, 1979; Drane, 1982; Gladding, Remley, & Huber, 2001; Hare, 1981; Kitchener, 1984). According to Gladding, Remley, and Huber, this level is composed of three tiers.

Tier One is the mandated ethics tier, referred to in Chapter Seven. At this level, what the code specifically states is what guides the professional's decision making. For instance, various mental health professional codes of ethics prohibit sexual relations with clients. A Tier One approach would be sufficient to determine action here, and professionals would not need to rely on intuition or aspirational ethics for guidance. It is prohibited, and professionals are clearly mandated to adhere to that code. Because the exemplified consultation in Case Study Two was a crisis consultation, the therapist had to proceed and act according to how she was assessing the situation *as it was developing.* Based on the nature of consulting situations in general, consultants will often have to act spontaneously according to their intuition and knowledge of the codes, the goals of the consultation, and the context in which the consultation is taking place. When the mandated and/or intuitive level of decision making is not sufficient, one needs to go to Tier Two.

In *Tier Two,* ethical decisions are based on a more general and profound understanding of the ethical principals. Gladding, Remley, and Huber (2001) describe the situation in which a professional might behave according to her or his understanding and subscription to the notions of a client's right to "self-determination" or the need for a client to "respect the rights of others." In Case Study Two, the *right of self-determination* related to the wife's right to lie to her husband. The issue related to respecting her husband's rights to not be subjected to that pain became an issue when his history with suicide was introduced into the case. The therapist conceptualized some line of hope or some window of opportunity that lay between these two rights. The client system or marital culture had grown accustomed to and tolerated such actions. Concomitantly, the therapist herself was balancing her own rights of self-determination while addressing her need to respect the rights of her clients. In essence, that was her battle throughout the crisis. Interestingly, even Tier Two was insufficient to handle the therapist's case in the most appropriate manner.

Tier Three is characterized by the appeal to ethical theory. According to some ethicists (e.g., Abelson & Nielson, 1967; Baier, 1958; Toulmin, 1950), ethical actions should emanate from a deeper well-spring of philosophy and theory whenever ethical principles are in conflict. At this level of decision making, *professional behaviors are based on what the professional determines that he, she, or significant others would want if the situation were reversed as well as what would produce the least amount of avoidable harm.* Tier Three is a tier in which the construct of "beneficence" is central. The therapist in the example based her decisions partly on the issue of producing what she believed to be the least amount of avoidable harm to everyone concerned. That included her value and belief that she was also helping the courts by keeping her clients out of the system that would have likely dismissed the case after a long process. In this manner, the therapist was valuing the objective of the grant, which was aimed at keeping divorcing couples out of the court system. That her values came into play in the case segues into the third process of Kitchener's ethical decision-making model.

Process 3: Integrating Personal and Professional Values

In this process, the mental health professional's personal and professional values begin to shape and texture the decision-making process. As the process moves forward, there is a shift from the concrete ethical considerations to a process that involves the more abstract, individual understandings and interpretations of the ethical standards. This is accompanied by a shift in the position of values as they move from the background to the foreground in the decision-making process. For consultants, this third process is the one in which their professional values—including those related to gender, disabilities, racioethnic diversity, finances, ambition, and self-interest—become influential. As you might suspect, the manner, direction, and intensity in which these values will present themselves in the decision-making process is largely based on the psychological contract between the consultant and consultee—and to a greater or lesser extent between the consultee and the client/client system. Gladding, Remley, and Huber (2001) mention the importance of the level of the professional's *virtue ethics*—willingness to follow the spirit of the law. In the example, the psychological (and legal) contract included the therapist helping both clients concomitantly.

Process 4: Implementing an Action Plan

Gladding, Remley, and Huber (2001) believe that it is not enough to have knowledge of virtue ethics, nor is it enough to be simply concerned about ethics and ethical decision making. Consultants must assume responsibility, take action, and hold themselves accountable. These same authors point out the necessity of mental health professionals' abilities to tolerate ambiguity in ethical decision making because total clarity and certainty are elusive. In addition to the complex issues involved in many consultations, consultants must also assume responsibility for the duality of relationships inherent in working with consultees and clients simultaneously. In many cases, the boundaries between consultees and clients and multiple client systems can become somewhat blurred. A good rule of thumb is for consultants to ensure that any ethical decision making respects individual rights and does not promote the enhancement of some clients over the welfare of other clients and consultees. This should and can be accomplished while consultants are respecting their primary obligations to the consultee.

The clinician in Case Study Two held herself accountable for her actions. She knew the stakes, knew the codes of ethics, was aware of the inherent conflicts, was able to project various outcomes to different scenarios, and acted the best that she could. Although it is very risky and likely inappropriate to evaluate the propriety of a given ethical decision based on the outcome, one cannot help but be thankful that the outcome in the case example worked well for all concerned. No one individual in the case seemed to have gained an advantage over the other in the process of being helped. Clearly, the clinician had some obligation or duty to both consultees as well as to both clients. One of the problems was the layering effect of having two consultees (one being the agency that hired the clinician to do the work, and the other being the law enforcement agency that awarded the mental health agency money to hire the clinician). This "double layering" of consultees meant that the clinician had to juggle a triple obligation. She was obliged to the mental health agency as a consultee, to the law enforcement agency consultee that awarded the money, and to her clients. A question is: To whom was the clinician primarily obligated? Before an answer can be provided, one must consider the relationship the clinician had with her clients. She clearly had some obligation to them individually as well as to them as a couple. In simple terms, she had a relationship with (1) the mental health agency, (2) the granting agency, (3) the male client, (4) the female client, and (5) the couple as a conjoint client system. In this example, it seems as though the welfare of her clients was the overriding obligation. This conceptualization seemed to subsume the other obligations under it.

If one were to conceptualize this case as a simple counseling case, the issue of obligation may be greatly minimized, but not eradicated. Even if this case were configured as counseling, there remains the issue of counseling the two individual family members as well as counseling those two conjointly. The "counselor" would have some obligation to honor the individual family members even when working with them as a couple. The problem is that if the clinician decided to consider herself a "counselor" in this case, then she would need to have followed the marriage and family counseling code of ethics throughout her time with the clients. The counseling paradigm has some limitations, however. The purpose of counseling was to help diminish the instances of family violence. This was in part the mission statement of the grant. Thus, the clients were not actually driving the counseling agenda. The counselor and consultee were promoting the agenda and, as such, a simple counseling paradigm would be insufficient to explain the nuances of the situation. Because the agenda was based on a third party who was paying the money, the paradigm was a consulting one.

The implications of this paradigm are enormous. A counseling paradigm meant that the clinician's primary (and only) responsibility was to the clients. In such a venue, her primary responsibility was to protect the clients' welfare. Her response to the law enforcement officer, although not totally truthful to the letter of the law, did seem to protect the client welfare, since there was such a small window that was left open until the female left the next day. Nevertheless, the clinician was not fully forthcoming with her disclosures about all that she saw, and that presented an ethical dilemma that included the perceived goodness achieved by a lack of full disclosure and the risk of harming the client system by being totally forthcoming. Here, the ethic and the law were in conflict. Since the clinician was schooled in consultation and consultation ethics, she was able to conceptualize the entire case, and subsequent crises, as a consultation. In such a conceptualization, she adhered to the larger aim of the granting agency, which was to diminish family violence in order to decrease the court caseload. In a consulting paradigm, the clinician was discharging her duties in a congruent fashion with the wishes of the granting agency. By assessing the crisis situation clearly and with conceptual forethought, the clinician recognized the fact that the court would not have to deal with this family in family violence since the female client was presently leaving town with no plans to return.

SUMMARY

Cottone and Claus (2000) reviewed the professional literature from 1985 to 1998 and referenced nine models of practiced-based ethical decision-making for counselors (p. 279). These models can be effectively translated into ethical guidelines for consultants. The first step identified in many decision-making models calls for consultants to gather information, describe the parameters, and/or identify the ethical problem (e.g., Corey, Corey, & Callanan, 1993; Steinman, Richardson, & McEnroe, 1998). There are a few models that have steps that are pre-problem identification. For instance, Welfel (1998) wants helpers to develop ethical sensitivity before defining the problem. Stadler (1986) believes that it is important for helpers to identify the competing principles involved. Tymchuk (1981, 1986) wants helpers to identify all of the "stakeholders" in the situation as a first step. In almost every case, there is a need for helpers to consult the ethical codes and guidelines early on in the process.

Once the initial steps have been taken toward making a decision, most models advocate helpers obtaining consultation from other professionals during the course of generating potential solutions (e.g., Corey, Corey, & Callanan, 1993; Stadler, 1986; Tarvydas, 1987, 1998; Welfel, 1998). In addition, all models reviewed by Cottone and Claus (2000) see the need for helpers to generate potential courses of action and alternatives, and all models include the evaluation of potential consequences of various courses of action. It is also not surprising that all models suggest the need for helpers to evaluate the action and reflect and modify actions in the future if need be.

Professionals are expected to maintain the highest possible ethical standards possible. According to Parsons (1996), ethical decision making in consultation is a complex process and involves consultant competence, consultant sensitivity to values and culture, and knowledge and awareness of the various relationship issues that surely surface during the course of the helping process. In terms of consultant competence, Parsons asserts the importance of consultants understanding and embracing the limits of their competence, seeking ongoing training and supervision, knowing when to seek support and consultation from colleagues, and having the ability to make referrals to other professions when it is appropriate for the welfare of the consultation (Parsons, 1996).

Regarding consultant values in consultation, Parsons (1996, p. 230) indicates the necessity of consultants understanding the range of options available and the identification of those options most congruent to the consultants' value structures. In addition, consultants need to attempt to help consultees and clients identify their own operative values. Finally, through the process of collaboration, consultants must determine the congruence of both the intervention goals and the strategies to be employed as they relate to the value structure of the consultee, client system, and the consultants' own orientations. According to Parsons (p. 232), the ethical consultant is one who is sensitive to the cultural makeup of the consultee/client system and who attempts to design interventions aimed at being compatible with the system's cultural values. In that process, consultants need to be aware of their own culture while understanding the limits of a single-culture "mainstream" approach. Consultants need to be sensitive to alternative worldviews and need to employ ethical decision-making skills that reflect respect and sensitivity for other cultures.

QUESTIONS

1. How would you have conceptualized both case examples in terms of their ethical implications?

2. In your conceptualizations, what prevailing elements of the cases were punctuated?

3. Analyze both case examples in terms of the consultant "making" or "allowing" events to happen.

4. How did these case examples differ along the lines of "making" and "allowing"?

5. What would you add to or eliminate from the list of "consultant core competencies"?

6. How do you think law enforcement would have reacted if the clinician had revealed everything she saw?

7. If the various professional organizations that make up the codes of ethics are not comprised of minorities, what are the ethics involved with that?

■ ■ ■ ■ ■ ▬▬▬▬▬▬▬▬▬▬▬▬▬▬▬▬▬▬▬▬▬▬▬▬▬▬▬▬▬▬▬▬

CHAPTER NINE

MENTAL HEALTH CONSULTATION

TRADITIONAL MODELS OF CONSULTATION

Popular graduate-level textbooks on consultation as well as a plethora of research appearing in professional journals for mental health professionals contain similar tables of contents and/or frequently cite the works of certain authors or researchers. For example, a review of the table of contents of four texts currently used to train graduate-level mental health professionals in consultation all reflect discussions about organizational consultation approaches, behavioral consultation, and mental health consultation approaches—in addition to some discussion of the stages of consultation (see Brown, Pryzwansky, & Schulte, 2001; Dougherty, 1990; Parsons, 1996; Hansen, Himes, & Meier, 1990).

Additional approaches may also be included, such as the discussion of Adlerian and family-based consultation in the Brown, Pryzwansky, and Schulte (2001) text, the medical consultation approach discussed by Hansen, Himes, and Meier (1990) in their text, or the systematic consultation approach of Myrick (1977). Although these approaches are informative and likely effective, they are not consistently discussed across texts. In addition to discussions of approaches, most texts will include specific models, such as the process consultation model of Schein (1969, 1987), the behavioral consultation model of Bergan (1977), and the mental health consultation model of Caplan and Caplan (1993; see also Caplan 1970). These are the first systematically described models of consultation for mental health professionals, and they remain today as seminal works used to train professionals in the mental health field.

Caplan and Caplan's (1993; Caplan, 1970) original mental health consultation model was founded when Caplan was working with immigrant children in Jerusalem in the late 1940s. The model was refined over the years and today is one of the basic conceptual and methodological systems that underlie the development of school psychology (Caplan & Caplan, 1993). The behavioral models of consultation—specifically, the works of Bergan (1977) and Bergan and Kratochwill (1990)—utilize a detailed problem-solving approach that is familiar to those working in most K–12 educational settings. The tenets of behavioral consultation are grounded in behavioral psychology. In addition, behavioral approaches in the helping professions are widely understood and used in educational settings. The process consultation approach of Schein (1969, 1987) emphasizes a collaborative approach in working with consultees and clients in organizations, and Caplan and Caplan punctuate the importance of having a "coordinate interdependence" (p. 60) with consultees. The lateral positioning with consultees is similar in structure to many counseling models that emphasize nonhierarchical relationships between counselors and clients.

Researchers across both counseling and consultation agree that these skills include holding consultees and clients in positive regard, being genuine, and being empathic (e.g., Kurpius, Fuqua, & Rozecki, 1993; Rogers, 1951). Although clearly divergent in actual process, some counseling and consultation models also share similar assumptions related to the initiation, building, and transforming of relationships. The emphasis on relationship-building skills and on mutual exploration of problems and their solutions is emphasized in most, if not all, consulting models. For instance, one of the major assumptions of Schein's (1969) process consultation model of organizational development is the fact that neither managers nor consultants can accurately diagnose problems independently of each other. There needs to be a process of joint diagnosis (Schein, 1969, p. 5). Foundational to this process of joint diagnosis is the assumption of good relationship-building skills on the part of consultants. So, when conceptualizing models of consultation, it can be helpful to note the categorical need for effective relationship-building skills on the part of professionals across both helping processes. However, remember that counseling and consultation operate in significantly different ways. The following discussion is not in-depth enough for one to go out and practice mental health consultation. The purpose of this chapter is to acquaint you with Caplan's (1970) and Caplan and Caplan's (1993) mental health consultation model and to discuss the relevant issues related to diversity. Their book, *Mental Health Consultation and Collaboration* (1993), is excellent reading, although some criticisms of it will be addressed here.

Generic Theoretical Structure

Similar to models of counseling, the structures of consulting models should be soundly based on a theoretical framework. However, consultation approaches have been criticized for being atheoretical (Gallessich, 1982), which, in practice, can lead to difficulties in focusing the process in a coherent fashion and/or may also emphasize techniques over integration. In addition, researchers such as Bardon (1985) and Glaser (1981) believe that a lack of theoretical grounding can cloud the role descriptions that need to be clear between consultant and consultee. Gallessich's (1982) research did pose a strong argument reflecting the state of consultation at the time. However, Brown, Pryzwansky, and Schulte (2001) reviewed the literature on the topic and concluded that there is no shortage of models and theories in consultation (p. 10). For instance, these same authors quickly point to the fact that the roots of behavioral consultation are grounded in behavioral psychology (p. 48). Other examples of grounded theory in consultation are mirrored in the works of Brown and Schulte (1987), Bergan (1977), Bergan and Kratochwill (1990), Myrick (1977), Caplan and Caplan (1993; Caplan, 1970), and Schein (1969, 1987).

It seems more likely that the real issue in the debate centers on the difficulty of how to accurately ground the consulting process more than to the actual models themselves being weak. Regardless of which side of the debate one is on, more research is needed to help clarify the issue. The structural components of sound theories and the models that emanate from them reflect core assumptions about human nature, the universe, and people's places in it. Clarifying the core assumptions of theories and models in consultation is an important task.

Flexibility of Traditional Model Structures

Excellent reviews and analyses of the organizational, behavioral, and mental health models and approaches in consultation are provided in various texts (e.g., Brown, Pryzwansky, & Schulte, 2001). However, little attention has been devoted to an examination of the applicability of the structural tenets of these models and approaches in terms of their applicability for women, persons with disabilities, and racioethnic minorities whose beliefs about nature, time, and meaning in the universe differ vastly within and across various populations. These assumptions and values help form worldviews (Ivey, Ivey, & Simek-Morgan, 2002). It should go without saying that consultants need to be culturally aware and sensitive at all points along the consulting process and, as previously discussed, this includes being aware of one's worldviews. Researchers such as Carter (1991), Richardson and Molinaro (1996), and others also stress the importance of this self-awareness.

The presence or absence of theory in any given approach is debatable, but the presence of one's worldview in the process of consultation is not. Fortunately, there has been increased research interest into the area of diversity and consultation (e.g., Brown, Pryzwansky, & Schulte, 2001; Dougherty, 1990; Helms, 1990, 1992). As mentioned, much of this research has centered on consultant characteristics or consultant skills in terms of how cross-cultural consultation is conducted; little, if any, has focused on an analysis of the structural assumptions of various models that impact the process. It is possible that the popular models of consultation that are described in various texts may not be structurally flexible enough to incorporate current views of women, persons with disabilities, and racioethnic minorities. The implications have profound ethical and moral implications in terms of the level of change that is affected. Although Brown, Pryzwansky, and Schulte (2001) present an analysis of the assumptions of mental health and behavioral consultation, such an analysis has not been advanced examining the influence of assumptions on various diverse groups. This is not to diminish the worth or utility of these existing models of consultation; quite the opposite is intended.

The first attempts to systematically organize consultation and the consulting process—found in the earlier works of Schein (1969), Caplan and Caplan (1993; see also Caplan, 1970; Bergan, 1977; and Myrick, 1977)—have withstood the test of time while spawning numerous offshoots in the research and practice of consulting. All four models have undergone revisions and refinements and continue to be accepted in the field (see Bergan & Kratochwill, 1990; Caplan & Caplan, 1993; Myrick, 1977; Schein, 1987). However, the results of quantitative and qualitative research appearing in the professional literature regarding strides made in multicultural competence in general would suggest a need to examine these approaches to help clarify their usefulness and appropriateness for these populations.

For example, a consulting model that philosophically and structurally assumes (or requires) the superior position of the consultant either in terms of skills and/or knowledge inadvertently (and categorically) places the consultee, and perhaps clients, in a structurally subordinate position. This may violate the psychological contract. The issue relates to whether that structural position is deemed acceptable given the consultee's or client's worldview. Such a structure may appear to bring about change, but there may be other levels of change that may be deleteriously affected. For instance, a consultation model that advocates consultants not only being experts but also positioned in a hierarchical relationship with consultees and clients may achieve some success in the short term in terms of immediate change on the part of the consultee and/or clients. However, the long-term effects of hierarchies may weaken the consultees' and/or clients' safety needs. As a result, both productivity and feelings of security and self-worth can be diminished. Productivity may go up in the short term and fall off over the long term.

Potential problems are similarly reflected in any number of gender or racioethnic configurations in consultation, such as having a female African American consultant, a Euro-Caucasian male consultee, Asian American female employee (client), and so on. However, it may not be the structural integrity of the models themselves that lead to situations such as just described. There is a plethora of research describing the effects of consultant characteristics and skills that influence the success of cross-cultural consultations (e.g., Brown, Pryzwansky, & Schulte, 2001; Caplan & Caplan (1993; Caplan, 1970), Conoley, Conoley, Ivey, & Scheel, 1991; Horton & Brown, 1990). As suggested, the issues of hierarchies can be handled effectively in cross-cultural consultations. Nevertheless, when discussing emerging dimensions in consultation, it seems relevant, if not mandated, that an examination of the very models and approaches of consultation be undertaken in order to help advance a more incisive understanding of the foundations of effective practice.

CAPLAN AND CAPLAN'S MENTAL HEALTH CONSULTATION

Caplan published the first edition of *The Theory and Practice of Mental Health Consultation* in 1970, and the revised edition, *Mental Health Consultation and Collaboration*, written with his daughter, was published in 1993. The model was one of the earliest systematically described models to appear in the literature and today remains a seminal work in the field due to its systematic thoroughness, attention to detail and process, and overall comprehensiveness.

Characteristics of Mental Health Consultation

Caplan and Caplan (1993, pp. 21–23; Caplan, 1970) summarize the characteristics of their mental health consultation model. A more incisive consideration of these characteristics will be discussed in later sections of this chapter.

1. Mental health consultation is a method of communicating and does not imply the emergence of a new profession.
2. Mental health consultation takes place between professionals: a professional mental health consultant and a consultee from another professional field.
3. The consultant usually comes in from the outside.
4. Consultants have no coercive or administrative relationship with consultees.
5. Consultants are under no mandate to change consultees' conduct.
6. Consultees are under no obligation to accept consultants' suggestions.
7. The consultant must have expert knowledge in mental disorders, the promotion of mental health, and/or interpersonal aspects of the work environment, and the consultees must define problems in terms of these mental health areas.
8. There are two main goals of consultation: one is to help consultees with the current situation and the other is to increase their capacities to handle similar situations in the future.
9. The consultant/consultee relationship is coordinate or nonhierarchical.
10. The consultant's aim is to improve job functioning; personal enhancement is seen as a healthy side effect.
11. Consultation is usually conducted in two to three short interviews and then the relationship between consultant and consultee is terminated until further consultation is needed.
12. Consultants do not focus on consultees' personal problems, but do devise ways to minimize the impact of such personal issues in the workplace.
13. Consultants remain focused on the problem situation at hand and have no predetermined body of information to impart.
14. There are infrequent times when consultants need to put aside their roles as consultants and provide direct advice to consultees when clients' welfare is in jeopardy.

Using the preceding list of characteristics to frame the overall structure of mental health consultation, Caplan and Caplan (1993) distinguish four types of consultation:

1. Consultee-centered case consultation
2. Client-centered case consultation
3. Program-centered administrative consultation
4. Consultee-centered administrative consultation

The titles of the types of consultation indicate the consultant focus as well as the consultation process. Two consultation approaches, client centered and program centered, have different foci and goals than those approaches emphasizing the consultee-centered approaches. In the consultee-oriented consultations, efforts are aimed at enhancing the consultee's level of functioning through the dissemination of new information or through various direct and indirect consultant interventions. The interventions are aimed at improving the consultee's current and future problem-solving capabilities (Caplan & Caplan, 1993, p. 20). The client-oriented approaches emphasize solutions to the client and/or administrative systems and focuses less on enhancing the skills of consultees. The importance of the consulting relationship is crucial in all four consulting configurations. In fact, Caplan and Caplan devote three chapters on relationships and relationship building in consultation, which underscores the essential nature of these skills in their view.

Client-Centered Case Consultation

This is the most familiar type of consultation. In client-centered case consultation, the primary goal is to have the consultants communicate effectively to consultees about how a particular client can be helped (Caplan & Caplan, 1993, p. 19). This type of consulting structure is similar to Schein's (1969, 1987) "purchase" and "doctor-patient" models of consultation. An example of this occurs when is a psychiatrist is enlisted to evaluate a client's mental status. In essence, this service is purchased from an expert in the field for a specific purpose. A client may be presenting in an unusual way such that it impedes a clinician's abilities to conceptualize the issue adequately or to form a plan of action. The clinician may request a consultation from the staff psychologist. Most, if not all, of the consultant focus is oriented toward the client rather than on the consultee. One of the assumptions in this consulting configuration is the fact that the client's difficulties are remarkable, and future cases would likely need consultation as well. So, it is not simply a matter of education or skill building with the consultee. In fact, Caplan and Caplan maintain that the more time consultants spend with consultees while collecting information about their clients, the more it approximates consultee-centered case consultation (p. 86).

This consulting configuration usually requires a high level of expertise or some specific content knowledge on the part of consultants. More often than not, client-centered case consultation will require consultants to have some diagnostic understanding of the client. Infrequently, this is done face to face. More often than not, the consulting process takes place by reviewing documents related to the case or by exploring the issue with the consultee. For instance, a school psychologist may attend an individualized educational plan (IEP) for the purpose of interpreting test scores for other IEP team members. There are times when the consultant would want to examine the client in person and times when gleaning information from consultees is appropriate. In some cases, both client and consultee must be assessed for successful consultations to occur. Basically, there are two areas of assessment: Focus on the client's problems and focus on the consultees' liabilities, resources, and work situations relative to the client (p. 89). It is critical to remember that the responsibility for the case rests on the shoulders of the consultee, not on the consultant (p. 98). In a fashion similar to collaborating relationships, which will be discussed later in the book, consultants take responsibility for their diagnoses and for the soundness of their recommendations to consultees.

Program-Centered Administrative Consultation

Client-centered case and program-centered administrative approaches have similar primary goals, which are to prescribe effective courses of action to consultees. However, program-centered administrative consultation is a type of organizational development for human service organizations. In this type of consulting, consultants need to possess knowledge of general organizational theory and practice and need expertise in several areas from finance to planning and administration (p. 224). As is the case with client-centered case consultation, the consultant will be responsible for the assessment and recommendations (p. 227) in this administrative approach as well. Caplan and Caplan (1993) draw parallels between the mental health specialists and OD consultants and contend that both types of consultants are often equally qualified to perform the job. However, these same authors point out that there might be occasions when a mental health consultant may be more appropriate if the issue(s) deals with a mental health program content area or if the issue involves a particularly difficult employee who may have psychiatric concerns (p. 224).

A program-centered administrative approach can be delineated from the client-centered case approach in that the latter has consultants focusing on presenting a plan for administrative action rather than recommendations for case management. Another difference between these two approaches is the potential manner in which data can be gathered. In the client-centered case approach, the consultant can, upon occasion, examine the client directly, as in face-to-face interviews, or, as in the example of the IEP, indirectly by basing recommendations on a review of the client's records, test results, and other pertinent databases. Although direct observation is clearly a method available to consultants in the program-centered administrative approach, most of the data are gathered by the staff of the consultee institution and presented to the consultant. Hence, the bulk of the consultant's information will be gathered indirectly, which, in some cases, creates the use of considerable staff time. It is critical to understand that during time spent with the staff, the purpose of the consultant is to gather data and not necessarily to help the group process and generate solutions to problems. This process would move the consultation into consultee-centered administrative consultation. The time spent with staff obviously requires more time across a longer period. Thus, it would not be unusual for consultants in this type of consultation to be working with consultees and clients for weeks or even months at a time. In client-centered case consultation, the time period is dramatically shorter—minutes or hours.

Consultee-Centered Administrative Consultation

As you might expect, the consultee-centered administrative approach is both similar to and different from the program-centered approach. It also has some similarities to the consultee-centered case approach. The consultee-centered administrative approach is an organizational approach in which consultants focus on the consultees and their abilities to generate new ways of dealing effectively with problems (Caplan & Caplan, 1993, p. 264). It is more of a "drawing solutions out" of consultees rather than a "moving solutions into" consultees process—as is more the case with the client- and program-focused approaches.

For Caplan and Caplan (1993), consultee-centered administrative consultation is the most demanding type of consultation. There are several reasons for this. First, these consultations can take from months to years to complete. Second, consultants need numerous skills. For example, in addition to general knowledge of organizational development, the authors suggest that consultants need knowledge of individual and group skills as well as specialized knowledge of social systems and administration. Moreover, consultants would need to have knowledge of the overall mental health of its community and more specialized knowledge of the potential impact that these issues would have on the psychological health of the staff members themselves (p. 265). Third, this type of consultation may have a broader focus, and the interventions may extend beyond the boundaries of specified consultees. For instance, although the interventions may be aimed at a specific individual, group, or groups, there might be a significant collateral impact. For this reason alone, Caplan and Caplan assert the categorical importance of consultants needing to be flexible in choosing consultees (p. 264).

The issues related to the data collection methods available to consultants in this approach differ from the methods of other approaches. Consultants routinely enjoy administrative support guaranteeing staff cooperation in program-centered consultation. However, in the consultee-centered administrative approach, no such legitimacy exists. Consultants are generally left on their own to generate cooperation from staff, and this constraint may be more punctuated in some situations than in others. The data available to consultants are also mitigated by the fact that consultants are concurrently gathering information and building relationships that will influence the intervention. Another issue relates to the scope of the problem. Consultants and consultees alike often do not know what will be uncovered in the course of consultee-centered administrative consultation. Whatever unforeseen issues arise, consultants need to match the needs of the consultees and their resources and capabilities (Caplan & Caplan, 1993, p. 273).

Consultee-Centered Case Consultation

The most clinical of the consultation approaches in Caplan and Caplan's (1993) mental health consultation model is the consultee-centered case consultation. Similar to consultee-centered administrative consultation, the consultant's focus is on the consultee. However, the setting is a clinical one, not an organizational setting as in the administrative approaches. *The consultee-centered case approach requires consultants to focus exclusively on the consultees' narrative or description of the problems they are having with their clients.* The purpose of this type of consultation is to improve the professional functioning of consultees with the current case, while concomitantly helping them develop a capacity to resolve similar situations in the future (p. 20). According to Caplan and Caplan, helping the client is of "secondary" importance. Clearly, this is not to suggest that consultants have no concern for the welfare of consultees' clients. This simply reflects a shift in consultant focus. If the client is in clear and immediate danger of not receiving adequate help from the consultee, the mental health consultant will set aside the role of consultant and move directly toward resolving the client's issues. Even though the consultee-centered case consultation approach can be used in a group format as well with a group of consultees, the researchers spend their efforts discussing issues related to singular consultees.

Sources of Consultee Difficulties

The most detailed discussions and analyses provided in Caplan and Caplan's (1993) work involve the processes that can occur during consultee-centered case consultation. According to Caplan and Caplan, the problems that consultees have with clients will most often emanate from one of four places: There will either be

1. A lack of knowledge
2. A lack of skill
3. A lack of self-confidence
4. A lack of objectivity

The lack of knowledge can be dealt with through the consultant imparting information to consultees. However, in working with consultees who are lacking skill, consultants should be careful to not give advice or provide alternative solutions. It helps to have the consultant assess the pervasiveness of the problem and then "energize the agency's training system" (p. 105) in these situations. Consultants should endeavor to provide "nonspecific ego support" (p. 107) while attempting to find the ways and means for consultees to move toward gathering that support from others in the organization. Working with consultees who experience a lack of objectivity, the fourth source of consultee problems, is a more complex task.

Sources of Consultee Lack of Objectivity

When consultees get either too close or too distant from clients and are not able to perceive the client accurately enough to be effective, the consultee is seen as not being objective (Caplan & Caplan, 1993, p. 107). The lack of objectivity can occur when

- Consultees become too involved with clients ("direct personal involvement")
- Consultees identify too much with the client's story rather than empathizing with it ("simple identification")
- Consultees conceptualize the client's story into a pattern of roles similar to those of consultees ("transference")
- There is a minor but enduring pattern in the consultees where they are not seeing the client accurately or broadly enough (characterological distortions)
- Consultees have more major transference issues with a client or clients (theme interference)

In general, efforts to address a consultee's lack of objectivity include verbal and nonverbal methods. The nonverbal method focuses on the consultant's use of such nonverbal behaviors as facial expressions, various body movements, and type and amount of eye contact directed toward consultees. The purpose of such gesturing is to essentially dissuade the consultee from his or her maladaptive stance toward the client. Verbal methods include consultants diffusing the issue by sharing an appropriate parable with consultees and through theme interference reduction.

Theme Interference and Reduction

A major concern when consultees lack objectivity is that they may be experiencing theme interference. *Theme interference* is the product of major transference reactions that can occur in the workplace among consultees (Caplan & Caplan, 1993, p. 121). In a detailed discussion, the authors point out that consultees who are experiencing theme interference are not necessarily uncommon. Therefore, personal issues that interfere with one's optimal work performance should not be regarded as highly unusual. According to Caplan and Caplan, a *theme* is a cognitive constellation centering on a consultee's unresolved conflicts that may or may not have actually occurred. In either case, the unresolved conflict looms just below the surface or deeper in the unconscious (p. 122). An indication of when consultees are experiencing theme interference occurs when consultants hear consultees stereotyping their clients. When clients are the recipients of such consultee confounding issues during the course of their working together, this would be referred to as "theme interference" on the part of the consultee. When consultants diagnose this condition in consultees, efforts to reduce the interference are undertaken by the consultant.

There are two approaches that consultants can use to help consultees become more objective when they are experiencing theme interference. Caplan and Caplan (1993) believe that consultees can become compulsive in their thinking about the negative overtones of their unresolved issues and that, cognitively, this repetition takes the form of a syllogism: "All *A* inevitably leads to *B*" (p. 122). The authors describe how consultants listen to consultees for information that can then be conceptualized by consultants into an "if this happens, then this and only this will happen" argument. Assessing this syllogism is accomplished through the process of establishing an "initial category" (the "if" component) and the "inevitable outcome" (the "then" component).

Once the consultant has conceptualized the syllogism, there are two avenues open for action. Consultants can help consultees to remove the client from the initial category. For instance, consultants may have consultees review the case in such detail that the client no longer "fits" the initial category. This is known as *weakening the link* or *unlinking* the initial category from the inevitable outcome. Consultants can also accept the initial category as a "test case" (Caplan & Caplan, 1993, p. 126) and work toward increasing the number of possible outcomes. In either case, the hope is that the consultees not only learn how to manage the current situation, but, through the process, learn how to avoid losing objectivity with similar cases in the future. At the same time, however, it is expected that consultees will also learn how to continually differentiate similar situations from those situations still requiring further consultation (p. 216).

■ ■ ■ ■ ■ ▬▬▬

CASE STUDY ONE
THE PREACHER'S WIFE

A newly hired mental health counselor requested my help with a case about which she was very concerned. She was rather well known around the clinic as having been married to and divorced from a Pentecostal preacher, whom she had variously described as controlling and emotionally abusive. This particular therapist was friendly, but would waste little time in letting others know of her former married life and the extent to which she and her four children felt liberated after having left him. It was also known that she had considered suicide a few times during her tenure as a "preacher's wife."

In general, the therapist had good entry-level counseling skills, but seemed to be somewhat glib when discussing her clients. Although friendly to others, she did not seem to lack self-confidence. Because she was very eager to do good clinical work, she was open to new ideas with regard to how to work more effectively with clients. During the initial discussions about the case, the therapist stated that she frequently tended to intervene inappropriately by giving advice to her client. This caused her client to withdraw during counseling sessions. The therapist/consultee "did not know why" she did this, and it caused her some discomfort in that she did not feel in control of her verbal interactions.

After sharing the particulars about the client and the client's story, one issue seemed to stand out: The consultee continually referred to the fact that the client had recently joined a church in which she had found solace. Frequently, in her dialogue with me, the therapist/consultee mentioned that she actually feared for her client's life if the client did not leave the church. Specifically, unless the adolescent client broke away from the church and her current circle of friends who also belonged to the church, the counselor was "certain" that her client would eventually commit suicide. She said she "knew" this because the church was unhealthy and would lead the client down a path of depression and despair.

In this case, I structured the syllogism as: "All young girls who follow the church rules unquestionably (initial category) will eventually become depressed and commit suicide" (inevitable outcome). In discussing the issue with the therapist, I was surprised by how little recognition the therapist had about the parallels in this case with her own experiences. Through mutually expanding the list of additional possible outcomes, she was able to weaken the link between the initial category and the categorical outcome. She no longer saw the client's suicide as an automatic and categorical action. In the process of discovering those other alternatives, it was hoped that the therapist would be able to generalize the issue in her future work.

CRITICAL ISSUES IN MENTAL HEALTH CONSULTATION

As can be seen from the preceding discussion, Caplan and Caplan's mental health approach to consultation is a well-integrated model, and a meta-analysis of 24 consultation outcome studies conducted by Medway and Updyke (1985) demonstrated the effectiveness of mental health consultation. The fact that the model is comprehensive and effective, concomitant with its longevity, has kept the mental health consultation approach in the forefront of modern-day consultation practice. However, research that is aimed at examining and "updating" the fundamental propositions of this model is needed for it to remain as a giant among peers in the consulting field. The following sections briefly outline some the issues. Nevertheless, it is not intended to be a comprehensive analysis or exhaustive critique of the model itself.

Implications of Medical/Disease Models

Primarily, Caplan and Caplan's mental health consultation model is a "medical" model as opposed to a "mental health" model. There is research in the mental health field examining the differences between "medical" or "disease-oriented" models and "developmental" philosophies and perspectives of change (e.g., Green, 1999; Vacc & Loesch, 2000). Many of the philosophical criticisms of the medical/disease model will be similar to those issues already raised by researchers on feminism. From a developmental perspective, the disease model sees the "glass as half-empty" first and then perhaps as "half-full." The mental stance in the developmental perspective likely organizes the same glass in a different order: the glass is seen as being half-full first and, if needed, the glass can be seen as half-empty. A philosophical implication of such a perspective presents itself in an interesting manner for diversity concerns. Individuals and cultures embracing an "inclusive" worldview perspective, such as those individuals following the principal tenets of Taoism, for example, might not even consider the question on a philosophical basis alone. For some of these individuals, the very structure of the question itself presupposes a split in the universe or, in this example, a splitting of the glass into two parts. Hence, one would be attempting to solve a problem that, for some Taoists, does not even exist (on that level).

Medical/disease-oriented perspectives hold on to a fundamental worldview embracing the "powerfulness" of humans and their abilities, through technology, to control, or, in some cases, restore nature. At its logical end, this philosophical position reflects a deterministic belief in a perfect world that is totally controllable. In such a worldview, technology is simply the logical and overt symbol of change that reflects the need for power and control. Essentially, a lack of control simply reflects a lack of technology (Habermas, 1970). From a medical perspective, if a virus invades a body, then it is essentially only the limits of medical technology—and not the properties of the virus itself—that impede the cure. The implications of such notions of technology as the presupposition of imperfection, power, and control for women and racioethnic minorities are significant (e.g., Plumwood, 1993). In general, disease-oriented perspectives might be considered as owning the term *patient,* whereas developmental models might be said to own the term *client.* Caplan and Caplan (1993) use the term *patient* throughout their discourse. The connotation of "patient" in relation to power and control is a direct one. That is, as individuals become "patients," they are temporarily turning some control of themselves over to another person (qualified professional). As mentioned in Chapter Seven, researchers on feminist theory criticize the very construct of "power" as it has been traditionally defined. These researchers believe "power" to be defined through a masculine male model that does not incorporate the worldviews of many women and many racioethnic minorities.

A related issue concerns another term used throughout Caplan and Caplan's (1993) book: the masculine pronoun. Since Caplan and Caplan's work is so well known and respected, concomitant with it being both theoretically and practically comprehensive, the consistent and categorical use of the terms *he* and *him* is anachronistic and would seem to suggest the need for an obvious rewrite of the original work. Such a rewrite would only continue to enhance the influence of this model in the mental health field. It would remain on the cutting edge of "best practice" in consultation. To their credit, Caplan and Caplan explain that the process of changing pronouns would create "clumsy sentence structure." Nonetheless, they oppose sexist stereotyping. Due to the inherent structures of disease-oriented perspectives as well as those perspectives structuring psychodynamic theory itself, such a rewrite would not alter the basic construction of the model. Not only would the practice of mental health consultation be positively facilitated, the academic issues could be affected positively as well. For instance, an elimination of sexist language in their text could address at least one major source of potential criticism by researchers into feminist concerns. Clearly, a shift in pronouns to more egalitarian pronouns would deemphasize the dominant male voice. It could also diminish the subtle, but nevertheless profound, implications that such a generic structure has for oppression of others while, at the same time, engage a more inclusive or "different voice" (Gilligan, 1982).

Implications of Psychodynamic Theory

In light of the plethora of recent research on diversity, the theoretical structures of Caplan and Caplan's model also need to be examined and perhaps extended in order to more accurately reflect current research on cultural concerns and values. For instance, the mental health consultation model is based on psychodynamic theory, and the assumptions built into the foundations that drive this psychoanalytic approach have received criticism in the professional literature (e.g., Firestone, 1979; Irigaray, 1985). In addition, researchers find it paradoxical that apparently bizarre productions of the unconscious, such as found in dreams, can be rationally deciphered by an analyst. Moreover, the social work perspective of "person-in-environment," and particularly the emphasis on role theory (Hamilton, 1958), also take umbrage with theme interference. As you know, psychodynamic theory is essentially a drive theory focusing on the interplay of opposing psychic forces within individuals (Goldenberg & Goldenberg, 1996). Researchers in feminism and feminist theory decry Freudian concepts as paternalistic, oppressive (e.g., Figes, 1970; Millet, 1977), and reinforcing a maladaptive and dangerous male model worldview (Caldecott & Leland, 1983; McAllister, 1982; Plumwood, 1993; Reuther, 1975; Statham, 1996). The issues gravitating around male oppression of women extend into the larger issue of oppression of racioethnic groups, and the popular and professional research into this area is obviously plentiful. So, researchers in the feminist field join with those researchers writing about "white oppression" in questioning the relevance of Freud's work in today's world.

Caplan and Caplan's emphasis on the intrapsychic experiences of consultees as a source of theme interference in the consultee-centered case approach is perhaps the most recognizable and conspicuous example of Freud's influence. However, psychodynamic theory influences the entire model, and this is also reflected in the discussions of relationship building. Interestingly and ironically, the extended discussions offered by the authors in their text on how consultants should go about initiating, building, and maintaining relationships with consultees and clients is brilliantly conceived, empathic, and exceptionally presented in terms of its detail and process. Nonetheless, the centrality of the consultees' internal psychic experience as a source of dysfunction assumed in "theme interference" may be incongruent for those consultees holding vastly different worldviews. For instance, in some traditional Native American populations, one's inner world is explained in terms of it being congruent with a larger entity or force as opposed to it being explained as a source of psychic tension and drive. Fisher and Harrison (1997, 2000) assert that many Native Americans and Native Alaskans advocate the need to harmonize with rather than control nature (p. 57). Psychodynamic theory incorporates an "oppositional stance" in its structural paradigm by the pitting of psychic forces against each other. The notion of "opposition" implies a need to control, and it is this "need to control" implication that can foster criticism of Caplan and Caplan's consultation model. Aside from the powerful implications that this connotation of control has to the oppression of women and racioethnic minorities, control runs counter to many traditional Native Americans and Native Alaskans who embrace an inclusive and harmonious stance in their worldview.

EMERGING CONSTRUCTS IN MENTAL HEALTH CONSULTATION

Cognitive Theory and Theme Interference

The works of Sandoval (1996) and Maital (1996) on theme interference reduction have profound implications on the structure of Caplan and Caplan's model. These implications can enhance the model's appropriateness for women and racioethnic minorities. Sandoval and Maital both agree that it is uncommon for workers to displace unfinished business onto tasks at work, which produces temporary ineffectuality. Hence, neither researcher takes umbrage with Caplan and Caplan on that issue. However, Sandoval believes that theme interference results from faulty conceptualizations about clients. The interference does not necessarily originate from the consultee's countertransference issues with clients. These conceptualizations are usually preconceived assumptions about clients and are not flexible enough to allow consultees to be as helpful to clients. In Sandoval's view, since the issue is about faulty conceptualizations, cognitive interventions can be aimed at correcting these incorrect cognitions. These interventions should result in the enhancement of consultees' effectiveness. Maital also conceptualizes theme interference as resulting from faulty cognitions rather than countertransference issues. Maital sees theme interference resulting from irrational beliefs. They do not emanate from faulty conceptualizations per se. Using more of a cognitive-behavioral perspective, Maital believes that correcting irrational beliefs is an effective means to enhance consultees' effectiveness with clients.

Recall the case example of the female counselor's faulty thinking related to church and suicide. The consultee's experience could easily have been reconceptualized into a cognitive paradigm. Instead of seeing the consultee as behaving in unconscious ways that impeded her progress with her client, the consultee's difficulties could be seen as problems in faulty thinking about the client. According to Maital (1996), the consultee's problem could have been identified as a faulty belief that her client was going to commit suicide when, in fact, there was a dearth of objective information suggesting the probability of such an action. Instead of theme interference, consultants can intervene with their consultees in helping them examine the logic of such conclusions.

Role Theory and Theme Interference

Central to a social work behavioral person-in-environment perspective is role theory (Hamilton, 1958). Role theory assumes that the relationships occurring between humans are reciprocal by nature. Moreover, human behavior is guided by set of culturally bound beliefs, attitudes, values, and expectations inherent to the relationship structure (Thomson & Greene, 1994, p. 93). According to these same authors, the concept of role addresses how individuals learn what behaviors are permitted, expected, and/or prohibited in both their families and in the social groups to which they belong. Thomson and Greene assert that the concept of role also considers human behavior as flowing from the internalized social prescriptions that are motivated by the nature of group identification, and yet are bounded by the status to which they are assigned (p. 93).

Role theory has an interesting relationship with consultation and with Caplan and Caplan's work in particular. Nelson, Nelson, Sherman, and Strean (1968) published findings that counter the psychoanalytic notions of theme interference. These researchers also shift the focus away from the individual's intrapsychic world to an external, social world. In their book on roles and paradigms in the therapeutic setting, Nelson and colleagues conceptualize the counselor/client relationship as "paradigmatic treatment," whereby the treatment venue becomes a representation of the world in which every possible drama and role may be played out (p. 123). When applied to the ideas of theme interference in Caplan and Caplan's mental health consultation model, this role theory perspective sees consultant/consultee/client relationships as the "paradigmatic treatment." Although Caplan and Caplan and others believe that interference is somewhat normal in the workplace, the psychodynamic tenets cast theme interference as somewhat pathological. Role theory reconceptualizes theme interference as less negative and more naturally occurring. In fact, transference issues would be expected to be a natural part of the consultant/consultee/client relationship. As mental health professionals are consulting with consultees, consultants and consultees are acting out roles and dramas on a stage of their own. It is the unexamined role conflicts occurring between consultant, consultee, and client (in whatever configuration) that can become an area of concern.

SUMMARY

Caplan and Caplan's approach to consultation can be likened to looking through four panes of glass in a single window. Each pane of the window shares some common characteristics of relationship building, and each pane also differs on either consultant focus or consultation setting. The four-pane window metaphor comprises all of the structural variations for mental health consultation. In *client-centered case consultation*, consultants work directly with consultees to determine ways that consultees can better help their clients. This is a form of the familiar doctor/patient type of consulting. In this situation, most of the consultant's focus is on the client, although it would be unusual for the consultant to actually see the client face to face.

Program-centered administrative consultation is similar in structure to the client-centered approach. However, the program-centered approach is more organizational in nature. The consulting intervention is aimed at administrative action rather than on a consultee's management of the client's case. In the discussion of program-centered administrative consultation, Caplan and Caplan raise questions about the particular perspective of the consultant. In situations where an organization that is experiencing problems does not have a "mental health product" (a company that manufactures chairs or carpets, for example), there does not appear the need for the consultant to possess mental health expertise. Thus, there would appear to be little need for a "clinical perspective" on the part of the consultant because it would appear on the surface that the consultant would need to possess extensive knowledge of industrial psychology and manufacturing. Nonetheless, Caplan and Caplan (1993) maintain that such problems may involve "a significant human relations factor—poor leadership, lowered morale, or communication blocks" (p. 225). These same authors state that consultants using an industrial/organizational perspective and those consultants from a clinical or mental health perspective would probably agree on the salient issues that need to be addressed. Additionally, both would likely agree on the recommendations forwarded to the consultees.

Another organizational approach in mental health consultation is *consultee-centered administrative consultation*. In this approach, consultants focus on the consultee's abilities to effect new ways of dealing with administrative issues. Whereas program-centered administrative consultation focuses on the program(s) per se, the consultee-centered administrative approach focuses on administrators themselves. In consultee-centered administrative consultation, consultants are interested in the larger organizational system and aim to help administrators find new ways to work more effectively with their staff. In program-centered administrative consultation, consultants work with administrators to develop more effective policies and procedures. The differences between the two major structures of consultation (case centered or administrative centered) are differences in numbers and focus. In case-centered approaches (consultee-centered case consultation and client-centered case consultation), the consultant's focus is on the single triad: consultant, mental health professional (consultee), and client. In consultee-centered case consultation, the consultant works directly with the consultee and indirectly with the client. In contrast, the consultant works directly with the client and indirectly with the consultee in client-centered case consultation. In both administrative consultation paradigms (program centered and consultee centered), consultants utilize a broader perspective. Helping consultees figure out new ways to deal with problems in organizational planning and/or personnel management both require consultants to focus on the larger system in which individuals operate.

Consultee-centered case consultation is the fourth approach in Caplan and Caplan's mental health consultation approach. The focus of this approach in on the consultee's difficulties with the case. There are four sources of consultee difficulties identified by the researchers: lack of skill, lack of knowledge, lack of confidence, and lack of objectivity. The consultee's lack of objectivity is seen as the most serious of the difficulties, and the researchers discuss theme interference and its reduction as a means of helping consultees work more efficiently with their clients. Interestingly, although the traditional theoretical framework structuring Caplan and Caplan's mental health consultation model is clearly psychodynamic, Caplan and Caplan advocate the use of cognitive restructuring techniques throughout their discussions of theme interference and theme interference reduction. For example, one of the ways that consultees can come to different conclusions about their cases is to have them examine the case in detail. By going over the case in more and more detail, more and more information emerges, which changes the ways that consultees can conceptualize clients. Using a gestalt framework to explain the phenomena, gestalt theory assumes that by going over the story in more and more detail, one begins to "finish" (or gestalt) the story. In the process, the background and unattended details come to the foreground of the consultee's experience and reflects a more accurate picture. Once this contact boundary has been made, this changes the consultees' conceptualizations about the client and/or the client's story.

In many ways, it is easy to see how Sandoval and Maital see theme interference as resulting either from the consultee's difficulties in conceptualizing the case or in the consultee's faulty logic used to construct conceptualizations. As shown, the etiology of the theme interference is indeed debatable. The traditional views of themes originating out of unresolved issues in the unconscious are met with the vigorous counterperspectives of researchers of cognitive theory. In short, cognitive theorists hold that conceptualizations and beliefs, no matter how irrational or rational, are mental processes. For cognitive theorists, the origin of theme interference is of lesser importance than the understanding of the mental processes at work that deter the consultee's enhanced functioning with clients. In addition to the issues raised by cognitive theorists, traditional behavioral theorists would reject the very notion of the unconscious. Thus, behaviorists would reject the notion of theme interference as traditionally explained by psychodynamic theory in much the same manner as any Taoist would not be able to conceptualize the issue of the glass being half empty or half full because it presupposes a split in the world that does not fundamentally exist for them. These different worldviews shift the locus of the problem away from the reality or unreality of the unconscious to a more phenomenological conceptualization.

Although the implications of such a cognitive perspective would seem to deconstruct mental health consultation as traditionally defined through psychodynamic theory, the opposite actually occurs. The shift from a psychodynamic structure to a cognitive structure demonstrates the broad "explanatory" power that Caplan and Caplan's mental health consultation model has on the practice. To say that psychodynamic theory is the only theoretical structure inherent in mental health consultation inappropriately limits the tenets of this consultation model. Clearly, Caplan and Caplan's model seems to borrow from many different theoretical structures. Their notion of the necessity of the consultant and consultee having a "coordinate" relationship is in direct contrast to traditional views of the medical model. It is obvious that their consultation model is heavily influenced by psychodynamic thought, but its structure is flexible enough to incorporate the theoretical tenets of other worldviews.

QUESTIONS

1. What are your views of the relevancy of psychodynamic theory to contemporary practice?

2. Since mental health consultation is popular, why is it important to examine its theoretical structure?

3. Do you believe in the unconscious? Why or why not?

4. Do you prefer to intervene directly or indirectly with consultees, such as would be the case if you were to follow traditional interventions to reduce theme interference?

5. How do the traditional perspectives of mental health consultation help or hinder diverse populations?

6. What do you like about Caplan and Caplan's model of consultation?

CHAPTER TEN

BEHAVIORAL PERSON-IN-ENVIRONMENT APPROACHES

PERSON-IN-ENVIRONMENT PERSPECTIVE

Caplan wrote the original mental health consultation model in 1970, and it was published during a time when the mental health field was continuing to reel from major transformations in the counseling and therapy field. For instance, Rogers (1951) had revolutionized traditional psychodynamic therapy, and the therapeutic relationship in particular, with his client-centered approach. B. F. Skinner (1953) countered with the publication of his works on scientific behaviorism. A decade later, in 1963, the United States government enacted a comprehensive community mental health centers act that led to the deinstitutionalization of mental health patients. Nowhere would Rogers's and Skinner's disparate worldviews seemingly clash more than in the treatment approaches designed to help manage the influx of these newly released mental health patients. That intersection was the self-actualizing philosophy of Rogers and the deterministic worldview of Skinner.

Caplan (1970) seems to have captured the best of both worlds in the descriptions of the consultant and consultee relationship and in the belief in the medical model approach to consultation, which assumes consultants' expertness. However, at the time that it was written, the theoretical foundation of Caplan's model did not appeal to every professional or to every professional group. In the 1960s, social workers were becoming increasingly dismayed about the ability of the Freudian medical and psychodynamic model to extend itself toward a more comprehensive understanding of human behavior. The social upheaval in the 1960s, concomitant with this theoretical ambivalence toward psychoanalytic thought, shifted social workers' emphasis from the diagnostic, treatment, and cure approach to a social learning theory oriented toward a behavioral person-in-environment perspective (Greene, 1994). In this paradigm, the individual is conceptualized as an inextricable component who interacts with numerous and varied social systems. The relationships formed through these interactions are reciprocal in nature. That is, they mutually influence each other. At the time of its conception, this behavioral social work perspective recognized the powerful influence that cultural group membership had on behavior, and therefore it was thought to be more explanatory of human behavior than the psychodynamic model (Janchill, 1969). Greene maintains that this social learning perspective has been the theoretical foundation guiding behavioral social work practice for over 30 years.

During the same time period, the intrapsychic tensions asserted in traditional psychodynamic theory were also being challenged in the counseling and therapy field, which had now moved past the central debate between Rogers and Skinner to embrace its own versions of the person-in-environment perspective. The 1960s and 1970s saw a spate of new brief therapy approaches and new perspectives in marriage and family therapy being heralded. Von Bertalanffy's (1950) work in general systems theory revolutionized some aspects of marriage and family therapy and extended the therapist's perspective from the individual to the family system. The Mental Research Institute (MRI) in Palo Alto (CA), with its emphasis on communication/interaction, was center stage among family therapists during the 1960s. It was also during this time period that Satir (1964) first published her works on conjoint family therapy. This publication and her energetic and embracing style did much to popularize family approaches to treating problems. The timing was right. Families with mental health concerns in the mid-1960s would need family treatment now that the federal government had authorized block grants to set up local community mental health centers to handle the influx of patients that would be released. (It comes as no surprise that much of the early family therapy work and research was conducted on families who had family members diagnosed with schizophrenia.)

The 1970s also witnessed extensions of traditional behaviorism with the arrival of Bandura's (1977) social learning theory, Meichenbaum's (1977) cognitive-behavioral therapy, and the behavioral ecology perspective (Willems, 1974). In the end, these various mental health centers would need psychiatrists to oversee the clinical case management of patients. The administrators would need consultants' help, too. This is the Zeitgeist in which Caplan's mental health consultation model, Myrick's systematic consultation model, and Bergan's (1977) behavioral model became prominent. All of this took place at the time when there would be widespread interest in the person-in-environment perspective.

Broadly speaking, the term *person-in-environment* denotes a generic professional-behavioral worldview that recognizes the person and the environment. This includes the person, and all of the interactions occurring within that person(s) and between that person(s) and the various environments. Although this perspective may be symbolic of the learning theory structure for behavioral social work, it is not behavioral social work's exclusive domain. Nor is it the categorical possession of the behaviorists in the counseling and therapy field. A person-in-environment perspective is incorporated into the various learning theory-based approaches in consultation as well. Most notably is the behavioral consultation model, first promulgated by Bergan (1977), then revised by Bergan and Kratochwill (1990). The social learning theory model of Brown and Schulte (1987) is another example of a behavioral person-in-environment consultation approach. Both models are problem-solving models for consultants emphasizing behaviors and the environment, and both have demonstrated effectiveness with a variety of problems in a variety of settings (Brown, Pryzwansky, & Schulte, 2002). Another behavioral approach is Myrick's (1977) brief problem-solving systematic consultation model.

These three approaches are referred to in this chapter as behavioral person-in-environment approaches for several reasons. In the first place, the term describes the important constructs considered in each of the structures of these three behavioral models. More significantly, the use of the traditional social work perspective allows for a meta-structure to frame and therefore orient the various behavioral approaches to ensure their relevancy and effectiveness for diverse groups of people. Hence, this perspective is used to provide a professional orientation to behavioral consultation approaches. This is a crucial perspective for consulting effectively in contemporary U.S. culture.

The behavioral person-in-environment perspective in consultation lies in direct opposition to the psychodynamic orientation of Caplan and Caplan's mental health consultation model. In general, behavioral approaches can be considered to be behavioral problem-solving models. This includes traditional behavioral-oriented as well as social learning theory consultation models. Behavioral consultation approaches assume that overt behavior is more influential in determining a consultee's success than an unconscious theme.

According to Gallessich (1982, p. 177) and Keller (1981), the early behavioral consultants in the 1970s and 1980s typically came from clinical behavioral backgrounds. Due to their training in experimental psychology, consultants often treated consultees from that clinical perspective. It would not be surprising then to learn that the focus of early behavioral consultation was almost exclusively on individual cases or clients. Currently, behavioral consultation approaches are also used to produce changes in organizations (Bergan & Kratochwill, 1990). In its broadest context, behavioral consultation is a problem-solving activity whose goal is to change the client's and/or consultee's behaviors. When used in organizations, the goal is to produce change in those organizations as well. As the name suggests, behavioral consultation focuses primarily on behaviors and relies on the systematic use of learning theory to solve problems. As you would expect, behaviorists believe that since most behavior is learned, it can also be unlearned and replaced with a new behavior. Even though behavioral consultation is a method all unto its own, Gallessich (1982) suggests that all consultants use behavioral approaches at points in the consulting process.

CHARACTERISTICS OF BEHAVIORAL CONSULTATION APPROACHES

The term *behavioral consultation* refers to a general approach in consultation as well as the specific works of Bergan (1977) and Bergan and Kratochwill (1990). So, when "behavioral consultation" is being used, it could refer to Bergan's model exclusively or to more generic behavioral consultation approaches, unless there is clarification. The following list summarizes many of the central tenets in behavioral consultation approaches.

1. Behavioral consultation approaches are indirect services and usually focused on cases and clients even when conducted in organizational settings (Gallessich, 1982; Keller, 1981; Dougherty, 1990).

2. Behavioral consultation approaches are most often used to problem solve as well as enhance consultee competence (Bergan & Kratochwill, 1990; Vernberg & Reppucci, 1986, p. 50).

3. The goals of most behavioral approaches are to alter the client's behaviors, to change the consultee's behaviors, and to produce changes in organizations (Brown, Pryzwansky, & Schulte, 2001, p. 48).

4. The length of the consulting relationship varies from minutes to months (Bergan & Kratochwill, 1990; Brown, Pryzwansky, & Schulte, 2001; Myrick, 1987).

5. In all cases, consultants should have a degree of expert knowledge in learning principles and utilize social learning theory and behavioral technology principles to design, implement, and assess interventions (Bergan & Kratochwill, 1990; Gallessich, 1982; Vernberg & Reppucci, 1986, p. 50).

6. The consultant/consultee relationship ranges from collegial to the consultant having some control in the relationship (Bergan & Kratochwill, 1990; Myrick, 1977).

7. The consultant's major role ranges from facilitator (Myrick, 1977) to expert who imparts psychological information and principles to consultees (Bergan, 1977; Bergan & Kratochwill, 1990).

8. A primary task of the consultant ranges from helping the consultee problem solve (Myrick, 1977) to enhancing the probability that the consultee will accept the consultant's recommendations (Bergan, 1977; Bergan & Kratochwill, 1990).

9. In behavioral consultation approaches, the client and/or consultee "goals" need to be defined in behavioral terms (Bergan, 1977; Bergan & Kratochwill, 1990; Dougherty, 1990; Gallessich, 1982; Myrick, 1977).

10. Most approaches emphasize direct observation techniques (Keller, 1981, p. 64) and focus on present, current influences on overt behavior (Bergan, 1977; Dougherty, 1990; Myrick, 1977).

11. In most cases, the interventions and evaluations lend themselves to empirical testing (Bergan, 1977; Bergan & Kratochwill, 1990; Vernberg & Reppucci, 1986).

BERGAN AND KRATOCHWILL'S BEHAVIORAL CONSULTATION MODEL

Bergan's (1977) seminal work, *Behavioral Consultation,* was not the first behavioral model to be published in the field, but it was the most comprehensive model pertaining to the actual consulting process. Bergan's (1977) model approximated that of Caplan's (1970) mental health consultation model in terms of depth, scope, and the amount of detailed analysis given to the consulting process itself. Bergan and Kratochwill (1990) extended and revised Bergan's earlier model in their book, *Behavioral Consultation and Therapy.* As with other behavioral approaches, the major steps in Bergan and Kratochwill's (1990) problem-solving consultation model are:

1. Problem identification
2. Problem analysis

3. Plan implementation
4. Problem evaluation

Some other models include additional major steps. For example, the systematic consultation model of Myrick (1977), discussed later in this chapter, identifies seven steps. However, the four steps identified by Bergan and Kratochwill serve as generic phases in almost all behavioral consultation practice. Currently, behavioral consultation is widely accepted as an indirect service for helping consultees, clients, and consultee/ client systems.

When consultants utilize Bergan and Kratochwill's model with consultees who have concerns about clients, the process is referred to as *behavioral case consultation* (Bergan & Kratochwill, 1990) or *case focused behavioral consultation* (Gallessich, 1982). Consultants can also use behavioral consultation in their work with organizations, which is called *behavioral system consultation*. Regardless of the setting, behavioral consultants can use a developmental perspective or a problem-centered perspective in working with consultees about client concerns. The goal is consultee and/or client behavioral change. Developmental behavioral case consultation occurs when the consultant's interest in the consultee/client system is more long term. Problem-centered behavioral case consultation focuses on consultees and clients in the acute or short term. Behavioral case consultation is not the only approach to behavioral consultation, but it is the most frequently used form (Dougherty, 1990, p. 261).

Behavioral Case Consultation

Behavioral case consultation is conceptually similar to and obviously different from Caplan and Caplan's model. In the first place, behavioral case consultation has components similar to both client-centered case consultation and consultee-centered case consultation. In Caplan and Caplan's client-centered case consultation model, the consultant gathers data about the client either from the consultee or directly from the client. Generally, in behavioral case consultation, consultants do not work directly with the clients. Instead, they train the consultees in the principles of learning theory so that the consultees can go about the task of working directly with clients. At the same time, both mental health and behavioral consulting models are considered indirect services, which means that there is almost always an "odd person out." This person could be the client when the consultant is working directly with consultees, or the consultee when consultants work directly with clients. The consultee is receiving direct service in the first case and receiving indirect service in the latter. Essentially, behavioral consultants "manage the consultee's management of the case" (Dougherty, 1990, p, 262). This perspective is different from that of Caplan and Caplan, who would likely not consider themselves managing cases. Finally, if theme interference and theme interference reduction are the hallmark of Caplan and Caplan's work, consultant verbal interactions are the hallmark of behavioral case consultation.

In behavioral case consultation, consultants manage the process through consultants' uses of verbal skills in restructuring the consultant/consultee relationship (Conoley & Conoley, 1982). Caplan and Caplan do use verbal skills in intervening with consultees' theme interference. In fact, this is "the most usual technique" (Caplan & Caplan, 1993, p. 140). However, the management of the case through the use of the consultant's verbal skills in the mental health consultation model involves a joint examination of the facts of the case. The focus of this type of verbal intervention is on the idiosyncratic details of the client and the client's situation (p. 141). Caplan and Caplan also warn consultants about the proper type and timing of their verbal responses so as to avoid increasing the consultee's anxiety. Although Caplan and Caplan do discuss verbal skills of the consultant in some detail in their chapter on theme interference reduction (pp. 140–151), they do not place the emphasis on it that behavior case consultation does. In behavioral consultation, the consultant's verbal interactions are central. The specific manner in which the consultant helps consultees manage the case is through these verbal interactions.

Consultant/Consultee Verbal Processes

Bergan (1977) and Bergan and Kratochwill (1990) emphasize the need for consultants to glean information from consultees in a strategic fashion. That is, consultants utilize selected types of verbalizations in an attempt to encourage consultees to produce specific categories of information that will lead to successful resolution of the client situation. Dougherty (1990) sees behavioral consultants as selecting subcategories of verbalizations in attempting to control the topics discussed at any given time as well as control the kinds of verbal action that occur (p. 265). The detail provided in Bergan and Kratochwill's (1990) work is comprehensive and organized. The detail is meant to provide specific steps that behavioral consultants should utilize to enhance the successes of consultation.

Bergan (1977) and Bergan and Kratochwill (1990) outline seven subcategories of consultee verbal content, and each subcategory has the same five verbal processes occurring. The consultant's remarks are seen as being either eliciting or emitting. According to Brown, Pryzwansky, and Schulte (2001), *elicitors* are seen as having a controlling effect on a listener, whereas *emitters* are statements about content in the consultee's story and about process issues (p. 51). Both types of responses can be in the form of statements or questions. *Eliciting remarks are designed to be more broad based and open ended and are seen as more controlling, whereas emitting remarks tend to focus the consultee into specified areas but are not seen as controlling.* In essence, consultants use elicitors to set the boundaries of a given topic for discussion and use emitting responses to focus the discussion. Another way of conceptualizing these two types of responses is to consider the eliciting responses as aimed at gathering information, and the emitting responses as aimed at getting the consultee to respond.

Subcategory One: Background/Environment.   The content of this subcategory is comprised of the historical and environmental conditions that may have bearing on the case. During this discussion, consultants use eliciting and emitting remarks in an attempt to control the structure of the interactions with consultees. At the same time, consultants use various verbal subcategories to organize the specific and appropriate data they need to help consultees strategize plans for successful resolution. In discussing the background and environmental issues related to the case at hand, consultants need detailed information from consultees (**specification subcategory**). During the course of the discussion, consultants will use questions or statements designed to control the type and level of detail gleaned from consultees. Depending on the specific case, these factors could include specific medical, family, psychological, and social histories as well as specific remote environmental conditions that are seen as related to the client's or client system's behavior. For example, in the course of discussing the client's medical history, a behavioral consultant might use an *eliciting* remark in the form of an open-ended question, such as, "Why do you think your client wants to be hospitalized again?" This might be followed by an *emitting* remark, such as, "So, that is the fourth hospitalization in five months."

While the consultant and consultee are interacting and discussing the case, the consultant would be attempting to evaluate (**evaluation subcategory**) the consultee's values and emotional content surrounding the case. Understanding the consultee's values and attachment to the case can help consultants focus the type of intervention most likely to be embraced by the consultee. In this process, the consultant can use an *eliciting* remark, such as, "How did you feel when you saw that your client needed to be hospitalized again?" Such a remark would be designed to focus the consultee on an area that the consultant can use for developing a better understanding of the consultee's affect related to the case. The consultant's eliciting remark might then be followed by clarifying the consultee's feelings: "So, the way you see it over the past couple of years, your client is playing the game" (*emitting* response).

Dougherty (1990) considers the **inferences subcategory** as the consultant and consultee playing "hunches" rather than acting on pure fact (p. 265). The consultant might use an *eliciting* remark with the consultee, such as, "How good is this client at playing the hospital game?" and then an *emitting* response, such as, "It seems as though this client goes into this helpless mode and sometimes needs hospitalization whenever feeling abandoned by someone important."

The **summarization category** consists of the consultant's attempts to condense the data into a manageable statement or statements aimed at ensuring the accuracy of his or her understanding of the case. Continuing with the example, the consultant might employ an *eliciting* remark, such as, "From all that we have discussed so far, what would you consider to be your client's real agenda in this current situation?" An emitting response, such as, "You're considering this call for help as your client acting in a malingering fashion similar to before" could also be employed effectively.

The final process that would close out the background/environmental subcategory is the **validation subcategory**. Here, the behavioral consultant could invoke an *eliciting* remark that asks the consultee to agree or disagree with the summarization. An example might be, "Do you think we have covered the important background points?" The consultant could also use an *emitting* response, such as, "Well, we can certainly consider seriously that this client is asking for something other than hospitalization this time. Would you agree?"

The same five processes, with consultants utilizing eliciting and emitting responses strategically throughout the discussion, are recycled as consultants go about the task of gathering data from the remaining six subcategories. Brown, Pryzwansky, and Schulte (2001) and Bergan and Kratochwill (1990) believe that elicitors can be used to increase the specificity of the data gathered from consultees, to provide feedback to consultees, and/or to summarize data regarding the consultees' values and affect as they relate to the client's situation. In addition to helping focus consultees within a given domain elicited by the consultant, emitters can be also used to communicate personal evaluation of the case at hand or to communicate information about the level of consultee functioning (Brown, Pryzwansky, & Schulte, 2001, p. 52).

Subcategory Two: Behavior Setting.   There is a shift in time from the background/ environmental subcategory to the behavior-setting category. In this subcategory, the consultant is more interested in the immediate, rather than remote, environmental cues. The behavior-setting subcategory is structured at gathering **specific** and detailed information regarding the antecedent, consequent, and sequential aspects of the environmental conditions. The consultant's verbalizations in this subcategory are among the most frequently used (Bergan, 1977; Bergan & Kratochwill, 1990). As in the verbal process outlined in the background/environment subcategory, consultants would strategically use eliciting responses to control the venue of information asked from consultees. Emitting responses are used to clarify the content and process concerns. During this process, the consultant would be **evaluating** the values and affective aspects of the consultee's experiences as they relate to the case at hand. In learning how the consultee conceptualizes the experience, the consultant can be more effective as he or she and the consultee draw **inferences** from the facts. To weed out irrelevant information and to punctuate relevant issues and concerns, consultants would use eliciting responses to **summarize** the situation and emitting responses to ensure accuracy. Dougherty (1990) refers to the **validation subcategory** as consultants checking to see if they are on the right "wavelength" with consultees.

Subcategory Three: Client Behaviors.   The success of the consultation outcome depends on an accurate understanding of the client's problematic behaviors (Bergan, 1977; Bergan & Kratochwill, 1990; Gallessich, 1982; Myrick, 1977). So, this is a very important step in the process. Here, consultants endeavor to have consultees describe their concerns with clients in behavioral terms. Consultants would want to gather a **specific** description of the behavior and determine what occurs when, how long it occurs, and under what conditions it occurs. The accuracy of information gathered in this subcategory is a categorical imperative.

Consultees are encouraged, through the consultants' use of eliciting and emitting responses, to describe clients' thoughts, feelings, overt behaviors, as well as their intensity and duration. As consultees describe their clients, consultants are provided with a plethora of data about how the consultees are processing the case. This helps consultants **evaluate** courses of actions with consultees. For example, a consultant might use an eliciting response in asking a consultee to describe the client's reactions to a particular intervention. During this exchange, the consultant is paying attention to the number of times the consultee says "totally shutdown" to describe the client's openness to help. This might clue the consultant into using a particular plan of action with the consultee. An *eliciting* response made by the consultant, such as, "What do you think prompts this behavior?" is an example of the **inference subcategory**. In order to ensure that the verbal process is flowing along accurately, consultants will use **summarizations** and validations. An *emitting* summarization in this subcategory might be when the consultant says to the consultee, "You have mentioned that the client usually asks questions in groups of threes." Some of the **validations** might be reflected in both consultant and consultee agreeing on the facts of the case and the conclusions drawn.

Subcategory Four: Client Individual/Special Characteristics.   Information to be included in this subcategory ranges from basic demographic information, such as age, height, weight, eyesight/glasses, and auditory considerations, to more complex psychological constructs, such as IQ, neurological concerns, learning disabilities, alcohol-related problems, and remarkable features in the client's mental status. Consultants can use an *eliciting* response in asking consultees to describe the idiosyncratic features, such as, "What is unusual about this client?" In attempting to get more **specific** information, a consultant might ask the consultee to be more descriptive (*emitting* response) about something the consultee identified. As the consultee is conversing with the consultant in describing the client's demographic or remarkable features, the consultant is focusing on learning more about the consultee and evaluating his or her values and feelings about the client **(evaluation subcategory).**

Consultants attempt to control the flow of discourse with consultees with eliciting responses in an endeavor to put together a picture of the client replete with the client's demographic variables, unusual characteristics, quirks, and behaviors. Consultants and consultees attempt to **draw inferences** about what certain features might mean, even though there may not be actual facts to corroborate the hunches. **Summing** up what is known and **validating** the facts and the consultee close the verbal interactions in this subcategory.

Subcategory Five: Observations Made.   In this step, the behavioral case consultant will simply gather a sufficient amount of information directly from the consultee or will help devise a manner in which more data can be gathered by the consultee. In the **specification subcategory**, the consultant would use eliciting and emitting responses to determine what was observed and how it was observed. In this process, it may be that the consultee has not systematically observed the client's behaviors. If this is the case, efforts could be made to help the consultee gather more data. Again, the consultant would want to listen to and **evaluate** the consultee's affect and values surrounding the client's behaviors as well as evaluating the consultee's preferences for the types of observations made. The consultant might ask the consultee to describe how he or she observed the client (*eliciting* response) and perhaps follow directly by asking if it would have been possible to observe the client is another way or in another setting (*emitting* response).

In the drawing **inferences subcategory**, the consultant and the consultee might begin to predict the efficacy of certain interventions. For example, in using an *eliciting* response, a consultant might ask the consultee, "What do you think would happen if you were to leave the room?" Assuming the consultee describes a potential consequence of leaving the room, the consultant might then employ an *emitting* response in stating, "I wonder if the client would even notice. Do you think your absence would even be noticed?" Throughout the process of discussing observational data, consultants should always **summarize** and **validate** their findings in their interactions with consultees. The strategic use of eliciting and emitting responses will endeavor to lay important foundation for the verbal interactions that will occur as a plan is created.

Subcategory Six: Strategies and Plans.   Characteristic of this subcategory is the focused discussion between the consultant and the consultee regarding what has already been tried by the consultee. A simple *eliciting* question, "What have you tried?" is a good way to open the door to this discussion. The process of narrowing down what exactly has been tried and the detailed discussion of the impact of those efforts **(specification subcategory)** helps move the process. In the **evaluation** verbal process, the consultant might choose an *emitting* response to feed information back about how angry the consultee seems: "Gosh, it sure seems as though you are pretty exasperated with the client at this point. Does it seem that way to you?" Consultants and consultees should endeavor to draw **inferences** about clients from plans that have already been tried and failed. This could be done through the consultant's use of *eliciting* responses, such as, "From what you have tried and we have discussed, what does that say about your client's issues about power and control?" During the dialogue, the consultant would **summarize** relevant data and important issues to ensure accuracy as well as to **validate** the efforts of consultees.

Subcategory Seven: Additional or Other Data Needed.   In order to be all inclusive, Bergan (1977) and Bergan and Kratochwill (1990) structure this subcategory as a "catch-all" for anything not identified and categorized previously. Dougherty (1990) states that this category could even include "talk about the weather" (p. 265). In general, this subcategory might include the general rapport-building verbal skills conducive to a strong consultant/consultee psychological contract. One of the advantages of having this subcategory is that it allows for the behavioral model to be flexible without compromising its structural integrity. In other words, this category allows for all data to be organized, but the fact that it is nonspecific allows for the vagaries that naturally occur in the consulting process to become "accountable."

The seven subcategories naturally flow from subcategory one to subcategory seven. However, it is important to understand that in the course of a conversation, the content of consultant/consultees' interactions will likely move from topic to topic in no given order. These subcategories allow consultants to be able to follow along with consultees in a more or less normal manner while organizing the information flow into preset subcategories. Most behavioral problem-solving consulting models have four or five steps, and the verbal interactions outlined above will generally be concentrated, but not limited to, the first two steps. As mentioned, the consulting steps include (1) problem identification, (2) problem analysis, (3) plan implementation, and (4) problem evaluation. The first two steps, problem identification and problem analysis, are those in which the consultant will attempt to gather data and organize it into the seven subcategories. From that discussion, consultants and consultees will devise a plan and then evaluate it. Gallessich (1982) reviewed the works of Bergan (1977), Bergan and Tombari (1976), and Tharp and Wentzel (1969) and identified five steps in the behavioral consulting process: First, the problem is identified. Next, provisions are made for observing and recording the problem behavior (if it has not already been done). Third, the consultant analyzes the behavior. Fourth, a program is designed, implemented, and evaluated. Finally, the consultant systematically withdraws from the consultation. The verbal interactions occurring between consultant and consultee in these five steps would likely be concentrated in the first three steps.

Controversy in Behavioral Consultation

The reason so much attention has been given to the consultant/consultee verbal interactions is because the need to identify the problem behavior specifically and correctly is paramount to the success of the consultation (Bergan, 1977; Bergan & Kratochwill, 1990; Myrick, 1977). However, compliance with the consultant's professional point of view is also important to the success of behavioral consulting. In Bergan's model as well as in Bergan and Kratochwill's model, one of the main foci of consultants is consultee compliance with consultants' recommendations (Brown, Pryzwansky, & Schulte, 2001, p. 48). This segues into the controversial issue of consultant control in the process. As mentioned previously, some behavioral consultants advocate the position of "control" in the consulting process as being the most efficacious. Although there has been no dearth of professional debate on the issue of control, the consultee's compliance with the agreed upon plan is necessary for successful resolution. The five verbal processes of specification, evaluation, inferences, summarizing, and validating will do much to enhance consultee compliance. A main reason for this is structural: Specification mandates detail, and the more detail consultees and consultants have, the greater the probability that they will not miss important issues relevant to the case at hand.

A remarkable, but predictable, feature of the behavioral case consultation model is the structure by which consultants can systematically organize their data. It is easy to understand how important it is for consultants to be fully prepared and skilled in the use of these various techniques. In gathering data from consultees, consultants methodically attempt to organize the verbal interactions occurring between them in order to increase the probability that the consultation will be successfully executed. Clearly, consultants will not be robotic in their verbal interactions. However, Bergan (1977) and Bergan and Kratochwill (1990) believe that consultants need to control the interaction. When criticism is aimed at behavioral case consultation, the issue of control is the target. Bergan and Kratochwill soften Bergan's original stance on consultant control while continuing to assert the primacy of the consultant's responsibility as being the eliciting of certain, specific information deemed necessary to the resolution of the case.

It would seem that Caplan and Caplan's client-centered case consultation model would be similar to the generic behavioral case consultation model. However, behavioral consultants conceptualize consultants as being experts in learning theory. These expert consultants attempt to alter clients' behaviors by teaching consultees how to make positive changes in clients' behaviors. Caplan and Caplan see consultants as experts in a broader scope. They see mental health consultants as experts in mental health and, when appropriate, experts in organizations and systems. Moreover, the fact that consultants "teach" consultees in behavioral case consultation runs counter to Caplan and Caplan in two ways. First, in behavioral case consultation, it is assumed that the consultant, if not teaching, will be at least supervising the knowledge base of consultees as far as their understanding of learning theory is concerned (Dougherty, 1990, p. 262; Gallessich, 1982, pp. 180–181). Caplan and Caplan (1993) identify consultees' "lack of skill" as only one of four types of consultee problems in consultee-centered case consultation (pp. 103–108). So, the teaching role is greatly diminished in the mental health consultation model. Second, Caplan and Caplan state there is usually little need for consultee-centered case consultation occasioned by a lack of knowledge because of the likelihood of already having a professional staff that is adequately trained (pp. 103–104). In this manner, what seems central to behavioral case consultation is almost structurally dismissed in Caplan and Caplan's model.

It could be argued that Caplan and Caplan's model offers more flexibility in that consultants have two options in which to proceed: consultee-centered case consultation and consultee-centered client consultation. These two options are mitigated by the consultee's request and concerns and the client's acute needs. Caplan and Caplan conceptualize consultants working directly with clients only on occasion—specifically, for a specified reason such as providing a diagnosis. Although consultations are conducted on an ongoing basis, each is conducted for the short term. Behavioral case consultants will usually exercise only one option, and that is to work directly with consultees.

Behavioral Consultation and Diversity

Whereas Caplan and Caplan's mental health consultation model borrows heavily from traditional psychodynamic thought, the behavioral social work person-in-environment perspective utilizes learning principles to explain human behavior. In general, a behavioral analytic approach such as that exemplified by the behavioral social worker person-in-environment perspectives differs dramatically from traditional stage theories such as is used to structure Caplan and Caplan's mental health consultation model. Instead of postulating a subjective hierarchy of intrapsychic stages, such as those identified in traditional psychodynamic thought, researchers advocating the behavioral person-in-environment perspectives are more *objectivist* in their approaches and emphasize the *application of universal, scientific principles of learning* (Thyer, 1994). This perspective is a social perspective in that it conceptualizes individuals as inextricable components of social systems and emphasizes the reciprocal nature of all relationships. These relationships are found in all organized groups, including families, and within each group there is a division of labor and roles.

Role Theory and Behavioral Consultation

In the behavioral person-in-environment perspective, roles are important to understand and are therefore a central construct in this paradigm (Hamilton, 1958). According to Greene (1994), one of the strengths of role theory is that cultural relativity is inherent in the structure of the theory (p. 95). That means that roles cut across all racioethnic and gender lines. Roles are roles in whatever environment they are found. The particulars of any given role vary only by culture. Role theory softens the pathology of theme interference. On a more global scale, role theory reflexively addresses the inherent structure and nature of "pathology" and asserts that pathology is culturally bound. For instance, there is professional research debating the construction of the *Diagnostic and Statistics Manual (DSM-IV-TR)* (American Psychiatric Association, 2000). The main criticisms relate to the traditional view of pathology and how this manual is a symbol for the dominant male model (Plumwood, 1993). The impact of such a philosophy on these groups is similar to that described in the discussion of feminism and environmental mastery.

Bergan and Kratochwill's (1990) model incorporates the term *role relationships* to partly describe the interactions that occur between consultant and consultees. This term blankets a critical component of their consultation model in which the consultee carries out the joint agreed upon plan. Nonetheless, the issue of roles, and especially the role of the behavioral consultant, has been contentious. Not surprisingly, there has been vociferous objection to Bergan's (1977) earlier notions that the behavioral consultant had "control" in the relationship with the consultees. However, Bergan was not alone. Erchul (1987) and other researchers corroborated those findings and saw that hierarchical stance as effective (e.g., Erchul & Chewning, 1990). However, a plethora of researchers advocate the collegial approach as most effective (e.g., Caplan & Caplan, 1970, 1993; Gutkin, 1996; Houk & Lewandowski, 1996; Myrick, 1977, 1987). Nonetheless, in later published works, Bergan and Kratochwill (1990) and Erchul and Martens (1997, 2002) maintain their original positions in believing that consultants have and should have some control in the relationship with consultees. This is especially true with the use of consultants' verbal structuring techniques, which are designed to elicit specific data and the systematic reinforcement to enhance compliance with the consultant's perspective (Brown, Pryzwansky, & Schulte, 2001, p. 48; Gallessich, 1982; Henning-Stout, 1993).

The essential line of the debate gravitates around differing worldviews. On one side stand the behaviorists, who believe in a deterministic world in which the existence and valuating of "control" is appropriate. This notion is the same as contained in the structure of all medical models, which have been discussed. On the opposite side of the debate lie those who deplore the very idea that someone has control over them and reject any theory based on that assumption. The debate is not likely to be settled. Hence, it might be helpful to note what two behavioral social work researchers have stated. Thyer and Hudson (1987) maintain that behavioral social workers may or may not embrace any particular aspects of behaviorism to be effective in their interventions (p. 1).

When considering a discussion of behavioral approaches in consultation, credit needs to be given to the person-in-environment approach and role theory in particular. Its underlying learning theory is applicable to almost everyone, almost everywhere. Although not purported to be value free, a clear advantage of a person-in-environment and role theory perspective over the psychodynamic school is the flexibility of the learning theory perspective to more easily embrace diverse populations (Greene, 1994).

Learning Theory and Behavioral Social Work

According to Thyer and Hudson (1987, p. 1), *behavioral social work* is defined as a professional endeavor in which there is an informed use of intervention techniques founded on empirically derived learning theories. The theories utilized in behavioral social work include but are not limited to operant conditioning, respondent conditioning, and observational learning. As mentioned, behavioral social work does not necessarily subscribe strongly to traditional stage theories of human development in attempting to understand culturally diverse clients (Greene, 1994, p. 139). The human development theories utilized in social work often encompass knowledge about biopsychosocial development across the life span, and attempt to address the range and hierarchy of social systems in which individuals live. These systems include families, groups, organizations, institutions, and communities (CSWE, 1992). Social learning theory explains human behavior within and across those systems. In social work, the social learning theory perspective emphasizes that the practitioner need not apply behavioral principles differentially, because they are based on universal principles of human learning. According to Greene (1994), the psychosocial environments in which individuals operate clearly vary, but the learning principles remain the same.

Behavioral Social Work and Diversity

The following is a summary of some basic assumptions of behavioral social work that highlight the culturally sensitive person-in-environment perspective (Greene, 1994, p. 136):

1. Human behavior includes everything that a person does, and this will include observable behavior as well as an individual's cognitive and affective domain.
2. Considerable weight is given to the principle that human behavior is learned.
3. The similar underlying biological processes by which people acquire behavior apply to all people across all racioethnic and gender lines as well across social classes.
4. Similar learning processes take place across different environments within an individual's life span, within a cultural environment, and across history.
5. The three major biological processes by which people learn are respondent learning, operant conditioning, and modeling or imitating others.

These assumptions level the playing field in terms of racioethnic differences in how behavior is learned. Essentially, people learn different things the same way across cultures. Clearly, social learning theorists do recognize that clients differ. Social learning theorists also agree that these differences need to be taken into account when working with diverse clients (e.g., Greene, 1994). In fact, not only is there agreement but there is also a strong emphasis in behavioral social work on individualized assessment. According to learning theory, all people essentially learn the same way, yet each person is an individual. Thus, the need for individualized assessments seems to be obvious, and research in diversity has underscored the need for such individualized approaches. For instance, Wyche (1993) asserts that most applied research involving African American women has not had representative samples or the samples were limited. Moreover, Zuckerman (1990) states that most studies involving racioethnic differences focus on between-group variances while ignoring important within-group or individualized differences. It may well be the case that various groups have much more in common than they have differences. Hence, from a social learning perspective, an adolescent who is Caucasian and middle class might have more in common with a middle-class African American than with an adolescent coming from a poor family in Appalachia (Greene, 1994, p. 139).

The behavioral social work perspective and the learning principles that form its structures are important to keep in mind when reviewing behavioral approaches to consultation. The fundamental structures of the learning principles have always been relatively culture free (e.g., Bandura, 1977; Bergan, 1977; Bergan & Kratochwill, 1990; Meichenbaum, 1977; Skinner, 1953). Nonetheless, during the 1950s, 1960s, and, to some degree, the 1970s, the learning principles guiding behaviorism were seen as dehumanizing principles while substituting a mechanistic and deterministic veil over free will.

The result was somewhat ironic, but clearly understandable. During the 1960s, a time when there was great social upheaval, there was a need for greater understanding of human behavior on everyone's part. Learning theory provided just that way to understand vastly diverse populations and people's behaviors. But, the consternation it caused by the implications for free will precluded an appreciation of how it could be used to help understand others, and their behaviors, while functioning to bring people together. As shown throughout the previous chapters, the need for embracing diversity in consultation is only increasing. As such, it provides fertile ground for new perspectives on traditional learning theory. Behavioral social work understood the flexibility of learning theory for diversity early on. Using that approach to frame current behavioral approaches in consultation should help diminish objections to some of the traditional as well as current notions contained in behavioral approaches, and in behavioral consultation in particular.

A SYSTEMATIC BEHAVIORAL CONSULTATION MODEL

Myrick (1977) developed a behavioral model that is especially useful for school counselor/consultations that has been revised and updated through the works of Vacc and Loesch (2000). According to Myrick, one of the main advantages of behavioral consultation is that it relates to diverse populations and is relatively simple, direct, and concrete. The same author goes on to say that behavioral consultation does not require complex interpretations such as those found in Caplan and Caplan's model. Moreover, behavioral approaches are systematic, and because they focus on specific behavioral changes and the maintenance of appropriate behavior, the results are easier to evaluate (p. 61). This is clearly one of the distinct strengths of Myrick's model as well. Although developed mainly for use in the schools, Myrick's problem-solving behavioral model can be applied to a variety of situations with a variety of consultees and clients. In comparing

Myrick's consulting model with Bergan and Kratochwill's, there is at least one major difference: Consultants in Myrick's model as well as in Vacc and Loesch's model do not engage in teaching social learning principles to consultees. Instead, the structure of consultation is more traditional in that consultants can "help consultees help clients" through a variety of means. Myrick is similar to Caplan and Caplan in stating that an in-service workshop, focusing on learning about behavior change, might be appropriate for those consultees who need instruction on behavioral learning principles (pp. 64–73).

Ingredients of Effective Consultation

Myrick (1977) cites the works of Dinkmeyer and Caldwell (1970), who outlined several general conditions that are necessary for consultation to be successful. Some of the characteristics are structural and some are interpersonal. A significant feature of Myrick's model is the balance between consultee and client behaviors and the consultant/consultee relationship. According to Dinkmeyer and Caldwell as well as Myrick, the responsibility and decision as to how to proceed in any given consultation case must be left up to consultees. Also, the consultant and the consultee must align the goals and the purpose of the consultation. So, the process is seen as a joint venture. Additionally, consultees must also be "ready" for the consultation to be successful. These three conditions are all congruent with aspects of mental health and behavioral case consultation models.

Myrick (1977) and Dinkmeyer and Caldwell (1970) believe that the consultant should be perceived not only as competent to handle the situation but seen also as caring and empathic. This is not such a dramatic departure from the emphasis in behavioral case consultation, but it does underscore a structural difference in how the relationship between consultant and consultee is conceptualized or perceived. Another emphasis in Myrick's model is the presence of counseling core conditions as necessary to the relationship. Caplan (1970) and Caplan and Caplan (1993) would not use the specific term *core conditions.* However, those authors would not take umbrage at Myrick's or Vacc and Loesch's discussion of the importance of such facilitative conditions. Current behavioral consultants would not likely take issue with this either.

Even though it is clear that the consultation model advocated by Myrick does not incorporate the issue of "consultant control" in the relationship with consultees, consultants are seen as having the ability to "influence" consultees. Whereas Bergan (1977) and Bergan and Kratochwill (1990) use the term *control,* the term is not referred to in Myrick's works. The best that consultants can do in Myrick's model is *attempt to influence* consultees through the use of facilitative responding and structured "leads." This "attempt to influence" may continue to be perceived as a form of control, but Myrick would likely be quick to point to the efficacy and power of Rogerian approaches in counseling and consulting while also maintaining that Rogerian approaches could hardly be described as "controlling." Nonetheless, the argument raised by Myrick's emphasis on consultants being warm, empathic, respectful, genuine, sincere, and expert does not reflect a nondirective approach in the consulting process. Being an active participant in the consulting process is seen as a critical component. This active participation involves helping consultees clarify the issue(s) by having consultants focus on the communication that occurs in consultation.

Facilitative Communication and Responding

Myrick (1987, 1993), Myrick and Bowman (1981), Wittmer and Myrick (1974, 1989), and Wittmer (1992) researched significant aspects of the communication process and outlined six responses that tend either to facilitate or not facilitate a helpful relationship with consultees. These consultant responses essentially form the structure of the consultant's leads in the consulting model. The six responses are as follows:

1. Advice
2. Analyzing and interpreting
3. Untimely reassurance
4. Open/closed questioning
5. Clarifying, paraphrasing, and restating
6. Feeling-focused responses

When applied as the structure for the consultant's verbal "leads," these six responses form the core facilitative conditions through which consultants can genuinely care and be effective, while maintaining a focus on problematic behaviors in clients. One of the powers of Wittmer and Myrick's research is its structural flexibility. This allows the model to address gender, disability, and racioethnic concerns as well as holding stable across time. That is, the timely use of the six responses form the conditions for facilitating relationships with peoples of diverse worldviews. Wittmer's (1992) later research in facilitative communication skills and diversity, particularly with the Amish, supports this assertion.

According to the earlier research of Myrick (1977) and Wittmer and Myrick (1974, 1989), the six responses can be conceptually aligned along a continuum from "less facilitative" to "more facilitative." All responses are considered appropriate, but it is the timing and the frequency that are significant. Briefly, **advice** is on the less facilitative end of the pole, and **feeling-focused responses** lie at the other end. Advice occurs when there is an overt or implied suggestion of what consultees "should do or ought to do." This is a response that is least facilitative and one that should be used sparingly.

Analyzing and interpreting another's experience (although legitimate in counseling) is seen as the next least facilitative response in terms of frequency. An example of an interpreting response is, "The reason you are having trouble with the client is because you do not like him." Myrick (1977) and Vacc and Loesch (2000) advocate that consultants be parsimonious with the frequency with which they use this type of response to consultees because it tends to put consultees on the defensive by indicating an intent at "teaching them what they should do" (Myrick, 1977, p. 68). There are exceptions, of course. The above comment might well be accurate, and there might be times when such feedback is necessary or preferable. Nonetheless, analyzing behaviors has a high probability of closing off open communication on the part of consultees. The researchers suggest caution in using this type of response. This is not to suggest that consultants should be passive and never analyze the situation. They should and do. The analyzing and interpreting of the situation should be done continuously and mostly silently in the mind of consultants. Bergan and Kratochwill (1990) do think that analyzing, interpreting, and making inferences about clients' behaviors is an important component of the consulting process. Yet, it is not likely that behavioral consultants would verbalize their analysis and interpretation of the consultees' behaviors. If anyone, Caplan and Caplan would be more interested in analyzing than would either Bergan or Myrick.

Reassurance is the next "less facilitative" response along the continuum. Clearly, everyone, including consultees, wants to be reassured from time to time. A key concept with reassurance is noting a difference between reassuring a consultee that things will be okay while not taking away the consultee's experience. Being aware of that distinction and being sensitive to the timing of the response can help make it more effective. An effective way that this reassurance can be accomplished is through the use of more facilitative responses on the part of consultants. This is a central construct in counseling, where beginning counselors are taught or (firmly) encouraged to avoid imparting the certainty that the client's situation will resolve itself. One reason is that such untimely or "false" reassurance refocuses the power of change in the counseling process onto the counselor while covertly or overtly disempowering the client in the process.

Even though consultants do have power in consultations (a major delineation between counseling and consultation), Myrick (1997) is saying that consultants ought not to use this power indiscriminately through the untimely use of these three types of responses. Instead of advising, consultants can use **questions**—both open and closed questions. The use of such techniques in counseling and therapy with a variety of populations is well documented, and consultants are encouraged to use open-ended questions, such as "how, when, where, and what" with consultees. This helps gather data and information from and about consultees.

Open questions might be followed by **clarifying, paraphrasing, and/or summarizing** responses. These responses are similar to summarizing responses utilized in Bergan and Kratochwill's model. However, a significant departure from the behavioral case consultation model occurs in Myrick's advocacy of the use of "feeling-focused" responses in communicating with consultees. Here, it is clear that the models of Myrick and Caplan merge closer conceptually while separating from the models advocated and outlined by Bergan (1977) and Bergan and Kratochwill (1990). Yet, significant structural differences continue to exist between Caplan and Caplan and Myrick on the issue.

Caplan and Caplan (1993) see the consultant as focusing on the feelings of the consultee by paying attention to the consultee's anxieties about the case, about the consultation, and about the consultant. The personal feelings of consultees are taken into consideration as they relate to a lack of objectivity, but are not considered to be an appropriate focus of consultation. Myrick would agree in theory, yet would assert the need to "debrief" consultees' feelings about clients, the situation itself, and perhaps, if necessary, the consultant and consultation process itself. Although these feeling-focused responses are aimed at the consultee's experiences, they are multipurposed. The use of such responses by a skilled consultant is seen as creating an atmosphere of trust, mutual respect, reassurance (that things will, in fact, be okay without ever saying the words directly), and empathy. The last element, empathy, is seen as a cornerstone of effective consultation in Myrick's model, and another purpose of using feeling-focused responses is to help enhance that empathy. Taken together, the three facilitative responses of open questioning, paraphrasing and summarizing, and feeling-focused responses form the foundation of the systematic consulting process outlined next.

The Seven Steps in Systematic Consultation

In his original work, Myrick (1977) outlines seven steps of consultation that are sequential in nature. In using this approach, consultants will find that there is a significant flow to these steps. They seem to sequence themselves naturally in the normal course of consulting dialogue. Moreover, a particularly useful aspect of these seven steps is their simultaneous brevity and profundity.

Step One: Identify the Problem.   Identifying the problem at the beginning of the consulting process is an obvious initial task. This step is congruent with almost every other consulting mode. An emphasis in Myrick's model is on consultants being listeners during the process. Being good listeners means that consultants will reflect back to consultees what they hear consultees saying.

Step Two: Clarify the Consultee's Situation.   In this step, consultants focus on examining the consultee's experiences with the client as well as identifying the consultee's expectations. Consultees are encouraged to discuss feelings they have about clients while they are discussing in detail their experiences related to the client. Naturally, consultants want to get an accurate picture of exactly what is happening with the client. Oftentimes, consultees do not have specific expectations about what they want to see happen. This can be the result of misperceiving the client in much the same way as Caplan and Caplan would see consultees experiencing theme interference.

However, instead of punctuating the psychodynamic approach, Myrick utilizes de Shazer's (1985) "exception to the rule" approach. This approach is in agreement with other studies. For instance, research conducted by Downing and Harrison (1992) suggests that it might be important also to identify positive assets in clients. For instance, when processing the consultee's feelings and experiences, he or she might tend to see the client in dualistic or absolutist terms. For example, a consultee might describe a client as "totally out to lunch every time we have our meetings." This extremist perspective generates feelings that may well cause the consultee to be less than effective with the client. In other words, the consultee is saying that the client was never mentally there during sessions, and that there were no exceptions to the consultee's experience. Caplan and Caplan might impose a theme interference perspective on the situation and attempt to organize the consultee's experience into the Initial Category and Inevitable Outcome. Downing and Harrison cite the work of de Shazer (1985) in noting the advantage of using the "exception to the rule" technique as a means to generate "hope" in those attempting to change self or others. This technique is based on the idea that there is always an exception to the rule. (Ironically, there are no exceptions to this rule. It is a categorical structure.) So, if consultees see their clients only in absolutist terms with no exceptions, then generating possible solutions is all the more difficult because the situation would appear more hopeless than it might in fact be. Sensing little hope or self-efficacy, consultees might be reluctant or find it difficult to generate creative solutions.

Step Three: Identify the Goal or Desired Outcome.   Identifying the goal or expected outcome is as significant as identifying the problem. First, this detailed understanding of what is expected will act as a baseline for evaluating the results of the consulting process. Second, it allows consultees to identify with the process by which the goal(s) will be reached. This helps consultees trust consultants. Furthermore, it is important to note that the goal(s) or desired outcome(s) can be general or specific. This is a departure from models that want the goals to be identified in very specific terms, such as might be the case where a student's time on task is measured every 30 seconds. In systematic consultation, the consultee might simply want the student to pay more attention during classroom instruction. Although this would likely be operationalized during the discussions between consultant and consultee, the goal of paying more attention is sufficient enough.

Myrick implores consultants not to give advice or interpret the client's behaviors in this step. Advice tends to shut down the process, and interpreting the client's behaviors is based only on conjecture. Whatever goals or outcomes are determined, Myrick believes that they must be stated in positive terms. For example, the goal of paying more attention during classroom instruction could have been, and often is, stated as "not having the student leave the desk during instruction." "Not leaving the desk" is stated in negative terms: It is something the student *will not do*. A more positively framed goal would see the student as "paying more attention." This is something that the student *will do*. According to Myrick and others (e.g., Wittmer & Myrick, 1974, 1989), this positive orientation works better in shaping client behaviors.

Step Four: Record and Observe Existing Behaviors.   Recording behaviors can either involve actual observation or simply detailing the client's behaviors through discussion with consultees. A key to this process is identifying observable behaviors—those that can be measured. It does not include interpreting nonverbal behaviors of clients. School counselors can go into a classroom and observe the student(s), and this observation can fall short of a formal behavioral analysis.

Step Five: Develop a Plan.   This component of Myrick's model is interesting in that the process involves a brainstorming session with consultees. The major purpose of this brainstorming is to involve the consultee in the process of solution. However, there are several other reasons for invoking this approach. For instance, having the consultee generate potential solutions allows the consultant to see in more detail what has already been tried. Moreover, it is easier for the consultant to make appropriate suggestions after knowing what has already been tried. It generating solutions, it is critically important that both the consultant and the consultee attempt to predict outcomes that segue from potential solutions. For instance, if the consultee suggests a solution that the consultant sees as having problems, asking the consultee to identify the probable outcome allows for this type "error detection" to occur and adjustments to be made. As a result, the proposed solution may be eliminated altogether or may be altered to effect a better outcome. This process of identifying a plan is a joint process.

Step Six: Initiate the Plan.   Once a plan for intervention has been discussed and agreed upon, determining when, where, and how the plan will be implemented is the next step. Again, it is important that consultants and consultees get very specific about this issue. Asking a consultee when, where, and how not only helps with the consultee's adherence to the plan but it also allows for a plan to be more realistic in its execution. Consultees will know the actual situation better than consultants and will therefore have a more incisive understanding of how to do it.

Step Seven: Follow Up.   Following up on a consultation seems to be a rather obvious step; it is another term for evaluating the results. Following up with a consultee in a school might simply mean making sure that the consultant asks how the plan went. This discussion does not have to be long, but it could be. Myrick advocates that the consultant follows up so that the consultee knows the consultant cares. This acts to reinforce consultation as an effective method of help. Following up allows for consultants and consultees to see what, if any, alterations to the original plan need to be made.

Lead and Focus in Systematic Consultation

Myrick believes that consultant "leads" are intended to help facilitate a relationship with consultees. The relationship should be structured to be natural and sensitive to the personalities involved. Similar to Bergan and Kratochwill's model, the consultant's leads are aimed at encouraging an interactive discussion in which a mutually agreed upon diagnosis, evaluation, and set of goals is a result. Even though there is a mention of consultees becoming more aware of how their behavior interacts in the problematic situation, Myrick agrees with Caplan and Caplan (1993), Bergan (1977), and Bergan and Kratochwill (1990) in saying that personality reorganization is not a goal of the consultation process.

In their model, Bergan and Kratochwill emphasize the paramount importance of consultant/consultee verbal interactions replete with the controversial issue of "consultant control." Myrick also places strong emphasis on the consultant/consultee relationship in saying that communication is important in consultation. However, Myrick places a stronger emphasis on the relationship between consultant and consultee rather than on the structural power of the consultant's verbal interactions inherent in the relationship. Myrick (1977) cites the works of Dinkmeyer and Carlson (1973) and outlines consultant verbal and nonverbal techniques. This same researcher punctuates the necessity of consultants in establishing an atmosphere for the open sharing and exploring of ideas (p. 29). Similar to Bergan and Kratochwill's idea of consultant "leads," Myrick maintains that consultants can influence the responses of consultees through the use of consultant leads and focus. In general, in systematic consultation, consultants can utilize the following (Dinkmeyer & Carlson, 1973; Myrick, 1977, pp. 29–30):

■ Techniques that focus on the content of the situation
■ Techniques that elicit affect and encourage the expression of feelings

- Techniques designed to facilitate self-understanding and an awareness of one's own part in the transactions
- Techniques designed to analyze the purpose and the dynamics of behavior to develop insight
- Techniques designed to facilitate new responses and procedures for improving the consultee/client relationship along with facilitating new methods for modifying behavior

The verbal leads in Bergan and Kratchowill's model are focused on helping the consultee *see the consultant's light,* as it were. The verbal leads in Myrick's model are focused on having the consultee *see their own light.* That is the nondirective aspect of Myrick's model. Moreover, in traditional behavioral case consultation, there is an emphasis on consultants needing to be able to accurately organize data into subcategories. The manner in which this is accomplished is through the use of five verbal responses. For Myrick, the verbal techniques that are designed to influence consultees do not lead to a categorization of data. Rather, the leads are designed to facilitate the consultee's understanding and abilities to enhance change in her or his client. Although this clarifies a difference in focus in the two models, the leads in each accomplish essentially the same thing. The goal in both models is to facilitate a relationship with the consultee in order to clarify and detail what is happening with the consultee and the client so that effective plans for action can be agreed on and implemented.

The Four Steps in Vacc and Loesch's Model

Both Bergan (1977) and Myrick (1977) updated the content and some concepts in later research (Bergan & Kratochwill, 1990; Myrick, 1987, 1993). Vacc and Loesch (2000) provided an abridged version of Myrick's 1977 works. Vacc and Loesch (who, incidentally, were colleagues of Myrick's at the time) collapse Myrick's seven steps into a four-step problem-solving model. Vacc and Loesch maintain every important component of Myrick's original model. Moreover, they state that this model is "particularly well suited for professional counselors" (p. 103). In their version, Vacc and Loesch outline the four consulting problem-solving steps into "intent" and "purpose" (p. 105).

Step One: What Is the Problem or Situation?   The identification of the problem is clarified through the use of active, facilitative listening skills. According to the authors, the purpose of this first step is to establish rapport with the consultee, stimulate discussion, tentatively identify aspects of the problem, allow the consultee to "vent," and to identify the boundaries around "who owns the problem." Critical to the efficacy of this step toward problem resolution is the ability of the consultant to **empathize** with the consultee while defining the problem. Most likely, the consultee will have feelings about the issue at hand, and it is important to allow him or her to vent. Caplan and Caplan would not take umbrage with this approach.

Myrick (1977) and Vacc and Loesch (2000) believe it is important to use **feeling-focused responses** that identify, clarify, and affirm the feelings and experiences of consultees. These feeling-focused responses do not necessarily need to be direct. For example, imagine that an executive of a small company requests help with staff morale as a result of forced layoffs in her company. In the initial conversations with the consultant, she remarks, "I think I am going to go crazy." The consultant responds, "Yes. I can well imagine that a trip to Hawaii looks pretty appealing right now." This type of indirect identification of feelings can be useful if the personal culture or organizational culture values holding feelings inside.

A rationale for allowing and/or encouraging consultees to express their feelings is that it can help clear the way for more rational thinking. For Caplan and Caplan, if consultees are not able to return to more rational (albeit "male" model) ways of thinking, they are more likely suffering from a more severe form of distortion and theme interference. Although discussed in Caplan and Caplan in greater detail than in either Bergan's or Myrick's models, all three authors would agree that consultees who are experiencing personal problems that otherwise prohibit thinking differently about a case should be referred out to the appropriate and qualified professionals.

In Step One of Vacc and Loesch's model, consultants might find themselves using a plethora of **open questions, summaries, and paraphrases** to detail the issue(s) at hand. For instance, the consultant might ask the consultee, "What happened? How did you respond? When did you first notice the behaviors?" These open questions would be followed by summaries, paraphrases, and/or restatements aimed at clarifying what the consultee has said. An example would be, "So, you are saying that you first noticed the behavior the day after the holiday." Throughout this process, Myrick as well as Vacc and Loesch agree that the well-timed use of **feeling-focused responses** will be effective in helping consultees vent as well as be effective in facilitating a sound working relationship with consultees. In empathizing with a consultee who has just described her response to a student's aberrant behavior, a consultant might say, "Sounds like you are frustrated and feel like there's no where else you can turn **(feeling-focused).** It's a tough situation **(clarification and reassurance).** Let's see what can we can do about it."

Step Two: What Have You Tried?   Once a solid relationship with consultees has been attained and the problems have been identified, consultants and consultees need to focus on what has already been tried. In Bergan's model, this would take place in subcategories five and six—the discussions about data that have already been collected and/or observed (five) as well as what consultees have already tried (six). Vacc and Loesch see this step as purposeful in obtaining data, eliciting perceptions, and identifying issues. The major focus of this step is to clarify the consultee's situation along several dimensions. For instance, it is of interest to know what the consultee has already tried and how the consultee feels about what has been tried. When consultees have many feelings about a situation, there may be a tendency for them to go off on tangents. Consultants should be aware of this and make appropriate compensations to try to help consultees remain focused. It is also important for consultants to avoid overgeneralizations as well as being too myopic in their need for information. For instance, the process of getting specific descriptions of the client's behaviors is critical to the consulting process, and consultants are encouraged to use open questions and clarifications, summaries, and paraphrases in an effort to get an accurate picture of the lay of the land. Asking an **open question,** such as, "What is it about that behavior that is of concern?" or "What happened next?" are examples of attempting to help consultees become more specific while keeping the discussion focused appropriately. Again, this question might be followed by a clarifying response, such as **restating or paraphrasing** what was heard: "You are saying that you have had some success in the past."

Another important component of Step Two is to have consultants and consultees become aware and agree on the expected outcome as well as any expectations of the consulting process seen as needing attention by either party. Similar to Myrick's approach, Vacc and Loesch's model allows for the identified outcome(s) and goals to be either general or specific. "What would you like to see happen in this situation?" is an effective open-ended question to use for this purpose. These researchers also believe that it is usually more effective to set goals that are positive, that can be operationally defined, and that encourage an action in clients rather than an inaction (Vacc & Loesch, 2000, p. 40).

The example of a school counselor/consultant helping a teacher identify ways to improve a student's behaviors during classroom instruction depicts this consulting value. Instead of setting the goal of the student needing to be obedient and not interrupting, the consultant helped the teacher identify a goal of focusing on having the student raise her hand. The new positive-action goal reflects a student-in-action: raising her hand, as opposed to "not doing" something which was, in this case, not interrupting. All during this process, Vacc and Loesch (2000) as well as Myrick (1977, p. 40) maintain that consultants need to "call upon the very best communication skills." In this case, this is tantamount to using a plethora of more facilitative responses with consultees.

The final purpose of Step Two is to have the consultant identify positive attitudes and behaviors of the consultee. This is a "positive assets" approach characteristic of Rogerian thought as well as of effective behavioral therapies. One of the benefits of this positive assets approach is that is has an inherent motivational factor to it, according to social learning theory. That is, consultees are more likely to engage in behaviors in which they feel a high degree of self-efficacy or ability to accomplish the task (Bandura, 1977; Brown, Pryzwansky, & Schulte, 2001).

Step Three: What Else Could You Do?   In this step, consultants want to help consultees determine what else can be done about the situation in addition to what has already been tried (Step Two). Myrick and Vacc and Loesch again stress the importance of the relationship between consultant and consultee so that there is a "mutualization" of realities (Vacc & Loesch, 2000, p. 105). This mutualization should not be confused with a blending of realities. Rather, the process leads to a more accurate identification of issues, behaviors, and outcomes or plans of action. Seeing a blending of realities is likened to seeing diversity as a "melting pot" as opposed to a "salad bowl" (or some other metaphor). The mutualization connotes the nature of the relationship in which both consultant and consultee connect positively in the helping process. This is achieved through the empathic responses of **open questions, clarifications and summaries, and feeling-focused responses** on the part of consultants.

Similar to Bergan (1977) and Bergan and Kratochwill (1990), it is important in this stage to infer possible outcomes of potential courses of action. The process by which options are identified is important. Brainstorming ideas is advocated by Myrick (1977). Consultants can help consultees with ideas, should they run out of ideas or not generate potentially effective options. Bergan, Bergan and Kratochwill, Myrick, and Vacc and Loesch would all agree on the need for consultants to "guide" consultees toward solutions that may be more efficacious. The difference is in the manner in which this is done. Bergan leans more toward control, whereas Myrick and Vacc and Loesch lean more toward influencing through facilitative communication and brainstorming.

An example of how a consultant might go about helping a consultee brainstorm is, "What else do you think you can do that might work?" (open-ended question). After a list has been generated, the consultant and the consultee can go through the list and evaluate and make inferences about the probability of success in a similar fashion, as advocated by Myrick's model as well as by Bergan and Kratochwill's (1990) model. During this process, it would not be uncommon for a consultant to reflect a consultee's reaction to a particular strategy with a feeling-focused response like, "Wow. That sure generated a response from you. Sounds like you feel more comfortable with this plan than the other." Even though consultants empathize with consultees in this fashion, there remains a strong emphasis on detailing specific behaviors in this step as with other problem-solving behavioral consulting models.

Step Four: What Is Your Next Step?   The consulting process is now at a point where consultants and consultees can develop a plan of action. This plan will essentially include *what can be done, what will be done, how it will be done, and when it will be done* (Vacc & Loesch, 2000, p. 105). One main strength of this step is reflected in obtaining a "commitment" from consultees through the process of specification. The point is to collapse the "next step" into a manageable step. Following traditional approaches to behavioral change, Myrick's (1977) original model and Vacc and Loesch's (2000) abbreviated version of it both advocate behavior change through small steps. This helps ensure success on the part of consultees. Both this model and that of Bergan and Bergan and Kratochwill emphasize the importance of having this commitment to action on the part of consultees.

Open-ended questions, such as, "When do you think this plan can start?" and "How will you go about setting this plan up?" are good examples of how to start Step Four. Following a similar formula as that advocated by Bergan and Kratochwill, open-ended questions might be followed up with a **clarifying** response, such as, "I hear you saying that next week would be good. What day do you think you can start?" A technique utilized when assigning homework in therapy can be used here to help ensure the consultee's compliance to the agreed upon action. As in Myrick's (1977) original model, Vacc and Loesch (2000) see identifying potential barriers to the plan as a way to help predict unanticipated obstacles that may come up that could impede success. Asking consultees to discuss any barriers is reflected in this statement: "Between now and Tuesday, what can happen or come up that would make it difficult for you to carry out your plan?" This could be followed by, "It sounds like there might be many things that can occur between now and Tuesday, and you are not feeling confident that you pull this plan off. What if you target another day to start?"

Vacc and Loesch's (2000) abbreviated version of Myrick's (1977) model is simple and straightforward, yet very effective. Myrick's original model has seven steps, and the only one not addressed directly in Vacc and Loesch's condensation of it is the last step: following up. Nonetheless, Vacc and Loesch advocate strongly that there be some type of follow-up to the consulting process for similar reasons as stated by Myrick.

SUMMARY

The systematic consultation model of Myrick and the abbreviated version of it by Vacc and Loesch essentially reflect a two-pronged model in which facilitative communication is used by consultants as they guide consultees through either a seven-step or a four-step process. Although not punctuated with the same emphasis as in Bergan's (1977) behavioral case consultation, the use of facilitative responding in Myrick's model is no less requisite to the success of the consulting process. Through the use of the term *influence,* Myrick has been able to avoid the vociferous criticism leveled at Bergan and Kratochwill's model for their emphasis on consultants controlling the flow of consultees' responses as well as controlling the flow of consultation. Moreover, even though Myrick's model is considered "atheoretical" by Vacc and Loesch, a scrutiny of Myrick's work reveals a strong influence from both the behavioral as well as the Rogerian schools of thought. Neither Myrick nor Vacc and Loesch are proposing that consultants be nondirective, as is a hallmark in the Rogerian person-centered therapy (Rogers, 1950). In fact, it may be somewhat of a misnomer to associate Rogers with Myrick's and Vacc and Loesch's models except for the fact that the core facilitative conditions of warmth, respect, positive regard, and empathy are so central to the efficacy of both consulting models.

Myrick's model is not a nondirective model. In essence, Myrick, as well as Vacc and Loesch, utilize a straightforward behavioral problem-solving approach while placing the strongest emphasis on the consultant/consultee relationship in attempting to identify the issues in behavioral terms. Both behavioral case consultation as well as the systematic approach advocated by Myrick and Vacc and Loesch utilize similar structures. The subcategories of Bergan and Kratochwill's model are reflected in the process steps outlined in the latter model. Moreover, both models see consultants' verbal skills as categorically important.

A central advantage of Myrick's model over the behavioral case consultation model is its flexibility to incorporate diverse consultees without having to address the limitations of a deterministic and objectified approach to consultation. Behavioral case consultation is very effective. So, one should not dismiss this approach. In reality, effective behavioral consultants will employ good relationship-building skills, too. The issue lies more with the ability of Myrick's and Vacc and Loesch's models to be more "neutral" in their approaches with consultees. Caplan (1970) writes about a consulting atmosphere referred to as "entre nous" or "We two professionals are talking together about this lay client" (p. 136). The atmosphere alluded to by Caplan is similar to what Myrick believes to be essential to the consulting process.

Behavioral consultation has its roots in the educational system (Gallessich, 1982; Myrick, 1977; Vacc & Loesch, 2000). As such, behavioral consultation approaches seem to fit easily into the behavior-driven agenda of public education. Whereas Bergan and Kratochwill's behavioral consultation model can be and is used with systems, Myrick's model is general enough to form a sound structure within which organizational functioning can be understood. As Schein states, all organizational problems are inevitably human problems (E. H. Schein, personal communication, July 6, 2000). Even problems with the copier can be traced back to a human-made paper jam, lack of machine service by humans, and the like. This perspective on organizational problems concurs with that of Skinner, who stated, "What could be more human than behaviors?" (B. F. Skinner, personal communication, May 10, 1981). Yet, even conceptualizing organizations in such a "human" manner may not allow for the generalized use of the behavioral consultation for all organizational (human) problems. There may be consultees who are not well suited to being taught behavioral principles. There may also be consultees for whom a deterministic worldview is not congruent with their own worldview or for whom a behavioral approach might seem "too simplistic."

Whereas Myrick's and Vacc and Loesch's models are more gender neutral and may work well with consultees in a variety of organizational settings, Brown and Schulte (1987) outlined a social learning model of consultation (SLM) based on the works of Bandura (1977). According to Brown, Pryzwansky, and Schulte (2001), this social learning model extends many of Caplan and Caplan's ideas and focuses on consultees' behaviors and skills, cognitive self-efficacy expectations, and environment. Part of the assessment process involves understanding the environmental culture of consultees in order to gain an accurate depiction of the idiosyncratic norms that are operating. This model seems to be more conducive to working with organizations than the more restricted behavioral case consultation model. Nonetheless, the traditional behavioral case approach is effective in a variety of settings. The debate over the issue of "control" and/or "influence" aside, behavioral approaches are excellent ways in which consultants can formulate ideas as well as strategies for effective change.

Myrick considers consultants to be specialists in human relations. Therefore, it is important that consultants be aware of the multifaceted messages that take place during consultation (p. 28). These messages can include events and feelings that occur in the consulting process, and it is very important that consultants be able to concomitantly hear both the words and the affect of consultees in order to accurately comprehend the messages from consultees. Myrick's concern with the messages received and sent in the consulting process is similar to and dramatically different from the verbal interactions of Bergan and Kratochwill. In a behavioral case consultation model, one of the consultant's primary tasks is to enhance the effectiveness of verbal skills so that the consultee will be more likely to follow the consultant's leads and "arrive" at the desired and shared plan for problem resolution.

Myrick also focuses on the consultant's behaviors in the relationship with consultees. Both Bergan and Kratochwill and Myrick refer to consultants' verbal interactions as "leads," and both approaches adhere to the belief that consultants influence consultees' responses. However, Myrick's as well as Vacc and Loesch's approaches can be considered "behavioral approaches with empathy." Although oversimplified, this phrase captures Myrick's and Vacc and Loesch's dual emphases on social learning behavioral principles and a person-oriented approach to the consultee relationship. The issue of "consultant control" is not directly discussed in Myrick's monograph, but it is clear that the consultant/consultee relationship is not structured in the same philosophical orientation as is the model of Bergan and Kratochwill. Although Myrick believes in the power of behaviors and observation, it is crucial that consultants understand the *feelings* and *experiences* of consultees for a successful resolution to the issue. Distinctly different from Bergan and Kratochwill's case approach, Myrick's model does allow for direct observation of clients when appropriate and jointly agreed on with consultees.

Recall that Myrick's (1977) original model was developed for use in schools. The school counselor/consultant would not only have the opportunity for direct observation but might also have the structural responsibility to do so because of the status of being a school employee and responsible to a principal. Although this difference between behavioral models may be due to settings in Myrick's case, there is a fundamental orientation toward a collaborative relationship that is not emphasized in the behavioral case consultation model. Myrick's model provides details regarding consultant interactions and, in particular, specific "pitfalls in consultation" (pp. 81–90), which outlines ways to avoid problems. These problems include such things as consultants eliciting excessive guilt and defensiveness in consultees, failing to recognize consultees' efforts to sabotage the process, failing to provide proper support, being too expert and talking down to consultees, using nonfacilitating jargon, failing to take time or to follow up, and being too bottom-line oriented.

The philosophical orientations between mental health consultation, behavioral consultation, and systematic consultation are at once similar and vastly different from each other. Caplan and Caplan's as well as Bergan and Kratochwill's models are medical models, which reflect consultant control on either a philosophical basis, as is the case with the former, or control on a phenomenal basis, as is the case in behavioral case consultation. Both models emphasize on hierarchical structures while at the same time attempt to define the consultant/consultee relationship as either *clearly* a collaborative one (in the case of Caplan and Caplan) or *perhaps* a collaborative one (in the case of Bergan and Bergan and Kratochwill). Myrick's and Vacc and Loesch's advocacy of and emphasis on behaviors reflects a phenomenological approach, and at the same time reflects an advocacy toward a relationship that clearly is aligned with that of Caplan and Caplan. Finally, Myrick's model is considered "atheoretical" by Vacc and Loesch (2000). That reiterates the concern by Gallessich (1982). Yet, Myrick's model is less "atheoretical" than it is simply structurally flexible. It is a generic problem-solving consulting model that is applicable to and can be adapted to diverse populations.

QUESTIONS

1. What are your views of behaviorism?

2. Why do many people seem to feel threatened at the mention of behaviorism?

3. Given that all three behavioral models emphasize the relationship between consultant and consultee, which model(s) seems to fit better for you? Why?

4. Why do behavioral approaches in general have such strong and benevolent implications for diversity?

5. Even though both Myrick as well as Vacc and Loesch like the empathy skills of Rogers (1951), how are these consulting skills different from those used in counseling?

6. Knowing that all three models emphasize a consultant's leads and focus, to what extent would you agree and disagree with Bergan's and Bergan and Kratochwill's perspectives on consultant "control"?

CHAPTER ELEVEN

PROCESS CONSULTATION IN ORGANIZATIONS, INSTITUTIONS, AND AGENCIES

Schein (1969) introduced process consultation (PC) into the realm of organizational development the year before Caplan published the first version of his mental health consultation model and eight years before Bergan's model was first published. This means that Schein's process consultation model also came at a time when there was keen and widespread interest in the nature of the relationship that occurred between mental health professionals and their various clients. Caplan's interest in the relationship and the amount of attention given to it is a hallmark of the mental health consultation model.

The actual *relationship* that was built between consultant and consultee in Bergan's (1977) and Bergan and Kratochwill's (1990) behavioral case consultation model is not discussed in the same fashion nor given the amount of detail as that provided by either Caplan and Caplan (1970, 1993), Myrick (1997, 1987, 1993), Vacc and Loesch (2000), or Schein (1969, 1987, 1999). Obviously, behavioral consultants are very interested in the relationship that they have with consultees. The interest in the relationship in the behavioral case model is aimed more at the effects of verbal exchanges on the consultee's compliance with the consultant's suggestions than it is on the psychology or study of the "relationship" per se. Moreover, the focus on the consultee's compliance in the relationship (and the subsequent controversy that it stirs up) in the behavioral case consultation model is clearly different from the focus of Caplan and Caplan, Myrick, Vacc and Loesch, and Schein. With regard to PC specifically, consultee compliance is not an issue. The ultimate goal in Schein's model of organizational consulting is to establish an effective helping relationship (1999, p. 1). In that pursuit, the process consultant and consultee embark on a joint venture of diagnosis and intervention.

In my the experience, many mental health professionals do not consult in what is traditionally referred to as organizational development (OD) as a normal course of professional endeavor—unless specifically trained to do so. In general, mental health professionals might conduct workshops, training sessions, and retreats for organizations. However, as mentioned in earlier chapters, many of the larger corporations have their own in-house consulting departments that conduct the various technical trainings and organizational consultancies needed by their parent organization. Although these consultants may be considered professional consultants, their training is likely more specifically focused on organizations and organizational behavior and not necessarily on consulting in the mental health field. Nonetheless, aside from the organizational context in which consultation takes place, almost every mental health professional will undoubtedly consult with clients in traditional organizations at one time or another. For this reason, Schein's process consultation model in organizational development is presented. One of the main reasons for choosing to outline Schein's process consultation model is that the philosophy, principles, and structure of the model closely parallel a generic philosophy of helping relationships while clearly retaining its organizational consulting perspective. A result of this parallel is that mental health professionals may find it easier to employ a process consultation approach when conceptualizing the very complex issues inherent in organizational consulting

DEFINITIONS OF PROCESS CONSULTATION

Similar to the evolution of other consulting models, Schein shifted his emphases when attempting to define process consultation over the years. In the earlier versions (1969, 1987), Schein, characteristically brief, defines *process consultation as a "set of activities" on the consultant's part that are aimed at helping clients understand their internal and external environment better so that they can act on the process events that occur.* In the 1999 definition, Schein clarifies that *the "set of activities" is actually the "creation of a relationship"* with clients in which clients can better perceive, understand, and act on the process events that occur* (p. 20). The significance on the "relationship" is reflected throughout the 1999 version of process consultation. In reviewing the evolution of the definition of PC, the only real difference is reflected in the emphasis on the clear articulation of the "relationship." The ensuing definitions are consistent with respect to the need for consultants to help clients help themselves. Schein uses the adage, "Instead of giving people fish, teach them how to fish" to characterize the essential foundation of his model (1999, p. 19). The implications of this saying are woven into a set of assumptions and principles around which Schein builds the 1999 version of process consultation.

EARLY ASSUMPTIONS IN PROCESS CONSULTATION

Schein has presented several assumptions in the earlier works on process consultation (1969, 1987). First, Schein's experience is that managers do not often know what is wrong, and they need a special form of help in order to diagnose problems. Clearly, managers have some sense of what is wrong and how to go about fixing it, but, in many cases, they have been advised not to go to their bosses unless they know exactly what kind of help they need. For many, the risk of being seen as inept is too great. Moreover, in the same vein, managers themselves may not know exactly what the problem is, even though they know something is not right. Second, managers are often confused or misinformed as to what any particular consultant can offer. Consultants need to help clients determine what kind of help is needed. Third, most managers or clients will demonstrate a constructive intent to help in attempting to improve things. Nonetheless, they need help in the identification of which things need to be improved and the ways to do it. Fourth, no organizational form is perfect. Every organization will have inherent structural weaknesses for which compensatory mechanisms must be prescribed. Fifth, no consultant could possibly be expected to learn enough about the organization's culture in the client system to suggest viable courses of action without exhaustive and time-consuming efforts. Hence, organizations are better off if they learn to diagnose their own problems. For the same reason, an "outsider" does not have a great chance of remedying the situation unless these very processes are worked out jointly with the client. Sixth, clients and managers are much less resistant to the process of implementation when they are more involved in the process. Moreover, should the same or similar problems occur or recur, managers are better equipped to handle the situation. In all cases, decisions must be made and assumed by the client even though consultants can be active in the process and can provide challenging alternatives in the process.

The seventh and final assumption is interesting because the wording varies across all three versions (1969, 1987, 1999). In the original version, Schein (1969, p. 8) states that the "prime importance" in process consultation is that the helper needs to be an expert in how to diagnose and how to establish effective helping relationships with the client and client system. Effective PC is seen as involving the intentional passing along of these two skills. In the 1987 (p. 11) version, Schein believes it to be the "essential function" to pass along these diagnostic skills so that clients can themselves learn how to improve the organization. In the 1999 version (pp. 18–19), Schein proposes that the passing along of these skills is the "ultimate function" of PC. Schein also asserts that the purchase (expert) and doctor/patient models of consultation are primarily remedial models. The process consultation model is both remedial and preventive.

According to Schein, the assumptions underlying process consultation also underlie a fundamental and general theory of helping. Similar to the models of Myrick, Vacc and Loesch, and Bergan and Kratochwill, Schein clearly believes that various clients' worldviews must be understood by consultants in order for process consultants to be effective in organizational change (Schein, 1992). In addition, the centrality of joint problem solving in PC clearly implies a potential to empower consultees and consultants alike throughout the process of the consultation.

Another significant reason for examining the process consultation model of Schein is the simplicity with which the model is presented in its original and revised forms (Schein, 1969, 1987, 1999). This is also a strength of Myrick's (1977) and Vacc and Loesch's (2000) models. All three are parsimonious and profound in practicality and application. Schein addresses this issue of practicality directly by stating that what a consultant or manager needs to know is a practical model that simplifies and is easy to understand while capturing the essence of the significant insights (Schein, 1987, p. 61). The benefit of this approach for women and racioethnic minorities is the fact that one could consider Schein to be "anti-technology" on that level (only). The philosophical and structural criticisms aimed at technology by various research on feminism and racioethnic groups thus wane when discussing process consultation.

Schein (1999, p. 219) believes that process consultation is best thought of as a skill that any helper must have rather than identifying oneself as a "process consultant." The emphasis on "process" reflects an interest in *how* things are done between people and between groups rather than *what* is actually done. The reason for this, according to Schein, is that the "how" or the "process" usually says more to consultants than the "what" is or will be done. This is especially true in organizations. For mental health professionals, the emphasis on "process" is similar to the emphasis in counseling on the relationship and the "helping process." While clearly not counseling, PC can be conceptualized as a "helping process" used in organizational consulting that has a categorical emphasis on the relationship with the "client" (i.e., consultee).

Schein's philosophy parallels two central principles of gestalt theory: the "here and now" and "how" the person is experiencing the events (Perls, 1969). Process consultation emphasizes the "here and now" in that Schein believes that to be effective, a consultant must stay in touch with the current reality (1999, p. 6). This means that consultants need to be continuously diagnosing the current situation and treat every interaction as current and ongoing data. Although the parallel between process consultation and gestalt theory may be topical, the similarity between PC and Rogers's (1951, 1980) work is more profound in terms of the amount of significance placed on the helping relationship. Even though counseling and consultation are categorically distinct, both person-centered counseling approaches and process consultation are focused on the helping relationship as a categorical imperative. Nonetheless, if one limits the scope of comparison between PC and counseling to the specific parallels mentioned, one would miss the essence of "helping" in the process consultation model. Schein (1987, p. 21) asserts that the process consultant's role is a "general role" that is applicable to many roles in a variety of personal and professional situations. Relationships of all configurations (e.g., parent/child, friendships, supervisor/supervisee) can be affected by a process consultant role. Process consultation works in situations where one party is seeking some kind of help because it is as much an *attitude* as a consulting model.

STAGES AND PROCESSES IN PROCESS CONSULTATION

The emphasis on "process" in PC has profound implications for a discussion of traditional notions of stages in consultation. Central to Schein's model of consultation is the fact that diagnosing and intervening is constantly ongoing. So, Schein sees consultation projects as evolving in numerous and complex ways. As such, it is impossible to identify simple, discrete, and sequential stages such as "scouting," "entry," "diagnosing," "contracting," and "intervening" (Schein, 1999, p. 219). Instead, Schein sees consultation as intervening with contact clients initially and then moving on to other clients in the system, who may have an entirely different set of issues and clients. In essence, the process starts all over again at that level. Thus, rather than exacting discrete stages, process consultation involves entering and then determining the settings in which to work as well as identifying a method of work. According to Schein, this is all accomplished by developing appropriate and helpful psychological contracts. The process of consultation does not require consultants to bring in a standardized method of work. Instead, they engage in a process of joint diagnosis, which in turn lead to interventions. However, *Schein states that the most difficult idea to grasp in process consultation is that diagnosing and intervening are considered to be one and the same process* (p. 241). The view that diagnosis and intervention are one and the same process clearly underscores the centrality of the consultant/consultee relationship in process consultation. Moreover, by collapsing the traditional stages of "diagnosing" and "intervention" in process consultation, the traditional view of stages in consultation is also impacted.

Myrick, Vacc and Loesch, Schein, and, to some degree, Caplan and Caplan have writing styles that suggest a relaxed and easy-to-understand approach. Yet, these models are profound in their respective applications. In a sense, the seeming "lack" of explicit detail in the Myrick, Vacc and Loesch, and Schein models requires consultants to construct a base of expertise that, upon examination, clearly rivals that of the expertise required in Caplan and Caplan's and Bergan and Kratochwill's models. Schein, Bergan, Bergan and Kratochwill, as well as Caplan and Caplan all provide much detail into the manner in which consultants can go about assessing consultees and their difficulties with clients. In mental health consultation, this assessment is based on four categories of the consultee's need for help: lack of skill, lack of knowledge, lack of confidence, and lack of objectivity. Caplan and Caplan's mental health consultation model is clearly the most clinical. At the same time, Caplan and Caplan's clinical approach is akin to the clinical approach of the behavioral case consultation model. Schein's work is not clinical. It is organizational in perspective.

If one were to line up the consultation models of Caplan and Caplan (1993), Bergen and Kratochwill (1990), Myrick (1977), Vacc and Loesch (2000), and Schein, and compare them along various dimensions, interesting trends emerge that can aid in a deeper understanding of these consultation processes. For instance, using a scale measuring directive versus nondirective dimensions, one could immediately categorize the behavioral case consultation model as being more directive—likely followed by Myrick, Vacc and Loesch, Caplan and Caplan, and Schein. Since information given by consultants to clients/consultees on how to handle any given case is not usually effective in and of itself, it is often better to assure consultee adherence to whatever plan is proposed. The efficacy of any model rests to varying degrees on the strength of the consultant/client/consultee relationship.

Process consultation also utilizes a collaborative perspective, and to varying degrees, so do all four other models. Of those who stand out in front advocating collaborative relationships, Schein would again lead the group. Schein's collaborative approach would be followed by Myrick, Caplan and Caplan, and then Bergan and Kratochwill. The rationale for this placement along a continuum is that Myrick, Vacc and Loesch, and Bergan and Kratochwill are all interested in the ways that consultants can go about influencing consultees/clients toward a particular outcome. Schein places less emphasis on a specified or particular outcome. Myrick and Vacc and Loesch believe that consultees/clients can be influenced when consultants utilize facilitative communication skills, which include open questions, clarifications, summaries and paraphrases, and feeling-focused responses. Bergan and Kratochwill advocate the consultant's use of emitters and elicitors in a five-step verbal interaction process. All three models are designed to influence consultees/clients. However, Myrick and Vacc and Loesch see facilitative responses as helping enhance the relationship with consultees/clients so that they can essentially help themselves. Bergan and Kratochwill see their verbal processes more as helping focus the consultee/client into thinking along the same lines as deemed appropriate by the consultant. Schein's views on communication are no less profound. However, he is much more interested in establishing a functional and effective working relationship than he is in determining a particular outcome of consultation per se.

TASKS AND ROLES OF TRADITIONAL OGANIZATIONAL DEVELOPMENT CONSULTANTS

In organizational development (OD) consultants perform a variety of tasks and assume a variety of roles. Schein (1987) maintains that many of the functions that are assumed by organizational development consultants are the same functions that most managers would assume in their roles in the workplace. The multifunctional dimensions of the managerial roles can confuse consultees, clients, and client systems to the point that it is difficult to figure out what kind of help is actually needed. Process consultation works well when *individuals do not know what the problem is nor do they know what kind of help should be sought* (p. 20). Hence, while the person in difficulty may be the most vulnerable and likely to be resistant, PC becomes a preferred method of work.

According to Schein (1987, p. 20) and others (e.g., Massarik, 1990; Silvester, Anderson, & Patterson, 1999), traditional organizational development consultants need to provide numerous tasks when working with organizations. Among these tasks is the need to *provide information* to consultees and clients that is not otherwise available. The information can be varied, depending on the needs of the consultees and clients. Organizational consultants also *analyze information* with sophisticated tools that are not available to clients or subordinates. Consultants then begin to *diagnose* complex organizational and business problems, and design interventions. In addition, OD consultants often train clients or subordinates to use diagnostic models that enhance decision making at various levels in the organization. Consultants also *contract to be available* to listen to clients and to provide support, comfort, and counsel when appropriate. Furthermore, consultants also exercise their *ecological power base*. For instance, in many cases, OD consultants help implement difficult and unpopular ideas or decisions. In the same vein, organizational development consultants can reward and punish particular behaviors by using status as an "outsider" along with legitimate coercion. When it is appropriate to do so, consultants can carry or transmit information up the ladder if it is not otherwise available to higher or lateral levels. When consultants have been granted the legitimate authority by consultees, they can *make decisions and give commands* as to what to do if line management is not able to do so. Finally, traditional OD consultants get paid to *take responsibility for decisions* while absorbing the anxiety and uncertainty of how things will turn out. This is in addition to *finding and providing the emotional strength in order to help others* in the process. A review of the professional literature might reflect few exceptions and/or additions to Schein's list, but for the most part, the list embraces the broad field of traditional organizational development (Beer, 1980; Brief, 1998; Massarik, 1980, 1990).

STRATEGIC GOALS OF PROCESS CONSULTATION

In contrast to the traditional OD paradigm, *process consultation does not assume that the manager or the organization knows what is wrong or how to go about fixing it.* Schein believes that all that is required for the process to begin constructively is some intent on the part of a person in the organization to improve on how things are going (p. 21). According to Schein (2000), there are three strategic goals of process consultation:

- *Strategic Goal One:* To provide help and/or create a situation in which the client will get help
- *Strategic Goal Two:* To diagnose and/or create a situation in which information will surface that will permit consultants and clients to understand better what is going on
- *Strategic Goal Three:* To build an intervention team and/or create a situation in which the client will at all times feel ownership of the problem and any further interventions that are made to work on the problem

Clearly, these are broad goals. Yet, remember that Schein believes strongly in the most simplistic approach to complex issues. Reflection on these three goals indicates a rather comprehensive and all-embracing structure for process consultation. For instance, the first goal relates to asking for help and identifying ways in which that help can be described and potentially addressed. The second goal relates to defining the issue that needs addressing. The third goal relates to the "ownership" issue. *This means that it is central to the process consultation model that the client owns both the problem and the solution throughout the process.* This third goal is perhaps a revolutionary one for many traditional OD consultants. Nonetheless, the goal certainly rings familiar when compared to models of counseling. Clients "own" their own problems in counseling, and this "ownership" of problems and solutions drives the structural dynamics of process consultation. The same is true for PC consultation. Thus, although these goals appear broad, they do describe the essence of PC. When one considers the minimal skills needed and the principles of process consultation, these broad goals take on a more specific and pragmatic meaning.

MINIMAL SKILLS FOR PROCESS CONSULTATION

Similar to the preceding broad goals, Schein (2000) believes that process consultants need broad skills, including:

- An ability to be able to see and hear what is going on with the client and the client system

- Skill in active inquiry
- An ability for instant diagnosis and re-diagnosis
- Flexibility in intervening
- An ability to design learning experiences
- An ability to work with (organizational) culture
- An ability to work with individuals, relationships, groups, and larger systems

Obviously, this list is simplified and partially obscures the skills and expertise required of PC consultants. At the same time, these basic skills are congruent with Schein's ideas of simplicity in theory and practice and should seem attainable and manageable for most mental health professionals. Moreover—and perhaps more important—is the idea that Schein considers these minimal skills to be actually skills toward becoming a better human being (E. H. Schein, personal communication, July 6, 2000). When put in this perspective, mental health professionals will readily notice the similarity with Carl Rogers, who believed in his works on exemplifying "a way of being" (Rogers, 1980). In fact, Schein (1999, p. 10) believes that *the process consultation mode is necessary at the beginning of any helping process because this is the only mode that will allow clients to reveal what the situation really is and what kind of help is needed.* Thus, you will see that Schein's list of minimal skills is indeed a prescription for successful living, and the ensuing discussion will focus on the skills needed from a consulting perspective.

An Ability to See and Hear

This first skill identified by Schein pervades his entire work in process consultation. From a consulting perspective, this is an obvious skill. So, the question becomes, "What is it that process consultants need to see and hear?" Schein believes that it is important to "see what really is." This means that consultants need to assess the situation from many levels simultaneously in order to understand the "what is" of the situation. This does not necessarily mean that consultants will be speaking with all levels of organizations. At the same time, it does not preclude that act from occurring. What is important is getting a feel for what is going on by listening with as few preconceived notions as possible. (Schein suggests that artistic training is an excellent way to improve one's ability to see. He uses the example of concentrating on an art object for 10 minutes to see what really is there [E. H. Schein, personal communication, July 6, 2000].) In process consultation, consultants can and will need to share what is seen and heard. The imparting of information is a question of timing.

Skill in Active Inquiry

Active inquiry is central to process consultation, and one way of conceptualizing its centrality is to parallel Schein's "active inquiry" with Bergan and Kratochwill's "verbal skills." Another parallel, but one with categorical exceptions, is the notion of consultant "control." Myrick (1977) sidestepped the issue by using the term *influence* instead of control, but Bergan (1977) hit it head on. For Bergan, the initial presentation of "consultant control" was met with harsh and vociferous rebuttal from professionals as well as practitioners. Even the later works of Bergan and Kratochwill (1990) and Erchul and Martens (1999), include the term *control*. However, the later works focus on different aspects of the consultant/consultee interactions and emphasize more of a collaborative approach (Erchul & Martens, 1999).

A helpful manner in which to conceptualize the issue of "control" and to understand its prominence in consultation in general is to see consultants, at best, controlling structures in the intentional interaction in which they engage. Because consultants most often come in after a problem has been experienced (not necessarily identified), they inherently need information. Theoretically, if a consultant engaged in an organization for a lengthy period of time and listened long enough, the story and the problem would emerge. Because that is not an efficient use of time, consultants need to help focus consultees and clients. This "effort at focusing" consultees and clients is another way of describing the "control" used by the various consulting theorists.

Because of the inherent need to focus consultees and clients, it is also helpful to conceptualize control in consultation as a focusing effort, where the distinction is in the narrowness of focus rather than the presence or absence of focus. That is, behavioral case consultants focus their consultees rather specifically and narrowly. The process through which this focus is accomplished is structured by consultants. One main benefit is the concrete identification of the problem and built-in evaluation of change. Myrick's use of "influencing" techniques is comprised of the more narrowly focused approach of Bergan and Kratochwill in terms of identifying behaviors. Nonetheless, Myrick's notions are clearly closer to those of Schein in terms of the emphasis on a facilitative relationship and the belief in the consultee's and client's abilities to solve their own problems. For his part, Schein uses the term *control* as well in his process consultation model. However, instead of the issue of "control" being aimed at the consultant, Schein notes that in pure exploratory inquiry, *clients control* both the process and the content of the conversation. The role of the consultant is to prompt the story and listen carefully and neutrally (Schein, 2000). Hence, "control" remains in the venue. Yet, the concept of control is posited with the consultee and client in PC as opposed to being the property of the behavioral consultant.

Schein (1999, p. 43) believes that active inquiry builds up the client's status and confidence while allowing consultants to gather information about the situation. Active inquiry also involves the client in the process of diagnosing as well as the action planning. Schein believes that clients are more likely to reveal critical information related to the situation when they feel more emotionally safe. Thus, there are two strategic goals of active inquiry. The first goal is to *build a relationship with the client so that diagnostic insights can make sense.* This is accomplished by establishing a common language between the consultant and the client. Active inquiry increases the probability that this can occur. The second strategic goal is to *have a relationship with clients at such a level that any remedial measures taken under consideration are realistic.* Having clients participate in the process through active inquiry tends to make the remedial considerations derived from the client's own organizational culture.

Pure exploratory inquiry involves asking questions that minimize the process consultant's presence while maximizing the client's control (Schein, 2000). Process consultants might generally be focused on identifying the situation. For example, process consultants might ask such questions as, "What is the situation? What is going on? Can you describe the situation? What is an example? Can you give me some detail?" According to Schein, these types of questions still allow clients to control the content and process. Since it is central to Schein's views of diagnosis and intervention being one and the same, it is not surprising to find that the consultant's silence and body language are interventions occurring inherently in the pure exploratory inquiry.

If pure exploratory inquiry is characterized by the identification of the situation at hand, the *exploratory diagnostic inquiry* is characterized by an intentional narrowing of the process into more specifics. The key in this phase is to not move too fast nor insert content into the process (Schein, 2000). In other words, consultants should not provide solutions in this phase. Exploratory diagnostic inquiry reflects a shift as consultants are seen as beginning to manage the process of how the content is analyzed and elaborated. In other words, the client continues to control the content.

There are three versions of exploratory diagnostic inquiry. Consultants can (1) explore emotional responses, (2) explore reasons for actions and events, and (3) explore actions, past, present, and future. Schein warns consultants that these are powerful interventions, and these do interfere and distort the client's experience. Regarding the exploration of the consultees' and clients' emotional responses, one needs to be careful because neither may have thought about feelings. Consultees and clients may also have repressed or suppressed their emotional responses. Examples of emotional inquiry are: "How did you feel about that? What was your reaction? How did others feel or react?" Examples of inquiries into reasons for actions and events are, "Why did you do that? Why do you think that would happen? Why did the other person do that?" (Myrick frowns on "why" questions, believing them to put consultees on the defensive. Schein, disagrees and uses "why" questions frequently.) Examples of the third type of exploratory diagnostic inquiry are: "What did you do about that? What did others do about that? What are you going to do?"

Noting that some clients do not want to be confronted, Schein sees *confrontive inquiry* occurring when consultants begin sharing their ideas and reactions to both the content and process of the consultee's or client's story. The ideas that are shared by consultants provide opportunities for both helpees to think about the situation from a new perspective (Schein, 2000). It is in this way that Schein refers to the inquiry as confrontive: In essence, anytime a new perspective is introduced to clients, it is inherently confronting to their cognitive status quo. The two kinds of confrontive inquiry relate to process ideas and content ideas. *Process ideas* are focused more on the dynamic events that occur, whereas *content ideas* refer to the static experiences. Examples of such static experiences are clients' emotional and behavioral reactions, their overreactions, and their reactions to exploring specific strategies. Through the use of confrontive inquiry, a client's conceptual field shifts to include that of the consultant. For example, Schein might ask clients, "Did you confront him (her, them) about the situation as you saw it?" This implies what should have happened. (I prefer to ask, "What happened when you confronted him or her?" This presupposes that such an action would have already occurred because it is an obvious thing to do. Both responses get the job done.)

Providing potential insight could be another strategy, and an example of this would be, "Did it occur to you that you (she, he, they) did that because you might have been anxious?" Other questions might include direct suggestions such as, "Could you do this?" In shifting the client's conceptual framework, the client now is faced with dealing with his or her own content, not just the process. In any and all cases, timing is a critical element with confrontive inquiry, as is the issue of how to do it (Schein, 1999, pp. 47–48).

Flexibility Skills in Instant Diagnosing, Re-Diagnosing, and Intervening

Related to the skill of timing in confrontive inquiry are the skills of remaining flexible, diagnosing, and intervening. In many cases, consultants need to be able to provide some type of instant diagnosis for consultees. This is because consultees will often ask consultants, "Well, what do you think?" When this question is asked too early in the process, consultees are probably feeling too vulnerable to continue to tell more of the situation. Moreover, the consultees' requests for instant diagnosis is also borne out of a combination of their need to test consultants as well as expressing a genuine need for instant relief and help. When this early request for diagnosis occurs, consultants may not have had time to develop an incisive understanding of what is actually going on. Nonetheless, consultants need to be flexible enough to be able to provide what the consultees need while, at the same time, preserving the integrity of the consulting process. As such, process consultants need to trust their initial impressions of the organization and trust their aperçus in order to be able to respond reasonably accurately early on in the process. If consultants do not respond in a helpful manner, they may be viewed as out of touch with the current reality of the situation and therefore seen as less effective.

It is important for consultants to understand that when consultees ask this question, the question becomes a test of trust. This is true because they are often assessing a variety of consultant/consultee-related issues. As such, the question becomes a significant one in the formulation of the psychological contract because it helps establish some structures and guidelines for continuing the consulting process. Moreover, since Schein (1999) sees diagnosing and intervening as one and the same, the question also invites consultants to intervene. Consultants' responses intervene in the consultees' perceptions, expectations, goals, visions, and conceptualizations of the situation. For example, by asking, "What do you think?" the consultee is usually assessing the goodness of fit (discussed earlier) as well as assessing the skill and expertise of the consultant. The goodness of fit will likely relate the request for diagnosis with the manner in which the consultant handles the request. First, the goodness of fit in this situation will primarily include the consultee's impressions of the approachability of the consultant. Approachability essentially reflects the degree of openness on the part of the consultant. Openness is not only interpersonal, it is the degree to which the consultant will allow the consultee to participate in the process. Second, the goodness of fit will include the consultee's impression of how much ownership the consultant is willing to assume in the solution. When the consultant simply hands the question back to the consultee by asking, "Well, what do *you* think?" the consultee gains a quick insight into the way he or she will likely be involved in the process. Third, the goodness of fit tests the consultant's general interpersonal skills. Here, the consultee is simply getting a feel for the relationship. Essentially, this relates to whether the consultee likes the consultant and the way the consultant communicates. For instance, the terms, language, and concepts used by the consultant in response to the consultee's question will help establish the workability of the consultation. If consultants are too pedantic, do not assume enough responsibility in the consultee's eyes, or are not able to respond to the question in a meaningful way, the consultation will have a difficult time proceeding until these issues are addressed in some fashion. Finally, and perhaps, more important, the goodness of fit will include an assessment of the degree to which the consultant and consultee agree about what the issue is.

Abilities to Work in Various Cultures and to Design Learning Experiences

Congruence is also a factor in working with an organization's culture. Consultants need to match up reasonably well with both consultees' conceptualizations of the problem and their expectations of consultation. When working in organizations, consultants do not want to stick out like sore thumbs. Consultants need to be genuine, following the organizational dress code, ideas of proper etiquette, notions of time, among other things. Clearly, the consultant is not an employee. At the same time, being seen as too different can be deleterious to the consulting process.

Moreover, consultants need to be flexible in that they can work in a variety of settings and situations during the consultation. These various situations include working with individuals, relationships, groups, and larger systems. Sometimes, situations can include working with all these dimensions simultaneously. By being flexible and sensitive to the organization's diurnal "way of doing things," consultants can learn enough from the organization's culture to design meaningful learning experiences. The learning experiences are based not only on valid learning theory but they are also based on what would work in a particular organization's culture. It is a given that consultants have at least some knowledge in learning theory. Skills at being flexible means being able to apply learning theory to a variety of situations in which they will be helpful and meaningful. Hence, the issue here is not so much how much do consultants know as it is how well they can infuse meaningful learning experiences into a dynamic organizational culture.

THE TEN PRINCIPLES OF PROCESS CONSULTATION

The idea that it is not so much what consultants know as it is how they go about getting the work done is echoed throughout Schein's (1969, 1987, 1999) work on process consultation. This unique idea in organizational consulting is summarized in 10 principles. These principles are used to structure Schein's (1999) most recent notions of process consultation.

Principle 1: Always Try to Be Helpful

Schein (2000) states that if there is no intention of wanting to be helpful, there is little chance that a helping relationship will ever develop. Moreover, the intention of wanting to help another person is the best guarantee of a rewarding relationship that leads to mutual learning. In every instance, it is crucial to try to be helpful. Clearly, this suggests that consultants need to hone their listening skills. Specifically, recall the discussion in Chapter One that focused on the doctor/patient model and the purchase or expert model. These are different forms of consulting that can be utilized in a flexible manner so that consultants can remain helpful. Nevertheless, there may still be some resistances from racioethnic minorities and women when using the doctor/patient model because of the hierarchical structure that is inherent in this process. Nonetheless, the dictum of "always try to be helpful" should mitigate some of this resistance, by implying that consultants would be very sensitive to this issue of diversity.

Principle 2: Always Stay in Touch with the Current Reality

This principle requires that consultants need to decipher what is going on within themselves, in the situation at hand, and in the consultee and client system. Schein (1999) believes that every contact with consultees, clients, and the client system needs to yield diagnostic information about the "here-and-now" state (p. 6). The reality of the situation is the key for Schein. Part of the current reality may include the need to provide an answer for clients, and consultants should not hesitate to provide answers when appropriate. *However, Schein cautions consultants to provide at least two answers so that clients can choose their own answer.* This allows clients to remain active participants in the process (E. H. Schein, personal communication, July 7, 2000). Moreover, in terms of working with clients of varying racioethnic backgrounds, this collaboration stance is respectful of differences that will exist. Staying in touch with the current reality also means consultants need to stay open to realities that may be very different from their own.

Principle 3: Access Your Ignorance

Schein (2000) believes that the only way to discover one's own inner reality is "to learn to distinguish what one knows, from what one assumes one knows, from what one truly does not know." Schein states that it is generally most helpful to work on those areas where "one truly does not know." One of the implications of this principle relates directly to racioethnicity and gender differences: Accessing one's ignorance requires consultants to remain open to data that are transmitted from individuals as well as data gleaned about the organization itself. When it comes to individual differences, consultants need to develop a relationship with clients so that the deeper nuances of disability, racioethnicity, and gender can emerge in such a manner as to help shape a meaningful exchange in which both consultant and consultees and clients are personally enhanced.

Schein also believes that this ignorance can be accessed. This is especially important when it comes to the doctor/patient model of consulting. Schein points out that this particular model puts more power into the hands of consultants in that they diagnose, prescribe, and sometimes administer the cure. This can be counterproductive, however. For example, all consultants have or will have the experience in which their recommendations are politely accepted and then shelved. One of the reasons for shelving the recommendations may be that the client did not believe that the consultant really understood the situation. This can be deleterious in situations of diversity where a consultant may not truly understand or want to understand the cross-cultural implications of a given consultancy. Even though the advice or recommendation may be valid or have good potential, if clients do not think consultants understand them, much information may be consciously or unconsciously withheld.

Principle 4: Everything You Do Is an Intervention

Schein states that every interaction reveals diagnostic information. As such, every interaction has consequences for both consultants and clients. Because of this, consultants need to own everything that they do. This will also include the necessity of consultants to continually access their ignorance as well as the consequences for the situation at hand. This helps ensure that the consequences fit the goals of creating a helping relationship. One direct result of both the doctor/patient and purchase or expert models is that these two models propel consultants to "fix" the problem. Process consultation has the aim of helping clients to help themselves. Hence, when using the doctor/patient or purchase/expert models, one needs to be very careful in assessing the short- and long-term effects of this posture.

Schein advocates that consultants need to "calibrate their interventions" (personal communication, July 8, 2000). To be successful in this endeavor, consultants need to continually assess their "roles" in each situation of the consultation. Since everything is an intervention, consultants need to remain in touch with the realities of the situation (Principle 2). Clearly, another implication of this principle relates to racioethnicity and gender differences. Principle 4 essentially underscores the necessity for consultants to access their ignorance about issues of diversity before entering into the consulting relationship. If consultants wait until they are forming the psychological contract to learn about the deeper nuances of diversity, it may be too late to establish an effective foundation.

Principle 5: It Is the Client Who Owns the Problem and the Solution

In principle, this posture of ownership is consistent across most models of consulting. As has been pointed out, the doctor/patient and purchase/expert models may have a line of responsibility that suggests otherwise. However, similar to counseling, most consulting models adhere to the theory that clients and consultees own their own problems. Schein admits that this may not be as true for consulting in technical areas, such as computer engineering. Short of these situations, Schein believes that consultants can truly never know enough about an organization to really give advice or tell clients what can be done differently. This is a strong rationale for involving the client and client system in the consulting process. This also parallels generic counseling theory in that it is the client who lives with the consequences of the problem and solution. Therefore, consultants need to be careful so as to not "take the monkey off the client's back" (Schein, 1999, p. 20).

Principle 6: Go with the Flow

Schein (1999) believes that all consultee and client systems develop cultures and attempt to maintain the stability of those cultures. In that consultants really do not know the consultee's or client's reality, consultants should be careful to not impose their own sense of flow on an "unknown" situation. Again, assessing the potential consequences of all actions in the consulting process can help anticipate where the relationship with consultees and clients might go. Schein (2000) believes that as the consultant/consultee/client relationship reaches a certain level of trust, each begins to share insights about what is going on, and flow becomes more or less a shared process. It can be helpful for consultants to ask themselves a series of process questions. For instance, consultants can ask themselves: "Is this conversation helpful? Am I getting to the problem? Are we talking about the right issues?" (Schein, 1999, p. 39).

Principle 7: Timing Is Crucial

According to Schein (1999, p. 49), any given (verbal) intervention might work in one situation and not in another. So, when consultants ask clarifying questions, suggest alternatives, or however else introduce their conceptual scheme into the client's conceptual scheme, they must synchronize their interactions/interventions to those moments when the consultee/client attention is most available (Schein, 2000). Schein believes that the criterion for assessing the propriety of timing is to listen to when consultees and clients mention something that consultants have already thought about. When this situation develops, clients are more available to new information. Consultants need to be continuously assessing the helpee's availability and time themselves accordingly. It is critical for consultants to be aware of the diverse conceptualizations of "time" in order for them to be "on time" as it were. For instance, all individuals have their own sense of time and timing when it comes to relationships. Some relationships take longer to develop than others. When the racioethnic or gender differences are considered, the issue of "timing" becomes even more complex. So, timing a shift in focus or a shift in the method of inquiry is mitigated by many factors. Each factor is a significant variable.

Schein (1999) discusses the notion of "constructive opportunism" and relates it to consultants sensing when to shift focus. In the process of shifting, consultants will need to seize opportunities and take risks. Even when errors are made in the timing, Schein believes this to be an opportunity for new and diagnostic information about oneself and the client and client system.

Principle 8: Be Constructively Opportunistic with Confrontive Interventions

This principle is related closely to the principle of timing. Schein states

> When the client signals a moment of openness, a moment when his or her attention to a new input appears to be available, I find I seize those moments and try to make the most of them. In listening to those moments I find it most important to look for areas in which I can build on the client's strengths and positive motivations. Those moments also occur when the client has revealed some data signifying readiness to pay attention to a new point of view. (E. H. Schein, personal communication, July 5, 2000)

Clearly, in order to be constructively opportunistic, consultants need to find and build on the existing motivations and cultural strengths of consultees and clients. This is an example of "going with the flow." Consultants balance this with their risks in intervening. The reason for this is that as consultants listen to the consultee's and client's stories, consultants may have strong feelings and ideas that might be highly relevant. These can potentially enhance the client's understanding of the situation (Schein, 1999). The issue is not whether the consultants should reveal themselves; it is only a question of when. Thus, being constructively opportunistic is both something that consultants can help "make" as well as something that requires consultants to be "waiting and watching for." This concept is similar to the notions of "making" and "allowing," discussed in Chapter Eight.

Principle 9: Errors Are Inevitable

It is Schein's (2000) belief that one can only really learn by trying to change something. Thus, although consultants can follow the previous eight principles that guide process consultation, there will be many times when unexpected results occur. In some cases, these situations will be created by something that the consultant says or does. The results can be undesirable. In other cases, these situations will result directly from the inherent errors in process consultation. This is due to the assumption that consultants can never really know enough about an organization or its culture to categorically avoid errors. In process consultation, consultants need to avoid defensiveness, shame, or guilt when these misfires occur. Again, as long as consultants stay open to the flow of ongoing data that emanate from these "errors," process consultation can proceed successfully.

Principle 10: When in Doubt, Share the Problem

This principle relates directly to Principle 3, which advocates consultants accessing their own ignorance. Schein (2000) acknowledges that there will be times in the consulting relationship when consultants will "run out of gas, don't know what to do next, feel frustrated, and in other ways get paralyzed." In process consultation, it is advisable to share the consultant's "problem" with the client. A confrontive inquiry that consultants should use on themselves is, "Why should I assume that I know what to do next?"

Because process consultation is built on the notion that the client owns the problem, Schein believes that it is entirely appropriate for consultants to involve the client in the consultant's own efforts to be helpful. Clearly, this principle is directly related to the principle of timing, in that sharing the problem with clients and client systems without having built up the relationship might leave clients with the impression that consultants are not expert enough to be effective. Moreover, with respect to timing, it is important that consultants also assess the consequences of such sharing to help ensure the propriety and efficacy of this intervention. In any case, Schein states that if consultants can keep this principle in mind, especially the fact that sharing the problem enhances the client's involvement, and incorporate this into the psychological contract, then the consultant's conceptual approach to process consultation will likely be congruent and helpful.

SUMMARY

In summarizing these 10 principles, Schein (1999) asserts that the principles do not tell consultants what to do. Instead, these principles are seen as reminders of how to think about any given situation. When the situation is unclear and consultants are not sure of what to do next, reviewing these principles can be helpful in providing clarity and more direction. The 10 principles discussed by Schein are generic in that they can be used to guide a variety of consulting processes, including the models of Bergan and Kratochwill (1990), Myrick (1977), and Caplan and Caplan (1970, 1993). The one notable exception might be found in Principle 10: When in Doubt, Share the Problem. It is doubtful that consultants utilizing a behavioral case consultation model or a model of mental health consultation based on Caplan and Caplan would share the problem they might be having in the consultation. This is not to say that this sharing would never occur. It is to say that the structures of these two models themselves do not readily incorporate such an intervention. To share the problem with the consultee might be seen as obviating the need to be perceived as "expert" in the behavioral case and mental health consultation models. All consulting theorists see the need for the consultants to be perceived as "expert." The main difference between them is that Caplan and Caplan and Bergan and Kratochwill are clinical experts. Myrick, Vacc and Loesch, and Schein would be considered expert at building relationships with consultees as opposed to being clinical experts per se. All models can be used with groups and organizations, and all models have similar aims, which is to help clients/consultees. In general, Caplan and Caplan as well as Bergan and Kratochwill can be seen as helping consultees manage their clients. Myrick, Vacc and Loesch, and Schein might be seen as helping consultees/clients help themselves.

Process consultation is an attitude as much as it is an intervening style with organizations. Although Schein focuses his model on organizations, he does suggest that the skills necessary for appropriate implementation of his model are really skills that effective human beings possess or strive to possess. As with the other models discussed, Schein also emphasizes the importance of building an effective helping relationship. He is interested in structuring conversations that have focus, meaning, and purpose. He would likely advocate the facilitative communication style of Myrick and Vacc and Loesch. Schein would likely be intrigued by the detailed approach to relationships described in the behavioral consultation model. Yet, in the final analysis, Schein advocates going with the flow rather than getting caught up in the details of emitters and elicitors.

QUESTIONS

1. How does Schein's PC approach help in settings other than OD consulting?

2. If you had to collapse the definition of *process consultation* down into its most simple form, how would you define it?

3. How do Schein's 10 principles relate to school or agency consulting?

4. What role does "flexibility" have in PC?

CHAPTER TWELVE

SCHOOL-BASED CONSULTATION AND COLLABORATION

Those in their middle years may remember an American educational system that assumed that learning really mattered only for a select few. The select few were those whose high natural ability would lead them to college and the professions. At that time, these select few fortunate individuals were comprised mainly of white males with a smattering of exceptional minority men. Minority women were the rarest of creatures on a college campus. White women were assumed to be attending college for the purpose of contracting a suitable marriage, perhaps earning a degree in nursing or teaching to help out until their husbands got established in business or a profession. Before the advent of the knowledge economy, there were plenty of good jobs for high school graduates and even dropouts.

Today, the connection between education and earning power is so obvious and dramatic that students have no logical grounds for questioning the practical value of education. However, historian Richard Hofstetter (1970) pointed out years ago that a strain of anti-intellectualism had infected American culture since its beginnings:

> I think that it [anti-intellectualism] is a problem of more than ordinary acuteness here [the United States]. . . . I am disposed to believe that anti-intellectualism, though it has its own universality, may be considered a part of our English cultural heritage inheritance, and that it is notably strong in the Anglo-American experience. (p. 20)

Despite the central role that learning plays in U.S. economy, America's adolescents are strangely lacking in intellectual interests and values. In a study of more than 20,000 high school students, Steinberg (1996) concluded that the peer culture of the American high school "demeans academic success and scorns students who try to do well in school" (p. 19). Eighty percent of students in the Steinberg study told investigators that their friends did not think that grades mattered and that most of the respondents never discussed schoolwork among themselves. Sports, extracurricular activities, employment, and socializing with peers fill the days of the American teenager, leaving no more than an hour or so for homework per day. Only 5 of every 100 American teenagers commit to 20 or more hours of study outside of school every week. The average amount of time that teenagers spend reading for pleasure is less than 1hour per week.

The value system that guides the American adolescent is at odds with economic realities. The ability to make large amounts of spending money, the notoriety of athletic success, and the desire to "fit in" with the values of one's friends all combine to lessen the appeal of the world of learning and ideas. To counter such dismal trends, counselors must enlist many allies in the struggle to modify the teenage ethos of hedonism and anti-intellectualism. Counselors need their consultative and collaborative skills in working with students and parents about the economic importance of academic success while understanding the prerequisites to that success. This is especially challenging in working with families that do not have a history of valuing education, and are not personally aware of the changing demands of the new economy. Employers of student labor need to be educated about the deleterious effect of excessive working hours by teenagers. Teachers and administrators must be sure that athletic training and events do not consume a disproportionate amount of the time. Moreover, recognition of academic achievement must be set at a level equal to or greater than the recognition of sports accomplishments.

Changing values is a long and arduous task. Yet, the facts are overwhelmingly on the side of establishing a healthy balance between academic endeavors, extracurricular activities, and part-time work. Counselors and their collaborators can help students succeed by persistently educating the public about the facts and consulting with students, parents, and the community regarding the new economy and its relationship to education.

DIVERSITY AND SCHOOLS

Certainly, all students benefit from increased focus on learning, but it is especially important to bring poor and minority students to high levels of achievement. One of the insidious myths of American education is that poor and minority students lack the ability or value system to learn at high levels. Significant gains in academic performance by minority groups are possible when students are provided with effective teachers and a challenging curriculum. Counselors need to be particularly vigilant about collaborating with lower socioeconomic/racioethnic groups and those with disabilities to make sure that they take rigorous classes that prepare them for higher education and postsecondary training.

Counselors perform a variety of functions in the school setting—coordination of the comprehensive guidance program, individual and group counseling, classroom guidance, interpretation of group test results, and other activities to promote student development (Gysbers & Henderson, 2001). However, counselors increasingly report that consultation is the most effective use of their time. As discussed, school counselors have a unique opportunity to function as consultants because of their abilities to access many people within the consultee's and client's environment, such as teachers, administrators, parents, and community agencies. The opportunities to help must not be overlooked in today's schools. As a nation, it is critical to offer all students the opportunity for maximum growth and development. The philosophy driving these considerations acknowledges that such goals are difficult to achieve. This is especially true when one considers the scope and nature of difficulties confronting American children. For instance, there are some alarming facts about child abuse (Children's Defense Fund, 2001a):

- Some 2.8 million cases of child abuse or neglect have been reported since 1990 and 900,000 confirmed. African American and Hispanic American children were victims at twice the rate of their presence in the national population.
- The number of children in foster care has increased by more than one-third since 1990. More than half of the children in foster care are children of color.
- Only about half of those children who leave foster care in their late teens graduate from high school.
- Most cases of child abuse are associated with parental drug or alcohol problems, but existing treatment programs meet only one-third of the need.

Equally disturbing are recently compiled data on children in poverty (Children's Defense Fund, 2001b). In the world's wealthiest nation, more than 12 million children lived below the poverty line in the year 2000. This figure represents over 17 percent of American youth. Children under age 5 comprised one in five of this group. In contemporary America, children are more likely to be poor than adults. Poverty is especially widespread among African American children (33.1 percent) and Hispanic American children (30.3 percent). These figures are more than double the rate of white and Asian children (Children's Defense Fund, 2001c). The Census Bureau defines poverty as a family of three living on $13,500 and a family of five living on $16,400 per annum. Poverty seriously affects a child's chances for personal success and reduces the general level of economic productivity by billions of dollars. Left unchecked, there is a real danger that school systems may let a generation of minority students remain confined to the lowest rungs of the socioeconomic ladder when an adequate education would allow them opportunities to better themselves.

Given these alarming statistics, many school counselors believe that the philosophy behind the standards of personal/social growth, academic achievement, and career development must be inextricably woven into the fabric of each student's daily life. To help combat these unfortunate statistics, more effective ways of working together for the benefit of U.S. students in all three major areas of their development need to be implemented.

According to Sparks (1999, p. 220), if all of America's children are to succeed in school and life, then reform efforts must address the fact that "achievement cannot be met without addressing a variety of social and physical stressors on learning." For instance, the child with limited English proficiency, whose attention in class is distracted because of the pain of untreated dental cavities, will not be helped by admonitions to work harder. The real cause of the child's difficulty and its remediation may require sensitive work to identify the problem and effective collaboration with family and health professionals. The young person whose emerging sexual orientation is at odds with the culture of her or his school will need the counselor to consult and collaborate with staff to develop a supportive school environment that does not tolerate harassment. The middle-class child, overwhelmed with parental expectations for academic "excellence" and participation in a schedule of sports events that would stress an adult, may deteriorate from chronic tiredness to clinical depression.

SCHOOL-BASED CONSULTING

According to Sparks (1999), children's abilities to learn and succeed grow out of a biosocial, linguistic, and familial matrix that precludes monolithic and simplistic answers to complex problems. These conditions require counselors to collaborate and coordinate the resources of families, teachers, and community agencies to address multifaceted problems. In some cases, counselors may need to coordinate their work with the school district's legal division to make sure that staff and students understand the serious consequences of harassment or toleration of harassment. Social conflicts can arise when staff and community values systems are at odds with student needs and safety. Serious problems can be avoided when school counselors are successful in consultation with the various agents in a student's life. Clearly, today's student needs to be understood in the context of a culture that makes extraordinary demands on its young people to cope and succeed in an intensely competitive environment that can be insensitive to their natures, needs, and personal limitations. Counselors are the members of the school staff in the best position to bring the available resources of the school/community nexus to bear on the problems of youth. Counselors can play a role in helping improve the life chances of America's children and make strides to the goal that all children will learn and become the kind of adults they have a right to be.

Historically, school personnel conceptualize counseling as something done in isolation and behind closed doors. The previous discussion arguing for reconceptualizing school counseling as school consulting is an attempt to more accurately reflect what counselors actually do in the schools outside of their offices. Even in spite of—and perhaps because of—that argument, the school counselor must view consultation as a primary job function. Student, staff, and parent expectations of counselors need to be consistent with a collaborative/consultative style of problem solving. Counselors will continually need to educate the school community about mutual responsibilities in solving problems. Consultation, coordination, and collaboration allow counselors to deal with the very real problems that are often beyond the scope of a single professional working in a traditional venue of isolation.

The adoption of the National Standards of the American School Counselor Association established consultation as a primary function of school-based counseling (Dahir & Campbell, 1997). According to these standards, consultation may be delivered individually or in small or large groups. In all cases, counselors as consultants primarily help parents and teachers become more effective in working with others. More specifically, consultation helps both parents and teachers to think through problems and concerns, acquire more knowledge and skill, and become more objective and self-confident.

According to the national standards, schools counselors must be concerned with student progress in three broad areas: academic development, career development, and personal/social development. To help meet these concerns, consultants can provide information and impart skills to parent/guardians, teachers, and the community in order to assist them in helping students achieve in their academic, career, and personal/social development. In this fashion, counselors serve as a liaison between teachers, parents, support personnel, and community resources to facilitate successful student development (p. 12). Specific to *academic development,* school counselors help students acquire positive attitudes and dispositions that lead them to value knowledge and become life-long learners. They help students understand the relationship of knowledge to their own economic and personal development and that of their communities. In helping students in their *career development,* counselors help students gain an understanding of their own abilities and interests. Moreover, they help them select career paths and postsecondary options that lead to success and achievement. Regarding their *personal/social development,* counselors help students deal with personal problems, develop interpersonal skills, and learn to function effectively in school and the community.

Generic School Consultation Stages

Since counselors perform many functions in the school that have some degree of overlap, it may be helpful to staff and parents if, at a formal meeting, the counselor is allowed to define the process of consultation as part of the role of the counselor. As emphasized earlier in general models of consultation, school counselors should "do their homework" by making an effort beforehand to learn what previous counselors in the school have done and the extent to which they used different models of counseling. This is useful because parents and school staffs may differ in the role that they think counselors should play. A school counselor who learns the culture of a particular school may have a better chance of dealing with staff resistance to his or her efforts. Establishing successful consultation services requires that the counselor stress collaboration and build trust.

Similar to the portrayal of generic stages and phases of consultation, the consulting relationship in school-based consultation may be broadly conceptualized as occurring in several sequential stages or phases. Initially, a *request for help must be communicated* to the counselor, and the definition of what can be expected in the consultative relationship needs to be established. At this point, it is critical to *determine boundaries* and *determine who owns the problem.* Next, *information* needs be gathered to understand the problem and then *goals* set to determine the desired change. *Strategies must be selected, implemented, evaluated, and modified* as necessary. Finally, the consultation must be *terminated* to the satisfaction or at least acquiescence of all parties.

For example, imagine that an eighth-grade teacher named Mrs. Danforth referred a student, Billy, to the counselor for serious behavior problems. Mrs. Danforth said that he was threatening other children and refused to complete assignments or to follow classroom rules. She didn't know what was wrong. She said that her contact with Billy's mom has been unproductive. The teacher expressed great frustration with Billy and his mother and wanted to know what the counselor could do about the situation or if Billy could be transferred out of her class. The counselor discussed the details of the situation, reviewed the teacher's previous interactions with the parent, and clarified her role as a consultant. The counselor said that she did not have the authority to move students and that the teacher would have to talk with the principal if that were her goal. The counselor stated that she would meet with the student, observe the student in class, and confer with the parent to get a better understanding of the problem. *While expressing sympathy with the discomfort of the teacher, at no point did the counselor she say that she would solve the problem for the parent or the teacher.* After the preliminary assessment of the situation, the counselor set up a meeting to discuss the problem and guide the participants to set some goals and create interventions.

On paper, the stages of consultation look neatly linear. However, surprisingly new information may quickly change the definition of a problem. A father's impending separation from the family, a student's substance-abuse problem, or a student's avoidance of academic work by disrupting the classroom may suddenly and unexpectedly present themselves as major factors. In the case of Mrs. Danforth's student, any of these factors could have been present and could most likely have been discovered by utilizing a collaborative/consultative approach. Each issue would lead the team in a different direction to help solve the problem.

For school counselors, it is obvious that their jobs involve working with students, parents, school staff, and professionals from other disciplines for the benefit of students. In a consulting/collaboration relationship in the schools, a counselor works with other adults to help them locate and utilize resources in the solution of the problem. An important point to reiterate is the fact that in a consultative relationship in the schools, the counselor does not own the problem. This is congruent with other nonschool-based models of consultation. In consulting with a teacher about the behavior of an unruly child, the counselor can help the teacher do a number of things. Among them is to create a plan to deal with the problem. Another helpful task is to help the teacher locate needed resources that exist in the community. In another instance, the counselor can help the teacher facilitate a parental collaboration on the child's problem that includes all of these things. In all of these instances, the counselor does not pluck a troubled child out of a classroom and return a "cured" one. Even if such fortuitous results were occasionally attained by a counselor working alone with a student, the resulting expectations of the staff for quick and painless "fixes" could not be met. The main reason for this proclivity is reflected in the fact that solving a problem usually requires analysis and change by everyone involved in a pattern of behavior—child, parent, teacher, and classmates.

The results of school-based consultation may be satisfactory initially. However, the school consultees and clients may later revert to unproductive patterns of behavior. This does not mean that consultation does not work, but rather that it is similar to most kinds of human problem solving. It involves error and feedback and modification until the desired result is achieved. Of course, most problems are not solved categorically. At the same time, many human difficulties may be significantly ameliorated by honest and intelligent effort (Harrison, 2000). In addition, there may be other effective means that school counselors can utilize in effecting change, such as collaboration.

CONCEPTUALIZING COLLABORATION

Definitions and Generic Approaches

The term *collaboration* has been defined in different ways, and the descriptions of collaboration can be specific or quite broad. Brown, Pryzwansky, and Schulte (2001, pp. 266–268) review the literature on collaboration and cite, among others, Idol, Paolucci-Whitcomb, and Nevin's (1986) definition that collaboration is *a reciprocal arrangement between professionals that allows diverse expertise to generate creative solutions to mutually defined problems.* Pryzwansky (1974, 1977) defines collaboration as *an indirect service in which consultant and consultee engage in a process of joint problem identification and joint problem solving, with each professional assuming some responsibility for the outcome.* Fishbaugh (1997) proposes the concept of the "collaborative school" in which *collegiality, professionalism, and shared decision making are central to the climate of a school that invokes a wide range of practices.* One problem with all of the variations of meanings with the term *collaboration* is the fact that the term is often linked to the educational system so inextricably that professionals can make "consultation and collaboration" synonymous with "teacher consultation and collaboration" (Brown, Pryzwansky, & Schulte, 2001, p. 257).

The Context of Collaboration

It can be seen from the definitions described above, no matter how broadly or definitively it is defined, *collaboration* has some elements of consultation included in its structure. Because of that, it is not surprising that some professionals prefer the concept of "collaborative consultation," whereas others prefer to posit collaboration as a separate form of professional service (e.g., Dettmer, Thurston, & Dyck, 1993; Friend & Cook, 1996). These different orientations essentially ask the same question: "Does collaboration describe a particular type of relationship in consulting, or does it describe a separate consulting role?" Although the answer to this is conceptual and academic, the answer one ascribes to the question has practical implications. Dougherty (1990) sees collaboration as a subset of consultation. For Dougherty, collaboration is a role that consultants employ. Other researchers view the relationship between consultation and collaboration differently. In essence, these researchers believe that if the counselor in counseling focuses on the relationship with the individual client, and the consultant focuses on the relationships with the consultee and client, then the collaborator focuses on the consultee, client, and the collaborating partners. Given this structural disparity, it follows that consultation and collaboration differ in professional responsibility, differ in the role of the consultee, differ in the relationships and assumptions of change, and differ in the goals (Brown, Pryzwansky, & Schulte, 2001, p. 257; Conoley & Conoley, 1982; Fishbaugh, 1997; Mostert, 1998; Pryzwansky, 1974).

Clearly, collaboration has a similar structural configuration in comparison to consultation. At the same time, the differences in contexts provide a significant line of demarcation. Exactly like the context of consultation, the context of collaboration is the organization. Yet, the organization in collaborating relationships is categorically punctuated to a level of significance that is clearly not mandated in consultation. Even though the "preparing ground" in collaboration is similar to that of consultation in terms of process issues such as entry, developing relationships, and obtaining sanctions to work, these process concerns are categorically *necessary* in a collaborative relationship. The reason for this is that there is more than one individual involved in the diagnosis and treatment process. Moreover, each individual may or may not have equal status, decision-making ability, or sanctioned roles in the host institution or organization. Yet, an effective working relationship with each individual is critical to the successful outcome for all, including the client.

Triangulation Effect.   Since the consultative and collaborative relationship consists of working with parents, teachers, and other adults to deal with a student's behavior or academic problem, it is important that the counselor avoid the triangulation effect where the parent or teacher feels that the counselor is siding with the other party. Marriage and family therapists address this triangulation effect through the various ways that they "join" with their client families (Nichols & Schwartz, 2002). The counselor needs to establish the consultative role and utilize counseling and mediation skills to respond to concerns on both sides, always being respectful of the knowledge of the parent and the teacher and the needs of the student. Sometimes, if the relationship is volatile between parties in a consultation, the counselor may need to meet individually with each participant. In these situations, the counselor serves as an intermediary who brings together warring factions (Harrison, 2000). Hopefully, this situation is averted before it ever becomes an issue. This is due to the emphasis in collaboration on an introductory phase where such issues can be addressed and worked through as well as addressed throughout the process (Christenson & Sheridan, 2001; Sheridan, Kratochwill, & Bergan, 1996).

Models of Collaboration

Collaboration has been the subject of a rising number of professional articles (e.g., Friend & Cook, 1996; Lusky & Hayes, 2001). In addition to Fishbaugh (1997), many others have written books on the subject (e.g., Dettmer, Thurston, & Dyck, 1993; Conoley & Conoley, 1982; Mostert, 1998). Caplan and Caplan (1993) revised the original works on mental health consultation to include mental health collaboration, devoting four chapters to the topic. According to Brown, Pryzwansky, and Schulte (2001), most of the blossoming literature on collaboration is found in the area of mainstream and special education and points to the advantages of collaboration. These same researchers cite Babcock and Pryzwansky (1983) and Pryzwansky and White (1983), who found that mainstream teachers, special education teachers, and school administrators prefer a collaborative relationship with school counselor/consultants.

Fishbaugh (1997) describes three models of collaboration: consulting, coaching, and teaming. In the first instance, Fishbaugh defines the consulting model of collaboration very similar to the doctor/patient and purchase models of consultation. In the *consulting* model of collaboration, the consultant is seen as prescribing expert advice to others. The *coaching* model of collaboration is essentially the same situation in a non-hierarchical relationship mode. The difference between the consulting model and the coaching model is that in the latter the consultant still gives expert advice through a nonhierarchical relationship structure. In describing Fishbaugh's work, Brown, Pryzwansky, and Schulte (2001, p. 267), assert that a *teaming* model of collaboration is "the interaction of professionals responsible for the groups' problems and their solutions." According to Fishbaugh (1997, p. 102), the teaming model is completely interactive, which sets it apart from the one-on-one nature of the consulting model. The teaming model is also different from the coaching model, where the participants take turns owning or assisting with a problem. In the coaching model, team members share ownership of the purpose and outcomes of their collaborative efforts.

Furthermore, Fishbaugh (1997) describes three specific types of teaming in schools: coteaching, team support, and team problem solving. *Coteaching* is when two or more teachers team up to instruct a group of students in a specific course or class. *Team support* refers to teams of teachers supporting each other. Examples of *team problem solving* relate to the prereferral or special education individualized educational plan (IEP) processes. It is obvious that some clarification of roles and relationships needs to take place whenever a collaborative effort is undertaken.

Responsibility in Collaboration

Responsibility in collaboration is conceptualized significantly different from responsibility in consultation. In consultation, consultees are responsible for the ultimate outcome of the situation. It is the same in collaboration except for the fact that "responsibility" itself is separated into (1) professional responsibility among the collaborating partners and (2) the responsibility for the ultimate outcome in the situation. The responsibility for the outcome is shared among the collaborating partners involved. According to Caplan and Caplan (1993, p. 281), *the fundamental difference between consultation and mental health collaboration is that in collaboration, the consultant accepts responsibility for the outcome.* Caplan and Caplan (1993) delineate this distinction sharply. In devoting several chapters on the subject, these authors maintain that mental health collaboration is an

> inter-professional method in which a mental health specialist establishes a partnership with another professional worker, network, group, or team of professionals in a community field or a human services institution. The mental health specialist, by agreement with his colleagues, becomes an integrated part of their evaluation and remedial operations, and accepts responsibility for contributing his specialized knowledge and for personally using specialized diagnostic and remedial skills in dealing with their cases. He takes part in the process of making decisions about the diagnosis, management, and treatment of the clients. He is professionally responsible for the mental health outcome. He may himself play a direct role in investigation or treatment, or he may act as an advisor to other workers who share assessment or remedial assignments. (p. 295)

All of this is predicated on the consultee accepting the recommendations of the collaborators, including the consultant who is engaged in collaborating. Caplan and Caplan (1993) maintain that recommendations may ultimately fail due to ineffective implementation. Thus, whereas each professional who is engaged in collaboration may be responsible for his or her assessment(s) and recommendation(s), each is not responsible for the ultimate outcome of the case. That responsibility continues to rest with the consultee, who is responsible for setting the tone of the organization and who makes the final decisions.

As discussed, the responsibility in collaboration is shared across collaborative partners. It is critical to understand that although shared, it is at the same time divided according to each professional's expertise. For example, in an individualized educational plan (IEP) at school, a teacher is not expected to be responsible for the student's mental health any more than a counselor is responsible for how well the student performs academically. They share responsibility. Going further, the school psychologist or the assistant principal may be the person running the IEP meeting. This creates a situation in which there is some elevation of status among a group of partners sharing responsibility. It can be seen that although there is a shared responsibility among a group of professionals who jointly agree on a diagnosis and treatment plan, the relationships themselves are concomitantly equal, unequal, and hierarchical. This is certainly an interesting notion, indeed.

According to the mental health collaboration model of Caplan and Caplan (1993), the actions of the collaborating specialist must improve the conditions of the client and not merely the attitudes and performance of the participating staff, as is the aim in consultation. Hence, the responsibility of the collaborator may be broader than that of the consultant. Collaborators must attend to the client's needs, their fellow collaborators' needs, and to the needs of the consultee. At the same time, collaborators will not only be improving their own handling of similar cases in the future but they will also be helping colleagues improve theirs as well during the course of collaborating.

Relationships in Collaboration

As is the situation with consultation models, almost all definitions or approaches to collaboration refer to both the issue of responsibility and the importance of relationships. Although the emphasis on relationships seems obvious at first, collaborating relationships are interesting and different from those present in consultation. There is a strong emphasis on developing relationships with consultees in consultation. Effective relationships with consultees is seen as required in order to increase the chances that the consultee will adhere to the consultant's suggestions. The sole responsibility for the outcome remains with the consultee. The same generally holds true for collaboration, except that the relationships in collaboration include those with the consultee and with those collaborating professionals of the host institution. There can be any reasonable number of these individuals. In collaboration, the context of an "effective relationship" includes gaining clarity on what Caplan and Caplan (1993) refer to as status issues, decision making, and sanctioned roles.

Perhaps the most simplistic, yet profoundly descriptive, delineation of the collaborative relationship is reflected in Fishbaugh's (1997) work. In that in-depth research on collaboration in special education, Fishbaugh defines collaboration as "working together for the common end" (p. 4). Dougherty (1990, p. 12) believes that collaboration is an approach in consultation where consultees and consultants work in a type of relationship that structurally minimizes the "danger of too much domination by the consultant." Other approaches do not emphasize danger as the agenda driving a collaborative approach. For example, Parsons (1996, p. 33) sees both the consultee and the consultant playing an active role in a collaborative mode, and the reasons are more for effectiveness than reasons borne out of fear of consultants' influence. For Parsons, the consultant and consultee share responsibility for data gathering, analysis, goal setting, and intervention planning. In doing so, Parsons assumes that through "such an expansion of resources," the efficacy of the consultation is enhanced. Dettmer, Thurston, and Dyck (1999, p. 6) portray collaborative school consultants as facilitators of effective communication, cooperation, and coordination. These collaborative consultants work with teachers, administrators, parents, and families as "one team" for addressing the needs of students.

Freedom.   Collaboration still encompasses the collaborator's abilities to provide indirect services to a client. This remains true even if there is some type of direct service to the client. An example of this is when a school psychologist assesses a student for special education. At the same time, the structure of collaborating does not allow for the same amount of "freedom" as does that of consultation (Caplan & Caplan, 1993). In consultation, consultants can essentially choose which problems or issues are to be the focus of concern. However, in a collaborative structure it is the collaborator, through mutual consent of the collaborating partners, who essentially chooses which situations on which to focus. At the same time, each specialist is "equally tied to the well-being" of a given client or client system (Caplan & Caplan, 1993, p. 282). The result of this is a group process that is aimed at helping a client or client system, and a process that is guided by dimensions of decision making and professional responsibility. Although consultants deal with these same issues, they do so outside of this same group process dimension. Moreover, the interplay of information from various specialists throughout the collaborative process shapes and molds each individual professional's assessment and opinions as to how to proceed.

From a traditional Euro-American perspective, individual freedom in collaboration is, in effect, restricted in that it is mitigated by various aspects of group process. From a collectivist perspective, collaboration includes the group process as a component of its structure and, as such, individual freedom gives way to collectivistic mindsets. In yet another issue related to freedom, Parsons (1996) sees that each collaborating partner is free to accept or reject any part or whole of the interaction. All of these considerations have cultural overtones that will impact the various assessments of benefits. In the final analysis, it is probably most appropriate to say that freedom is influenced in a host of ways in collaboration.

Status, Decision Making, and Sanctioned Roles

As one would suspect, the mention of group process components in collaboration segues into at least some consideration of status, roles, and decision making. Collaboration is generally indicated as a potential intervention process when the well-being of large numbers of clients is at stake. Although the numbers of potential benefactors of collaboration may be large, the process can be effectively used when there is only a single, individual client, such as a student in an IEP meeting. School-based intervention teams such as student assistance programs (SAPs) most often employ a collaborative approach to identify and help students who meet the qualifications established by the collaborators. Special education students also benefit from collaborative approaches in their schools. When such a collection of professionals come together in collaboration, relationships are influenced in ways unfamiliar to consultants.

The effective working relationships in consultation are characterized as coordinate in structure. When collaborating as a primary service, consultants have a range of what Caplan and Caplan (1993) refer to as "status relationships." For these researchers, the relationship with the collaborating colleagues is *coordinate,* whereas the relationship is *hierarchical* with the consultee. This is because each collaborator has specialized knowledge and skills that, although perhaps overlapping to a degree with others' expertise, is otherwise unduplicated elsewhere in the collaborating group. At the same time, the collaborating group has some hierarchy related to the agenda of the student or client. For example, if a student is potentially in need of special education services, the expertise of the school psychologist will likely be punctuated in the group's process of decision making. In mental health collaboration, regardless of who is the designated lead collaborator, that individual is still subject to the consultee's overriding authority and decisions. In the final analysis, collaborators not only have to consider the well-being of the client, they have to embrace the desires of the consultee at the same time. To help ensure that the recommendations are congruent with the desires of the consultee, it is important that collaborators are able to exchange information rather freely and frequently about complications that are incurred.

Goals and Interventions

Collaborators are convened to help clients. That is their main goal. It is a bonus if other collaborators are helped in acquiring new and useful knowledge in the process. In the process of effecting change, the goals of the collaborative process necessarily include *relationship goals* and *treatment goals:*

- A primary goal of collaboration is to have effective working relationships with other members of the collaboration.
- The second goal of collaboration is to arrive at the best possible solution for the client(s).

Regarding goals related to relationships, collaborations need to be effective decision-making entities or the process will become inefficient. Although these goals sound familiar to those in consultation, an effective relationship with the consultee does not guarantee an effective relationship with fellow collaborators. Collaborators need to have effective working relationships with both consultees and fellow collaborators. Since the ultimate goal is to help the client(s), the process of developing effective working relationships becomes a main objective.

To achieve these goals, a variety of roles and functions can be utilized. Caplan and Caplan (1993, p. 307) assert that taking part in staff meetings in order to provide mental health information is helpful for mental health collaborators. It is in these staff meetings that the collaborator initiates the focus on the mental health aspects of specific cases. In schools, counselors can do this with teachers, parents, and other school personnel. Collaborators contribute their specialized knowledge and skills in a way that helps others learn new and effective ways of enhancing client well-being. Finally, specific to mental health collaboration, these same authors suggest that collaborators provide psychosocial and emotional support to other staff members as they grapple with mental health aspects of their work.

Collaboration in Schools

One of the benefits of collaborative problem solving is the knowledge and confidence participants gain. By giving up the hope that other professionals will solve difficult problems for them, members of the collaboration expand the boundaries of their own competencies in ways they could not accomplish working in isolation. Every member of a collaboration team learns something new with each collaboration, and the collective wisdom of the group grows dramatically (Harrison, 2000). The collaborative nature of consultation is not just a style. It is an acknowledgment of the fact that a student's behavior emerges out of *two relationship systems:* the school and the home. For instance, Amatea and Brown (2000) state,

> Each [school and home] has its own distinctive memberships and activities, predictable ways of interacting, shared values and beliefs, and coherent identity as separate units. However, when a student enters school, these two distinctive human systems join forces to carry out the aims of educating and socializing the student and thus become interconnected. (p. 193)

According to Amatea and Brown (2000), counselors, by collaborating with families, can do much to facilitate productive and harmonious home/school relationships. Many potential conflicts arise if either or both parties fail to recognize and respect the other as coequal in the task of educating the child. The adults in the home and school need to be explicit about their expectations and work out their differences so that the student is faced with a consistent set of standards. The parent who regards reading as a recreational activity, with no educational value, needs to reach an informed understanding with the school about the importance of self-directed reading in the child's education before she or he is ready to moderate the child's commitment to chores or television.

Collaborative/Interdependent School-Based Model

The school counselor is in an ideal position to employ a collaborative model to marshal support in the school staff and community. According to Peterson and Skiba (2001), counselors can coordinate the development of peer mediation programs to reduce school violence, deal with interpersonal conflicts, and prevent bullying. Counselors should always begin their efforts by utilizing the resources available in the school itself, such as parents, teachers, and students. Programs such as peer mediation empower students and staff to create a safe and supportive environment in which to learn. Besides working with school programs and the families of perpetrators and victims, counselors may need to scour the community to find programs to help normalize violence-prone children. Too frequently, violent children spend too much time in unsupervised youth groups or gangs. Such children need to have their out-of-school time structured into involvement in adult-supervised club and sport activities. The counselor and school staff may find such resources in the community or create social action pressure groups to bring them into existence. Coordinating these various constituencies so that they become a reality can enhance the learning environment for diverse student populations.

The counselor and teacher may need to actively educate parents about violence and its effect on children. Members of the community may be fatalistic about preventing violence because the media may be lax in reporting about programs that successfully minimize school violence. Counselors, school staff, mental health professionals, and community leaders may need to collaborate about school violence and present the information to state legislators so that additional support may be obtained. Whether at the individual school or at the community or state level, the counselor's main role is collaborative.

The seriousness of the problems that today's youth bring to school—gang and community violence, substance abuse, poverty, family disintegration, and homelessness—are beyond the problem-solving powers of the school working in isolation (Lerner, 1995). According to Keys, Bemak, Carpenter, and King-Sears (1998), such extreme distress calls for a new model of counselor consultation. Such a model is referred to by the researchers as the *collaborative/interdependent (CI)* model of school-based consultation.

In the collaborative/interdependent model, the job of the counselor is to facilitate a variety of agents to take an active and collaborative role in the solution of a problem. Research by Erchul and Martens (1997) supports the idea that small group collaboration on a problem leads to reciprocity and higher levels of involvement in problem solving. In such collaborations, schools may form alliances with professionals from other agencies, such as parks and recreation, community-based mental health services, substance-abuse programs, families, and grass-roots neighborhood improvement associations. In collaborative/interdependent consultation, it is the sharing and transferring of knowledge and information among all team members that enables the group to determine and carry out a more comprehensive plan (Keys et al., 1998).

Similar to other collaborative models (e.g., Christenson & Sheridan, 2001; Sheridan, Kratochwill, & Bergan, 1996), success in collaborative/interdependent consultation requires certain factors to be in place. First, the team must define and agree to mutual goals. The participants are volunteers and, even though different levels of expertise, education, and power will exist in the collaboration, all members must have an equal say in decision making. Each person on the team has a role and a responsibility. Team members share whatever resources they can in the solution of the problem. All members of the team are accountable for the results (Keys et al., 1998; Friend & Cook,

1996). Tourse and Sulick (1999, p. 68) have summarized eight prerequisites for successful collaborative/interdependent efforts:

1. Understand basic nomenclature of the participating disciplines.
2. Trust the unique contributions of each team member.
3. Respect the theoretical perspective of each profession.
4. Acknowledge a shared responsibility to promote learning.
5. Recognize and understand the cultural differences that exist among professions and professionals, as well as such differences that exist among students and their families.
6. Devise models, goals, and strategies that promote empowerment of children and families.
7. Maintain open communication across disciplines by means of established scheduled meetings.
8. Accept that all professions have different outcome orientations.

Social workers, juvenile probation officers, and marriage and family therapists are no strangers to the school community, but in the past they have come to do their jobs more as individual practitioners rather than as members of a team. The concept of working as a team, which may include parents without formal education or credentials, may alarm some professionals. Professional collaboration does not deny the importance of specialized and formal learning, but it recognizes that many problems have so many dimensions that one field's limited outlook may be inadequate to the task. A parent may not know any theories of child development. Yet, all parents are likely to be experts on the histories of their own children and the ethos of their neighborhoods. The jealous guardians of professional boundaries may have difficulty adapting to collaborative problem solving. Learning even the fundamental concepts, operations, and vocabulary of another field of professional practice will require more time and effort than most busy professionals can comfortably spare, but given the high cost to children of failure, it would seem to gather strong moral support as the right thing to do.

Stages and Phases

Collaborative/interdependent (CI) consultation begins with a coming together of concerned parties from the school and community who meet and develop a shared vision of a better future. In the vision stage, goals and objectives are established and participants define the responsibilities in the collaboration. During this phase, each collaborator explains his or her agency's mission, operating procedures, and constraints. In the next stage, a strategic plan is developed to bring the assembled resources of the team to bear on the problem. This may involve a change in traditional ways of doing things in both school and agencies. In the action phase, the plan is put into practice. Finally, the participants evaluate their progress toward goals and make adjustments as needed. The CI intervention requires much flexibility and a willingness to accept innovation. Participants may have difficulty accepting the fact that others see problems and solutions in different terms. Time and resources may be an issue with some who feel overwhelmed with the demands being made. Additionally, the collaborators' respective agencies and institutions may outwardly espouse collaboration, while covertly resisting any innovations that tend to diminish their autonomy and control (Keys et al., 1998). The issues of resistance notwithstanding, collaborative stances have great potential to help. Another popular and effective collaborating model is offered by Sheridan, Kratochwill, and Bergan (1996) and Christenson and Sheridan (2001).

CONJOINT BEHAVIORAL CONSULTATION

Christenson and Sheridan (2001) see problem-solving strategies that empower parents to become meaningful contributors to the education of children as very effective. According to these same researchers, an empowering perspective sees the failure of social systems, including schools, to create opportunities for a family's strengths to be displayed (p. 163). Christenson and Sheridan maintain that parents must believe that changes are a result of their own efforts. In other words, parents need to see that their efforts impact the system—especially those who may be in control of making decisions or sanctioning action. Sheridan, Meegan, and Eagle (2002) and others (e.g., Pianta, 1999) see the formation of positive relationships among parents and teachers and homes and schools as central in structuring pathways for student success.

A particularly effective manner in which parents can feel empowered while helping their children is conjoint behavioral consultation (CBC; Sheridan, Kratochwill, & Bergan, 1996). This consultation model is "a structured indirect form of service delivery, in which parents and teachers are joined together to address the academic, social and/or behavioral needs of an individual for whom both parties bear some responsibility" (Sheridan & Kratochwill, 1992, p. 122). Conjoint behavioral consultation is a model through which partnerships between homes and schools can be fostered. Constructive communications among home and school systems can also be established (Sheridan, Meegan, & Eagle, 2002, p. 316).

In terms of its core basic assumptions, CBC rests on ecological as well as behavioral theories. Conjoint behavioral consultation utilizes a behavioral theoretical base that recognizes the importance of conducting direct behavioral observations, collecting data in a continuous manner, performing functional behavioral assessments, and employing validated interventions as a crucial element of educational and behavioral programs (Christenson & Sheridan, 2001, p. 165). The behavioral orientation is joined by a person-in-environment or ecological perspective that addresses the meso-level of the child's environment. This level includes the interactions among primary systems in the child's life, such as the home, school, and other immediate surroundings. This theoretical orientation also advocates the bringing together of the child's important primary caregivers, such as parents, teachers, and other significant individuals who are involved in the system. The result is an effective and empirically validated model that advocates a consultation/collaboration approach to problem solving in today's schools.

Goals of Conjoint Behavioral Consultation

There are two sets of goals in CBC: outcome goals and process goals. The outcome goals include:

- Obtaining comprehensive and functional data
- Establishing consistent treatment programs across settings
- Improving skills, knowledge, or behaviors of all parties while developing skills and competencies to promote further independent conjoint problem solving between home and school
- Monitoring behavioral side effects systematically
- Enhancing the generalization and maintenance of treatment effects across the different settings

In discussing the relationship goals in CBC, it is helpful to recall the discussion about the criticisms of consultant "control" levied against Bergan's (1977) and Bergan and Kratochwill's (1990) behavioral case consultation model. In CBC, there is a strong emphasis on the verbal interactions among team members, including the consultant, which can be construed as "controlling" behaviors. For instance, researchers such as Sheridan, Kratochwill, and Bergan (1996) and Christenson and Sheridan (2001) describe very specifically the ways in which group members should interact with one another during their attempts to achieve the goals of developing effective relationships. These goals and verbal processes include:

- Increase the understanding of the family through the identification of strengths in the child and the family. This also includes eliciting ideas, information, and perspectives through the use of effective communication skills such as those described by Myrick (1977, 1987, 1993) and Wittmer and Myrick (1989).
- Establish a home/school partnership by identifying the goals for families based on current family needs. In doing so, it is important to provide rationales and expectations for families and schools to work together. This, according to Christenson and Sheridan (2001), is accomplished by emphasizing a team concept as well as through the use of inclusive words such as *we, us,* and *together.* Moreover, it is also critical to highlight similarities across home and school settings as a way to embrace both environments.
- Promote a shared ownership for problem solution. Typical of behavioral approaches, there are specific behaviors that need to be undertaken for this feeling of shared ownership to occur. For instance, there needs to be shared eye contact and verbal encouragement. It may also be helpful to structure interventions in such a way as to require cooperation and communication. An example the researchers use is to employ a series of home/school notes (Christenson & Sheridan, 2001).
- Promote a greater conceptualization of problems as well as increase perspective taking. In reaching this goal, a description of the rationale and expectations of the home/school problem-solving efforts should be discussed with the team members. During the process, one should use nonverbal and verbal listening skills that convey understanding, respect, and empathy.

- Strengthen the relationship among participants. This is accomplished through the use of verbal skills and in the positive reframing of problems into being opportunities for skill development. It is also critical to utilize a strengths approach in reinforcing the efforts of parents and teachers. Additionally, the researchers encourage the use of physical spaces for meetings that are conducive to good eye contact and discussion. Sitting in rows, as in a classroom, is not advisable.
- Recognize the need to address concerns that occur across settings. The meso-level approach is emphasized in such a way as to encourage an exploration of out-of-school opportunities to achieve success.
- Increase parent and teacher commitments of educational goals. It is advisable to involve team members in projects. Another manner in which this goal can be reached is by developing plans that are consistent across settings and that support achievement in and out of school.
- Increase the diversity of expertise and resources available. Christenson and Sheridan (2001) think it is important to have students actually involved whenever possible. Moreover, other family members can be involved, too. Once convened, the researchers see it as critical to involve the participants in the process. This is accomplished by asking for help and by encouraging the expression of ideas or perspectives that can be incorporated into the interventions.

Stages of Conjoint Behavioral Consultation

Conjoint behavioral consultation includes four generic elements that are consistent with most problem-solving team-based models. The four elements include (1) an introductory phase between members of the school and family environment that sets the stage for problem solving, (2) a collaborative brainstorming of concerns, (3) a joint selection of an immediate concern on which to focus the discussion, and (4) an implementation of a solution that is agreed on by everyone. Each of these phases requires effective communication skills and assumes some competence in problem solving. In the process, both parties share a primary goal of empowering parents, while helping to create partnership between home and school (Christenson & Sheridan, 2001, p. 164). In addition to these four elements, Sheridan, Kratochwill, and Bergan (1996) outline specific procedural stages contained in CBC. These four stages are similar in nature to all behavioral consultation models with one major exception: It is a group problem-solving model. The stages include:

- Conjoint problem identification
- Conjoint problem analysis
- Treatment plan implementation
- Conjoint treatment plan evaluation

Phase One: Conjoint Problem Identification. In the conjoint problem identification phase, there needs to be a description of the parents' and teachers' concerns as they relate to the child's primary behavioral, academic, or social concerns. This is conducted through the Conjoint Problem Identification Interview (CPII). This structured interview aims to get clear and objective definitions of the target concerns from the collaborating partners. Often, these descriptions of behavior will identify the specific behavior in terms of what time it occurs, in what setting, and with what subject matter it is associated. Thus, this phase also allows parents and teachers to explore the conditions that may be contributing to the problem as well as explore the conditions that seem to exacerbate the problem. Information from home and school is shared. It is also important during this phase to agree on a procedure through which data about the problematic behavior(s) can be collected.

Phase Two: Conjoint Problem Analysis.   Once the goals of Phase One have been accomplished, attention turns to the conjoint problem analysis phase. This phase is also initiated with a structured interview, the Conjoint Problem Analysis Interview (CPAI). According to Sheridan and colleagues (1996), there are two distinct phases that occur here: data analysis and plan development. In the *data analysis phase,* the consultant, parents, and teachers examine the baseline data. The group then conducts a functional assessment of the target behavior across both home and school settings. Once the behavior is isolated in its context, it is time to plan an intervention.

During the *plan development phase,* hypotheses are offered about the possible functions of the behavior. From these hypotheses, the team of parents, teachers, and consultant discuss an intervention plan. During the development of this plan, it is important that all team members participate. Whatever plan is agreed on, it should be reasonable and not so complex for teachers and parents that it becomes difficult to follow through (Yeaton & Sechrest, 1981). Regarding the intervention, Sheridan and colleagues (1996, p. 169) believe that plans that span across home and school do not necessarily need to be identical. One reason for this is the fact that a given behavior may have different functions at home than at school. For instance, a child might use vulgar language at school to get attention from classmates and use the same language at home to intimidate a younger sibling.

Phase Three: Treatment Plan Implementation.   Unlike the previous phases, there is no structured interview during this phase. Nonetheless, there are important issues that need to be addressed in order to help enhance the efficacy of the implementation. For instance, Christenson and Sheridan (2001) believe that the consultant needs to remain in close contact with both teachers and parents throughout the implementation process. There are several reasons for this. In the first place, it may be that the intervention itself is not fully understood. This can result in errors and misunderstandings. Second, it is important to monitor the plan to ensure that it is being implemented correctly. Third, the consultant needs to be able to offer assistance or otherwise provide support and reinforcement for the implementation. Finally, it is important to remain in close contact in order to be able to make adjustments to the original plan, if need be.

Phase Four: Conjoint Treatment Plan Evaluation.   The Conjoint Treatment Evaluation Interview (CTEI; Sheridan et al., 1996) is used to determine whether the goals of the consultation have been met across settings. All team members are encouraged to discuss the results and, if need be, make recommendations for the continuation, modification, or termination of the intervention. In successful cases, it is important to review the strategies that help reinforce a solution-oriented approach.

According to Sheridan and colleagues (1996), CBC is a structured, indirect form of service delivery. The process includes involving parents, teachers, and other support staff in an effort to work together to address the academic, social, or behavioral needs of an individual for whom all parties bear some responsibility. As such, CBC models partnerships of children, parents, teachers, and other professionals in an effort to promote positive outcomes. Although both the collaboration/interdependent and conjoint behavioral consultation can be effective, there are barriers to overcome.

GENERIC OBSTACLES IN SCHOOL-BASED COLLABORATION

The collaborative nature of effective consultation may be undermined if one-sided, power-centered relationships between parents and the school are allowed to replace mutuality and collaboration. Teachers and parents might avoid each other, meeting only when a situation becomes intolerable. In another instance, parents may be intimidated into accepting the preference of the school without being solicited to give the kind of information that may shed light on the problem. A third example of obstacles that need to be overcome is reflected in situations when a troubling competition emerges in a home/school conflict, where each side adamantly demands compliance with its wishes. Sometimes parents feel so overwhelmed by a child's problems that requests by the staff to deal with the problems are met with increased feelings of fear, frustration, and helplessness. As a result, teachers may face unrealistic demands from parents.

On a meso-structural level, a barrier that counselors face in instituting collaborative approaches is that school staff are seldom given any training in the purpose and rationale of the collaborative process. Other demands on the time and energy of teachers, such as training in high-stakes testing and training in the utilization of technology, are present. These can compete with the time teachers may be able to devote to collaboration and collaboration training (Reinhaller, 1999). The many demands on school staff time and energy must be considered in any rational planning for change. Counselors should explain that collaboration is an effective means of realizing individual goals through the synergy of group problem solving. All participants in the collaboration process need to learn that the more they give, the more they will get out of the process of collaboration.

On a macro-level, the issues are equally complex and equally significant to the culture of collaboration. In some violence-prone schools, collaborative problem solving may be a matter of life and death. Astor, Pitner, and Duncan (1998) quote a teacher from their study: "Almost every child in my class knows someone who was murdered or shot. I know it gets to them and they can't always think about the lesson or school—but it's hard for me to think about lessons, too" (p. 336). According to Astor and colleagues, despair under such circumstance is pervasive, inducing feelings of helplessness in students, teachers, and parents. People may be so overwhelmed that available resources are ignored or no effort is made to mobilize social and political forces in support of the school's efforts to protect and nurture children. Under such unfavorable circumstances, the academic, personal/social, and career development of students becomes sidetracked.

To help offset the potentially negative impact of such situations, counselors need to bridge the gap between home and school and to replace these ineffective and nonproductive relationships with *collaborative* relationships where the home and school work together in a commensurate manner (Amatea & Brown, 2000). The team can be encouraged to evaluate the situation and focus its energies on dealing with the issues that prevent the school from performing its mission.

SUMMARY

The challenge of educating students today is far greater than the abilities of any one person or discipline. Personal/social, career, and academic success for students builds a firm foundation for their entire lives. School counselors and school psychologists, through consultation and collaboration with school personnel, students, parents, other professionals and community members, can build a process of group problem solving whose synergy will multiply the efforts of each individual. School counselors working with individual students, their families, their schools, and the larger world may find their greatest effectiveness in consulting and collaboration.

If the trademark structural configuration of consultation is the triad, collaboration can be configured as triadic as well, with some internal variations. Consultants who collaborate still work with consultees and clients. What changes is the number and types of potential relationships that are configured within the structure of "consultee" and "client." Whereas consultation has one consultee, collaboration may have one consultee and several designates of the consultee. Recall from the discussion in Chapter Two about the context of consultation being the organization. The "organization" was always in the background of any consultation to some degree. That discussion pointed out that sometimes the organization mattered significantly, and sometimes it did not. In collaboration, the organization is present to a significant degree because collaboration involves the interactions of many different individuals from the organization.

According to Caplan and Caplan (1993), the basic mandate of school counselors and school psychologists inherently incorporates collaboration in partnerships with other staff members. This is in addition to the traditional duties of specialized testing and therapeutic duties for which each professional is responsible. Both school counselors and school psychologists are perceived as integral members of the school staff, and are seen as partially responsible for students' welfare at school. What varies from school to school is the ratio of time spent on testing and therapy versus the time spent in collaboration with other school professionals. Sometimes the culture of the school will dictate the roles and responsibilities of both the school counselor and school psychologist. In other situations, this is influenced by the personal preferences of the professionals themselves. For instance, Caplan and Caplan (1993) mention that population-oriented school psychologists may spend more time in collaborative activities because they are seen as having an impact on the broadest collection of individuals, including students, staff, administration, and the community (p. 338). On the other hand, more traditional school psychologists, who are individual oriented, may spend more time with individual cases that utilize their specialized testing skills. In any case, at some point, other staff will be brought into the contextual foreground, and the effectiveness of the relationships that have been developed with them will be tested.

The same caveats pertaining to counselors and consultants relating to their knowing which mode of operation they are in at any given time applies to collaborators as well. Brown, Pryzwansky, and Schulte (2001), together with Schulte and Osborne (1993), caution professionals to be clear about which mode, either consultation or collaboration, they are in. For example, Caplan and Caplan (1993) state that school psychologists are likely using mental health collaboration whenever they are a part of a task force aimed at dealing with a particular case (p. 336). Caplan and Caplan also believe that the effectiveness and efficiency of the host institution directly influences the outcome of collaborative efforts and assert that the techniques used in collaborating "must be geared to the host institution's level of effectiveness" (p. 297). The reason for this is that the consultant who is collaborating has to rely on the host institution's personnel to agree to plan and carry out the recommendations.

Some institutions do not operate efficiently enough to implement change effectively. Because of the potential deleterious effects of working with an ineffective institution, it is important for those mental health professionals who are employed as "outside" consultants to assess what Caplan and Caplan (1993) refer to as *salience* and *feasibility*. Salience refers to whether the benefits of collaboration impact significant numbers of clients. In other words, collaborating relationships are better indicated if it is seen as impacting significant numbers as opposed to only one or two clients. The issue of feasibility relates to the assessment of how well the effective working relationships can be formed in the process. Although these two issues are choices for the "outside" consultant who is free to accept or not accept the offer to work with the host institution, school counselors and other inside consultants are not free to choose in the same sense. Instead, they are structurally placed together and, hopefully, can develop effective collaborating relationships.

Collaborative problem-solving models offer the best chance of dealing with the serious and pervasive problems and distractions that inhibit school success. The counselor is in an ideal position to facilitate this process. The importance of school success in the age of the knowledge economy can hardly be minimized. In the long run, the efficacy and efficiency of collaborative problem solving will become apparent. Eventually, counselors will understand the skills and constraints of law enforcement officers. Teachers will learn to speak with parents in ways that make them allies and sources of information. Psychologists will explain the implications of test results in ways that make the knowledge useful to all members of the team. The synergy effect may require months or years of work. Mistakes and misunderstandings are an inevitable part of the collaboration process, but pursued with integrity and real commitment, great achievements are possible.

QUESTIONS

1. What is the basic difference between collaboration and consultation?

2. What is the relationship between collaboration and consultation?

3. How is the issue of "responsibility" different in collaboration?

4. What are the basic elements in conjoint behavioral consultation?

5. How different are these elements from behavioral case consultation?

6. Why is there such an emphasis on the relationships in collaboration?

7. What are some of the resistances to collaboration?

8. If there is one caveat to collaboration, what would it be?

CHAPTER THIRTEEN

AGENCY-BASED CONSULTATION AND COLLABORATIVE CULTURES

Understanding the essential tenets of collaboration that were discussed in the previous chapter will help you conceptualize some of the necessary processes and structures of collaborating and consulting in a community setting. State and local agencies, community-based organizations, businesses, families, health-care and mental health providers are all examples of potential consultees, clients, and client systems. Although not reported in the literature to any great degree, collaborative efforts in community settings aimed at helping promote the mental health of clients, is an effective approach. For example, ask almost any mental health practitioner treating anorexia, bulimia, or a substance-abuse issue about the need for collaborative efforts among professionals, and you will likely get a resounding "There needs to be more of it!"

The general models of consultation, such as mental health and behavioral case consultation, apply to consulting situations occurring in mental health agencies. So, a review of those models is not warranted. Instead of reviewing such models, this chapter will introduce you to specific consulting situations that occur in mental health agencies. A specific type of effective consultation with agencies is a purchase/expert model in which a consultant develops and evaluates a program. This approach is known as *program consulting* (Dougherty, 1990; Hansen, Himes, & Meier, 1990). This chapter will extend the discussion of collaboration, and apply it to mental health agencies. Particular attention will be placed on collaborative cultures. In addition, an introduction to program development and evaluation will be presented. A discussion related to the substance-abuse field will be outlined, depicting both collaborating and consulting in the mental health agency field.

COLLABORATING IN SUBSTANCE-ABUSE TREATMENT

Currently, there are numerous opportunities for collaboration and consulting in the substance-abuse prevention and treatment field. The alarming rise of alcohol and other drug-related illnesses and their associated problems, including the direct and indirect impact on communities, have been well documented (Fisher & Harrison, 2000). These same researchers have also noted a concomitant rise in community treatment facilities as well as an increase in treatment modalities.

As in other consulting relationships, the purpose of consulting or collaborating with these entities is to enhance the services and outcomes for clients. Specific to drugs and alcohol, collaboration and consultation are aimed at those who have been impacted or may be impacted in the future by the consequences of alcohol and other drug abuse. The type of consultation that is required in this field points toward the use of preventive, developmental, and family approaches conducted through such venues as workshops, program development and implementation, and clinical consultation. The target population of consultees includes communities as well as individuals. As you will see in the ensuing discussion, there are interesting consultee characteristics that will challenge consultants. Many of the consultant skills that are needed to facilitate change are easily transferable from the traditional models of consultation discussed in this book. Other skills and issues are more idiosyncratic to the field of prevention and treatment of substance abuse. Some of the specialized skills relate to the consultant having a degree of content expertise in addition to experience in working with diverse groups. Because of the state of the substance-abuse prevention and treatment field in serving its clientele, consultants will often find use specific types of approaches.

In an outpatient agency or inpatient venue, substance-abusing clients may be seeing multiple professionals. The prevalence of substance-abuse problems, which are complicated in many cases by co-occurring disorders in that population concomitant with the ensuing inhibiting treatment costs associated with it, increase the likelihood that collaborating partnerships will be deemed as a necessity. Whether the venue is outpatient or inpatient, the primary clinician will collaborate with other professionals who are involved in the case. The collaborating partnerships in these cases can include family members, agencies, physicians, social workers, institutions, and other counselors and professionals. These partnerships will take place in both inpatient and outpatient venues. In both venues, the collaborating teams will be comprised of individuals who differ along vertical dimensions and horizontal dimensions. With respect to the vertical dimensions, collaborating members will differ in educational level and in status. The horizontal dimensions relate to differing orientations in the field as well as idiosyncratic biases held by individual collaborating members.

POTENTIAL CHALLENGES

There are challenges to working with individuals being treated for substance abuse. For instance, individual family members themselves may differ on their attitudes and opinions on substance abuse. The same can be true of the collaborating partners. For example, the collaborating partners in addiction cases will probably include professional specialists in the addictions field. These collaborating individuals can hold strong and differing beliefs about the use of medication, controlled use of the substance by the client, the use of recovering addicts as counselors, natural recovery, and spirituality in the treatment of substance abuse.

Outpatient Issues

Disconnect during Treatment.   When a substance-abusing client relapses and needs inpatient treatment, it would logically follow that the treatment team would include the client's primary outpatient therapist as well as the primary inpatient therapist. However, this is not often the case. The outpatient therapist usually is put "on hold" until the client is treated and released. In many cases, the inpatient unit does not request the therapist's records or notes. Instead, it chooses to rely only on its own staff's assessment of the client. While it makes sense to do that for many reasons, the flow of information stops or is greatly impeded. At the end of treatment, the same thing happens in the other direction: No notes follow the client back to the client's outpatient therapist. This disconnect is troublesome and is experienced as being more serious in some cases than in other cases.

The disconnect does not usually happen when it comes to the family. Family members can be involved in family therapy with the client or through consultations with the family or be involved during family weekends. During treatment, the inpatient unit will likely have a treatment team of collaborating professionals who might include a psychiatrist, nurse, chemical dependency counselor/specialist, social worker, and others (e.g., vocational rehabilitation specialist), as deemed appropriate. Sometimes, during family weekend visits, this team, or individual team members, will consult with the client's family members to update them on such things as the substance abuser's progress and transition planning. Meetings between helpers and family members can also be convened to answer questions and allay unfounded fears and anxieties. Aside from the therapeutic benefits of such family inclusion into the process, these family visits and periodic consultations attempt to address the issue of disconnect between the inpatient unit and the family.

Leadership Concerns.   In their work, Caplan and Caplan (1993) see the role of the mental health collaborator as being responsible for the mental health aspects of the case. In the mental health field, and in the substance-abuse treatment field specifically, this "mental health" responsibility can be subdivided among clinicians. There may even be a lawyer involved to handle the legal concerns of the client. For example, imagine that a substance-abusing client and the client's family are seeing a licensed marriage and family therapist for the family concerns because of substance abuse. At the same time, the client may be seeing a licensed alcohol and drug abuse counselor for the substance-abuse issues, a psychiatrist or psychologist if there is a co-occurring disorder with substance abuse, and perhaps an attorney to help the client deal effectively with legal issues (e.g., driving under the influence).

The questions of leadership among those professionals responsible for the client's mental health are usually established structurally, as is the case with inpatient treatment facilities. However, in outpatient settings, the structure is not always clear. In many cases, there is an appeal to more traditional and hierarchical leadership structures. Problems can ensue. For example, suppose the client had a working diagnosis of substance-abuse disorder and was seeing a alcohol counselor while at the same time seeing a psychiatrist for depression. The alcohol dependence might be the primary working diagnosis, which would then suggest that the mental health collaborator leader would be the substance-abuse counselor. The psychiatrist is relegated to a secondary role by virtue of the diagnosis. Nonetheless, the psychiatrist may become overly assertive and attempt to manage the mental health aspects of the case anyway. Struggles for power over the management of the client's mental health can become a focus of the group's energies rather than the focus on the real task at hand.

Structural Concerns.   Imagine three working mental health professionals. Assume that these three professionals have full-time practices. One is a psychiatrist, one is a private practice mental health clinician, and one is an alcohol and other drug counselor. Imagine that a client, diagnosed with substance-abuse disorder, bipolar disorder, and relationship problems is seeing all three for various reasons. This situation clearly calls for some form of collaborating relationships between the various parties. Further detailing the example, assume that the client receives some personally distressing news. In response, the client relapses and decides to drink alcohol. Suppose the combination of alcohol and other drugs creates a situation in which an ambulance is called and the client is admitted into the local emergency room. Imagine that coincidently the primary psychiatrist and mental health therapist are on vacation. Now there are several more professionals involved in the case, and it is entirely possible that none of these professionals have ever met or even heard of each other. It may also be the case that these professionals are not the most appropriate ones to be treating the case. One result is that the collaboration may not ever take place. It can be seen by potential collaborators as too complicated to attempt, given all of the professionals involved. Moreover, the effort can also be seen as an "add-on" to an already heavy professional caseload. A result is the potential for phone collaboration. This would seem to be the easiest way to go about it. However, conference calls would almost certainly not be possible due to scheduling problems. When attempts are made to collaborate over the phone, it usually involves two professionals. Any other professional involved in the case will get the information secondhand. This can create some potential for misinformation.

Inpatient Issues

Given some of the challenges to collaboration in the outpatient setting, it would seem as though collaboration among a group of professionals who work in the same building or unit together would be easy. This is not the case. The inpatient setting has its own set of challenges to collaborating efforts.

The Unit's Organizational Culture.   As you would imagine, inpatient units and hospitals that function to treat substance-abuse clients are similar to any other organization and are subject to organizational behavior. The fact that collaborating partners in these units also "work together" make this type of setting different from a collaborative relationship convened in an outpatient setting. Components of organizational behavior that can directly affect collaborative efforts include status issues, gender equality, racioethnicity, power and control issues, opportunities, and the like. Problems in any one of these areas can impact the collaborating relationship.

Most of these units or hospitals are founded on the medical model by virtue of being medical facilities. As such, the collaborating partners will almost always include a medical professional, such as a psychiatrist or other physician. This medical professional often gains legitimacy as a leader of the collaborating partners because of legal and professional considerations. However, in the case of co-occurring disorders, this legitimacy can become blurry. For instance, if the addicted inpatient treatment client has also been diagnosed with depression, it can become a matter of philosophy as to which disorder came first. The implications of such a distinction, although academic to the practitioner directly treating the addict, are profound in terms of leadership. Caplan and Caplan (1993) advocate that the psychiatrist would be the mental health collaborator in charge of the group, which itself would be subject to the decisions of the administering consultee. Yet, in an inpatient treatment facility, the addictions counselor may believe that he or she has precedence in the case, and therefore the leading role, because of the manner in which the case has been conceptualized. At the same time, the psychiatrist may believe that the client's depression as ultimately what led to the addicted behaviors and may press indirectly or directly for a change of perspectives. All of these professionals share responsibility for the mental health aspects of the case, and all have the client's best welfare in mind. Yet, the psychiatrist has the ultimate responsibility and may preempt other partners' decisions and input by virtue of this structural and legitimate power. In this example, once the collaborating team has finished a particular decision-making process in which overt agreement has been reached, there may be very little covert support to carry the plan out. A result can be less than efficient client care.

The structural and process concerns in the treatment of substance-abuse disorders should not deter professional efforts to collaborate and consult. Although the barriers can seem arduous, establishing collaborative cultures, such as those discussed in a later section, can go a long way in helping create an environment in which these partnerships can flourish. Once collaborating partnerships are established, collaborators can discuss the difficulties that they may face beforehand, as a way of predicting outcomes and conceptualizing ways through difficult times.

PROGRAM CONSULTATION AND EVALUATION

Collaboration is one effective method of helping clients in a variety of mental health settings. Mental health agencies are also venues where consulting can take place. Aside from the clinical consultations, these agencies are usually funded through federal, state, and private grants. Many of these grants are for program development, implementation, and evaluation. Program consulting is growing because of influx of such grants (Kratochwill, Mace, & Bissel, 1987). Consultants can be hired as a result.

Definition

Gladding (1997) maintains that counselors and consultants in agencies need to be dedicated to the "greater good, recognizing that one's own health and well-being is connected with that of others" (p. 405). In many cases, agency counselors do not have the time to devote to the greater good through pro bono services or through their roles as consultants. Nonetheless, there are mental health problems that need addressing, and program consultation in the form of program development is an effective means of garnering support from communities in helping meet the mental health needs of clients in their communities. Dougherty (1990) sees program consultation as a purchase/expert model of consultation. In this case, the consultee is often a key figure in the agency or the organization. The consultant's expertise is purchased for the purposes of assisting in the planning of a new program, revising an existing program, or dealing with the factors that affect a current program.

Goals and Process

According to Dougherty (1990), the primary goal of program consultation is to provide an organization the technical assistance it requires in order for it to have successful programs and accomplish its mission (p. 203). Gallesich (1982) maintains that no new consultant skills are needed when conducting program consultation. Moreover, consultants do not need to reconceptualize the phases of the process. Nonetheless, Hansen and colleagues (1990) believe that this method of consulting is a more complex version of consulting with individuals because it is more expansive and comprehensive. At the same time, Dougherty cites Gallesich (1982), who sees program consultation as being different from other forms of consultation due to it being restricted to dealing with a specific program. Thus, program consultation is specific but at the same time quite expansive. This is an interesting concept for consultants to entertain and is partially what makes this approach appealing and challenging for consultants. The challenges inherent in program consultation do seem to scare off many consultants from undertaking these contracts (Hansen et al., 1990). This is particularly unfortunate because this type of consultation is sorely needed in the rapidly growing field of alcohol and other drug-abuse prevention and treatment.

Lusky and Hayes (2001) see generic program consultation models as consisting of four major phases:

- Planning
- Analyzing and designing
- Implementing
- Evaluating

Stage One: Planning.   A needs assessment is undertaken in this stage to determine the level of need. Needs are assumed to exist based on several different factors. These factors include institutional or personal philosophy, government mandate, available resources, history/tradition, and expert opinion (Gladding, 1997, p. 329). Any one or a combination of these factors can encourage the development of a program.

According to Lusky and Hayes (2001), successful change demands committed leadership and a supportive environment (p. 28). In the planning stage, it is important that consultants identify existing human resources as well as assess the levels of system support. In programs that center on school-aged children and adolescents, partnerships with schools are needed.

Hall and Torres (2002) and Dryfoos (1996) discuss three manners in which these school/community partnerships can be developed. According to these researchers, the least intrusive of the partnerships is the *school-linked services* approach. Here, schools are seen as coordinating formal agreements for services with community needs and resources. In *school-based services*, schools serve as the hosts for a wide variety of services. Examples of services include such things as a school-based health clinic or a family resource center. The *community school* model is the more inclusive of the three discussed. In the community school, comprehensive services are provided within the school setting in order to address the diverse needs of students (Dryfoos, p. 107).

Agencies can also be involved in the process. Depending on the program goals, infant nursing services, Head Start programs, juvenile justice authorities, family social services, rehabilitation services, and employment counseling agencies can be brought on board. This interagency consulting and collaboration process not only helps with the program development and implementation but it also provides opportunities for mental health counselors and consultants to become more familiar with resources in the community.

Hall and Torres (2002) believe that there is a need for prevention programs and community-based partnerships in order to impact mental health concerns. These same researchers assert that mental health counselors and school counselors can work conjointly in primary care settings to develop prevention programs that can positively impact the mental health of communities. Lewis and Lewis (1989) believe that program consultation aimed at prevention program development can effectively train paraprofessionals and/or community leaders to handle less serious mental health problems. These researchers maintain that paraprofessionals and community leaders can resolve many potential problems before they become serious. This allows the professional counseling staff to be utilized for situations involving more difficult issues.

Furthermore, Hall and Torres (2002) implore mental health agency counselors to forge partnerships with school counselors, parents, and community leaders in order to better plan and implement effective mental health treatment programs for communities. Standards for effective partnerships have been established by the Human Resources and Services Administration's Bureau of Primary Care in the U.S. Department of Health and Human Services (HRSA, 1996). First, the partnerships must involve community members in the actual design and delivery of services. Second, the partnerships need to identify the individuals at risk for problems during crisis events. Third, the partnerships must have the ability to reach out to the individuals in the target population. This is accomplished through the provision of coordinated services in accessible community sites. Fourth, the partnerships must also emphasize community ownership of the problems and of their resolution. Fifth, the partnerships must develop training mechanisms that reach across professional boundaries. The purpose of this is to help professionals and community members provide a more holistic and coordinated delivery of care. Finally, the partnerships must create new structures in order to integrate the fragmented systems of care that do exist in the community.

It is also helpful to review the agency's mission statement, philosophy, and direction, and to clarify the role of the program within this context. Similar to Pugach and Johnson (1995), Lusky and Hayes see the need for the establishment of a shared vision of the program in terms of its goals. Once set, a program philosophy can be developed that is consistent with the overall mission of the agency. This is an important issue due to the fact that resistance to the process is inherent, and almost any reason to thwart the development of a program can and is often used to maintain the status quo. It is not that the resistance is bad or that it connotes a lack of care and concern. Sometimes, it is simply a perception that another program will take away valuable and "indispensable" human resources and time. According to Margolis, Fish, and Wepner (1990), resistances to the process can include a fear of loss, miscommunications, low tolerance for change, and a general fear of the unknown. These same researchers maintain that these various resistances can be overcome through supportive measures (p. 77).

Stage Two: Analyzing and Designing.   Lusky and Hayes (2001, p. 28) maintain that any problem can be conceptualized as a difference between "what is and what can be." This understanding of what is and what can be is gleaned through the perceptions of others who are, or will be, a part of the program. In gathering data and other information, participants utilize their shared vision to determine potential outcomes. Once the information has been gathered and analyzed, efforts can be initiated to design the intervention program.

In talking about prevention programs, Ellis (1998) identifies three types of intervening: multi-factor, multi-system, and multi-level interventions. The *multi-factor intervention* plans include both the individual as well as collective concerns. The individual dimension means that the program will meet the individual needs. The collective dimension reflects the program's abilities to reach the needs of all individuals in the target population. *Multi-system interventions* are those interventions that address the factors existing in every social context in which the individuals interact. Ellis (p. 102) asserts that consultants need to know the role of each system in the life of the individuals in the target population. This is due to the obvious interaction effects that occur between individuals and the environment. *Multi-level interventions* address the need to provide resources at both the micro-level as well as the macro-level. At the macro-level, Ellis sees the need for consultants to ascertain if others know that the services exist. Another issue addresses whether people have access to the services. Finally, a main question for consultants is, "Do people know that they need the services that are offered?" (p. 102).

In designing the actual intervention plan, Lusky and Hayes (2001) state that sources include a comparison of a current program with the one that is being proposed, a survey measuring "customer" satisfaction, and prioritization of the program elements. Looking at programs already in existence can help consultants develop appropriate strategies to meet their goals, while diminishing the probability of failure. Atler (1995) reviews effective programs that exist in communities, and this can provide a framework for consultants to organize and analyze effective programs. In the programs noted, there was time and energy devoted to the program itself as well as to the financial resources. A significant component of these programs was the dedication of the counselors and consultants who were involved. Atler found the effective programs were characterized by:

- Intervening early and often
- Building a sense of character

- Busting the Kafkaesque bureaucracy
- Setting high standards
- Getting the community involved

During Stage Two, an evaluation procedure is identified, discussed, and formally agreed on. Daniels, Mines, and Gressard (1981) identify several types of evaluation models, and there are several that apply to the mental health field. For example, in systems analysis, the goal is to determine the efficiency of a particular program. Typical questions in this model would relate to whether the expected effects were achieved as well as determining the most effective programs. This approach assumes that goals are established at the outset and that they can be quantified. In using a behavioral objectives model, the questions relate to whether the population is achieving the goals and objectives of the program. This evaluation is used frequently in school systems to measure student achievement. Usually there needs to be a baseline of behavior with behavioral goals specified as the outcome measure. In a decision-making model of evaluation, the goal is to measure the effectiveness and assure quality control. Although similar to a systems analysis model, the decision-making model employs different means to measure success. For instance, surveys, questionnaires, and interviews are employed in the decision-making model as opposed to a cost-benefit analysis. House (1978) advocates that quantitative measures be used. Frey, Raming, and Frey (1978) herald the merits of qualitative evaluative measures—especially in counseling and psychology.

Stage Three: Implementing.   As the term suggests, this phase is reflected in the formal efforts to initiate a new, stand-alone program or to infuse an existing program into another program. The actions associated in this stage include focusing on the specific administrative tasks as well as initiating evaluative efforts. It will often be the details and those that are overlooked that will serve to diminish the success of programs. However, this is not always the case. So, communication is important in this stage, and getting the partnership together in order to help predict problems in advance of their occurrence is helpful. For instance, administrative help may be assigned to one partner or partnership, when, in fact, that service is not available. In another situation, it might be that a particular partnership undergoes an unexpected change that disrupts the flow of implementation. A principal might be reassigned, for example, and a relationship with the new one must be undertaken.

Stage Four: Evaluating.   Hosie (1994) and Oetting (1976) believe some type of evaluation should be made for every counseling program within an agency. The actual evaluation of a program should be an ongoing process. Hence, the formulation of questions for evaluation, the selection of an evaluation design and measuring instruments, and the development of data-collecting procedures need to be considered at each step of the process. This means that the evaluation process actually starts in Stage One and is inextricably tied to the design of the program itself. The evaluation needs not only to reflect the current status of the program's effectiveness, it needs also to suggest program areas that are in need of improvement. In this fashion of ongoing evaluation, the program is continuously being evaluated, reevaluated, and adjusted.

Evaluating a program is a complex undertaking, and consultants need to have expert knowledge of ways to go about accomplishing this task. Consultants without expertise might find themselves trying to assess a program without any clear goals. According to Burck and Peterson (1975), this approach is like a "shot in the dark."

Evaluation usually involves gathering meaningful data and information on various aspects of a given program that will act to guide decisions about the allocation of resources and to help ensure the effectiveness of the program (Wheeler & Loesch, 1981). According to Gladding (1997), evaluation has a quality of immediate feedback and utility. The process should be accomplished systematically and follow sequential steps. According to Burck and Peterson (1975), the first step in formulating an evaluation plan occurs during the needs assessment. So, this step actually occurs in Stage One of program development. Once needs have been identified, the program that is developed and its concomitant evaluation process should reflect clear goals and performance objectives. These goals include both short-term and long-terms goals, or what Gladding and Burck and Peterson refer to as *terminal* program and *ultimate* program outcomes. The importance of having clear goals is reflected in designing the program itself. Clear goals will assure that the clarity and focus of objectives and activities that will be employed are designed to meet those goals. These objectives can then be measured more easily.

Because evaluation is ongoing, the fourth step in the process allows for adjustments to be made to the program. According to the researchers, this step in the evaluation process includes examining the specific activities as well as the adequacy of the communication patterns used to keep the program going. The last step involves reporting the results of the outcomes of the program. Dissemination of the results to the partnerships, clients, and community-at-large occurs here. Oetting (1976) asserts that the evaluation team members need to convene often to discuss the process for there to be any efficacy to the program. The reason for this is that an evaluator who is involved is more likely to evaluate.

Hopefully, evaluation is performed meaningfully and appropriately. If done correctly, evaluation of a program allows clients to have systematic and positive input into the system that helps them. Clearly, there are things that can limit or render the process ineffective. For instance, Daniels, Mines, and Gressard (1981) identify several incorrect procedures that are often used in evaluation. These researchers see problems with evaluation occurring when consultants restrict the sampling of opinion by asking too few clients about their experiences. Also, consultants evaluating programs often make comparisons between nonequivalent groups. In addition, consultants often assemble a group of people for the purpose of having them write a committee report. In some cases, these group members do not have the necessary skills, background, or motivation to do so. For example, a consultee revealed recently to me that during a board meeting, she had been asked by the board members to write up a position statement. In private, she shared with me that she had no knowledge of how to write up a position report because she had never had to do one before. We worked on ways to involve the appropriate individuals—in this case, that meant soliciting the help of her legislative lobbyist.

As discussed, the incidence of substance abuse in the U.S. culture as well as the critical need for community prevention programs in other areas of mental health set the stage for numerous opportunities to consult and collaborate. By now, you can see how complex substance-abuse treatment can be as well as how complicated program development can be. The consulting and collaborative efforts across these two concerns require the staunch efforts of many individuals. Toward that aim, Hall and Torres (2002, p. 106) identify the necessary knowledge base and skill set for collaborating partners. The skills include:

- An ability to organize
- An ability to create resource packaging and budgeting
- An ability to conduct training and consultation
- An ability to participate effectively in outcome evaluation and cost analysis
- An ability in marketing
- An ability to help in building and sustaining new structures

No one partner can or needs to possess all of the skills. In fact, in keeping with the inclusive philosophy inherent in effective collaborative efforts, it is probably a good thing that not everyone does possess all the skills. The result is the opportunity for partners to share their respective expertise.

COLLABORATIVE CULTURES

Senge (1990) advocates collaborative cultures as a means of dealing effectively with the layering effect of bureaucracies. In describing business and industry as learning organizations, Senge identifies five disciplines of systems: systems thinking, personal mastery, mental models, and building a shared vision. In these innovative organizations, the fifth discipline is team learning. In organizations adhering to the fifth discipline, there is the practice of surfacing one's own defensiveness, acting as colleagues, suspending unexamined assumptions, integrating dialogue and discussion, and aligning the collective intelligence of organizational members.

If one were to reflect for a moment, it would be obvious that inpatient units and mental health agencies are ideal places in which a collaborative culture and the fifth discipline can exist. After all, as demonstrated in the previous discussion, both agencies and institutions are social units directed toward a multidimensional approach to treatment in which any number of professional staff interact and collaborate to varying degrees regarding many cases on a daily basis. The partnerships that are emphasized in program development and evaluation also seem to be able to benefit from a collaborative culture that enhances the commitment of members, improves the functioning among collaborators, and addresses the needs of consultees and clients more effectively. Fortunately, collaboration between professionals and between professionals and community agencies and/or schools is happening all the time. It is occurring as you read this chapter. If you are practicing in the field and seeing clients on an outpatient basis, chances are you are either engaged in collaborating efforts or have the potential to do so. If you are or will be involved in hospital inpatient treatment, either as staff or as a consultant to the unit, you likely will be involved in collaborating relationships on a daily basis, because that structure will be a component of the unit's culture.

Characteristics of Collaborative Cultures

Schein (2000) sees innovative cultures as characterized by several features. Primarily, there is *proactive optimism*. This is the sense that one can manage one's immediate and future environment. In this type of culture, learning and change are desirable. There is also a *commitment to all stakeholders*. This refers to valuing owners, principals, students, parents, customers, employees, suppliers, community, and the like as equals and as important. For inpatient units and mental health agencies, it might be the director, clinicians, clients, other staff, the medical team, custodians, parents and other family members, and the community who are identified as important to the process. It is also recognized that a total effort is needed and appreciated.

In terms of *theory and attitudes*, innovative cultures hold that people are capable and willing to work toward organizational, institutional, and agency goals and direct or control their efforts to that aim. There is *organizational slack,* which means that these cultures are able to generate some excess resources for creativity and innovation. This is especially necessary and helpful in the development and maintenance of collaborating partnerships. Excess financial resources are difficult to come by. Although this is clearly a challenge in a managed-care–driven treatment field, it is important for agencies and institutions to keep looking for grants and funding from various state and federal authorities. In these cultures, *power and influence* are derived from knowledge and skill. For collaborating partnerships that involve paraprofessionals and community leaders, this can be an issue. Some partners will have expertise and education; others may not. It is important to value the contributions of all members, and to make every attempt to include the ideas and perceptions of nonprofessionals, parents, and the like into the program development. When people feel included, motivation is enhanced.

In like fashion, there is a focus on task rather than on the accumulation of status or position. Egos need to be put aside for the common goals. Since this focus on tasks is paramount, group processes that are replete with jealously and resentment, which can result from status differences that go unaddressed or unchecked, can be a significant barrier to the collaborating process. There is also an emphasis on *building and maintaining trusting* relationships in these cultures. The relationship issues are held in equal esteem with the task at hand. *Open communication* needs to flow freely. In these progressive cultures, there is an efficient networking of relationships and information. Communication among and between collaborating partners is critical. Finally, there is *organizational diversity*. This reflects the structural ideal of collaboration in which variety and diversity in people and groups are necessary, and serve as a powerful source of motivation. This is especially true when the programs that are developed are aimed at minority groups. If a program is going to address a certain minority population, it only seems reasonable to include a significant number of collaborating partners representative of that population.

Pugach and Johnson (1995) also write about collaborative cultures. Although referring to schools, many of their concepts can be easily and effectively translated to mental health settings. According to the authors and Hargreaves and Dawe (1990), collaborative cultures in schools and agencies are characterized by evolutionary relationships where openness, trust, and support among the staff is valued. In their study of collaborating relationships and collaborating cultures in schools, Pugach and Johnson (pp. 16–19) identify member collaborators' characteristics and subsequent activities that help lead to collaborative cultures. This information can be useful in terms of guiding collaborating efforts in agencies and institutions. First, effective collaborative professionals recognize that the *goal is too complex and requires a joint effort* to achieve the goal. This is clearly the case in the substance-abuse field, where the presenting problems can be very involved and intricate. This is also true when attempting to develop programs on a communitywide basis. Second, collaborating professionals also need to naturally *enjoy the social nature of problem solving*. Third, collaborative relationships are not easy, and they do require both a *commitment* to common goals as well as a commitment to a level of social interaction that directs them toward that goal. Fourth, professionals who are effective at collaboration value the personal and professional growth that is a result of collaborating efforts. There is intellectual growth that adds to each professional's content knowledge and abilities to manage similar cases more effectively in the future. Last, collaborative professionals also are *reflective* in their practices. This means that time is taken by the collaborators to reflect on the actual process of collaboration to determine how the process is being experienced by all parties.

Activities and Roles in Collaborative Cultures

Schein (1999, p. 172) maintains that in ongoing collaborative situations, the task and interpersonal processes occur at the same time and are inextricably woven, creating a perpetual decision issue about which processes to focus on and when to intervene in the interpersonal issues. Schein as well as Pugach and Johnson (1995) address the need for collaborative groups to examine the task and process issues as they go about the business of making decisions. The reason is clear: The members of collaborative groups or collaborative cultures need to work together in such a way as to be able to focus on both the goals of helping the client and the group process goals necessary to achieve the client-related goals. Pugach and Johnson maintain that the issue relates to how one defines "working together."

The ultimate purpose of working in collaborative relationships is to improve the professional practice so as to enhance the effectiveness of service to the current client as well as to a wider range of clients who have similar concerns. "Working together" in collaborative cultures means engaging in collaborative activities and roles that include *supporting, facilitating, informing,* and *prescribing roles* (Pugach & Johnson, 1995). These approaches cover a broad range of interactions that take place among professionals. As you might expect, these four dimensions are not pure, static forms. Rather, collaboration moves dynamically between these roles and processes in much the same manner as school counselor/consultants change hats during the course of a normal day's work. According to these authors, although identifying a common goal established the purpose for collaboration, it is understood that different situations require different kinds of collegial roles and interactions. Therefore, collaboration is something that people come to accept (p. 20). This is especially true if the collaborating partners do not have much experience in the collaboration or the collaborating process. This might be the case in a situation where a treatment team that is convened to work with a substance-abusing client includes a newly licensed substance-abuse counselor or recently graduated marriage and family therapist intern.

A component of collaborating is educating the collaborating partners about mental health issues. This can include being sensitive to the actual workings of the collaborating group so that it can reflect on itself to a degree that enhances the decision-making process. Pugach and Johnson (1995) see the *supportive dimension* of collaboration as one of the most important and fundamental to the process. This supportive role is similar to that discussed by Caplan and Caplan in terms of paying attention to the mental health of the group. In this supportive role, the mental health collaborator can help group members learn to be interpersonally supportive of each other. This may include such things as helping the group to recognize accomplishments and/or helping collaborating partners become supportive of innovative approaches. Anyone of the mental health collaborating partners can offer this supportive expertise to the group and the group's functioning. Although sounding promising, this type of culture obviously may or may not exist in any given inpatient setting. The supportive efforts can also be aimed at helping administration officials and agency directors see the advantages of supporting such a culture. This can be aided through Caplan and Caplan's program-centered administrative consultation.

The *facilitative dimension* of collaborative cultures is closely related to the supportive dimension. In the facilitative dimension, colleagues take on the role of facilitating their peers' knowledge about the case while helping them deal independently with relevant issues that may arise in future situations. For example, imagine that a mental health clinician, who is also a member of the collaborating team, continually requests help and advice for similar situations. Other collaborating team members can help this clinician understand more about a particular case while fostering the clinician's independent action in the future. In such a manner, time can be spent on other difficult cases, rather than rehashing similar ones. The process by which this supportive and facilitative role is carried out does not necessarily include giving the clinician advice or prescribing directives.

The *information-giving* dimension encompasses the sharing of information among collaborating partners. This also includes what Schein (1999) refers to as "open communication," which was discussed earlier. This dimension involves moving appropriate information into the network so that meaningful and relevant information about the client's care or program is readily available to collaborating partners. For example, if a decision was made in a staff meeting about a particular course of action for a client, this needs to be communicated to those who are not in attendance at the meeting. The plan of action needs to detail what information is going to be available to whom, how, and when. Follow-up is a simple way to ensure that this communication happens. In the case of an inpatient unit, this open communication or information-giving dimension needs to include the coordination of information to outpatient settings. This would obviate the deleterious effects of the "disconnect" between inpatient and outpatient settings.

Another related issue to outpatient settings and information giving in collaborative cultures is the need for sharing knowledge about existing resources. These resources include identifying and sharing information about human resources as well as community and financial resources. For instance, it is often difficult for those who are in substance-abuse recovery to locate support groups if they are new to a community or new to the recovery network. Inpatient units and agencies have information about such services and are usually willing to share this information with professionals and the lay population alike in their efforts to include the community in their prevention and treatment. In situations where collaborating partners convene for the purpose of developing and evaluating a program, attention needs to focus on educating members about existing resources. This enables them to contribute more effectively their opinions and suggestions.

The final dimension of collaborating cultures is the *prescriptive dimension* (Pugach & Johnson, 1995). This dimension is the familiar and traditional approach to collaboration in which a specialist offers opinions to the group. Schein (1999) and Puguch and Johnson would both argue in favor of collaborating relationships needing to be based more on specialized knowledge and skills than on status or position. In collaborative cultures, this prescriptive dimension is invoked in appropriate situations for purposes of growth and resolution of client issues. It is not aimed at gaining power over other members of the group. The prescriptive function in collaborating groups can be exercised by members, who are seen as holding a certain specialized knowledge. At the same time, it is important that these "experts" do not distance other less expert members of the group. If this happens, fragmentation among the collaborating partners can begin to erode the structure of their relationships.

As consultants, it is important to have an understanding of the ingredients of effective collaborative cultures. This is critical because often the best attempts at collaboration fail (Fishbaugh, 1997). Fishbaugh believes that even though all of the collaborative pieces are in place, such as having similar goals and the same stated purpose, collaborating partners will frequently be playing the same game on different boards. According to the same researcher, "Just as the players may not realize that they are playing different versions of the same game, the collaborators may fail to understand that they have come into the collaborative endeavor from different perspectives" (p. 133).

Change is not easy. This is especially true in a bureaucracy, such as those found in agencies, hospitals, and institutions. Yet, the future of community mental health in all sectors, including public education and private businesses, will demand that change takes place through coordinated, collaborative, and consultation efforts (Fishbaugh, 1997). However, for some professionals, collaboration happens only in crisis situations. For others, collaboration happens when professionals are available. In some other situations, collaboration is a painful experience in which individuals share cases with condescending professionals. Some partners in a collaborative arrangement may start with enthusiasm only to have it wane for any number of reasons. It is important to help develop collaborative cultures that can enhance the collaborative environment and provide the necessary reinforcement for effective service delivery.

SUMMARY

Although most of the mental health issues of clients could be addressed effectively through consultation and collaboration, the rise of co-occurring disorders—in which one of the disorders is substance abuse—lends itself readily to indirect services delivery. During the course of collaborating in the substance-abuse field, barriers will present themselves. The ones described in this chapter range from inpatient issues to outpatient issues. The issue of "who owns the client" is determined by the client's primary diagnosis. Yet, the structure of many mental health agencies is such that psychiatrists are the ones with the most legitimate power base by virtue of their training and status in the mental health field. The collegial nature of collaboration is impacted by the hierarchical tendencies of the individuals who fail to see the necessity of working together. For some, the roles are defined by status and power. Innovative cultures and collaborative cultures do not value such role definition. In these progressive cultures, the roles are defined by expertise rather than by status or power. It is not that individuals shy away from their power bases. It is that in successful collaborative efforts, the main goal is to help the clients. It is not the accumulation of power and status. Hence, collaborative partnerships are fostered best when there is time to reflect on the actual process of the collaboration. Communication is revered.

Program development and evaluation consultation also values communication. Moreover, program development requires collaborative efforts as well. An interesting feature of program consultation is the fact that the evaluation process is inherently built into the program development from the outset. That is, as the needs are identified, the design of the plan must address the issues of evaluation. If this is not the case, it may well result in a situation where the program cannot be effectively evaluated. This would be due to several possibilities. There is a very real possibility that the goals of the program are diffuse or not clear. In this case, the objectives and activities may not be well defined either. As a result, the structure might not lend itself easily to evaluation because it would be hard to determine what to actually evaluate.

Another situation where evaluation might not be effective is when consultants and collaborating partners choose an inappropriate method of evaluation. There are several models of evaluation, such as systems analysis, behavioral objectives, and decision making. According to Daniels, Mines, and Gressard (1981), each model is aimed at a specific goal, contains idiosyncratic assumptions, and utilizes differing methods. For example, the behavioral objectives evaluation model for school achievement assumes that a baseline or criterion has already been established. A decision-making model would use surveys, interviews, and questionnaires. Consultants should have expertise in program development and evaluation. In collaboration, any one individual can possess that expertise. It does not necessarily have to be the professional consultant.

Collaborative cultures are not only occurring in many organizations, but they are the way of the future (Fishbaugh, 1997; Senge, 1990). They can exist in business, industry, agencies, institutions, and schools. A collaborative culture is an attitude of collegiality that is envisioned and shared among those involved. Yet, this attitude is extended into a core of supportive behaviors. Among these are an openness, a surfacing of defensiveness, the suspension of unexamined assumptions, a strong emphasis on building meaningful relationships, and a deep, sincere appreciation of diversity in every form one can imagine.

QUESTIONS

1. What are the main ingredients for effective collaborative relationships?

2. What are some of the reasons why collaborative efforts fail?

3. What are some of the barriers and challenges in working collaboratively with others to treat substance abuse?

4. What are the four generic stages of program consultation?

5. Why is it necessary to incorporate evaluation in the planning and designing stages of program consultation?

6. What are some of the characteristics of successful community-based programs?

7. How do status and power impede the process of collaboration?

CHAPTER FOURTEEN

STRUCTURING WORKSHOPS/ SEMINARS IN CONSULTATION

Workshop, training, and *seminar* are terms describing a particular learning venue in which participants pay a predetermined fee to learn in a group-type format. These terms usually reflect different venues. *Seminars* are often associated with graduate courses, and *workshops* are associated with professional continuing education. Both utilize a group format in order to accomplish their respective goals. Many mental health professionals are familiar with continuing education workshops designed to inform practicing and pre-practicing professionals about new or established theories, skills and techniques, and experiences in the field.

If asked for a description of a workshop or seminar, many mental health professionals might conjure up an image of a group of professionals sitting around in a formal manner and listening to an expert speak about an issue relevant to professional practice. If pressed for more detail, the image of a workshop would likely include some activities such as people moving around in small groups. The seminar might be depicted as occurring in a more formal, pedantic setting. These would not be total misperceptions. An argument could be made that seminars and workshops are more different than similar. However, practically speaking, examining advertisements for workshops and seminars that appear in various professional publications does not reveal that there is much difference between the two formats. The terms seem to be used interchangeably in the field. Hence, it is not purposeful here to make an academic delineation. The terms will be used conjointly in the following discussion for the purpose of broadening the consultant's knowledge and skills about how to manage the process of learning and change in a group format.

There are generic workshops/seminars designed to provide information or an experience in just about anything one can imagine. Some workshops are designed for professional practitioners, whereas others are designed for the lay population interested in a particular topic. For the general public, there are workshops covering topics such as assertiveness training, communication skills, ways to improve interpersonal relationships, weight loss, finding partners and keeping them, financial planning, how to buy a home, how to start a business, and the like. The offerings are as numerous for mental health professionals. A review of professional journals revealed workshops and seminars on the family emotional process, hypnosis, marital therapy, brief therapy, divorce mediation, narrative therapy, eye movement desensitization and reprocessing (EMDR), biofeedback, and a host of other offerings.

Workshops pertaining to professional development are led by professionals, whereas workshops open to the general public can be led by anyone who is considered credible enough to do it. There are, of course, "professional trainers" who work in the field. These individuals usually hold at least a bachelor's degree, and many of them have graduate education. These workshop specialists work in a variety of fields and organizations. For instance, the larger banks and business corporations often have their own in-house training departments who employ in-house consultants. These consultants conduct workshops, seminars, and trainings for their employees on a regular basis. Topics can include such things as an orientation for new employees, customer relations, sexual harassment prevention, affirmative action issues, and information regarding new benefits packages. Workshops can also be used to disseminate technical information within these large entities, such as that which might be required for engineers, accountants, logistics personnel, risk-management specialists, and others. Naturally, those leading these in-house workshops, seminars, and trainings will have expertise in the area.

In general, some workshop facilitators will also be formally trained in how to conduct workshops and seminars. Others will use their professional education and subsequent knowledge of human relations and the change process to guide their workshops. Those facilitators who are not formally trained can easily pick up skills by reading any number of popular paperback books on the subject. At the same time, some facilitators have never been trained and have spawned poorly conducted workshops as well as some very well designed ones. Even in the professional ranks, where the facilitators will likely have some professional training at least in the content, some workshops and seminars are better led or facilitated than others. Perhaps the range in facilitator training, which produces such a mix of effective and ineffective presentations, is the reason why a graduate student once mentioned in class, "I don't consider 'workshops' to be consultation."

The impression of workshops held by that particular graduate student may also be shared by many mental health professionals. Although an interesting theoretical inquiry, it is not the purpose of this discussion to argue pro or con on the issue. What follows is a presentation of how workshops/seminars can be conceptualized from a consulting perspective, because there clearly are times when a workshop/seminar type of format can be useful. Workshops/seminars might even be the intervention of choice in some cases. For instance, schools and school districts are often mandated by their respective state departments of education to allocate a specific number of teacher "in-service" days per school year in order for teachers to attend continuing education workshops. When these workshops are scheduled prior to the new school year (usually the week before school opens), they are referred to as *pre-service.* When they occur during the school year, they are usually referred to as *in-service.* The topics of these workshops vary widely, and sometimes attendance is mandated by the school or by the district administration. Proof of attendance for continuing education credits is usually confirmed by a certificate handed out at the end of the workshop or by other observable means, such as a sign-in sheet. Certified and licensed mental health professionals—

including psychologists, psychiatrists, social workers, mental health and professional counselors, school counselors, marriage and family therapists, and psychiatric nurses—are required to accumulate a specified number of these "continuing education" credits for renewal of their respective professional credentials.

CONCEPTUALIZING WORKSHOPS/ SEMINARS AS CONSULTATION

Consultants might also employ a workshop/seminar format as a formal intervention when using Caplan and Caplan's (1993) program-centered administrative consultation model. Likewise, consultants who are employing a behavioral case consultation model might suggest that the consultee attend a workshop on behavioral learning theory in order to help facilitate change in a particular case. Myrick (1977) and Schein (1987, 1999) might suggest consultees and clients attend a workshop or seminar in order to help them generate possible solutions to problems. In all of these cases, the workshop that is recommended is a component of an already established consulting process. The fact that it can be recommended as an intervention suggests that consultants need to be aware of the elements that enhance the success of this format.

Although the topics, participants, and reasons for attending workshops vary widely, workshops have a similar consulting structure: There is a consultant (presenter or workshop leader), consultees (the person/organization who pays), and clients (participants). In the case of school pre-service and in-service workshop trainings, consultants can actually be a member of that school's staff, such as counselors and/or various school administrators. The clients would be the teachers and other appropriate school personnel attending the workshop. The consultees in school examples would be the principals, since they handle the on-site financial responsibilities. Schools can also bring in local or national consultants to deliver a pre-service or in-service workshop to school personnel. Nonetheless, the consultee would still be the person or entity paying for the local or national presenter, and the clients would be anyone attending the workshop.

Similar to consultation in general, workshops can be preventive, developmental, educational, or crisis oriented in nature. For example, school districts might call for a pre-service workshop to go over new guidelines for competencies in middle school. This would be an educational workshop in which the imparting of information was the main agenda. The same school district might ask for volunteers who would be interested in establishing a "buddy" program matching fifth-graders with second-graders. This would be an example of a workshop aimed at preventing problems among the student body while enhancing school pride. A consulting experience in the early 1980s suffices as an example of a crisis-oriented workshop. At that time, I was asked to debrief a group of employees at an organization in which another employee had shot and wounded seven people. The executive director wanted a workshop aimed at debriefing the rest of the staff about this crisis while helping them cope with the stress and trauma. A one-day workshop was planned for the group. This included some debriefing exercises, some information on what to expect in terms of post-traumatic shock and stress, and some skills to help them work through their shock. This crisis workshop was to be followed up by individual sessions that staff members could request in order to help deal with the event at a more personal level.

In general, the structural format of workshops can be oriented more toward content or more toward process. Presenters can choose to deliver the workshop in a didactic or experiential fashion. Presenters can also utilize a combination of the two approaches. The delivery of the workshop is mitigated by the style/preference of the presenter, the content itself, and the population in attendance. The example of the shooting incident was one in which there was a combination of process and information/content, and the delivery included both didactic and experiential approaches. The debriefing component of that particular workshop was the main process/experiential piece. The information and the imparting of skills leaned more toward content and were delivered in a didactic fashion. The overall structure of any given workshop is also determined by the content of the workshop, the length of time allowed for the work, environmental factors such as room space, the number of participants, the request/preferences of the consultee(s), and the general orientation/skill of the presenter(s).

Primary-Level and Secondary-Level Clients

The distinction between levels of clients is a structural issue serving to distinguish workshops/seminars from other types of professional consultation. In a workshop/seminar format for mental health professionals, the term *clients* refers to the practitioners who are attending as well as to those whom the practitioners are attempting to help. In a workshop/seminar format, the *consultee* can be an organization who is paying for its employees to attend. In the case of an organization hiring the consultant, the clients are the organization's employees. In cases where professionals pay for themselves, they become both the consultees and the clients. Public school districts and mental health agencies and organizations often pay for employees to attend a workshop as part of their employment packages. A principal who hires a consultant to conduct an in-service for teachers on increasing student attendance is the consultee. The workshop participants in this case would be the *primary-level clients*. The participants' own clients and clientele would be considered the *secondary-level clients* in the consultation. The secondary-level clients would be the ones indirectly benefiting from the enhanced skills of the professional caregivers who participated in the workshop.

A second reason for drawing the distinction between levels of clients relates to how consultants will go about attempting to draw the clients/participants into a sense of working cohesion. Even though continuing education workshops/seminars are attended by those who have some interest in the given topic, the primary clients/participants may not all deal with the same type of clients. For instance, a workshop/seminar on the latest developments in narrative therapy might draw primary clients/participants from such settings as private practice, residential treatment centers, hospitals, local agencies, and graduate schools. Whereas all of the secondary clients might be mental health clients in some form or another, the secondary client population would likely reflect significant differences along social, political, economic, educational, and diagnostic lines. The more the consultant knows about this secondary-level client population, the better the primary-level clients/participants can be served. Otherwise, assuming that all narrative family therapy principles can be applied in the same manner across diverse populations may prove to be a divisive factor rather than a cohesive one. As suggested in the models of consultation discussed in this text, it is important for consultants to know about the consultees and clients with whom they are working.

Workshops/Seminars as Purchase Models of Consultation

Mostly, workshops and seminars can be considered to be purchase/expert models (Schein, 1999) of consultation. In describing this type of purchase consultation, Schein (p. 7) states that consultees purchase some information or expert service that they, for whatever reason, are unable to provide themselves. In the case of professional development workshops, participants usually self-select their attendance based on need and interest. However, sometimes attendance at a workshop is a stipulation for employment. For instance, the university where I work requires all faculty members to attend a sexual harassment workshop every two years. Not attending can initiate grounds for dismissal.

In addition to professional development/continuing education workshops/seminars, this purchase format can be used in other ways as well. For instance, an organization can decide that morale needs to be improved and hire a consultant to come in with a standard two-day workshop on team building/morale enhancement. In another instance, a consultant may be hired to come in and formulate a two-day workshop on morale/team building based on the results of interviews with the staff (the future workshop participants).

Preformulated and Formulated Workshops

Preformulated workshops are delivered by any number of professional institutes. Many of these institutes are put on or sponsored by various graduate and professional schools and universities. As in the case with many graduate school institutes, the seminars may be year-round. Many professional and lay journals on mental health have numerous advertisements for these institutes, some of which are international. Organizations such as school districts and businesses often use preformulated workshops/seminars as a means of enhancing productivity of its employees. For instance, a school district might choose a number of teachers to attend a workshop on building school morale. This workshop may be located in a different geographical area than the school district itself and may have attendees from a number of different school districts throughout the country. In another instance, an organization might send employees to a two-day workshop on building leadership skills. Again, this format is chosen precisely because it is preformulated and focuses its content on a specific area of perceived need by the organization. Often, the organization decides on the topic without the help of a consultant. In these situations, the success of these preformulated workshops is based on the specific organization having correctly identified the need or problem as well as on having selected the appropriate individuals to attend.

Clearly, in the case where the consultant is hired by a consultee to deliver a standard preformulated workshop, the success of the workshop depends on many things. According to Schein (1999, pp. 7–8), the likelihood of this mode (purchase/expert model) working is influenced by (1) whether the consultee has correctly diagnosed the issue, (2) the extent to which the issue has been accurately and adequately conveyed to the consultant, (3) the ability of the consultee to correctly assess the expertise of the consultant, (4) the extent to which consultees have adequately assessed the potential fallout of such a process, and (5) the extent to which the "issue" can be adequately and meaningfully described to participants.

For example, if employees/clients were suddenly told by their boss that they are being required to attend a workshop aimed at heightening morale, there might be immediate resistance due to the denotation and perceived connotations of the term *morale*. Morale means many things to many people, and a failure to adequately and accurately assess the problem can create more morale problems than there were before! However, from a consulting perspective, the utilization of a preformulated program may not be the best means of achieving the consultee's goals. For instance, imagine a principal wanting the school counselor to conduct a series of workshops aimed at improving student motivation. This simple example reflects the potential for numerous errors, and some of these errors may be fatal flaws that can increase the probability that the workshop will fail to meet the established goals.

For instance, the problem is identified as a lack of student motivation. If the problem has not been identified correctly, then there may well be numerous teachers for whom this workshop is not indicated because they do not have "student motivation problems" in their respective classrooms. Asking them to attend a workshop that they, in fact, do not want or need to attend is building in a structural resistance. As a result, the workshop may be perceived as a waste of time. If it is a waste of time for some teachers, the fallout from this may create problems with teacher motivation. Thus, while attempting to address a motivation concern among students, the consultant may be helping to simply move the motivation problem from students to teachers. Developing a flexible psychological contract with a consultee would allow a consultant to help the principal ensure that the problem had been correctly identified. This is the consultant's responsibility in intervening: to see the present situation, to see the future as best as can be seen, and to be aware and acknowledge the potential fallout of any intervention. This picture can help avert potential problems and can help with another type of error—the probability of solving the wrong problem.

A workshop/seminar format can also be effective when it is not sponsored by a university or set up as a preformulated program. One main difference between preformulated and formulated workshops/seminars is that the former is likely used for continuing education purposes and can attract a wide range of professionals, whereas the latter is mostly used as an intervention with an existing group. For example, organizations sometimes request a consultant(s) to come in from the outside and run or facilitate a retreat. The purpose of the retreat can be varied. A retreat can be used to review the mission of the organization or to formulate a new one, for example. A retreat can also be a time when an organization wants staff to come together for the purpose of building more cohesion. There are also occasions when retreats are used to set up the year's agenda or to work out differences among group members, as might be the case with a city council that is experiencing divisiveness among its elected members.

When there is not a predetermined agenda, consultants will need to formulate or generate one. This is often accomplished by interviewing the potential participants, which should come after having established a psychological contract with the consultee. In cases such as these, the images of a group of professionals sitting around listening to an expert might not be fitting. Instead, participants might be rather active in the process. There are also times when participants may become emotionally reactive, and the tension in the workshop can escalate. The clear difference between a preformulated workshop/seminar and generating a format to address a particular or specific organizational issue is the potential for emotional reactivity in the latter case. This is not to say that there will not be any tension in a preformulated workshop, however. For instance, in my experience, there are many times when participants may vociferously challenge the statements of facilitators and/or other participants. Emotions can run high in these situations, even when the participants do not know each other. However, when participants do not know each other, there may be little cross-over effect. That is, once the workshop/seminar is over, all clients/participants go their own ways. They may or may not change as a result of the emotionally charged experience. Participants who come from the same organization and experience emotional reactivity have a greater fallout potential because participants work together and may have unfinished business among them.

When consultants are asked to generate the structure and format of a workshop for an organization, consultants need to attend to the formulation of the psychological contract. The formulation and structure of the psychological contract used in workshops/seminars is the same as that developed in any other consulting arrangement. What could be different will be how much information consultees may provide to consultants during the initial planning stages of the workshop. It has been my experience that consultees who request a workshop (of any length) often have certain expectations about the amount of information they expect to give to consultants. It is important to have that clarified. At the same time, it is important that consultants gather information in order to better focus the structure and process of the work to help ensure its effectiveness. When this information is gathered, it is critically important that consultants have a conceptual schema in which to organize the flow of information. The conceptual schema will be based on whichever particular theories ground the various aspects of the workshop/seminar.

THEORETICAL GROUNDING OF WORKSHOPS/SEMINARS

Learning Theories

Effective workshops/seminars need to be grounded in theory (see Bardon, 1985; Brown, Pryzwansky, & Schulte, 2001; Gerber, 1999; Glaser, 1981). Workshops/seminars require theories that ground individual and group learning in both structure and the process. The structure of the process of learning in these workshops will be aimed at several levels: the individual, the subgroup, and the whole group.

Although the reasons that participants choose to attend a workshop/seminar vary, the general purpose of workshops/seminars remains relatively constant: to help participants learn something new, help them learn something different, and/or help them relearn what they already knew. The learning that takes place in a structured workshop/seminar format is both the same and quite different from that which takes place in a typical classroom. Traditional classroom teaching can clearly be configured structurally as consultation with consultees variously identified as principals and parents, and clients most often identified as students. However, a major difference between teaching in a traditional classroom and teaching in a workshop/seminar is that the former venue has an inherent hierarchy between teacher and student that is not necessarily useful or appropriate in workshops/seminars. In any case, such an overt hierarchy would run counter to most consultation models (and certainly the models discussed in this text) in terms of how to structure the consulting relationship. Participants in professional workshops and seminars are professionals, and although each may be thought of as a "student," the more appropriate conceptualization is "colleague." This allows for what Caplan (1970) and Caplan and Caplan (1993) refer to as a "coordinate relationship" with consultees and clients (workshop participants).

Sometimes the learning and change that take place will be reflected in a participant's behavioral change. Sometimes it is difficult, if not impossible, to accurately measure the learning and change that take place in workshops. In any case, participation in workshops/seminars is meant to be a learning process. As such, a critical question needing to be answered by consultant/facilitators is, "How do people learn?" The answer to this question theoretically grounds the workshop/seminar. Gerber's (1999, 2001) analysis of various learning theories used in counseling can prove useful to consultants facilitating workshops. Gerber's work on learning theories can be used to help organize the structure and process of workshops/seminars. Moreover, Gerber's presentation is sensitive to diversity.

According to Gerber (1999, 2001), there are four families of learning models: There are *association theories, reinforcement theories, cognition-perceptual theories,* and *cognitive rational/linguistic theories.* These four "families" of models belong to one of two classes based on whether the model has one or two stages. Association theories are considered as one-stage theories because they do not involve a subjective experience or cognitive mediator in the equation. On the other hand, two-stage theories include the person or subjective experience, such as would be described in Bandura's (1977) social learning model of change. Operant conditioning is an example of a learning theory based on reinforcement. Applied models are based on a cognition-perceptual foundation. Examples of applied models of learning include Seligman's work on learned helplessness (Seligman, 1975) as well as Rogers's (1951) and Maslow's (1962) work. Festinger's (1957) cognitive dissonance theory and Ellis's (1962) work on rational restructuring are representative of the fourth family, cognition-rational/linguistic.

These two classes (dividing models into either one or two stages) and four families of learning theory models have three contexts in which they occur: developmental, social, and spiritual. The contextual aspect of learning theories allows for individual differences to be understood, acknowledged, and incorporated into the process of change. The *developmental context* of change is explained in the works of traditional stage theorists such as Piaget (1952). The *social context* acknowledges the importance of the group or system in which an individual is operating. Group process (e.g., Corey & Corey, 2002; Jacobs, Masson, & Harvill, 2002; Peck, 1987; Posthuma, 1999) and family therapy (e.g., Bateson, 1958; Minuchin, 1974) are examples of models based on a social context for learning. The *spiritual context* of change is represented in the works of Fukuyama and Sevig (1997). This context includes issues that have spiritual implications, such as suicide, extramarital sex, criminality, homosexuality, and many others (Gerber, 2001).

The identification of two classes, four families, and three contexts in learning theory models embrace the essential dynamics that will be occurring for individuals during the course of the workshop/seminar. However, the context of workshops/seminars is the group. They have either paid themselves or have had their attendance paid for by a consultee. These individual participants/clients form subgroups during the workshop/seminar. Sometimes the basis for forming these subgroupings is homogeneous. For example, the participants/clients can be comprised of individual clinicians who work together at the same agency. On the other hand, these subgroups can be heterogeneous and comprised of any number of individual associations. No matter how these subgroups form, their sum total comprises and defines the larger, entire group. The group dynamics and change can be gleaned from the works of Peck (1987), Corey and Corey (2002), Jacobs, Masson, and Harvill (2002), and Posthuma (1999). In most cases, it is important to conceptualize the clients/participants more as a working group than as a counseling or therapy group. However, the phases that this working group will go through parallels those same phases established in the research on the process of counseling and therapy groups such as those described by Corey and Corey (2002).

Clearly, the dynamics of workshops/seminars are continuous and complex. In order to be able to work effectively with the multitude of dynamic interactions and processes, it is helpful to conceptualize the process of the change that occurs during workshops/seminars on a global level as well as on an individual level. A useful conceptualization needs to be broad enough in order to incorporate, organize, or subsume the specific dynamics that occur in workshops/seminars. Such a conceptualization of learning and change can help reduce the anxiety associated with undertaking this type of consultation.

A TRIADIC THEORY OF CHANGE

Myrick (1977, 1987) maintains that on a global scale the change process involves three components: discomfort, anxiety, and preparation time. This holds across individuals as well as for changes in a group. The components are sequential. However, similar to the "sequential" stages of consultation, change is not conceptualized as a linear process. Change is geometric and defies linearity in most cases.

Dissonance and Discomfort

Discomfort precedes any change process because discomfort implies a change in the status quo or equilibrium of the individual or group. Without discomfort, there is no need to change. For example, think of what happens when a person wants to initiate an exercise program, lose weight, or quit smoking. At some point, the individual who wants to lose weight decides that, for whatever reason, the weight he or she is at is no longer comfortable. Maybe the individual does not like how he or she looks or feels. Maybe the person no longer fits into favorite clothes comfortably. Perhaps the individual does not like how he or she is treated by others in a weight-conscious society. The same holds true for those desiring to initiate an exercise program or quit smoking. Individuals may not like how lethargic they feel or how out of shape they look. A person who smokes may become uncomfortable with the status quo of her or his health. This person may have become tired of the social pressures and/or the stigmatization attributed to those who smoke. The reasons for the newly experienced discomfort are numerous and idiosyncratic. The key is that the individual, at some point, begins to feel uncomfortable with her or his status quo. Clearly, in most cases, this discomfort has not been sudden. Rather, there has likely been some mild discomfort experienced for a period of time. At some point, this discomfort becomes punctuated and meaningful. In essence, the discomfort that has been experienced on a low-grade level becomes a difference that matters to the person's cognitive, affective, and/or behavioral domains. The individual's status quo becomes challenged to the point that she or he becomes motivated to change.

Cognitive Dissonance Theory.   From a purely cognitive perspective, experiencing discomfort is the same as experiencing cognitive dissonance (Festinger, 1957). According to Festinger's theory, when a person's attitudes, perceptions, beliefs, and opinions about one do not match the information from his or her external environment, the individual's cognitive status quo is disrupted, and he or she experiences dissonance or discomfort. At this point, the individual will attempt to rebalance the system by either resisting the information from the outside or by changing views of self to match the new external information. The individual then reexperiences cognitive consonance, and a new internal status quo is established. This process is cyclical and constant in the flow of the individual's experience.

The examples mentioned here can be conceptualized from a cognitive dissonance theory perspective. The three individuals held a certain view of themselves about how they either felt or looked. At some point, this internal view no longer was consonant with the information coming in from the outside. As a result, each person changed. Perhaps the individuals wanting to diet or begin exercising saw themselves differently when they looked in the mirror, and this dissonance created more motivation to change. Whatever view the person held (the status quo) was disrupted. The person who smoked may have been confronted by a lover enough times that it was no longer comfortable, which created dissonance in the relationship. To eliminate the dissonance and discomfort, the person decided to quit smoking. The relationship began to flourish again, and a new status quo was established.

What is important and relevant to workshops/seminars is the fact that consultants should expect participants to feel uncomfortable on some levels. Attempts to ensure that everyone feels "okay" is not indicated in the triadic theory of change because feeling "okay" implies a status quo that is not impacted by the process. Without discomfort, participants will not change. Clearly, there are levels of discomfort that are more conducive to change. This is similar to the concept of stress, helpful stress, and distress. Clearly, consultants want to help participants feel comfortably uncomfortable. Another critical notion is the fact that in order to learn and change in the process, consultants need to be able to invoke discomfort and monitor its level related to its intended purpose.

Anxiety

As soon as the person allows the discomfort to reach a meaningful level of challenge to the status quo, anxiety sets in. Anxiety is different from fear. Both are perceived threats, but fear is usually associated with a specific object or event. Anxiety can be about many things. It can range from the deeper levels of existential angst, such as that described by Tillich (1952) in *The Courage to Be,* to the anxiety experienced by athletes prior to competition, or to the ambient anxiety students feel throughout the course of their studies. An elder who is being pressured by family members to move into a residential home may experience a profound sense of existential anxiety over giving up independence and the implications surrounding such a move. While sounding ominous, a level of anxiety is also necessary for change.

Structurally, a change in the status quo is inherently an anxious experience. Change always incorporates an element of the unknown. Although discomfort with one's status quo may have reached a significant level, the accompanying overwhelming anxiety may push the individual back to her or his norm for a period of time (or forever) so that the change does not occur. In another instance, if the individual has attempted a similar change in the past and was unsuccessful, the anxiety might be associated with past failed attempts as well as anxiety about being successful and preclude the change. An individual can also be anxious about how the change will impact his or her quality of life and perspective of self, of others, and of the world. A person might also be anxious about how the change will affect intimate and social relationships. Sometimes the experience of anxiety can be so overwhelming that individuals decide to return to the status quo in order to quell their stress. Pondering leaving a long-term relationship and then deciding not to leave because of all of the anxiety associated with the unknown is another good example of how anxiety can inhibit change.

At the same time, not enough anxiety will preclude change in the same fashion as not being uncomfortable enough. The key here is that anxiety is an essential and given component in the process of change. It is the level and timing of anxiety that will mitigate change. In conducting workshops, consultants need to be aware of the levels of anxiety that are in the room. Some participants may ask numerous questions—so many that it affects the group. Other participants may not ask questions at all. Still others might wait until the break to discuss an issue with the workshop leader. In all of these cases, anxiety plays a part. It needs to be present for the workshop to be successful, and it needs to be infused into the structure of workshops and seminars. Activities or experiences during a workshop can be used as attempts to heighten or lessen the amount of anxiety experienced. As is the case with discomfort, there is an optimum amount of anxiety needed to produce change. The amount of anxiety needed for change is idiosyncratic both to individuals and to each group of participants. Asking participants to share something personal likely heightens anxiety, and this can be the case even though participants might know each other. The reason for this is that the sharing takes place in a group format. Consultants can help mediate the effects of too much anxiety by having participants share in smaller groups. These groups can be made up of those who are familiar or unfamiliar, and consultants need to take the time to structure these experiences with the issue of anxiety in mind.

Preparation Time

Preparation time (prep time) refers to the amount of time needed by the individual(s) in order to actually make the change. In the example of the person desiring to leave a long-term relationship, the person may have considered leaving for months or years before she or he finally decides to seriously consider that change to the status quo. For a person wanting to initiate an exercise program, he or she may have been thinking about it for days, months, or even years. The same holds true for the two other examples of individuals wanting to quit smoking or lose weight.

In graduate classes on consultation, I like to ask class members to think about a change that they have made. The change can be small, large, significant, or insignificant. After some typical clarifications regarding when the change process actually "started," the students are given a few minutes to reflect. I then ask the graduate students to determine how long it took them to actually make the change. They are then asked to reveal to the rest of the class only how long it took and whether the change was big or small. Invariably over the years, I have found that there is no set standard for the length of time and the level of change among students in the courses. Interestingly and quite significantly, some of these graduate students can make big changes using only a short amount of prep time. Others report taking a longer prep time in order to make the "same" change (leaving a relationship, for example). As you would expect, small or insignificant changes appeared to require less prep time among the graduate students taking the course over the years. What is important is the fact that change does require a certain amount of time to prepare for the process.

Preparation time is not the same as procrastination. The latter carries the judgment of guilt and irresponsibility. Actually, prep time is a reframe of procrastination and connotes a sense of hopefulness and responsibility. In discussing the topic of change with graduate students, I often suggest to them that since preparation and procrastination both involve time, it is simply a matter of choice as to which orientation one subscribes. Both terms refer to and account for the length of time needed before a change takes place. The difference between them relates to the varying self-prescribed and/or social judgments and the implications attributed to each. Also, prep time does not suggest a time frame in which there is a discrete beginning. It does not have a true ending point either, since humans are always in the process of changing. Nonetheless, prep time frames a period of time in the change process in which individuals (and groups of individuals) evaluate the necessary information to such a degree that they are able to decide, to act, and to change.

Preparation time occurs in two dimensions. Each activity or experience in the workshop needs to have a certain amount of preparation time built into its structure, and the entire workshop should leave participants with both the latitude to change at some future date as well as experiencing some change during the process. Consultants should attempt to "let go" of their expectations of participants' preparation time. Some participants will make significant changes immediately, and some will change later after they leave. It does not matter, because to ensure that everyone changes in the same direction at the same time is simply not realistic. Hence, in order to be more realistic, consultants can make every effort to create an atmosphere of trust and change, and then allow participants to determine for themselves when and how they want to change.

Consultants leading workshops can conceptualize prep time as beginning at the start of the workshop, because the participants need time to adjust to several things, such as the consultant, the format, each other, and expectations set for the day. This is why warm-up exercises can work well. It helps people acclimate to all of these issues. Consultants can also pay particular attention to the sequencing of activities and experiences and utilize debriefing procedures that can help minimize the amount of time needed to change. In terms of sequencing, consultants may sequence a series of activities in such a way as to mediate the amount of discomfort and anxiety and minimize the amount of prep time needed for a change. For instance, starting off with lower-anxiety experiences might help participants adjust to the experience and lessen the amount of time needed to change. On the other hand, high-anxiety experiences might push participants outside of their comfort zone, and in doing so, exacerbate the amount of time needed to change. Personalizing experiences also helps minimize the amount of time needed to change, because participants can readily relate the information to their own experiences and make adjustments quicker.

PSYCHOLOGICAL CONTRACTS
IN WORKSHOPS/SEMINARS

Aside from reframing guilt, irresponsibility, and procrastination, another value of using the concept of preparation time in the change process relates to how consultants will go about formulating psychological contracts with consultees and clients/participants. Workshops and seminars operate on the psychological contracts developed with consultees and the first-level clients/participants. As with any consultation, the psychological contract forms the boundaries around the workshop and helps define the work at hand. In formulating the psychological contract with the consultee, consultants will need to find out as much information as possible about the topic, goals, and information about the first- and secondary-level clients and clientele. In other words, consultants need to know as much as possible about who will be attending the workshop/seminar (first-level clients) and about the secondary-level clients who will indirectly benefit from those attending. Aside from this content information, there are process concerns as well. These will include forming understandings around the issue of consultant "expert and expertise." Some consultants are more versed in content; others are more skilled at the change process. Both may be considered expert, and it is important for consultants to assess the needs of the consultee and the consultant's abilities to deliver what is being requested. The psychological contract will also need to address the relationships that will be developed and the freedom afforded to the consultant to reframe the consultee's topic for the workshop.

Goals and Goal Setting

When a consultee contacts a consultant and requests a workshop, the topic and goals of the workshop will most likely be revealed during that first encounter. Consultants need to assess the plausibility of the goals set forth by the consultee and place that in a context of the amount of prep time that will be needed in order to accomplish the consultee's goals. If the goals are too lofty for the time allotted for the workshop, then adjustments need to be made. It may be that not enough prep time can be built into the structure of the workshop for the participants/clients to change. This would be a fatal flaw in the design of the workshop—especially if the evaluation that is filled out by participants at the end of the day is aimed at determining some behavioral change.

The administrator, discussed in an earlier chapter, who wanted a one-day workshop to enhance employee morale is a good example. The goal of the workshop was clear. However, the format and time allotted to attain the goal was not seen as sufficient in my estimation. A one-day workshop to boost morale may be seen as potentially deleterious. So, not only is it important to agree on the goals for the workshop/seminar, it is also critical for consultants/facilitators to assess the amount of prep time or workshop time needed to accomplish the stated goals. Goals and/or time can and should be adjusted in order to increase the probability of a successful endeavor.

As Schein (1987, 1999) suggests, consultees may or may not have some idea of what they want out of the consultation. As a result, the goals may not be clear to consultees or may not be appropriate for the situation at hand. Identifying and clarifying the goals of the workshop/seminar is a critical step to help ensure effectiveness. During this time, consultants will need to shape the goals to more closely match their preferences and delivery style.

Clearly, there are topics and ensuing workshops that lend themselves more easily to objective goals. For example, a consultant might be called in for a three-hour in-service to help middle and high school teachers develop better teacher-made tests. The advantages and disadvantages of multiple-choice tests can be presented. New information and skills about how to make up effective multiple-choice tests can also be a central component of the workshop. It is a reasonable goal to assume that teachers can make immediate changes in the format, type, and purpose of the tests they give. The same situation might hold true for other topics as well. However, as you would expect, there are topics where the goals and the expected behavioral changes are much more difficult to quantify and measure. For instance, a workshop where the goal is to enhance the classroom environment might be a difficult one to execute in a three-hour workshop, and even more difficult to measure the outcome. The consultant and the consultee need to agree on the topic as well as on the amount of time needed to accomplish the stated goals.

Goals for workshops can be narrowly focused, as in the case of the training to improve teacher-made tests. Goals can also be broad and ambiguous, too. For instance, I was hired to conduct a series of workshops for teachers, where the goal was to improve a particular school's overall school environment. The principal wanted the teachers to be more approachable and to exude a sense of cohesion and belongingness. In other words, the principal wanted to create a collaborative culture (discussed in the last chapter). In this case, the principal did not set any specific goals. Instead, she said she was sure that she would be able to sense a change and did not need to have the improvement quantified or measured. I conducted a series of all-day workshops throughout the school year over the course of three years. Although a formal evaluation was never conducted, the principal said that she liked the results. The psychological contract was effectively executed because this evaluation process was understood between the consultant and the principal.

Consultant Expertise in Workshops/Seminars

Another issue related to the psychological contract concerns the expertise of the consultant. A different way of saying this is, "What is the consultant actually an expert in?" For many mental health professionals, "expertise" can range from being an expert in content to being an expert at process. Ideally, it would be helpful if the consultant were expert in both content and process. The traditional purchase/expert model of consultation is more closely aligned with the content expert. For example, a consultee who has identified the issue as problems with student motivation might want a content expert. This person could be someone who is expert on the latest methods of motivating students in the classroom. In this hypothetical workshop, the consultant might present information to teachers directly related to enhancing their skills in classroom motivation. However, what if the consultant is expert in the process of change in groups and does not possess the same level of content knowledge about motivating students? Does that invalidate the consultant's expertise or preclude his or her ability to perform a workshop when the content does not match denotatively? Clearly, there is an element of ethics involved that relates to consultants practicing outside of their respective areas of expertise. It is precisely in situations such as these where a preformulated workshop/ seminar might stretch the ethics in another direction. That is to say, ethics are also involved in those situations where consultants have a specific area of content expertise that is infused into a preformulated workshop, yet fail to correctly help the consultee identify the problem. This can be another example of the type of error where there is a distinct possibility of delivering a prepackaged workshop aimed at solving the wrong problem. This can be handled in the formulation of the psychological contract.

Diversity in Workshops/Seminars

The question of expertness is important for a variety of reasons. For instance, there are advantages to "not being too expert" in working with some racioethnic minorities and women. Sometimes a content expert approach is not sufficient to create an environment of trust and collegiality. A result can be that the importance of developing meaningful relationships with participants does not occur, and preparation time can be lengthened. Being an expert in the change process suggests that consultants will develop an effective working relationship with consultees and clients/participants. This is consistent with Schein's (1987, 1999) approach to organizational consulting, which has also been argued to be an effective means in working in a diverse society.

Early research into social influence theory (see French & Raven, 1957), social influence theory and counseling (Strong, 1968; Strong & Matross, 1973), and more recent research into social influencer theory and consultation (Smaby, Harrison, & Maddux, 1996; Smaby, Harrison, & Nelson, 1995) provide insight into the issue. Essentially, these researchers and others (e.g., Dorak & Lacrosse, 1975; Strong, 1968; Strong & Matross, 1973) suggest that effective consultants need to be perceived as expert, interpersonally attractive, and trustworthy to consultees and clients. Having information or content knowledge is a component of being perceived as expert, and, at the same time, research suggests that the consultant should have a manner of delivery that is perceived as attractive and trustworthy to consultees and clients/participants (Egan, 1975; Martin, 1978; Martin & Curtis, 1980).

The inherent structure of workshops/seminars is such that the "client" will be comprised of numerous individuals (clients/participants) who may or may not ostensibly have much in common. Racioethnic and gender differences may be punctuated among the clients/participants, and there may be varied socioeconomic, educational, and professional differences. Conducting workshops through a lens of social influence theory helps focus consultants on the relationships with consultees and clients/participants as central to the success of the work to be done. This focus essentially advocates the prizing of individuals in the same manner as Rogers (1951). When this focus is utilized effectively, it allows for the enhanced expression of diversity among consultees and clients/participants at all levels. In this manner, the psychological contract existing between consultants and participants is formulated on a more solid foundation of appreciation, inclusion, openness, trust, and mutuality.

Developing the Relationship and Reframing the Topic

As mentioned, sometimes consultees will have an idea of what they want for a workshop. Sometimes, however, this is not the case. Schein (1999) asserts that consultees will not always actually know what it is that they want and may need some help in identifying and/or clarifying the issues, the goals, and/or the format or method of delivery. A component of the psychological contract in workshops/seminars relates to how consultants will go about reframing the topic with consultees so that the topic becomes more congruent with the consultant's expertise, while enhancing the advantages to the consultees. This component of the psychological contract in these cases requires consultants to focus on their knowledge and experience of learning theory and change in order to help ensure that the agreed on goals can be met.

When consultees request a workshop in which the topic seems to lie just beyond consultants' professionally circumscribed level of content expertise, consultants can draw on their knowledge and expertise of human behavior change and group process in order to effectively shape or reshape the topic to align themselves with the situation at hand. Reframing the topic is both natural and strategic. It occurs naturally in the course of identifying and clarifying the goals. Reframing also is a strategy used by a consultant/facilitator to move the topic "closer to the consultant's home." This is based on the assumption that the closer the topic is to the consultant's expertise, the more comfortable she or he will be. A result is a more effective workshop/seminar.

Another dimension of the strategic aspect of reframing the topic relates to the consultant's own discomfort and anxieties, and the amount of prep time needed to remain genuine and spontaneous during the actual workshop/seminar. Most mental health professionals have heard horror stories about a workshop gone awry. These horror stories can range from the poor structure of the workshop to the manner in which the workshop was conducted. Clients/participants might comment about how the consultant was nervous, condescending, ill-informed, rude, or "not really there." Comments about poor structure might include such references to no breaks, poor food service, and poor lighting or room temperature. Obviously, some of these issues are under the direct control of the consultant/facilitator, and some are not. Leading an effective workshop or seminar requires risk, and with risk comes discomfort and anxiety. Hence, consultants/facilitators need to pay attention to their own levels of discomfort and anxieties and anticipate how these will manifest themselves in the actual workshop/seminar.

Consistent with the principles of the triadic theory of change, consultants/facilitators will experience the change process during the workshop/seminar. So, consultants will need to be aware of how they themselves are being affected during the process of helping others to change. In athletics, it is common for athletes to acknowledge differences between the various levels of stress associated with athletic performance. There is an optimum level of stress or arousal for optimum athletic performance. Too little stress can produce sub-par performances, and too much stress can cause athletes to shut down. Similarly, consultants/facilitators who experience too much discomfort and anxiety during the actual workshop may be less effective than they otherwise could be. Reframing the topic helps consultants/facilitators bring their stress to optimal performance levels.

STRUCTURAL ISSUES IN FORMULATING WORKSHOPS/SEMINARS

Consultants can structure the format of the workshop/seminar in a variety of ways, such as employing a didactic format, an experiential format, or a combination of the two in order to attain the goals set for the workshop/seminar. A didactic presentation assumes that there is an expert facilitator who has some knowledge or information deemed important for the clients/participants to learn. An experiential workshop, one that has clients/participants involved in an activity or activities, assumes that clients/participants have the ability to glean or integrate the necessary information if given the opportunity to experience it. A workshop on gestalt techniques in which the facilitator asks clients/participants to actually experience the technique would be an example of an experiential workshop or activity.

Bandura (1977) believes that actually performing the behavior is the most efficacious manner in which clients/participants learn new behaviors. The next most effective means is what is referred to as *vicarious experience* in which clients/participants observe the new behavior to be performed. Verbal persuasion and emotional arousal are the third and fourth means of learning, respectively. These two are seen as less effective in creating behavior change. If the goal is to have the clients/participants change and try new behaviors, it would be important that the clients/participants have the in vivo opportunities to try out the behavior. In an example of a workshop designed to improve teacher-made tests, the consultant who bases the format on Bandura's learning theory might allow time for teachers to actually write test questions and then have the opportunity to review and discuss. In this fashion, teachers are learning from their performance accomplishments as well as vicariously from other teachers in the workshop. This type of double-looping format to learning would not only be congruent with the Bandura's model but it would also be combining different modes of learning. A result is an enhanced and effective workshop experience.

Location

The issue of location is a simple one on some levels and a rather profound issue on other levels. There are advantages and disadvantages to running a workshop or seminar "on site." Similarly, there are pros and cons of running a workshop "off site." In many cases, structural constraints (e.g., money, size of group, etc.) will dictate where the workshop will take place. Moreover, consultants/facilitators may or may not have the ability to determine or even have much input into where the workshop/seminar will take place. Running a workshop off site places it on neutral ground, where theoretically everyone starts off as "equals." Conducting a workshop off site also creates a type of "nonworking work atmosphere." It also helps employees see the commitment of management or the administrative team because of the effort taken to find a special place. Since conducting workshops off site often means that meals may or may not be provided at the site, consultants need to be prepared to build in travel time for meals.

On site may mean that the workshop is being conducted on the grounds of a mental health center or on school grounds as opposed to a neutral environment such as a hotel convention room. On site allows some members of the host organization to enjoy the convenience of attending. At the same time, these individuals will likely maintain access to their work-related duties, such as seeing emergencies, seeing clients that are difficult to see at other times, and attending meetings not associated with the workshop. Often, these individuals leave word to have them (and the workshop) interrupted if a certain client calls or if there is an emergency. Clearly, the number of potential interruptions can be numerous. However, if conducted on site at an agency, there are instances where professionals from other organizations attend and get a chance to actually see the agency and meet other staff with whom they may have had phone or email contact. It may be that many of the participants have heard of the center or actually refer clients to this particular center, and this is the first chance they have had to actually see the professional to whom they are referring clients. In this type of situation, the interruptions seem to be worth the trade-off of networking on site. Consultants need to be flexible and not attempt to control what cannot be controlled. Treating participants like the hardworking, dedicated, and competent clinicians they are by being flexible as they go about discharging their duties will help foster a good working relationship between consultant and consultees. Moving through the interruptions smoothly also lessens each interruption's impact on the learning process of the group.

Format

If the workshop will include some didactic material, it is best to get the information out early—certainly before lunch if possible. After lunch is reserved for activities and moving people around in order to keep up motivation and keep the adrenaline pumping. Wherever appropriate, try to present a demonstration of what is being presented. Either the consultant can demonstrate, or there can be volunteers from among the participants. Consultants can present information and then include an experience or they can initiate the experience and then debrief the participants with information. Sometimes it is best to have the exercise first and then debrief it. Other times, the reverse would be more appropriate. In setting up group exercises, consultants should give only minimal directions first, and these directions should indicate only how the groups should be convened. Once the groups have formed, then the detailed directions can be promulgated to participants. When consultants give directions for the exercise before the groups have been formed, it is almost always the case that the directions need to be repeated.

"Chips in the Bank"

Wittmer and Myrick (1974) use the term *chips in the bank* to allude to an overall approach to workshops/seminars that specifically addresses the relationship between the consultant and the consultees/clients/participants. Consultants should employ this global paradigm throughout the workshop/seminar presentation. Not surprisingly, "chips in the bank" is an analogy borrowed from the field of banking to describe the manner in which consultants/facilitators go about generating rapport and involvement during the workshop or seminar. A bank account is empty until one puts money into it. Likewise, the relationship consultants have with workshop participants is empty until the consultant begins putting "money" into it. As more and more money is put into it, the bank account becomes bigger and bigger. When the metaphor is translated into consultation, it demonstrates that consultants need to pay attention to the amount of positive reinforcement that they are invoking during the workshop. Every time something positive is reinforced by the consultant, the bank account grows.

When consultants need to more directly alter perceptions, correct misinformation, add new information, or confront participants at points during the experience, consultants "cash out or withdraw some of the money from the bank account" during the process. Confrontation usually "costs" the relationship something, however temporary or permanent. So, putting "chips in the bank" helps keep the ledger in favor of facilitative communication and change. This approach is simple and profound at the same time. On a more global scale, the concept of "chips in the bank" is a metaphor used to describe effective communication skills, including being warm, empathetic, nonjudgmental, respectful, and genuine. All of these facilitative conditions, when invoked, serve to put "chips in the bank."

Know the Audience

In the pre-entry preparation, it is very important that consultants learn about the people with whom they will be working. Not only is this common sense, but it is seen as professionalizing the consultation. This *professionalization* results from the consultant taking the time, as with any consultation, to learn about the consultees and clients. Even though not all of the following information will be available, consultants need to glean as much data as possible. That information includes, but is not limited to (1) the number of those attending, (2) the gender breakdown, (3) the age ranges and mode or mean age, (4) the racioethnicity breakdown, (5) the number of years in the field, (6) the number and type of disabilities among participants, and (7) the participants' specific jobs and job descriptions.

This demographic information is important for several reasons. Primarily, it allows consultants to "see" or visualize their participants before actually working with them. In addition, it allows consultants the ability to predict certain types of resistances that may occur. For instance, if the group of participants is made up of primarily veterans with only a few newcomers to the field, consultants can anticipate that this discrepancy may show up in those periods of the workshop where suggestions are given on ways to improve clinical service. Consultants might not be wrong in assuming that the veterans would jump at a chance to educate the newcomers. Previous knowledge of the participants also helps consultants conceptualize an approach that will be meaningful. For example, if there are more neophytes than veterans attending, the level of assumed knowledge changes. Consultants can gear information to the appropriate levels.

A second significant element of knowing the participants ahead of time allows for consultants to preconfigure groupings that might take place during the workshop. For instance, participants might be conceptualized as heterogeneous or homogenous. In some instances, grouping participants according to their differences is more appropriate than grouping them based on similarities. This would be the case in which the consultant/facilitator uses the veterans as fulcrums around which a group of newcomers to the field are convened in a group during the workshop. In this heterogeneous configuration, information is shared among participants and becomes meaningful because of the mix of veterans and neophytes. In another instance, a homogeneous group might be more indicated. For instance, a consultant might recognize how participants initially congregate together and decide to keep it that way for the workshop. A group of school counselors convening for a pre-service prior to the start of a new school year would probably want to sit together with other counselor/friends in order to catch up on the summer vacation news. In this situation, asking these friendly school counselors to sit with others with whom they do not regularly associate could be counterproductive. Skilled consultants/facilitators can work with whatever configuration is necessary.

Make No Assumptions

At the same time that one is gleaning information about the participants, it is also important that consultants not make assumptions about what participants know and/or do not know. Clearly, some assumptions will be necessary; these are not what is being referred to here, however. The issue with making assumptions about what participants know or do not know relates more to the pacing of the workshop. Consultants who assume that participants know something that they, in fact, do not know cause dissonance among participants who are not familiar with the information. This disrupts the flow of the experience. Consultants can be "way ahead" of the group by assuming things that are, in fact, not true for the participants. The problem is that each individual participant may assume that other participants know more or at least know what the consultant is talking about when this is not the case. If nobody says anything, there is a distinct possibility that no one gets the information because everyone assumed that everyone else knew what was being discussed. Think of how often that happens in a graduate class in counseling or social work. Unless someone speaks up, the consultant may only have minimal cues that suggest that the information is not being received. Asking participants if they are familiar with a certain concept or a certain work can be helpful, although some participants may not be forthcoming out of anxiety, fear, or embarrassment. Nonetheless, consultants can sense the group's knowledge simply by paying attention to the facial expressions of participants. Obviously, many perplexed faces would suggest something. Silences might as well.

The other element involved in not making assumptions relates to the level of presentation. Even though the participants may be well educated, this does not mean that everyone was educated in the same way or about the same things. An obvious example occurs in participants who graduate from different counseling or social work programs. Not all programs are alike. Social work programs can be generalist programs or more clinically oriented. One counseling program can emphasize a cognitive-behavioral approach, whereas another one might focus on gestalt or person-centered therapeutic approaches. Although all participants may have a passing knowledge of the basic principles involved, some will be better versed in certain areas than others. Assuming the lowest common denominator and working off that platform can be very helpful. In other words, when working with a group of mental health professionals, one can assume that all have some knowledge of counseling, and all will have a variation on a given theory. Using the platform of "counseling" and the common assumptions almost ensures that every participant can understand what the facilitator is talking about. Then, once the common platform has been discerned, consultants can begin branching off into specialized areas, such as gestalt or cognitive-behavioral approaches.

Warm-Ups

As mentioned, it is helpful to use a warm-up for workshops. This is true for almost every workshop or seminar. Granted, there will be occasions when it appears that there is not enough time to do a warm-up; however, something to start things off is advisable, even in tight time lines, because it helps participants adjust to their surroundings. For instance, an in-service for counselors might last only 45 minutes once a month. Even though the participants might be very familiar to the consultant (who might also be a school counselor), a short warm-up to get participants "in the room" can prepare the counselors for the information that will follow.

Warm-ups do not have to be long to be effective. In any case, it is helpful if consultants pay attention to warm-ups so that (1) they are somewhat personal, (2) they establish a sense of common ground or commonality with other participants, (3) they are relevant to the upcoming workshop, and (4) they set the tone and intensity of what is to follow. For example, a workshop on motivating students might be started off with a warm-up asking participants to share a time when they felt most motivated in school and then clarify the conditions that helped them feel motivated. A warm-up for school counselors meeting for the first time since school was out in order to plan the year's school spirit activities might ask them to share something they did during their time off that was out of the ordinary for them and left them feeling excited.

Some participants will have attended many workshops and will perhaps be resistant to or choose not to participate in warm-up exercises. In such a situation, it is permissible to have them pass on the exercise. Not only will this plant "chips in the bank" but it will also set the tone of voluntary participation for the other workshop participants. If the purpose of refusing to participate was to assess the level of consultant credibility, flexibility, and control issues, the test was passed. What is most helpful is to mention the voluntary nature of the warm-up or of the workshop as a whole.

Time and Breaks

Start on time and end early. Initiating the workshop on time will set the stage for what is expected during breaks and after lunch. Many times, participants will be attending workshops and will want time to discuss the issues, visit with others in the field, or just relax. If there are refreshments in the morning, allow time for the refreshments to complete their appointed task, which is to nourish and to promote connections. In order to start on time, it is important for consultants to know if refreshments will be served. In addition, start breaks on time and give the participants enough time to complete their break. Effective consultants/facilitators time their breaks to the participants' needs. In a workshop in which some recovering addicts will attend, they might still smoke. It takes about 10 to 15 minutes to smoke a cigarette, and breaks can accommodate this ritual or habit. Although smoking may go against the consultant's values, the participants will surely appreciate the empathy. A large number of female participants concomitant with a paltry number of restrooms or stalls will require a longer break to accommodate everyone.

Use breaks to make up time or to keep the workshop on time. In other words, if the workshop is running behind in time, shorten the breaks if possible to make up for it. If the workshop is going faster than anticipated, lengthen the break. An effective, if not unusual, method of keeping time under some control during workshop breaks and lunches is to ask participants to come back at a specific time. It is critical to make that specific time salient. Asking participants to return at the top of the hour or at 15 minutes past the hour, or to take a "10-minute" break will often have the result of not having everyone ready to start on time. By giving a salient time, such as "Take an 11½-minute break," or saying, "We will start up again after lunch at 1:06 pm" will tend to stick in participants' minds and will help ensure that they pay attention to the time because it is unusual or salient.

Goals and What to Walk Away With

A related topic to the issue of assumptions is the goal or goals that are desired. Given that there are numerous participants, it does not seem very reasonable to have everyone leave with the same level of knowledge or information. Moreover, in terms of the preparation time (discussed earlier in this chapter), it is not reasonable to expect that all participants will utilize the information presented in the workshop or seminar at the same time. Some participants will need a longer prep time to grasp the nuances of the information. Others will find more immediate face validity and be able to utilize the information readily. Having clear and specified goals for the workshop can help participants feel successful in terms of learning something new.

Consultants/facilitators need to look for a simple goal or goals that everyone can attain at the conclusion of the workshop. This does not mean that everyone will be operating at the same professional level of competence. It does suggest that having lofty goals might leave some participants out of the loop. Finding the lowest common meaningful goal can help ensure the feelings of success among participants. When participants feel successful, it seems likely that they would be more enthusiastic to try something new. Perhaps the most significant aspect of setting a simple goal or goals that are attainable by all participants relates to the fact that in most cases the participants are already successful at their work.

One final note: Imagine that you have worked very hard putting together a dynamic workshop that will include overheads or a computer presentation. Now imagine not being able to locate a plug. Imagine a lightbulb burning out in the overhead. Imagine a floppy disc malfunctioning in a power-point presentation. Imagine that you have planned the group activities to allow for groups to form in circles only to discover that the room reserved for the workshop is an auditorium with fixed chairs. Clearly, anticipate and plan for what can go wrong. By doing so, you will find that much will go right.

SUMMARY

Most of the time, workshops are considered to be purchase models of consultation. Consultees can purchase preformulated workshops as well as individually designed ones. When preformulated workshops are used, the assumptions of effectiveness rest on the extent to which the consultee has adequately and correctly identified the need. In all situations, there are primary- and secondary-level clients. Primary clients in the consultation are participants in attendance; secondary clients are the clients of the clients. Consultants should endeavor to glean as much information as possible about the characteristics of both client systems prior to the workshop or seminar.

Workshops/seminars can be effective means of consulting, and this is especially true when they are grounded in a learning theory. Gerber's (1999) analysis of learning theories suggests that there are four types: association theories, reinforcement theories, cognition perceptual theories, and cognitive rational/linguistic theories. Myrick (1977, 1987) also advances a simple learning theory that is helpful in conducting workshops and seminars. The triadic theory of change includes discomfort, anxiety, and preparation time, and consultants are urged to incorporate this conceptualization throughout their work with consultees and clients. It is important to remember that consultants, themselves, will be experiencing the change process as well.

The psychological contract needs to be formulated prior to the delivery of workshops/seminars services. During this process, consultants need to determine the extent to which the consultee has identified a goal and how flexible that goal is. Consultants can then embark on an exploration of their own expertise to deliver the service while helping the consultee reframe the goal into one that is more congruent with the time allotted and the tasks to be accomplished. Consultants can be experts in content, the change process, and/or a combination of the two. In any case, there are several pre-service considerations that consultants need to contemplate. These relate to location, format, awareness of the audience, warm-ups, timed breaks, and manageable goals. The amount of attention paid to the details of the pre-entry consideration often determines the success of the workshop or seminar.

QUESTIONS

1. In recalling a time when you have attended a workshop or seminar, what characteristics did the consultant have?

2. What learning theory seemed to be in operation?

3. What might be some reasons why workshops and seminars are not considered consultation?

4. What considerations make workshops and seminars consultation?

5. What is the triadic theory of change?

6. Why is the formulation of the psychological contract an important undertaking in developing workshops?

7. Who are primary and secondary clients?

8. What is one thing that you have learned from this chapter?

REFERENCES

Abelson, R., & Nielson, K. (1967). History of ethics. In P. Edwards (Ed.), *The encyclopedia of philosophy* (Vol. 3). New York: Macmillan.

Amatea, E. S., & Brown, B. E. (2000). Counselor and the family: An ecosystemic approach. In J. Wittmer (Ed.), *Managing your school counseling programs: K–12 developmental strategies* (pp. 192–199). Minneapolis: Educational Media.

American Counseling Association. (1995). *Code of ethics and standards of practice.* Alexandria, VA: Author.

American Psychiatric Association. (2000). *Diagnostic and statistics manual (4th ed.), text revised.* Washington, DC: Author.

American Psychological Association. (1973). *Ethical principles in the conduct of research with human participants.* Washington, DC: Author.

American Psychological Association. (1992). APA Counsel of Representatives adopts new AIDS policies. *Psychology and AIDS Exchange, 7*(1), 4–32.

American Psychological Association. (2003). *Ethical principles of psychologists and code of conduct.* Washington, DC: Author.

Argyris, C. (1957). *Personality and organization.* New York: Harper and Row.

Argyris, C. (1970). *Intervention theory and method: A behavioral science view.* Reading, MA: Addison-Wesley.

Astor, R. A., Pinter, R. O., & Duncan, B. B. (1998). Ecological approaches to mental health consultation with teachers on issues related to youth and school violence. *Journal of Negro Education, 65*(3), 336–355.

Astrachan, B. M., & Astrachan, J. H. (2000). The changing psychological contract in the workplace. In E. B. Klein, F. Gabelnick, & P. Herr (Eds.), *Dynamic consultation in a changing* workplace. Madison, CT: Psychosocial Press.

Atler, J. (1995, May 29). What works. *Newsweek,* 18–24.

Attneave, C. (1982). American Indians and Alaska Native families: Emigrants in their own homeland. In M. McGoldrick, J. K. Pierce, & J. Giordano (Eds.), *Ethnicity and family therapy* (pp. 55–83). New York: Guilford.

Babcock, N. L., & Pryswansky, W. B. (1983). Models of consultation: Preferences of educational professional at five stages of service. *Journal of School Psychology, 21,* 359–366.

Backer, T. E. (1991). *Drug abuse technology transfer.* Rockville, MD: NIDA.

Backer, T. E., David, S. L., & Soucy, G. (1995). *Reviewing the behavioral science knowledge based on technology transfer* (pp. 1–41). Rockville, MD: National Institute of Drug Abuse. Publication #155.

Backer, T. E., Liberman, R. P., & Kuehnel, T. G. (1986). Dissemination and adoption of innovative psychosocial interventions. *Journal of Consulting and Clinical Psychology, 54,* 111–118.

Backer, T. E., Rogers, E. M., & Sopory, P. (1992). *Designing health community campaigns: What works?* Thousand Oaks, CA: Sage.

Baier, K. (1958). *The moral point of view.* Ithaca, NY: Cornell University.

Ball, J. C., Corty, E., Petroski, S. P., & Bond, H. (1987). Treatment effectiveness: Medical staff and services provided to 2,394 patients at methadone programs in three states. *National Institute on Drug Abuse: Research Monograph Series #76,* 175–181.

Ball, J. C., & Ross, A. (1991). *The effectiveness of methadone maintenance treatment.* New York: Springer-Verlag.

Bandura, A. (1977). *Social learning theory.* Englewood Cliffs, NJ: Prentice-Hall.

Barak, A., & LaCrosse, M. B. (1975). Multidimensional perceptions of counselor behavior. *Journal of Counseling Psychology, 22,* 471–476.

Bardon, J. I. (1985). Toward a consultation meta-theory: On the verge of a breakthrough. *The Counseling Psychologist, 13*(3), 69–72.

Basseches, M. (1984). *Dialectical thinking and adult development.* Norwood, NJ: Ablex.

Bateson, G. (1951). Information and codification: A philosophical approach. In J. Ruesch & G. Bateson (Eds.), *Communication: The social matrix of psychiatry.* New York: Norton.

Bateson, G. (1958). *Naven, a survey of the problems suggested by a composite picture of a New Guinea tribe drawn from three points of view.* Stanford, CA: Stanford University Press.

Baxter, J., & Wright, E. O. (2000). The glass ceiling hypothesis. A comparative study of the United

States, Sweden, and Australia. *Gender and Society, 14*(2), 275–294.

Beauchamp, T. L., & Childress, J. F. (1979). *Principles of biomedical ethics.* Oxford University Press.

Beer, M. (1980). *Organizational change and development: A systems view.* Glenview, IL: Scott Foresman.

Bell, D. (1976). *The post-industrial society.* New York: Harper and Row.

Benhabib, S. (1992). *Situating the self: Gender, community and postmodernism in contemporary ethics.* Cambridge: Polity Press.

Bennett, J. (1993). *Negation and abstention: Two theories of allowing.* Chicago: University of Chicago Press.

Bennett, M. J. (1986). A developmental approach to training for intercultural sensitivity. *International Journal of Intercultural Relations, 10,* 179–196.

Bergan, J. R. (1977). *Behavioral consultation.* Columbus, OH: Charles E. Merrill.

Bergan, J. R., & Kratochwill, T. R. (1990). *Behavioral consultation and therapy.* New York: Plenum.

Bergan, J. R., & Tombari, M. (1976). Consultant skill and efficiency and the implementation and outcomes of consultation. *Journal of School Psychology, 14,* 3–13.

Bersoff, D. N. (1995). *Ethical conflicts in psychology.* Washington, DC: American Psychological Association.

Betan, E. J. (1997). Toward a hermeneutic model of ethical decision-making in clinical practice. *Ethics and Behavior, 7,* 347–365.

Bond, C. F. (1982). Social facilitation: A self-presentational view. *Journal of Personality and Social Psychology, 42,* 1042–1050.

Bond, T. (1993). *Standards of ethics for counseling in action.* London: Sage.

Boss, R. W. (1985). The psychological contract: A key to effective organizational consultation. *Consultation, 4*(4), 284–304.

Bowlby, J. (1969). *Attachment and loss* (Vol. 1: Attachment). New York: Basic Books.

Bowser, B. P., & Hunt, R. G. (1996) *Impacts of racism on white Americans.* London: Sage.

Brems, C. (2001). *Basic skills in psychotherapy and counseling.* Pacific Grove, CA: Brooks/Cole.

Brenner, O. C., Tomkiewicz, T., & Schein, V. E. (1989). The relationship between sex role stereotypes and requisite management characteristics revisited. *Academy of Management Journal, 32,* 662–669.

Brief, A. P. (1998). *Attitudes in and around organizations.* Thousand Oaks, CA: Sage.

Brooks, L. (1990). Recent developments in theory building. In D. Brown & L. Brooks (Eds.), *Career choice and development* (pp. 364–394). San Francisco: Jossey-Bass.

Brown, B. S. (1987). Networking between research and service delivery. *International Journal of the Addictions, 22,* 301–317.

Brown, B. S. (2000). From research to practice: The bridge is out and the water is rising. *Advancing in Medical Sociology, 7,* 345–365.

Brown, D. (1996). Brown's values-based, holistic model of career and life-role choices and satisfaction. In D. Brown, L. Brooks, & Associates (Eds.), *Career choice and development* (pp. 337–372). San Francisco: Jossey-Bass.

Brown, D. (2002). The role of work and cultural values in occupational choice, satisfaction, and success: A theoretical statement. *Journal of Counseling and Development, 80,* 48–56.

Brown, D., Minor, C. W., & Jepsen, D. A. (1991). The opinions of minorities preparing for work: Report of the second NCDA National Survey. *Career Development Quarterly, 40,* 5–19.

Brown, D., Pryzwansky, W. B., & Schulte, A. C. (2001). *Psychological consultation: Introduction to theory and practice* (5th ed.). Boston: Allyn and Bacon.

Brown, D., & Schulte, A. (1987). A social learning model of consultation. *Professional Psychology: Research and Practice, 18,* 283–287.

Brown, M. T. (1995). The career development of African Americans: Theoretical and empirical issues. In F. T. Leong (Ed.), *Career development and vocational behavior of racial and ethnic minorities* (pp. 7–30). Mahwah, NJ: Erlbaum.

Burbules, N. C. (1993). *Dialogue in teaching.* New York: Teachers College Press.

Burck, H. D., & Peterson, G. W. (1975). Needed: More evaluation, not research. *Personnel and Guidance Journal, 53,* 563–569.

Burke, R. J. (1994). Canadian business students' attitudes towards women as managers. *Psychological Reports, 75,* 1123–1129.

Burke, R. J., & McKeen, C. A. (1992). Women in management. In C. L. Cooper & I. T. Robertson (Eds.), *International review of industrial and organizational psychology* (pp. 245–283). New York: Wiley.

Burns, C. M., & D'Avanzo, C. E. (1993). Alcohol and other drug abuse in culturally diverse populations: Hispanics and Southeast Asians. *Faculty Resource.* Washington, DC: Cosmos Corporation.

Caldecott, L., & Leland, S. (1983). *Reclaim the Earth: Women speak out for life on earth.* London: Women's Press.

Caplan, G. (1970). *The theory and practice of mental health consultation.* New York: Basic Books.

Caplan, G., & Caplan, R. B. (1993). *Mental health consultation and collaboration.* San Francisco: Jossey-Bass.

Carter, B., & McGoldrick, M. (2000). *The expanded family life-cycle* (3rd ed.). Boston: Allyn and Bacon.

Carter, R. T. (1991). Cultural values: A review of the empirical literature and implications for counseling. *Journal of Counseling and Development, 70,* 164–173.

Center on Addiction and Substance Abuse. (1998). *Behind bars: Substance abuse and America's prison population.* [Online]. Available: http://www.casacolumbia.org.

Cheatham, H. E. (1990). Africentricity and the career development of African Americans. *The Career Development Quarterly, 38,* 334–346.

Chestang, L. (1972). Character development in a hostile environment. (Occasional Paper No. 3). School of Social Service Administration, University of Chicago.

Children's Defense Fund. (2001a, August 14). Child abuse and neglect, foster care, and adoption: Child abuse and neglect fact sheet. [Online]. Available: http://www.childrensdefense.org.child_abuse.htm.

Children's Defense Fund. (2001b, August 14). New data show high poverty levels for children in every state. [Online]. Available: http://www.childrens defense.org/release010806.htm.

Children's Defense Fund. (2001c, August 14). Poverty matters: The cost of child poverty in America. [Online]. Available: http://www.childrens defense.org/fair start-povmat.htm.

Christenson, S. L., & Sheridan, S. M. (2001). *Schools and families.* New York: Guilford.

Cimmarusti, R. A. (1996). Exploring aspects of Filipino-American families. *Journal of Marriage and Family Therapy, 22,* 205–217.

Clark, B. (1972). The organizational saga in higher education. *Administrative Science Quarterly, 17,* 178–184.

Cocks, J. (1989). *The oppositional imagination: Feminism, critique, and political theory.* New York: Routledge.

Conoley, C. W., Conoley, J. C., Ivey, D. C., & Scheel, M. J. (1991). Enhancing consultation by matching the consultee's perspective. *Journal of Counseling and Development, 69,* 546–549.

Conoley, J. C., & Conoley, C. W. (1982). *School consultation: A guide to practice and training.* New York: Pergamon.

Corey, G., Corey, M. S., & Callanan, P. (1979). *Professional and ethical issues in counseling and psychotherapy.* Monterey, CA: Brooks/Cole.

Corey, G., Corey, M. S., & Callanan, P. (1993). *Issues and ethics in the helping professions.* Pacific Grove, CA: Brooks/Cole.

Corey, M. S., & Corey, G. (2002). *Groups: Process and practice* (6th ed.). Pacific Grove, CA: Brooks/Cole.

Cottone, R. R. (2001). A social constructivism model of ethical decision-making. *Journal of Counseling and Development, 79,* 39–45.

Cottone, R. R., & Claus, R. E. (2000). Ethical decision-making models: A review of the literature. *Journal of Counseling and Development, 78,* 275–283.

Council on Social Work Education. (1992). *Curriculum policy statement for Master's degree programs in social work education.* Alexandria, VA: Author.

Cox, T. (1993). *Cultural diversity in organizations: Theory, research, and practice.* San Francisco: Berrett-Koehler.

Dahir, C. A. & Campbell, C. A. (1997). *Sharing the vision: The National Standards.* Washington, DC: American School Counselors Association.

Daniels, M. H., Mines, R., & Gressard, C. (1981). A meta-model for evaluating counseling programs. *Personnel and Guidance Journal, 59,* 578–582.

Darity, W. (1983). The managerial class and the surplus population. *Society, 21,* 54–62.

Davidson, M. (1983). *Uncommon sense: The life and thought of Ludwig von Bertalanffy (1901–1972), father of general systems theory.* Boston: Houghton Mifflin.

Deal, T. E., & Kennedy, A. A. (1982). *Corporate cultures: The rites and rituals of corporate life.* Reading, MA: Addison-Wesley.

Denison, D. R., & Mishra, A. K. (1995). Toward a theory of organizational culture and effectiveness. *Organization Science, 6(2),* 204–223.

de Shazer, S. (1985). *Keys to solutions in brief therapy.* New York: W. W. Norton.

Dettmer, P., Thurston, L. P., & Dyck, N. (1993). *Consultation, collaboration, and teamwork for students with special needs.* Boston: Allyn and Bacon.

Devine, P. G. (1989). Stereotypes and prejudice: Their automatic and controlled components. *Journal of Personality and Social Psychology, 56,* 5–18.

Devine, P. G., Monteith, M. J., Zuwernick, J. R., & Elliott, A. J. (1991). Prejudice with and without compunction. *Journal of Personality and Social Psychology, 60,* 817–830.

Devore, W., & Schlesinger, E. G. (1981). *Ethnic-sensitive social work.* St. Louis, MO: C. V. Mosby.

Dinger, T. J. (1997, April). *Do ethical decision-making models really work? An empirical study.* Paper presented at the American Counseling Association World Conference, Orlando, FL.

Dinkmeyer, D., & Caldwell, E. (1970). *Developmental counseling and guidance: A comprehensive school approach.* New York: McGraw-Hill.

Dinkmeyer, D., & Carlson, J. (1973). *Consulting.* Columbus, OH: Charles E. Merrill.

Dollarhide, C. T., & Saginak, K. A. (2003). *School counseling in the secondary school.* Boston: Allyn and Bacon.

Donagan, A. (1977). *The theory of morality.* Chicago: University of Chicago Press.

Dorn, F. J. (1984). The social influence model: A social-psychological approach to counseling. *Personnel and Guidance Journal, 62*(3), 342–345.

Dougherty, A. M. (1990). *Consultation: Practice and perspectives.* Pacific Grove, CA: Brooks/Cole.

Doweiko, H. E. (1990). *Concepts of chemical dependency.* Pacific Grove, CA: Brooks/Cole.

Downing, J., & Harrison, T. C. (1992). Solutions and school counseling. *The School Counselor, 39*(5), 327–332.

Drane, J. F. (1982). Ethics and psychotherapy: A philosophical perspective. In M. Rosenbaum (Ed.), *Ethics and values in psychotherapy.* New York: Free Press.

Drucker, P. F. (1969). *The age of discontinuity: Guidelines to our changing society.* New York: Harper and Row.

Dryfoos, J. G. (1996). Adolescents at risk: Shaping programs to fit the need. *Journal of Negro Education, 65,* 5–18.

Dunphy, D. C., & Stace, D. A. (1988). Transformational and coercive strategies for planned organizational change: Beyond the OD model. *Organizational Studies, 9,* 22–45.

Egan, G. (1975). *The skilled helper.* Monterey, CA: Brooks/Cole.

Egan, G. (2002). *The skilled helper* (3rd ed.). Pacific Grove, CA: Brooks/Cole.

Ekins, P. (Ed.). (1986). *The living economy: A new economics in the making.* London: Routledge.

Ellis, A. (1958). Rational psychotherapy. *Journal of General Psychology, 59,* 35–49.

Ellis, A. (1962). *Reason and emotion in psychotherapy.* New York: L. Stuart.

Ellis, A. (1973). *Humanistic psychotherapy: The rational-emotive approach.* New York: Julian Press.

Ellis, R. A. (1998). Filling the prevention gap: Multi-factor, multi-system, multi-level intervention. *Journal of Primary Prevention, 19,* 57–71.

Ely, R. J. (1995). The power in demography: Women's social constructions of gender identity at work. *Academy of Management Journal, 38,* 589–634.

English, J. T. (1992). Pluralism: Building community for the 21st century. *Counselor Education and Supervision, 32,* 83–90.

Erchul, W. P. (1987). A relational communication analysis of control in school consultation. *Professional School Psychology, 2,* 113–124.

Erchul, W. P. (1999). Two steps forward, one step back: Collaboration in school-based consultation. *Journal of School Psychology, 37,* 191–203.

Erchul, W. P., & Chewning, T. G. (1990). Behavioral consultation from a request-centered relational communication perspective. *School Psychology Quarterly, 5,* 1–20.

Erchul, W. P., & Martens, B. K. (1997). *School consultation: Conceptual and empirical bases of practice.* New York: Plenum Press.

Erchul, W. P., & Martens, B. K. (2002). *School consultation: Conceptual and empirical bases of practice* (2nd ed.). New York: Plenum Press.

Erdoes, R., & Ortiz, A. (1984). *American Indian myths and legends.* New York: Pantheon.

Everstine, L., Everstine, D. S., Geymann, G. M., True, R. H., Frey, D. H., Johnson, H. G., & Seiden, R. H. (1980). Privacy and confidentiality in psychotherapy. *American Psychologist, 35,* 828–840.

Fairbairn, W. R. D. (1946). Object relationships and dynamic structure. *The International Journal of Psycho-Analysis, 27,* 30–37.

Feigenbaum, M. (1981, Summer). Universal behavior in nonlinear systems. *Los Alamos Science, 1*(1).

Ferguson, M. (1980). *The Aquarian conspiracy.* London: Paladin.

Festinger, L. A. (1957). *A theory of cognitive dissonance.* Evanston, IL: Row, Peterson.

Figes, E. (1970). *Patriarchal attitudes.* London: Granada.

Fiol, C. M., & Lyles, M. A. (1985). Organizational learning. *Academy of Management Review, 10*(4), 803–813.

Firestone, S. (1979). *The dialectic of sex.* London: New Women's Press.

Fishbaugh, M. S. E. (1997). *Models of collaboration.* Boston: Allyn and Bacon.

Fisher, G. L., & Harrison, T. C. (1997). *Substance abuse.* Boston: Allyn and Bacon.

Fisher, G. L., & Harrison, T. C. (2000). *Substance abuse* (2nd ed.). Boston: Allyn and Bacon.

Fisher, L. (1986). Systems-based consultation with schools. In L. Wynne, S. McKaniel, & T. Weber (Eds.), *Systems consultation: A new perspective for family therapy* (pp. 342–356). New York: Guilford.

Fordham, S., & Ogbu, J. U. (1986). Black students' school success: Coping with the burden of "acting white." *Urban Review, 18,* 18–36.

Forrester-Miller, H., & Davis, T. (1996). A practitioner's guide to ethical decision making. [Online]. Available: http//www.counseling.org/site/pageserver?pagename=resources prac guide.

Fox-Genovese, E. (1996). *Feminism is not the story of my life.* New York: Doubleday.

Framo, J. L. (1992). *Family-of-origin therapy. An integrative approach.* New York: Brunner/Mazel.

French, J. R. P., & Raven, B. (1957). Group support: Legitimate power and social influence. *Journal of Abnormal and Social Psychology, 59,* 400–409.

Freud, S. (1962). *Civilization and its discontents.* New York: W. W. Norton.

Frey, D. H., Raming, H. E., & Frey, F. M. (1978). The qualitative description, interpretation, and evaluation of counseling. *Personnel and Guidance Journal, 56,* 621–625.

Friend, M. J., & Cook, L. (1996). *Interactions: Collaboration skills for school professionals* (2nd ed.). White Plains, NY: Longman.

Fukuyama, M., & Sevig, T. (1997). Spiritual issues in counseling: A new course. *Counselor Education and Supervision, 36,* 224–232.

Gabbard, G. O. (2000). Consultation from the consultant's perspective. *Psycholanalytic Analogues, 10*(2), 209–218.

Gabbard, G. O., & Lester, E. P. (1995). *Boundaries and boundary violations in psychoanalysis.* Washington, DC: American Psychiatric Press.

Gagliardi, P. (1986). The creation and change of organizational cultures: A conceptual framework. *Organizational Studies, 7*(2), 13–26.

Gallessich, J. (1982). *The profession and practice of consultation: A handbook for consultants, trainers of consultation and consumers of consultation services.* San Francisco: Jossey-Bass.

Gallessich, J. (1985). Toward a meta-theory of consultation. *Counseling Psychologist, 13*(3), 336–354.

Garfat, T., & Ricks, R. (1995). Self-driven ethical decision-making: A model for child and youth care. *Child and Youth Care Forum, 24*(6), 393–404.

Garmezy, N. (1991). Resiliency and vulnerability to adverse development outcomes associated with poverty. *American Behavioral Scientist, 34,* 416–430.

Gerber, S. (1999). *Enhancing counselor intervention strategies: An integrational viewpoint.* Philadelphia: Accelerated Development/Taylor & Francis.

Gerber, S. (2001). Where has our theory gone? Learning theory and intentional intervention. *Journal of Counseling and Development, 79,* 282–291.

Gilbert, J. A., & Stead, B. A. (1999). Stigmatization revisited. *Group and Organizational Development, 24,* 239–256.

Gilbert, J. A., Stead, B. A., & Ivancevich, J. M. (1999). Diversity management: A new organizational paradigm. *Journal of Business Ethics, 21,* 61–76.

Gilligan, C. (1982). *In a different voice.* Cambridge, MA: Harvard University Press.

Ginsberg, E., & Vojta, G. (1981). The service sector in the U.S. economy. *Scientific American, 244*(3), 46–53.

Gladding, S. T. (1997). *Community and agency counseling.* Upper Saddle River, NJ: Merrill/Prentice-Hall.

Gladding, S. T. (1998). *Family therapy: History, theory and practice* (2nd ed.). Upper Saddle River, NJ: Merrill/Prentice-Hall.

Gladding, S. T., Remley, T. P., & Huber, C. H. (2001). *Ethical, legal, and professional issues in the practice of marriage and family therapy* (3rd ed.). Upper Saddle River, NJ: Merrill/Prentice-Hall.

Glaser, E. M. (1981). Ethical issues in consultation practice with organizations. *Consultation, 1*(1), 12–16.

Glasser, W. (1965). *Reality therapy: A new approach in psychiatry.* New York: Harper and Row.

Gleick, J. (1987). *Chaos: Making of a new science.* New York: Viking.

Goldenberg, I., & Goldenberg, H. (1996). *Family therapy: An overview.* Pacific Grove, CA: Brooks/Cole.

Goldstein, J. (1993). Beyond Lewin's force field: A new model for organizational change interventions. In F. Massarik (Ed.), *Advances in organizational development.* Norwood, NJ: Ablex.

Gomez, M. J., Fassinger, R. E., Prosser, J., Cooke, K., Mejia, B., & Luna, J. (2001). Voces abriendo caminos (Voices forging paths): A qualitative study of the career development of notable Latinas. *Journal of Counseling Psychology, 48,* 286–300.

Goodyear, R. K., & Sinnett, R. (1984). Current and emerging issues for counseling psychology. *The Counseling Psychologist, 12*(3), 87–98.

Gordon, W. (1983, May/June). Social work revolution or evolution? *Social Work, 28*(3), 181–185.

Green, J. W. (1999). *Cultural awareness in the human services*. Boston: Allyn and Bacon.

Greene, R. R. (1994). A diversity framework for human behavior: Conceptual and historical reformulations. In R. R. Greene (Ed.), *Human behavior theory: A diversity framework*. New York: Aldine de Gruyter.

Greiner, L. E. (1972, July–August). Evolution and revolution as organizations grow. *Harvard Business Review*, 322–333.

Gushue, G. V., & Constantine, M. G. (2003). Examining individualism, collectivism, and self-differentiation in African American college women. *Journal of Mental Health Counseling, 25*(1), 1–15.

Gutheil, T. G., Bursztajn, H. J., Brodsky, A., & Alexander, V. (1991). *Decision making in psychiatry and the law*. Baltimore: Williams and Wilkins.

Gutkin, T. B. (1993). Conducting consultation research. In J. E. Zins, T. R. Kratochwill, & S. N. Elliot (Eds.), *Handbook of consultation for children: Applications in educational and clinical settings* (pp. 227–248). San Francisco: Jossey-Bass.

Gutkin, T. B. (1996). Patterns of consultant and consultee verbalizations: Examining communication leadership during initial consultation interviews. *Journal of School Psychology, 34*, 199–219.

Gutkin, T. B., & Curtis, M. J. (1982). School-based consultation: Theory and techniques. In C. Reynolds & T. B. Gutkin (Eds.), *The handbook of school psychology* (pp. 796–828). New York: Wiley.

Gysbers, N. C., & Henderson, P. (1988). *Developing and managing your school guidance program*. Alexandria, VA: American Association for Counseling and Development.

Gysbers, N. C., & Henderson, P. (2001). *Leading and managing comprehensve school guidance programs* [microform]. Greensboro, NC: Eric Clearinghouse on Counseling and Student Service, University of North Carolina at Greensboro.

Gysbers, N. C., Heppner, M. J., & Johnston, J. A. (1998). *Career counseling: Process, issues, and techniques*. Boston: Allyn and Bacon.

Habermas, J. (1970). *Legitimation crisis*. Boston: Beacon.

Hacker, H. M. (1951). Woman as a minority group. *Social Forces, 30*, 60–69.

Hall, A. S., & Torres, I. (2002). Partnerships in preventing adolescent stress: Increasing self-esteem, coping, and support through effective counseling. *Journal of Mental Health Counseling, 24*, 97–109.

Hamilton, G. (1958). "Foreword." In H. D. Stein & R. A. Coward (Eds.), *Social perspectives on behavior* (pp. xi–xiv). New York: Free Press.

Hamilton, N. G. (1989). A critical review of object relations' theory. *American Journal of Psychiatry, 146*, 1552–1560.

Handy, C. (1989). *The age of unreason*. Boston: Harvard Business School Press.

Hansen, J. C., Himes, B. S., & Meier, S. (1990). *Consultation, concepts and practices*. Englewood Cliffs, NJ: Prentice-Hall.

Hare, R. (1981). The philosophical basis of psychiatric ethics. In S. Block, P. Chodoff, & S. A. Green (Eds.), *Psychiatric ethics*. Oxford: Oxford University Press.

Hare, R. (1991). The philosophical basis of psychiatric ethics. In S. Block, P. Chodoff, & S. A. Green (Eds.), *Psychiatric ethics*. Oxford: Oxford University Press.

Hargreaves, A., & Dawe, R. (1990). Paths of professional development: Contrived collegiality, collaborative culture, and the case of peer coaching. *Teaching and Teacher Education, 6*, 227–241.

Harrison, T. C. (1983). Perceived expertness, trustworthiness, and attractiveness in counseling and consultation. Unpublished dissertation. *Dissertation Abstract International* (Publication No. AAT 8515124)), p. 1273.

Harrison, T. (2000). The school counselor as consultant/coordinator. In J. Wittmer (Ed.), *Managing your school counseling programs: K–12 developmental strategies* (pp. 183–191). Minneapolis: Educational Media.

Haskins, R., & Macrae, D. (Eds.). (1988). *Policies for America's public schools: Teachers, equity, and indicators*. Norwood, NJ: Ablex.

Hawkins, D. M. (1986). Understanding reactions to group instability in psychotherapy groups. *International Journal of Group Psychotherapy, 36*, 241–260.

Hawkins, J. D., Catalano, R. E., & Miller, J. Y. (1992). Risk and protective factors for alcohol and other drug problems in adolescence and early adulthood: Implications for substance abuse prevention. *Psychological Bulletin, 112*, 64–105.

Heilman, M. E., Kaplow, S. R., Amato, M. A. G., & Stathatos, P. (1993). When similarity is a liability: Effects of sex-based preferential selection on reactions to like-sex and different-sex others. *Journal of Applied Psychology, 78*, 917–927.

Helms, J. (1990). *Black and white racial identity: Theory, research and practice*. New York: Greenwood.

Helms, J. (1992). *A race is a nice thing to have*. Topeka, KS: Content Communications.

Hennig, M., & Jardim, A. (1977). *The managerial woman*. Garden City, NY: Anchor.

Henning-Stout, M. (1993). Theoretical and empirical bases of consultation. In J. E. Zins, T. R. Kratochwill, & S. N. Elliot (Eds.), *Handbook of consultation services for children* (pp. 14–15). San Francisco: Jossey-Bass.

Herlihy, B., & Corey, G. (1996). *ACSA ethical standards casebook* (5th ed.). Alexandria, VA: American Counseling Association.

Heron, T. E., Martz, S. A., & Margolis, H. (1996). Ethical issues in consultation. *Remedial Education, 17*, 377–385.

Heyel, C. (Ed.). (1973). *Encyclopedia of management* (2nd ed.). New York: Van Nostrand Reinhold.

Hill, M., Glaser, K., & Harden, J. (1995). A feminist model for ethical decision making. In E. J. Rave & C. C. Larsen (Eds.), *Ethical decision making in therapy: Feminist perspectives* (pp. 18–37). New York: Guilford.

Hines, P. M., & Boyd-Franklin, N. (1982). Black families. In M. McGoldrick, J. Pierce, & J. Giordano (Eds.), *Ethnicity and family therapy* (pp. 84–107). New York: Guilford.

Hofstetter, R. (1970). *Anti-intellectualism in American life*. New York: Knopf.

Holy Bible. (Red Letter Edition). London: World Bible Publishers.

Hong, Y., Morris, M. W., Chui, C., & Benet-Martinez, V. (2000). Multicultural minds: A dynamic constructivistic approach to culture and cognition. *American Psychologist, 55*, 709–720.

Hood, J. N., & Koberg, C. S. (1994). Patterns of assimilation and acculturation for women in business organizations. *Human Relations, 47*(2), 159–181.

Horner, M. (1969, November). Fail: Bright women. *Psychology Today*, 36–38, 62.

Horton, G. E., & Brown, D. (1990). The importance of interpersonal skills in consultee-centered consultation. *Journal of Counseling and Development, 68*, 423–426.

Horton, H. D. (1992). Race and wealth: A demographic analysis of Black homeownership. *Sociological Inquiry, 62*, 480–489.

Horton, H. D., & Burgess, N. J. (1992). Where are the Black men? Regional differences in the pool of marriageable Black males in the United States. *National Journal of Sociology, 6*, 1–19.

Horton, H. D., & Thomas, M. E. (1995). The impact of population and structural change on racial inequality in the United States: An examination of employment toward the 21st century. In G. E.

Thomas (Ed.), *Race and ethnicity in America: Meeting the challenge in the 21st century*. Washington, DC: Taylor and Francis.

Hosie, T. W. (1994). Program evaluation: A potential area of expertise for counselors. *Counselor Education and Supervision, 33*, 349–355.

Hotchkiss, L., & Borow, H. (1996). Sociological perspective on work and career development. In D. Brown, L. Brooks, & Associates (Eds.), *Career choice and development* (3rd ed., pp. 281–336). San Francisco: Jossey-Bass.

Houk, J. L., & Lewandowski, L. J. (1996). Consultant verbal content and consultee perceptions. *Journal of Educational and Psychological Consultation, 7*, 107–118.

House, E. R. (1978). Assumptions underlying evaluation models. *Educational Researcher, 7*, 4–12.

Hubbard, R. L., & French, M. T. (1991). New perspectives on the benefit-cost and cost-effectiveness of drug abuse treatment. In W. S. Cartwright & J. M. Kaple (Eds.), *Economic costs, cost-effectiveness, financing and community-based drug treatment* (NIDA Research Monograph #113). Rockville, MD: National Institute on Drug Abuse.

Hughes, J. N. (1986). Ethical issues in school consultation. *School Psychology Review, 15*, 489–499.

Human Resources Services Administration, Bureau of Primary Health Care, U.S. Department of Health and Human Services. (1996). *Models that work campaign*. Washington, DC: Author.

Idol, L., Paolucci-Whitcomb, P., & Nevin, A. (1986). *Collaborative consultation*. Rockville, MD: Aspen Systems.

Illback, R. J., Maher, C. A., & Kopplin, D. (1992). *Consultation and education competency*. Washington, DC: American Psychological Association.

Irigaray, L. (1985). *This sex which is not one*. Ithaca, NY: Cornell University Press.

Isaacson, L. E., & Brown, D. (2000). *Career information, career counseling, and career development* (7th ed.). Boston: Allyn and Bacon.

Ivey, A., Ivey, M. B., & Simek-Morgan, L. (2002). *Counseling and psychotherapy* (5th ed.). Boston: Allyn and Bacon.

Jacobs, E. E., Masson, R. L., & Harvill, R. L. (2002). *Group counseling, strategies and skills*. Pacific Grove, CA: Brooks/Cole.

Janchill, M. P. (1969). Systems concepts in casework theory and practice. *Social Casework, 15*(2), 74–82.

Jenkins, S. A., Fisher, G. L், & Harrison, T. C. (1993). Adult children of dysfunctional families: Childhood roles. *Journal of Mental Health Counseling, 15*, 310–319.

Johnson, G., & Scholes, K. (1984). *Exploring corporate strategy*. Englewood Cliffs, NJ: Prentice-Hall.

Johnson, L. J., & Pugach, M. C. (1996). Role of collaborative dialogue in teachers' conceptions of appropriate practice for students at risk. *Journal of Educational and Psychological Consultation, 7*(1), 9–24.

Keller, H. R. (1981). Behavioral consultation. In J. C. Conoley (Ed.), *Consultation in schools: Theory, research, and procedures* (pp. 59–99). New York: Academic Press.

Keys, S. G., Bemak, F., Carpenter, S. L., & King-Soaro, M. E. (1998). Collaborative consultant: New role for counselors serving at-risk youths. *Journal of Counseling and Development, 76*, 123–133.

Kitchener, K. S. (1984). Intuition, critical evaluation, and ethical principles: The foundation for ethical decision in counseling psychology. *Counseling Psychologist, 12*, 43–55.

Kitchener, K. S. (1986). Teaching applied ethics in counselor education: An integration of psychological processes and philosophical analysis. *Journal of Counseling and Development, 64*, 306–310.

Kitchener, K. S. (1991). The foundations of ethical practice. *Journal of Mental Health Counseling, 13*, 236–246.

Klein, M. (1952). The mutual influences in the development of ego and id. In R. Money-Kyrle, B. Joseph, E. O'Shaughnessy, & H. Segal (Eds.). (1975). *The writings of Melanie Klein: Envy and gratitude and other works 1946–1963*. London: Hogarth.

Kratochwill, T. R., Mace, F. C., & Bissel, M. S. (1987). Program evaluation and research. In C. A. Maher & S. G. Foreman (Eds.), *A behavioral approach to education of children and youth* (pp. 252–288). Hillsdale, NJ: Erlbaum.

Kurpius, D. J., Fuqua, D. R., & Rozecki, T. (1993). The consulting process: A multidimensional model. *Journal of Counseling and Development, 71*, 601–606.

Larkey, L. K. (1996). Toward a theory of communicative interactions in culturally diverse workgroups. *Academy of Management Review, 21*(2), 463–491.

Lawlor, R. (1993). Aborginal dreaming. *Parabola, 23*(3), 43–51.

Lazaras, A. A. (1971). *Behavior therapy and beyond*. New York: McGraw-Hill.

Leonard, H. S., & Freidman, A. M. (2000). From scientific management through fun and games to high-performing teams. A historical perspective on consulting to team-based organizations. *Consulting Psychology Journal: Practice and Research, 52*(1), 3–19.

Leong, F. T. L., & Serifica, F. C. (1995). Career development of Asian Americans: A research area in need of a good theory. In F. T. L. Leong (Ed.), *Career development and vocational behavior of ethnic and racial minorities* (pp. 67–102). Mahwah, NJ: Erlbaum.

Lerner, R. M. (1995). *America's youth in crisis: Challenges and opportunities for programs and policies*. Thousand Oaks, CA: Sage.

LeVine, R. A. (1967). *Dreams and deeds: Achievement motivation in Nigeria*. Chicago: University of Chicago Press.

Levy, A. (1986, Summer). Second-order planned change: Definition and conceptualization. *Organizational Dynamics, 15*(1), 5–23.

Lewin, K. (1948). *Resolving social conflicts*. New York: Harper and Row.

Lewin, K. (1951). *Field theory in social science*. New York: Harper.

Lewis, J. W., & Lewis, M. (1989). *Community counseling*. Pacific Grove, CA: Brooks/Cole.

Lex, B. W. (1985). Alcohol problems in special populations. In J. H. Mendelson & N. K. Mello (Eds.), *The diagnosis and treatment of alcoholism* (2nd ed., pp. 89–187). New York: McGraw-Hill.

Lippitt, G. L. (1983). *Organizational renewal* (2nd ed.). Englewood Cliffs, NJ: Prentice-Hall.

Lippitt, G., & Lippitt, R. (1986). The consulting process in action (2nd ed.). La Jolla, CA: University Associates.

Lloyd, G. (1984). *The man of reason: "Male and female" in western philosophy*. London: Methuen.

Longres, J. F. (1990). *Human behavior in the social environment*. Itasca, IL: F. E. Peacock.

Lounsbury, J., Roisium, K., Pakarney, L., Sills, A., & Meissen, G. (1979). An analysis of topic areas and topic trends in the *Community Mental Health Journal* from 1965–1977. *Community Mental Health Journal, 15*, 267–276.

Lusky, M. B., & Hayes, R. L. (2001). Collaborative consultation and program evaluation. *Journal of Counseling and Development, 79*, 26–35.

Maher, C. A. (1993). Providing consultation services in business settings. In J. E. Zins, T. R. Kratochwill, & S. N. Witt (Eds.), *Handbook of consultation services for children* (pp. 317–328). San Francisco: Jossey-Bass.

Mahler, M. S. (1975). *The psychological birth of the human infant: Symbiosis and individuation.* New York: Basic Books.

Maital, S. L. (1996). Integration of behavioral and mental health consultation as a means of overcoming resistance. *Journal of Educational and Psychological Consultation, 7,* 291–303.

Mandelbrot, B. B. (1983). *The fractal geometry of nature.* San Francisco: W. H. Freeman.

Mann, P. A. (1972). Accessibility and organizational power in the entry phase of mental health consultation. *Journal of Consulting and Clinical Psychology, 38,* 215–218.

Margolis, H., Fish, M., & Wepner, S. B. (1990). Overcoming resistance to prereferral classroom interventions. *Special Services in Schools, 6,* 167–187.

Markus, H. R., & Kitayama, S. (1991). Culture and self: Implications for cognition, emotion, and motivation. *Psychological Review, 98,* 224–253.

Martin, R. P. (1978). Expert and referent power: A framework for understanding and maximizing consultation effectiveness. *Journal of School Psychology, 16,* 49–55.

Martin, R. P., & Curtis, M. (1980). Effects of age and experience of consultant and consultee on consultation outcome. *Journal of Community Psychology, 8,* 733–736.

Maslow, A. (1962). *Toward a psychology of being.* Princeton, MA: Van Nostrand.

Massarik, F. (Ed.). (1980). "Mental systems:" Towards a practical agenda for a phenomenology of systems. In T. G. Cummings (Ed.), *Systems theory for organizational development.* New York: Wiley.

Massarik, F. (1990). Chaos and change: Examining the aesthetics of organization development. In F. Massarik (Ed.), *Advances in organization development* (Vol. 1, pp. 1–12). Norwood, NJ: Ablex.

Massarik, F., Tannebaum, R., Kahane, M., & Weschler, I. R. (1961). Sociometric choice and organizational effectiveness. In R. Tannenbaum, I. R. Weschler, & F. Massarik (Eds.), *Leadership and organization.* New York: McGraw-Hill.

Matuszek, P. A. (1981). Program evaluation as consultation. In J. C. Conoley (Ed.), *Consultation in the schools* (pp. 179–200). New York: Academic Press.

Maupin, R. J. (1993). How can a woman's lack of upward mobility in accounting organizations be explained? *Group and Organization Management, 18,* 132–152.

McAllister, P. (Ed.). (1982). *Reweaving the web of life: Feminism and nonviolence.* Philadelphia: New Society Publishers.

McCauley, C. D. (1986). *Developmental experiences in managerial work: A literature review* (Technical report No. 26). Greensboro, NC: Center for Creative Leadership.

McCauley, C. D., Ohlott, P. J., & Ruderman, M. N. (1989). On-the-job development: A conceptual model and preliminary investigation. *Journal of Managerial Issues, 1,* 142–158.

McCauley, C. D., Ruderman, M. N., Ohlott, P. J., & Morrow, J. E. (1994). Assessing the developmental job components of managerial jobs. *Journal of Applied Psychology, 79*(4), 334–365.

McConahay, J. B. (1986). Modern racism, ambivalence, and the Modern Racism Scale. In J. F. Dovido & S. L. Gaertner (Eds.), *Prejudice, discrimination, and racism* (pp. 91–125). Orlando, FL: Academic Press.

McGoldrick, M. (Ed.). (1998). *Revisioning family therapy.* New York: Guilford.

McGonagle, J. J. (1981). *Managing the consultant.* Radnor, PA: Chilton Book.

McGregor, D. M. (1960). *Human side of enterprise.* New York: McGraw-Hill.

McWhorter, J. H. (2000). *Losing the race: Self sabotage in Black America.* New York: The Free Press.

Medway, F. J., & Updyke, J. (1985). Meta-analysis of consultation outcome studies. *American Journal of Community Psychology, 13,* 489–504.

Meichenbaum, D. (1977). *Cognitive-behavior modification: An integrative approach.* New York: Plenum.

Melamed, T. (1995). Career success: The moderating effects of gender. *Journal of Vocational Behavior, 47,* 295–314.

Merrell, D. W. (1991). Back to basics: Things you have always wanted to know about consulting but tend to forget in the heat of the battle. *Consulting Psychology Bulletin, 43,* 64–68.

Mettler, D. W. (1999). Patterns of relational communication in conjoint behavioral consultation. *School Psychology Quarterly, 14,* 121–147.

Miller, D. (1982). Evolution and revolution: A quantum view of structural change in organizations. *Journal of Management Studies, 19*(2), 98–104.

Miller, D., & Friesen, P. H. (1984). *Organizations: A quantum view.* Englewood Cliffs, NJ: Prentice-Hall.

Millet, K. (1977). *Sexual politics.* London: Virago.

Minuchin, S. (1974). *Families and family therapy.* Cambridge, MA: Harvard University Press.

Mohrman, S. A., & Quam, K. (2000). Consulting to team-based organizations. *Consulting Psychology Journal: Practice and Research, 52*(1), 20–35.

Monteith, M. J. (1993). Self-regulation of prejudices responses: Implications for progress in prejudice reduction efforts. *Journal of Personality and Social Psychology, 65,* 469–485.

Monteith, M. J., Devine, P. G., & Zuwerink, J. R. (1993). Self-directed vs. other-directed affect as a consequence of prejudice-related discrepancies. *Journal of Personality and Social Psychology, 64,* 198–210.

Morrison, A. M. (1992). *The new leaders.* San Francisco: Jossey-Bass.

Morrison, A. M., White, R. P., & Van Velsor, E. (1987). *Breaking the glass ceiling: Can women reach the top of America's largest corporations?* Reading, MA: Addison-Wesley.

Mostert, M. P. (1998). *Interprofessional collaboration in schools.* Boston: Allyn and Bacon.

Myrick, R. D. (1977). *Consultation as a counselor intervention.* Ann Arbor, MI: ERIC Counseling and Personnel Services Information Center.

Myrick, R. D. (1987). *Developmental guidance and counseling: A practical approach.* Minneapolis, MN: Educational Media.

Myrick, R. D. (1993). *Developmental counseling and guidance: A practical approach* (3rd ed.). Minneapolis, MN: Educational Media.

Myrick, R. D., & Bowman, R. P. (1981). *Children helping children: Teaching students to become friendly helpers.* Minneapolis, MN: Educational Media.

National Association of Social Workers. (1996). *Code of ethics* (rev. ed.). Silver Springs, MD: Author.

National Office of Addiction Technology Transfer Centers. (1999). *The change book: A blueprint for technology transfer.* (Available from the University of Missouri–Kansas City, Addiction Technology Transfer Center, National Office, 5100 Rockhill Road, Kansas City, MO 64110–2499.)

National Organization on Disability. (2002). *The state of the union 2002 for Americans with disabilities.* [Online]. Available: http://www.namiscc.org/newsletter/January02/StateOfTheUnion.htm.

National Organization on Disability. (2003). *Economic participation: Technology.* [Online]. Available: http://www.nod.org/technology/index.cfm.

Nelson, M., Nelson, B., Sherman, M., & Strean, H. (1968). *Roles and paradigms in psychotherapy.* New York: Grune & Stratton.

Neukrug, E., Lovell, C., & Parker, R. J. (1996). Employing ethical codes and decision-making models: A developmental process. *Counseling and Values, 40,* 98–106.

Nevada Revised Statutes. (2003). *Chapter 641A.252. Adoption by reference of codes of ethics.* Carson City, NV: Nevada State Legislature.

Newman, J. L. (1993). Ethical issues in consultation. *Journal of Counseling and Development, 72,* 148–156.

Nichols, M. P., & Schwartz, R. C. (2002). *Family therapy* (6th ed.). Boston: Allyn and Bacon.

Nkomo, S. M. (1992). The emperor has no clothes: Rewriting race in organizations. *Academy of Management Review, 17,* 487–513.

Norton, D. G. (1978). *The dual perspective: Inclusion of ethnic minority content in the social work curriculum.* New York: Council of Social Work Education.

Nurco, D. N., & Hanlon, T. E. (1996). The linking of research and science. *Substance Use & Misuse, 31,* 1059–1062.

Oetting, E. R. (1976). Planning and reporting evaluative research: Part II. *Personnel and Guidance Journal, 55,* 60–64.

Oetting, E. R., Donnermeyer, J. J., Plested, B. A., Edwards, R. W., Kelly, K., & Beauvais, F. (1995). Assessing community readiness for prevention. *International Journal of Addictions, 30,* 659–683.

Ogbu, J. (1978). *Minority education and caste: The American system in cross-cultural perspectives.* New York: Academic Press.

Ogbu, J. (2001). Minority education in comparative perspectives. *Journal of Negro Education, 59*(1), 45–57.

Ogbu, J. U. (1988). Diversity and equity in public education: Community forces and minority school adjustment and performance. In R. Haskins & D. McRae (Eds.), *Policies for America's public schools: Teachers, equity and indicators* (pp. 127–170). Norwod, NJ: Ablex.

Ogbu, J. U. (1989). The individual in collective adaptation. In L. Weis (Ed.), *Dropouts from schools: Issues, dilemmas and solutions* (pp. 181–204). Buffalo, NY: SUNY Press.

Ohlott, P. J., Ruderman, M. N., & McCauley, C. D. (1994). Gender differences in managers' developmental job experiences. *Academy of Management Journal, 37,* 46–57.

O'Leary, V. E., & Ickovics, J. R. (1992). Cracking the glass ceiling: Overcoming isolation and emotion. In U. Sekerun & F. T. L. Leong (Eds.), *Women power* (pp. 7–30). Newbury Park, CA: Sage.

Osipow, S. H., & Littlejohn, E. M. (1995). Toward a multicultural theory of career development. Prospects and dilemmas. In F. T. L. Leong (Ed.), *Career development and vocational behavior of ethnic and racial minorities* (pp. 251–262). Mahwah, NJ: Erlbaum.

Owens, T. R. (1973). Educational evaluation by adversary proceedings. In E. House (Ed.), *School evaluation: The politics and process*. Berkeley, CA: McCutchan.

Parsons, R. D. (1996). *The skilled consultant: A systematic approach to the theory and practice of consultation*. Boston: Allyn and Bacon.

Parsons, S. F. (1996). *Feminism and Christian ethics*. Cambridge: Cambridge University Press.

Parsons, S. F. (2002). *The ethics of gender*. Cambridge: Blackwell.

Patton, M. Q. (1990). *Qualitative evaluation and research methods* (2nd ed.). London: Sage.

Peck, M. S. (1987). *The different drum*. New York: Simon & Schuster.

Perls, F. (1969). *Gestalt therapy verbatim*. Lafayette, CA: Real People Press.

Peters, T. (1987). *Thriving on chaos*. New York: Knopf.

Peterson, G. W., Sampson, J. P., & Reardon, R. C. (1991). *Career development and services. A cognitive approach*. Pacific Grove, CA: Brooks/Cole.

Peterson, J. V., & Nisenholz, B. (1991). *Orientation to counseling*. Boston: Allyn and Bacon.

Peterson, R. L., & Skiba, R. (2001). *Creating school climates that prevent school violence*. Minneapolis, MN: Educational Research Clearinghouse Publications (621131).

Pettigrew, A. M. (1985). *The awakening giant: Continuity and change in Imperial Chemical Industries*. Oxford, England: Blackwell.

Piaget, J. (1952). *The origins of intelligence in children*. New York: International Universities Press.

Pianta, R. C. (1999). *Enhancing relationships between children and teachers*. New York: American Psychological Association.

Plumwood, V. (1993). *Feminism and environmental mastery*. London and New York: Routledge.

Polich, J. M., Ellickson, P. L., & Reuter, P., & Kahan, J. P. (1984). *Strategies for controlling adolescent drug use*. Santa Monica, CA: Rand.

Posthuma, B. W. (1999). *Small groups in counseling and therapy*. Boston: Allyn and Bacon.

Pringle, R. (1988). *Secretaries talk: Sexuality, power and work*. Sydney, Aus: Allen & Unwin.

Prochaska, J. O., & DiClemente, C. C. (1982). Transtheoretical therapy: Toward a more integrative model of change. *Psychotherapy: Theory, Research, and Practice, 19,* 276–288.

Pryzwansky, W. B. (1974). A reconsideration of the consultation model for delivery of school-based psychological services. *American Journal of Orthopsychiatry, 44,* 579–583.

Pryzwansky, W. B. (1977). Collaboration or consultation: Is there a difference? *Journal of Special Education, 11,* 179–182.

Pryzwansky, W. B. (1993). Ethical consultation practice. In J. E. Zins, T. R. Kratochwill, & S. N. Elliot (Eds.), *Handbook of consultation services for children* (pp. 329–350). San Francisco: Jossey-Bass.

Pryzwansky, W. B., & Noblit, G. W. (1990). Understanding and improving consultation practice: The qualitative case study approach. *Journal of Educational and Psychological Research, 1,* 293–307.

Pryzwansky, W. B, & White, G. W. (1983). The influence of consultee characteristics on preferences for consultation approaches. *Professional Psychology, 14,* 457–461.

Pugach, M. C., & Johnson, L. J. (1995). *Collaborative practitioners, collaborative schools*. Denver: Love.

Quinn, J. B. (1977, Fall). Strategic goals: Process and politics. *Sloan Management Review, 19*(1), 21–38.

Quinn, J. B. (1980). *Strategies for change: Logical incrementalism*. New York: Irwin.

Rae, W. A., Founier, C. J., & Roberts, M. C. (in press). Ethical and legal issues in the assessment of children with special needs. In R. J. Simeonsson & S. Rosenthal (Eds.), *Clinical assessment in child and adolescent psychology*.

Ragins, B. R., & Sundstrom, E. (1989). Gender and power in organizations: A longitudinal perspective. *Psychology Bulletin, 105,* 51–88.

Reardon, R. C., Lenz, J. G., Sampson, J. P., & Peterson, G. W. (2000). *Career development and planning*. Stamford, CT: Brooks/Cole.

Reed, G. M., & Noumair, D. A. (2000). The tiller of authority in a sea of diversity. In E. B. Klein, F. Gabelnick, & P. Herr (Eds.), *Dynamic consultation in a changing workplace*. Madison, CT: Psychosocial Press.

Reger, R. (1964). The school psychologist and the teacher: Effective professional relationships. *Journal of School Psychology, 3,* 13–18.

Reich, R. (1991). *The work of nations: Preparing ourselves for 21st century capitalism*. New York: Knopf.

Reinhaller, N. W. (1999). Efficient and effective formats for collaborative consultation. *Journal of Educational and Psychological Consultation, 10*(2), 175–184.

Reschly, D. J. (1976). School psychology consultation: Frenzied, faddish, or fundamental? *Journal of School Psychology, 14,* 105–113.

Rest, J. R. (1983). Morality. In J. H. Flavell & E. M. Markman (Eds.), *Handbook of child psychology: Vol. 3. Cognitive development* (pp. 556–620). New York: Wiley.

Rest, J. R. (1984). Research on moral development: Implications for training counseling psychologists. *Counseling Psychologist, 12,* 12–29.

Reuther, R. R. (1975). *New woman new earth.* Minneapolis, MN: Seabury Press.

Richard, R. C., & Kirby, S. L. (1998). Women recruits' perceptions of workforce diversity program selection decisions: A procedural justice examination. *Journal of Applied and Social Psychology, 28*(2), 183 188.

Richardson, T. Q., & Molinaro, K. L. (1996). White counselor self-awareness: A prerequisite for developing multicultural competence. *Journal of Counseling and Development, 74,* 238–242.

Robinson, T. L., & Ginter, E. J. (Eds.). (1999). Racism: Healing its effects [Special Issue]. *Journal of Counseling and Development, 77*(1), 1–3.

Rogers, C. (1951). *Client-centered therapy.* Boston: Houghton-Mifflin.

Rogers, C. (1980). *A way of being.* Boston: Houghton-Mifflin.

Rokeach, M. (1960). *The open and closed mind.* New York: Basic Books.

Rosenberg, N. R. (Ed.). (1992). *Japanese sense of self.* Great Britton: Cambridge University.

Routley, R., Meyer, R. K., Plumwood, V., & Brady, R. T. (1983). *Relevant logic and their rituals.* San Francisco: Ridgeview.

Russell, C. (1998). *Racial and ethnic diversity.* Ithaca, NY: New Strategist Publications.

Rutter, M. (1987). Psychosocial resilience and protective mechanisms. *American Journal of Orthopsychiatry, 57,* 316–331.

Sandoval, J. (1996). Constructivism, consultee-centered consultation, and conceptual change. *Journal of Educational and Psychological Consultation, 7,* 89–97.

Satir, V. (1964). *Conjoint family therapy.* Palo Alto, CA: Science and Behavior Books.

Schein, E. H. (1969). *Process consultation.* Reading, MA: Addison-Wesley.

Schein, E. H. (1987). *Process consultation* (Vol. I). Menlo Park, CA: Addison-Wesley.

Schein, E. H. (1990). Back to the future: Recapturing the OD vision. In F. Masarik (Ed.), *Advances in organization development* (Vol. 1). Norwood, NJ: Ablex.

Schein, E. H. (1992). *Organizational culture and leadership.* San Francisco: Jossey-Bass.

Schein, E. H. (1996). Culture: The missing concept in organizational studies. *Administrative Science Quarterly, 41,* 229–240.

Schein, E. H. (1999). *Process consultation revised.* Menlo Park, CA: Addison-Wesley.

Schein, E. H. (2000, July 5–10). Notes of Cape Cod seminar, Orleans, MA.

Schneider, B., Brief, A. P., & Guzzo, R. A. (1996). Creating a climate and culture for sustainable organizational change. *Organizational Dynamics, 24,* 7–19.

Schulte, A. C., & Obsborne, S. S. (1993). What is collaborative consultation? The eye of the beholder. In D. Fuchs (Chair), *Questioning popular beliefs about collaborative consultation.* Symposium presented at the annual meeting of the Council for Exceptional Children, San Antonio, TX.

Schuman, H., Steeh, C., & Bobo, L. (1985). *Racial attitudes in America.* Cambridge, MA: Harvard University Press.

Schwallie-Giddis, P., & Kobyarz, L. Career development: The counselor's role in preparing K–12 students for the 21st century. In J. Wittmer (Ed.), *Managing your school counseling programs: K–12 developmental strategies* (pp. 211–218). Minneapolis: Educational Media.

Schwartz, H., & Davis, S. M. (1981, Summer). Matching corporate culture and business strategy. *Organizational Dynamics, 30*–48.

Scriven, M. (1972). Pros and cons about goal-free evaluation. *Evaluation Comment, 3,* 1–4.

Scriven, M. (1997). Truth and objectivity in evaluation. In E. Chelimski & W. Shadish (Eds.), *Evaluation for the 21st century: A handbook* (pp. 477–500). Thousand Oaks, CA: Sage.

Sears, D. O. (1988). Symbolic racism. In P. A. Katz & D. A. Taylor (Eds.), *Eliminating racism* (pp. 53–84). New York: Plenum.

Seligman, M. (1975). *Helplessness: On depression, development, and death.* San Francisco: Freeman.

Selznick, P. (1957). *Leadership in administration.* New York: Harper and Row.

Senge, P. M. (1990). *The fifth discipline.* New York: Doubleday/Currency.

Senge, P. M. (1999). *Organizational change.* Paper presented at the annual meeting of the Academy of Management, Las Vegas.

Shenhav, Y. (1992). Entrance of blacks and women into managerial positions in scientific and engineering occupations: A longitudinal analysis. *Academy of Management Journal, 35*(4), 889–901.

Sheridan, S. M., & Kratochwill, T. R. (1992). Behavioral parent-teacher consultation: Conceptual and research considerations. *Journal of School Psychology, 30,* 117–139.

Sheridan, S. M., Kratochwill, T. R., & Bergan, J. R. (1996). *Conjoint behavioral consultation: A procedures manual.* New York: Plenum.

Sheridan, S. M., Meegan, S. P., & Eagle, J. W. (2002). Assessing the social context initial conjoint behavioral consultation interviews: An exploratory analysis investigating process and outcomes. *School Psychology Quarterly, 17*(3), 299–324.

Shillito-Clarke, C. (1996). Ethical issues in counseling psychology. In R. Woolfe & W. Dryden (Eds.), *Handbook of counseling psychology.* London: Sage.

Shinagawa, L. H., & Jang, M. (1998). *Atlas of American diversity.* Walnut Creek, CA: Altamira.

Silvester, J., Anderson, N. R., & Patterson, F. (1999). Organizational culture change: An inter-group attribution analysis. *Journal of Occupational and Organizational Psychology, 72*(1), 1–23.

Simpson, D. D., Joe, G. W., & Brown, B. S. (1997). Treatment retention and follow-up outcomes in the drug abuse treatment outcomes study (DATOS). *Psychology of Addictive Behaviors, 11,* 294–301.

Sinha, D. (1990). Interventions for development out of poverty. In R. W. Brislin (Ed.), *Applied cross-cultural psychology* (pp. 77–97). Newbury Park, CA: Sage.

Skinner, B. F. (1953). *Science and human behavior.* New York: Macmillan.

Smaby, M. H., Harrison, T. C., & Maddux, C. D. (1996). Outcome-based supervision for working supervisors. *Consulting Psychology Journal: Research and Practice, 48,* 40–49.

Smaby, M. H., Harrison, T. C., & Nelson, M. (1995). Elementary school counselors as total quality management consultants. *Elementary School Counseling and Guidance, 29,* 310–319.

Smircich, L. (1983). Concepts of culture and organizational analysis. *Administrative Science Quarterly, 28,* 339–358.

Smith, C. G., & Vecchio, R. P. (1997). Organizational culture and strategic leadership: Issues in the management of strategic change. In R. P. Vecchio (Ed.), *Leadership: Understanding the dynamics of power and influence in organizations.* Notre Dame, IN: Notre Dame Press.

Snow, D. L., & Gersick, K. E. (1986). Ethical and professional issues in mental health consultation. In F. B. Mannino, E. J. Trickett, M. F. Shore, M. G. Kidder, & G. Levine (Eds.), *Handbook of mental health consultation* (pp. 393–431). Rockville, MD: National Institutes of Mental Health.

Sorenson, J. L., Hall, S. M., Loeb, P., Allen, T., Glaser, E. M., & Greenberg, P. D. (1988). Dissemination of a job seekers' workshop to drug treatment programs. *Behavior Therapy, 19*(3), 143–155.

Sparks, E. (1999). The role of counseling psychology in full-service schools. In W. C. R. Tourse & J. Mooney (Eds.), *Collaborative practice: School and human service partnerships* (pp. 59–78). Westport, CT: Praeger.

Stadler, H. A. (1986). Making hard choices: Clarifying controversial ethical issues. *Counseling and Human Development,* 19–10.

Statham, A. (1996). *The rise of marginal voices.* New York: University Press of America.

Steinberg, L. (1996). *Beyond the classroom: Why school reform has failed and what parents can do about it.* New York: Touchstone.

Steinman, S. O., Richardson, N. F., & McEnroe, T. (1998). *The ethical decision-making manual for helping professionals.* Pacific Grove, CA: Brooks/Cole.

Stern, D., & Eichorn, D. (Eds.). (1989). *Adolescence and work: Influences of social structure, labor markets, and culture.* Hillsdale, NJ: Erlbaum.

Stevens, G. E., & Brenner, O. C. (1990). An empirical investigation of the motivation to manage among Blacks and women in business school. *Educational and Psychological Measurement, 50,* 879–886.

Stevens, P. (Ed.). (1999). *Ethical casebook for the practice of marriage and family counseling.* Alexandria, VA: American Counseling Association.

Stinchcombe, A. L. (1990). *Information and organizations.* Berkeley: University of California Press.

Strong, S. (1968). Counseling: An interpersonal influence process. *Journal of Counseling Psychology, 15,* 215–224.

Strong, S., & Matross, R. P. (1973). Change processes in counseling and psychotherapy. *Journal of Counseling Psychology, 20,* 25–37.

Sturkie, K., & Bergen, L. P. (2001). *Professional regulation in marriage and family therapy.* Boston: Allyn and Bacon.

Sue, D., & Sue, D. (1999). *Counseling the culturally different: Theory and Practice* (3rd ed.). New York: Wiley.

Swim, J. K., Aikin, K. J., Hall, W. S., & Hunter, B. A. (1995). Sexism and racism: Old-fashioned and modern prejudices. *Journal of Personality and Social Psychology, 68*(2), 199–214.

Tarvydas, V. M. (1987). Decision-making models in ethics: Models for increased clarity and wisdom. *Journal of Applied Rehabilitation Counseling, 18*(4), 50–52.

Tarvydas, V. M. (1998). Ethical decision-making processes. In R. R. Cottone & V. M. Tarvydas (Eds.), *Ethical and professional issues in counseling* (pp. 144–155). Upper Saddle River, NJ: Prentice-Hall.

Tenkasi, R. V., & Mohrman, S. A. (1995). *Reviewing the behavioral science knowledge based on technology transfer* (pp. 147–167). Rockville, MD: National Institute of Drug Abuse. Publication #155.

Tharp, R. G., & Wentzel, R. J. (1969). *Behavior modification in the natural environment.* New York: Academic Press.

Thomas, G. E. (1995). *Race and ethnicity in America: Meeting the challenge in the 21st century.* Washington, DC: Taylor and Francis.

Thomson, K. H., & Greene, R. R. (1994). Role theory and social work practice. In R. R. Greene (Ed.), *Human behavior theory: A diversity framework.* New York: Aldine de Gruyter.

Thyer, B. A. (1994). Social learning theory: Empirical applications to culturally diverse practice. In R. R. Greene (Ed.), *Human behavior theory: A diversity framework.* New York: Aldine de Gruyter.

Thyer, B. A., & Hudson, W. W. (1987). Professional behavioral social work: An introduction. *Journal of Social Service Research, 10*(2–4), 1–5.

Tillich, P. (1952). *The courage to be.* New Haven, CT: Yale University Press.

Tinker, G. E., & Bush, L. (1991). Native American unemployment: Statistical games and cover-ups. In G. W. Shepherd & D. Penna (Eds.), *Racism and the underclass.* New York: Greenwood Press.

Tobias, L. L. (1990). *Psychological consulting to management: A clinician's perspective.* New York: Brunner/Mazel.

Tokunaga, H. T. (1984). Ethical issues in consultation: An evaluative review. *Professional Psychology: Research and Practice, 15,* 811–821.

Torres-Rivera, E., Smaby, M., & Maddux, C. D. (1998). Attitudes, values, and beliefs of Latino men: Implications for counselors. *Journal of Psychological Practice, 4,* 77–87.

Toulmin, S. (1950). *An examination of the place of reason in ethics.* Cambridge: Cambridge University.

Tourse, R. W. C., & Sulick, J. (1999). The collaborative alliance: Supporting vulnerable children in school. In W. C. R. Tourse & J. Mooney (Eds.), *Collaborative practice: School and human service partnerships* (pp. 59–78). Westport, CT: Praeger.

Trice, H. M., & Beyer, J. M. (1984). Studying organizational culture through rites and rituals. *Academy of Management Review, 9,* 653–669.

Tushman, M. L., Newman, W. H., & Romanelli, E. (1986). Convergence and upheaval: Managing the unsteady pace of organizational evolution. *California Management Review, 29,* 124–132.

Tushman, M. L., & Romanelli, E. (1985). Organizational evolution: A metamorphosis model of convergence and reorientation. In L. L. Cummings & B. W. Staw (Eds.), *Research in organizational behavior.* Greenwich, CT: JAI Press.

Tyler, M. M., & Fine, M. J. (1974). The effects of limited and intensive school psychologist-teacher consultation. *Consultation in the Schools, 12,* 8–16.

Tymchuk, A. J. (1981). Ethical decision-making and psychological treatment. *Journal of Applied Psychiatric Treatment and Evaluation, 3,* 507–513.

Tymchuk, A. J. (1986). Guidelines for ethical decision-making. *Canadian Psychology, 27,* 36–43.

U.S. Bureau of the Census. (1993). *Census.* Washington, DC: U.S. Government Publications.

U.S. Bureau of the Census. (2000). *Census.* Washington, DC: U.S. Government Publications.

U.S. Department of Labor. (1997). *Facts on working women.* [Online]. Available: http://www.dol.gov/dol/wb/public/wb_pubs/bwlf97.htm.

U.S. Department of Labor (1999, November). *BLS releases new 1998–2008 employment predictions.* [On-line]. Available: http://www.bls.gov.news.release/ecopro.nr0.htm.

U.S. Department of Labor. (2000). *Labor force statistics from the Current Population Survey.* [Online]. Available: http://stats.bls.gov/news.release/work.t02.htm.

Vacc, N., & Loesch, L. L. (2000). *Professional orientation to counseling* (3rd ed.). Philadelphia: Brunner-Routledge.

Van Hoose, W. H. (1980). Ethics and counseling. *Counseling and Human Development, 13*(1), 1–12.

Van Hoose, W. H., & Kottler, J. A. (1977). *Ethical and legal issues in counseling and psychotherapy.* San Francisco: Jossey-Bass.

Van Velsor, E., & Hughes, M. W. (1990). *Gender differences in the development of managers: How women managers learn from experience.* (Technical Report No. 145). Greensboro, NC: Center for Creative Leadership.

Varney, G. H. (1985). OD professionals: The route to becoming a professional. In D. D. Warrick (Ed.), *Contemporary organizational development* (pp. 49–56). Glenview, IL: Scott, Foresman.

Vernberg, E. M., & Reppucci, N. D. (1986). Behavioral consultation. In F. V. Mannino, E. J. Trickett, M. F. Shore, M. G. Kidder, & G. Levin (Eds.), *Handbook of mental health consultation* (pp. 49–80). Rockville, MD: National Institutes of Mental Health.

Vogel, S. A. (1998). Adults with learning disabilities. In S. A. Vogel & S. Reder (Eds.), *Learning disabilities, literacy, and adult education* (pp. 5–28). Baltimore, MD: Paul H. Brooks.

von Bertalanffy, L. (1950). An outline of general systems theory. *British Journal of the Philosophy of Science, 1,* 134–165.

Walsh, F. (1998). *Strengthening family resilience.* New York: Guilford.

Waring, M. (1988). *Counting for nothing.* Aukland, Eng: Allen & Unwin.

Warwick, D., & Kelman, H. (1973). Ethical issues in social intervention. In G. Zaltman (Ed.), *Process and phenomena of social change* (pp. 417–477). New York: Wiley Interscience.

Websdale, N., Sheeran, M., & Johnson, B. (1997). *Reviewing domestic violence fatalities: Summarizing national developments.* Reno, NV: National Council of Juvenile and Family Court Judges.

Weiner, Y. (1988). Forms of value systems: A focus on organizational effectiveness and cultural change and maintenance. *Academy of Management Review, 13,* 534–545.

Weis, L. (1985). *Between two worlds: Black students in an urban community college.* Boston: Routledge and Kegan Paul.

Weisbord, M. R. (1985). The organizational development contract revisited. *Consultation, 4,* 305–315.

Welfel, E. R. (1998). *Ethics in counseling and psychotherapy: Standards, research, and emerging issues.* Pacific Grove, CA: Brooks/Cole.

Westermeyer, J., & Baker, J. M. (1986). Alcoholism and the Mexican Indian. In N. J. Estes & M. E. Heinemann (Eds.), *Alcoholism: Development, consequences, and interventions* (pp. 273–282). St. Louis: Mosby.

Wheeler, P. T., & Loesch, L. (1981). Program evaluation and counseling: Yesterday, today, and tomorrow. *Personnel and Guidance Journal, 59,* 573–578.

Willems, E. P. (1974). Behavioral technology and behavioral ecology. *Journal of Applied Behavioral Analysis, 7,* 151–156.

Williams, D. L. (1972). Consultation: A broad, flexible role for school psychologists. *Psychology in the Schools, 9,* 16–21.

Winnicott, D. W. (1964). *The child, the family, and the outside world.* Harmondsworth, England: Penguin Books.

Wittmer, J. (Ed.). (1992). *Valuing diversity and similarity: Bridging the gap through interpersonal skills.* Minneapolis, MN: Educational Media.

Wittmer, J., & Myrick, R. D. (1974). *Facilitative teaching: Theory and practice.* Pacific Palisades, CA: Goodyear.

Wittmer, J., & Myrick, R. D. (1989). *Teacher as facilitator.* Minneapolis, MN: Educational Media.

Wolin, S., & Wolin, S. (1993). *The resilient self: How survivors of troubled families rise above adversity.* New York: Villard.

Wyche, K. F. (1993). Psychology and African-American women: Findings from applied research. *Applied and Preventative Psychology, 2,* 115–121.

Yeaton, W. H., & Sechrest, L. (1981). Critical dimensions in the choice and maintenance of successful treatment: Strength, integrity, and effectiveness. *Journal of Consulting and Clinical Psychology, 49,* 156–167.

Young, R. A. (1994). Helping adolescents with career development: The active role of parents. *The Career Development Quarterly, 42,* 195–203.

Young, R. J. (1991). Native American drinking: A neglected subject of study and research. *Journal of Drug Education, 21,* 65–72.

Zuckerman, M. (1990). Some dubious premises in research and theory on racial differences. *American Psychologist, 45,* 1297–1303.

INDEX